After Charlemagne

T0381883

After Charlemagne's death in 814, Italy was ruled by a succession of kings and emperors, all of whom could claim some relation to the Carolingians, some via the female line of succession. This study offers new perspectives on the fascinating but neglected period of Italy in the ninth century and the impact of Carolingian culture. Bringing together some of the foremost scholars on early medieval Italy, *After Charlemagne* offers the first comprehensive overview of the period, and also presents new research on Italian politics, culture, society and economy, from the death of Charlemagne to the assassination of Berengar I in 924. Revealing Italy as a multifaceted peninsula, the authors address the governance and expansion of Carolingian Italy, examining relations with the other Carolingian kingdoms, as well as those with the Italian south, the papacy and the Byzantine empire. Exploring topics on a regional and local level as well as presenting a 'big picture' of the Italian or Lombard kingdom, this volume provides new and exciting answers to the central question: How Carolingian was 'Carolingian Italy'?

CLEMENS GANTNER is Researcher at the Department for Historical Identity Research at the Institute for Medieval Research, Austrian Academy of Sciences, where his research is focussed on early medieval Italy and intra- and intercultural communication around the Mediterranean. He is the author of *Freunde Roms und Völker der Finsternis* (2014) and editor of *The Resources of the Past in Early Medieval Europe* (2015), and is preparing a monograph on Louis II, great-grandson of Charlemagne and emperor in Italy in the ninth century.

WALTER POHL is Professor of History at the Institute for Austrian Historical Research, University of Vienna and Director of the Institute for Medieval Research, Austrian Academy of Sciences. His research addresses many aspects of early medieval history, with a special interest in Italy. His publications include *The Avars: A Steppe Empire in Central Europe, 567–822* (2018), *Strategies of Identification: Ethnicity and Religion in Early Medieval Europe*, ed. Walter Pohl and Gerda Heydemann (2013) and over 200 journal articles. In 2004 he was awarded the Wittgenstein Prize, and he has been a recipient of an ERC Advanced Grant (2010) and a Synergy Grant (2019).

After Charlemagne

Carolingian Italy and its Rulers

Edited by

Clemens Gantner

Austrian Academy of Sciences

Walter Pohl

Austrian Academy of Sciences

Shaftesbury Road, Cambridge CB2 8EA, United Kingdom

One Liberty Plaza, 20th Floor, New York, NY 10006, USA

477 Williamstown Road, Port Melbourne, VIC 3207, Australia

314–321, 3rd Floor, Plot 3, Splendor Forum, Jasola District Centre, New Delhi – 110025, India

103 Penang Road, #05–06/07, Visioncrest Commercial, Singapore 238467

Cambridge University Press is part of Cambridge University Press & Assessment, a department of the University of Cambridge.

We share the University's mission to contribute to society through the pursuit of education, learning and research at the highest international levels of excellence.

www.cambridge.org
Information on this title: www.cambridge.org/9781108743921

DOI: 10.1017/9781108887762

First published 2021
First paperback edition 2024

A catalogue record for this publication is available from the British Library

ISBN   978-1-108-84077-4   Hardback
ISBN   978-1-108-74392-1   Paperback

Contents

Section III   Carolingian Rulers

Section IV   Cities, Courts and Carolingians

Contributors

GIUSEPPE ALBERTONI is Professor of Medieval History in the Department of Humanities, University of Trento. His main research interests concern the Carolingian world and early medieval societies (VIII–XI centuries) in a comparative perspective between political, cultural, and economic history.

FRANÇOIS BOUGARD is director of the Institut de recherche et d'histoire des textes (CNRS, Paris). Since 1996 he has been Director of Medieval Studies at the École française de Rome, and since 2004 Professor of Medieval History at the University of Nanterre.

TOM BROWN is an Honorary Fellow of the School of History, Classics and Archaeology at the University of Edinburgh. He is the author of numerous studies on early medieval Italy and Western relations with Byzantium.

PAOLO DELOGU is emeritus at the University of Rome "La Sapienza." He studied the Normans, the Langobards, mediaeval archaeology, and early mediaeval Rome, which is currently his main field of research.

CLEMENS GANTNER is a researcher at the Institute for Medieval Research at the Austrian Academy of Sciences in Vienna. His research is centred on early medieval Italy and intra- and intercultural communication around the Mediterranean.

STEFANO GASPARRI, professor of Medieval History emeritus at the University of Venice, studies the history of the Italian Early Middle Ages (Lombard and Carolingian age and the origins of Venice). He also studied chivalry in the Italian cities of the late Middle Ages.

CAROLINE GOODSON is senior lecturer in Early Medieval History at the University of Cambridge and a fellow of King's College. Her research focuses on the Western Mediterranean in the period c. 500 – c. 1100, examining the evidence from archaeology and material culture as well as a range of texts.

THOMAS F. X. NOBLE taught at the University of Virginia and then at Notre Dame. His research focused on Carolingian history, papal history, and the history of the city of Rome. He served as president of the American Catholic Historical Association and of the American Society of Church History.

WALTER POHL is Professor for Medieval History at the University of Vienna and Director of the Institute for Medieval Research at the Austrian Academy of Sciences. His main research focus is on early medieval identities in Latin western as well as central Europe.

IGOR SANTOS SALAZAR is a post-doctoral researcher at the University of Santiago de Compostela. His main research interest is the history of early medieval Italy. He specializes in European comparative history.

ELINA SCREEN is a Lecturer in Medieval History at Birkbeck, University of London. She is an established historian of early medieval Europe, with particular specialisms in the Carolingian world. She is also General Editor of the Medieval European Coinage project and publishes on medieval numismatics.

MARCO STOFFELLA teaches history at the University of Verona. His main research interests lie in early medieval social history, local societies, international relationships, minor local officers, and manuscripts, with an emphasis on the Verona Capitular Library and its networks in the early and high Middle Ages.

FRANCESCO VERONESE is charged with teaching activities in Gender History and Medieval History at the University of Padova. His research interests embrace relics' cults, hagiography, and gender relationships in the Early Middle Ages, especially in Carolingian times.

GIORGIA VOCINO is a post-doctoral researcher at the University of Orléans. Her work focuses on early medieval literary culture and her areas of expertise are manuscript studies, textual criticism, and intellectual history.

Map 1: The Apennine peninsula, c. 863 CE

Map 2: Topography of Italy

1   Italy after Charlemagne
Scope and Aims of the Volume

Clemens Gantner and Walter Pohl

The present volume is the fruit of a small conference held in Vienna in late April 2016 under the title 'Italy and Its Rulers in the Ninth Century: Was There a Carolingian Italy?'. It was the last event sponsored by the ERC Advanced Grant Project 'Social Cohesion, Identity and Religion in the Early Middle Ages' (SCIRE)[1] which very successfully ran in Vienna between 2011 and 2016. Its specific aim was to bring together researchers working on Italy in the times between the death of Charlemagne in 814 and the death of Berengar I in 924, the last emperor to be crowned until 962. The scope was widened to include the period since King Pippin of Italy, Charlemagne's second-oldest son, who was responsible for Italy until his premature death in summer 810. The ninth-century kingdom of Italy still lacks an in-depth study that avoids dealing with it merely as a time of transition. This is quite surprising, as, for example, the tenth century has received more studies that are comprehensive. The present volume aims to fill parts of this gap.

Italy was in a peculiar situation as part of the Carolingian commonwealth. At times, it seems as if the peninsula was one of the most prized objects of Carolingian interest. For example, in most divisions of the Carolingian realm, the imperial dignity remained attached to Italy. Most likely, this has to do with the personal attachment of the emperor in the first such division, Lothar I. For his rule and for his personal link to Italy, the contribution of Elina Screen in this volume will provide valuable new insights. In contrast, most north Alpine commentators saw the Italian kingdom as a mere appendix to the Frankish Empire. For them, Italy was not the place where the meaningful and important decisions for the fate of the Frankish realm were made. The core area of the Carolingian empire lay north of the Alps. The Carolingian rulers in Italy inspired very few histories or texts that depicted them in a favourable light and

---

[1] The research leading to these results has received funding from the European Research Council under the European Union's Seventh Framework Programme (FP7/2007-2013) / ERC grant agreement No. 269591.

came from the main part of the kingdom in the Po Plain. We should mention the History of Andreas of Bergamo, a quite short text, and the rather obscure *Libellus de imperatoria potestate*. Both texts were written after the death of Louis II of Italy and did not have a broad impact. Italy thus remained somewhat detached from official Carolingian historiography.

Carolingian rule introduced some momentous textual and administrative practices in Italy – capitularies, the Carolingian minuscule, counts, *placita*, to name just a few of the innovations. Nevertheless, in many respects, we may wonder how deep its impact on Italy really was. The position of Italian Carolingian rulers seems more precarious than in the core area of the empire. They were also depicted as quite weak kings or emperors, both by contemporaries and in modern research. The ninth-century kings did not become pivotal figures in 'national histories', much unlike the famous northern Carolingian kings Louis the German or Charles the Bald. In Italy, the only emperor of partly Carolingian descent to be counted as one of the early kings of Italy and thus as a 'forefather' of the Italian nation was Berengar I. Contemporary onlookers, too, like Archbishop Hincmar of Reims held the opinion that the rulers of Italy were no emperors, but rather petty kings.[2] Many north Alpine writers and commentators will have felt with Alcuin that real politics were made in the Carolingian places of power, far from Italy.[3]

Were the Italian Carolingians really so ephemeral? Probably not. It was just hindsight, from the fact that neither their rule nor their realm did endure, that shaped the historian's view on ninth-century Italy. Does that mean that the Italian rulers were the self-confident sovereigns we find Louis II's famous letter to the East Roman emperor Basil I? Famously, Louis II claimed there that 'we govern all Francia, as undoubtedly we own everything, which is owned by those with whom we are one flesh and blood and with whom we are one through the spirit of the Lord'.[4] This, too, was not a realistic assessment of the Italian *regnum* or of the whole western empire. Rather, the letter's author, the notorious Anastasius, librarian of the Roman church, invented yet another fiction that fit his purpose: creating a larger-than-life version of his protagonist, including as much Louis' hopes and aspirations in these lines as his own as a

---

[2] For example, *AB*, a. 856, p. 73, and *AB*, a. 863, p. 96.
[3] Costambeys, 'Alcuin, Rome'.
[4] Emperor Louis II, *Letter to Emperor Basil I*, ed. Henze, 388–9, writing about his uncles' kingdoms: *In tota nempe imperamus Francia, quia nos procul dubio retinemus, quod illi retinent, cum quibus una caro et sanguis sumus hac a unus per Dominum spiritus.*

Roman urban loyalist and imperialist. While his statement is thus true from a strictly legal point of view, it did not reflect the realities in the European political arena.

The aim of this volume is thus to show a multifaceted kingdom of Italy in the ninth century, touching on as many subjects as possible. How did the Carolingians, starting with Pippin of Italy, govern their Italian realm and how, if at all, did they try to expand it? How did they shape their relationship with the other Carolingian realms (at times there were up to four of them after all – in shifting degrees between alliance and open conflict)? How did they shape their relationship with the south or the papacy? How did the communication of the Italian Carolingians with the East Roman ('Byzantine') empire work? How did the Carolingian rulers in the century after Charlemagne (814–924) govern? And finally: How Carolingian was 'Carolingian Italy'?

The volume starts with a section bringing together three overviews covering ninth-century Italy from three different angles: with Thomas Noble, Paolo Delogu and François Bougard, three leading experts in the field give their respective takes on the topic. Noble writes from the grand general perspective and finds a lot of Carolingian influence on the north Italian 'kingdom of the Lombards'. Delogu looks at the names this kingdom in Italy was given by contemporaries, and, connected with it, which functions were ascribed to it. Bougard then rounds off the introductory section by assessing how far this kingdom had actually remained Lombard despite Carolingian rule. He analyses the organization of the kingdom and the literary, cultural as well as legal output of its writing centres and is able to show that the Frankish influence was indeed felt, but only in certain respects.

Drawing on these basic assertions, the second section is dedicated to the organization of the Frankish kingdom in the north. Stefano Gasparri looks at the easternmost regions of the realm, a territory that often seems peripheral to the interests of the rulers but was in fact very important to the Carolingians, who tried to get a closer grip on the duchy of Venice and Istria. To be effective, they had to build on strategies already employed by their Lombard predecessors, but had to refine and expand these to be successful in this region. Giuseppe Albertoni in his chapter then analyses the relations between rulers and high-ranking officers in Italy and their vassals. He detects different types of vassalage, which is reflected in the terminology used in the contemporary sources, and thereby provides important insight into the ways the kingdom of Italy was governed. Connecting with both texts, Igor Santos Salazar uses the two bishoprics of Parma and Arezzo as test cases and provides an in-depth analysis of their political fate during the latter part of the period in question, when loyalties were often tested and the 'right' king to support was not always obvious.

The third section looks at a succession of Carolingian rulers of Italy, illustrating, in addition to the special topics under research, an evolution of government in the early ninth century. Marco Stoffella delivers a detailed study of modes of charter production and specifically of the dating of charters in the time of King Pippin of Italy (787–810). He also focusses on the reactions to the premature death of Charlemagne's second-oldest son. Elina Screen then takes a closer look at the charters of Lothar I (emperor in Italy 817–855) and how he paved the way for his son Louis' envisaged rule in Italy. Clemens Gantner adds a study on Louis II's earliest outing as king of Italy (840/844–875), concentrating on Louis' expedition to Rome in 844 and the implication of this 'visitation' for his rule in Italy and for papal–Carolingian relations in the years to come.

The fourth and last section deals with more regional policies in ninth-century Italy, all addressing cities and courts. Thomas Brown first examines the very special case of Ravenna and its still quite 'Byzantine' political culture in a changed world of northern Italy. Caroline Goodson then looks at the oftentimes methodical development of urban centres in the south of Italy in our period, also looking closely at the transfer of saint cults and relics within the region. Francesco Veronese then works in a similar direction, analysing the appropriation of saints' cults and hagiography coming from important centres like Rome, appropriated in the north of the peninsula. And Giorgia Vocino rounds off the volume with a study on the development of rhetoric and court culture in Italy between the eighth and the tenth centuries. She addresses the learned discourse at the Italian courts and shows the high degree of sophistication that was indeed present – thereby connecting neatly with Bougard's contribution in the first section.

The editors would like to express their thanks to the many great people at Cambridge University Press as well as to the whole staff of the Institut for Medieval Studies at the Austrian Academy in Vienna. Without them, it would not have been possible to publish this book. Special thanks go to Lena Kornprobst and to Nicola Edelmann for their hard work on the technical aspects of this volume.

2 A Brief Introduction to Italian Political History until 875

Clemens Gantner

The Early Years

The years 773/774 brought profound change for the Italian peninsula. The Frankish king Charlemagne invaded the Lombard kingdom of Italy and succeeded in deposing the last Lombard king, Desiderius, who was taken into custody. Charlemagne, however, did not disband the kingdom – far from it. Instead, he had himself crowned king of the Lombards in Pavia.[1] Pope Hadrian protested this move, as he saw chances to take over Italy well into the southern parts of the Po Valley – but to no avail. Quite to the contrary, Charlemagne managed easily to get the important Lombard duchy of Spoleto under his direct control – and he also established Frankish suzerainty in Ravenna and its environs, despite papal claims to the old exarchate.[2] There were many in Italy who were not content with this policy, and already in 776, the Franks had to put down a serious rebellion led by the Friulian *dux* Hrodgaud.[3] While the insurrection could easily be overcome, it warned the Carolingians that they still had to establish their control over the peninsula more firmly. Accordingly, during his visit to Rome in 781, Charlemagne had his second-born son by his wife Hildegard (third-born overall it seems) re-baptized with the name Pippin and appointed the four-year-old as sub-king of Italy. This move brought two very interesting dynastical problems with it. First, the young boy had now received the same name as his oldest half-brother, later to be known as Pippin the Hunchback. This must have come as quite a shock to the older one, who still, surprisingly, remained at his father's court for over a decade until he unsuccessfully rebelled in Bavaria in 792, and accordingly was removed from succession. Second, Pippin was given a kingdom, whereas his older brother, Charles the Younger, was not. The latter is more easily explained, as the

---

[1] Gasparri, *774*.   [2] Noble, *Republic* , pp. 138–48.
[3] Krahwinkler, *Friaul*, pp. 119–43.

older brother was clearly to stay at the centre of the realm, close to the father.[4] The information we have on Pippin's rule is rather scarce and until recently he has received surprisingly little attention. Historians, however, have rehabilitated Pippin in recent years and shown that he, rather than being his father's puppet, exhibited his own agency in his later years as king, starting from the time he came of age in the early 790s.

Pippin and his Frankish entourage were instrumental in the first years of Carolingian rule on the Italian peninsula.[5] This can also be shown towards the end of his reign in communications with the papacy. It is crucial that Pope Leo III (796–817) felt the need to complain several times in 808 about Pippin to the latter's father. The letter shows Pippin as not seeking the counsel or approval of the papacy for his actions and insinuates that his policy was also independent of his father's. It likewise shows, however, that the pope expected Charlemagne to be able to make the young ruler show more respect for papal interests.[6] These interests intersected with Carolingian ones, for example, in the principate of Benevento. The popes had been interested in establishing some kind of overlordship in that area since 774, maybe even earlier. The Franks, in turn, felt that they should be the rightful lords in the old southernmost Lombard duchy, whose rulers now styled themselves princes. Pippin tried energetically to establish the old northern suzerainty, but was ultimately repelled by Prince Grimoald III (788–806) – gaining quite a bad reputation for himself in the southern chronicles.[7] Pippin likewise attacked Venice, a duchy nominally under Byzantine rule, but largely independent by the early ninth century. It was in the aftermath of his last campaign against the lagoon that he found his untimely death at about the age of 33 in 810 in Milan, dying of a fever he had contracted during the unsuccessful expedition. His death caused confusion on the Italian peninsula, as he had only left one son, Bernard, who even seems to have been illegitimate (see Chapter 9 in this volume for details on this transition). For the charters in Italy, Charlemagne resumed ruling the kingdom directly. He seems, however, to have accepted that his young grandson would succeed. Indeed, Bernard ruled as sub-king of Italy and continued to do so when his uncle, Louis the Pious, became emperor upon Charlemagne's death in 814. When Louis, however, divided his realm among his sons in 817, allotting the lordship over Italy to his oldest son, Lothar, who also was promoted to co-emperor, Bernard must have

---

[4] Nelson, 'Charlemagne – Pater optimus?'.   [5] Albertoni and Borri (eds.), *Spes Italiae*.
[6] Leo III, ep. 1 to Charlemagne, ed. Karl Hampe, *MGH Epp.* v, 87f. See *RI I*, 1, ed. Mühlbacher, no. 513k. See Gantner, 'The silence of the popes'.
[7] Erchempert, *Ystoriola* ed. Berto, pp. 92–3, c.6.

seen his position as seriously threatened. He rebelled the following year, but was quickly forced to submit to his uncle unconditionally. He was ultimately sentenced to be blinded, but did not survive the procedure.[8]

The Reign of Lothar and the Establishment of a Frankish Italy

With Bernard gone and his minor son unable to rule, actual power in Italy quite soon fell to Lothar, who was in his early twenties at the time. At first, Italy saw a short period of interregnum, as the new ruler and the emperor himself were absent from the peninsula until 822.[9] The official documents stemming from the 820s in general were issued in the name of his father, Louis the Pious.[10] This has led to Lothar and his advisors being seen as largely instrumental to Louis' policy. Indeed, in 822, Lothar was assigned his relative Wala of Corbie as his key advisor for Italy.

In theory, Lothar was thus a mere sub-ruler in this very important region of the empire. The realities on the ground, however, were soon very different. We can for example see this in the relationship with papal Rome. In 817, the *Pactum Ludovicianum* still very much bore the mark of Louis himself and his inner circle. By the early 820s, the situation had changed. Despite the pact with Louis, Pope Paschalis I (817–824) had not allowed for much Frankish influence in the eternal city. In spring 823, however, Lothar was crowned as king of Italy and as co-emperor in Rome. On this occasion, he also heard a court case between the monastery of Farfa and the papacy – and decided in favour of the abbey. Once Lothar had left Rome, Paschalis had two high-ranking papal officials first blinded and then executed, which led to a veritable diplomatic crisis.[11] Paschalis, according to Frankish sources, offered to clear himself of any participation in the 'murders', which was done accordingly. Interestingly, this event was held in the presence of imperial *missi*, but not of the young king. When Paschalis died shortly thereafter, the new Pope Eugenius had to accept Frankish terms: The *Constitutio Romana* was drawn up in 824 – and even if not all of its terms were implemented at this point, it gave the Carolingians and the emperor in particular far-reaching rights in the city of Rome. Most importantly, the election of a new pope could only be held in the presence of imperial envoys, and the emperor had to give his assent before the enthronization of a Roman

---

[8] Albertoni, *L'Italia carolingia*, pp. 34–7.   [9] Ibid., pp. 37–9.
[10] Screen, 'Lothar I in Italy'.   [11] Goodson, *Rome of Pope Paschal I*, pp. 30–4 and 270–2.

pontiff could be effected.[12] The *Constitutio* was agreed upon and signed in the personal presence of Lothar. He was of course again carrying out his father's orders and certainly not acting without advisors sent by Louis, but he proved to be a capable king during this crisis all the same. The *Constitutio* was also Lothar's success. It expanded Frankish dominance in central Italy and in a way rounded off the Carolingian sphere of influence in Italy.[13] Thus the 820s saw a decelerated, but steady expansion of Carolingian interests in Italy.

The big change was to come, however, in the 830s – and it was triggered by events largely happening north of the Alps. In 820, Louis the Pious, widowed in 818, had married his second wife, Judith, and a son was born of this marriage in 823, Charles the Bald. When it became abundantly clear that the youngest son would be allotted a sizeable share in the inheritance, the situation pitted the three older half-brothers – Lothar, Pippin of Aquitaine and Louis the German – against their father. The first rebellion in 830 had already alienated all the older sons, but especially Lothar, from the emperor. Lothar had been at odds with his father even earlier, when he was blamed for an unsuccessful campaign into the Spanish march in the late 820s.[14] He then successfully rebelled again in 833. Louis the Pious was deposed and Lothar styled himself sole emperor – until his brothers deserted him and the counter-revolution brought Louis the Pious back on the throne in 834. Lothar was the only son who was permanently disgraced by the events. This caused his retreat, together with his closest supporters and advisors, to Italy – and it caused the subsequent concentration of all his efforts on this region, which he could rule directly.[15]

This does not mean, however, that Italy was a kingdom in rebellion, as the differences never escalated to that extent: Louis the Pious did not attempt to deprive his firstborn of power in Italy, while Lothar recognized his father's suzerainty in principle – for example, Italian mints still produced their coins in the name of Louis. There are several signs, however, that relations were very strained: Lothar continued using his full imperial title in his charters after 834 and he refused to obey summons to meetings due in *Francia*, of course always offering excuses as to why he was unable to get to the north. The reconciliation with his father had to wait until 839, when Lothar was also given back his place in Carolingian succession as heir to the imperial title.[16]

---

[12] Noble, *Republic*, pp. 308–24.   [13] Ibid., pp. 308–19.

[14] Jarnut, 'Ludwig der Fromme, Lothar I. und das Regnum Italiae'.

[15] Schäpers, *Lothar I.*, pp. 299–343.   [16] Screen, 'Lothar I in Italy'.

The years between 834 and 839 then marked a period of intense Carolingization, if not Lotharization, of the kingdom of Italy. Lothar brought many of his close followers and their families with him to Italy. Despite an epidemic in 836 and 837 that swept away many of the leading figures, among them the aforementioned Wala, these families managed to hold on to power more or less directly, though some of them are at times hard to pinpoint.[17] The invaluable work of tracking nearly all of them down has been done by Eduard Hlawitschka.[18]

In his actions set in and for the kingdom of Italy (or the Lombards, as both names were still in use, see chapter 4), he was also aiming to allow as seamless as possible a transition to his son and main heir Louis II. Elina Screen analyses this driving force behind his deeds in chapter 10 in this volume. The young Louis, maybe fifteen years old at the time, was accordingly granted the role of sub-king of Italy by his grandfather Louis the Pious in 840.[19]

Another great wave of influx of Lotharian partisans from the north followed in the years 842/843. This again had its causes in Carolingian politics: After the death of Louis the Pious, dissent about the hierarchy among the three remaining sons and the grandson Pippin II of Aquitaine had swiftly broken out. Military hostilities were unavoidable and saw Pippin II by Lothar's side, fighting against Charles the Bald and Louis the German at the battle of Fontenoy. With heavy losses on both sides, Lothar lost this fierce civil war and once again had to retreat to Burgundy. In the aftermath of the battle, another group of Lothar's supporters, who had already lost or were about to lose their lands in western or eastern Francia, respectively, moved to Italy. This situation was confirmed in the Treaty of Verdun in 843, that saw a partition of the empire into three realms (Pippin II losing everything in the process).[20]

The example of one prominent family may help to illustrate the various phases of Frankish influx into the peninsula: the *Guidoni*, also Widones, named after Guy, who became *dux* of Spoleto in 842. Guy was the son of Lambert, count of Nantes. Both had been supporters of Lothar – and thus was among those who had to flee to Italy after 834. Lambert died in exile in 837, probably of the epidemic already mentioned. After 839, Guy had hopes of regaining or reclaiming his family's holdings in Francia; indeed, he managed to get the monastery of Mettlach back into his possession. In the aftermath of Fontenoy, however, he was forced to relinquish his claims and was back in Italy, where he was obviously

---

[17] Screen, 'Lothar I in Italy', esp. pp. 242–8.
[18] Hlawitschka, *Franken, Alemannen, Bayern.*   [19] Bougard, 'Ludovico II'.
[20] Schäpers, *Lothar I.*, pp. 345–449.

compensated for his family's heavy losses with the very rich and important duchy of Spoleto.[21] He must also have proven reliable enough to be entrusted with this region, which had been notoriously led in a very independent fashion by the Lombard officeholders in the eighth century. Guy would still prove himself as a valuable asset of Frankish rule in the coming decades.[22]

It is important to note, however, that Lothar not only brought personnel to Italy and kept on appointing the first generation of supporters for his oldest son, Louis II – the Franks also imported parts of their legal system and their culture, as has been thoroughly analysed by François Bougard for this volume. Especially in the field of legal culture, Italy seems to have been an important hotspot in the Carolingian commonwealth, however separated.[23]

Louis II and the Peak of Carolingian Italy

Nominally, as already mentioned, Lothar had in 840 already asked his father, Louis the Pious, to install his oldest son, Louis, as king of Italy. For the earliest years, we do not see Louis acting at all in Italy, not even when his father was absent for a long time, fighting the civil war and negotiating the separation of the empire. An important event in 842 was certainly a Byzantine mission that reached Lothar in Trier. There at the latest, Louis was betrothed to a daughter of the late Byzantine emperor Theophilos (d. January 842), and Lothar may have concluded an alliance that eventually required Louis to intervene against Saracens in southern Italy and maybe Sicily.[24] This alliance was probably concluded for the intermediate future, given that there was no Frankish army to speak of that could have fought in Italy at this point. Indeed, Louis' first real act as king followed only in 844, when we encounter him at the head of a larger army of Italian magnates, sent to Rome in order to lend weight to Frankish claims of overlordship over the papacy, which had clearly been neglected in the swift election of the new pope Sergius II earlier in the year. This show of force made an impact insofar as the Romans swore a renewed oath of allegiance to Lothar. The pope also crowned Louis as

---

[21] di Carpegna Falconieri, 'Guido di Spoleto'.

[22] For a rich discussion see still Hlawitschka, 'Die Widonen', and Hlawitschka, *Franken, Alemannen, Bayern* .

[23] See, for example, the very interesting legal collection in the manuscript Wolfenbüttel, HAB Blankenburgensis 130, on which future publications by Stefan Esders should be expected. For the longevity, see Gobbitt, *Lombard Law-Books*.

[24] See Gantner, '"Our common enemies shall be annihilated!"', and Gantner, 'Kaiser Ludwig II. von Italien und Byzanz'.

king of the Lombards at St Peter's and girded him with a sword belt.
A possible intervention against the Saracens in the south (and possibly
against Benevento) was not carried out, as one of the contenders for
princedom in Benevento, Siconulf, submitted to Louis in Rome. Instead,
only Guy of Spoleto intervened in the south with (possibly deliberately?)
limited success.[25]

Louis had to return to Rome only some two years later, when in
August 846 a Saracen plundering force attacked the outskirts of the city
and stripped the shrines of St Peter and St Paul of their wealth. Louis and
Guy marched to Rome individually, and both managed to halt the
plundering of central Italy. Louis then went on to meet his father at an
undisclosed place, probably in early 847 – and Lothar took action in
Italy. In a capitulary, he first ordered a general levy to support the
construction of a wall around St Peter – thereby taking part in the first
phase of the construction of the Leonine Wall. Second, a large expedition
to Benevento was organized, to be led by Louis and Frankish magnates
both from north and south of the Alps. The armies were to meet at Pavia
in late January 848 and then to march into the Beneventan principality in
spring of the same year.[26] Benevento itself, held by Prince Radelchis, was
besieged, and all Saracen auxiliary troops gathered there were executed
or dispersed. In the course of late summer or autumn, the principality
was then separated into two more or less equal parts, assigned to the two
factions that had been fighting a civil war in the region since the murder
of Prince Sicard in 839. Louis personally presided over the procedure
and claimed the position of guardian for the important monasteries of
Montecassino and San Vincenzo al Volturno for his father and himself.
More importantly even, he had finally gotten a foot in the door for his
family in the south, a task that both Charlemagne and Pippin of Italy had
not succeeded in completing.[27]

In 850 followed another milestone for the kingdom and the king: Louis
II was sent to Rome and crowned co-emperor by Pope Leo IV
(847–855), most likely on 6 April, Easter Sunday.[28] This was an important step, obviously, as Lothar, though not personally present, seems to
have handed over the administration of Italy to his son on this occasion.
Shortly afterwards, for example, Louis issued his first own legislation for
the peninsula in the typical Carolingian form of a capitulary.[29]

From that point onwards, Louis was the most active ruler Italy
had seen in a long time. He intervened even in regional and local

[25] See Chapter 11 in this volume.   [26] Gantner, 'Common enemies'.
[27] Gantner, 'Kaiser Ludwig II. von Italien und Byzanz'.
[28] *RI* 1,3,1, ed. Zielinski, no. 69.   [29] Ibid., no. 72.

conflicts.[30] And he started a lasting conflict with the papacy under Leo IV by supporting the young anathematized priest Anastasius. This already shows in the *Liber Pontificalis*, the semi-official papal history book, which, for example, omits Louis' coronation in the life of Leo IV. When Leo died in 855, the Romans elected Benedict III as pope, but Louis did not confirm the election, which had, after all, been held without imperial envoys being present. Instead, the ruler supported the anathematized Anastasius, who was even put on the papal throne for a few weeks with the help of imperial troops and Frankish *missi*. But the Romans threw him out again at the earliest opportunity.[31]

In the meantime, Lothar I had abdicated and left his realm to his three sons. He had then entered the monastery of Prüm, where he died after a few days on 29 September 855. Louis' ten years younger brother Lothar II inherited the bigger part of the north Alpine middle kingdom, whereas the youngest brother Charles, only about ten years old at the time, got a small kingdom in the Provence. Louis' holdings did not increase. This last division of the middle Frankish realm therefore angered both Louis and Lothar II, who tried to overthrow their father's plans at a meeting in the Jura region in 856. There, however, after fierce negotiations with the nobles of each region, Emperor Lothar's plans were observed after all. This was also possible through the personal intervention of Pope Benedict, who remarkably did not grasp the opportunity to get back at Louis, but rather helped to re-establish concord among the brothers.[32]

In 858, Pope Benedict died – and for the first time, the Carolingians exerted actual influence on a papal election. Louis was personally present in Rome when Pope Nicholas I (d. 867) was elected, and it was widely believed that Nicholas had been the imperial candidate. Accordingly, the exiled Anastasius was recalled to Rome and given an important position in the Lateran administration. The quite young and energetic pope proved to be far more independent than the Franks had hoped. In the early 860s, the pope was in a prolonged dispute with Archbishop John of Ravenna, in which Louis was practically forced to take Ravenna's side. The pope prevailed and forced John to submit to him in Rome at one point.[33]

Up until this point, north Alpine Frankish politics had not shaped the Italian ones as much as in prior generations – surely, because Louis II

---

[30] Stoffella, 'In a periphery of the empire'.

[31] For more information on Anastasius and his work, see Perels, *Papst Nikolaus I. und Anastasius Bibliothecarius*, and Forrai, 'Anastasius Bibliotecarius and his textual dossiers'.

[32] Gantner, 'Louis II and Rome'.

[33] Herbers, 'Der Konflikt Papst Nikolaus I. mit Erzbischof Johannes VII. von Ravenna'.

had been solely responsible for that *regnum* until 855/6. To a certain extent, and apart from short-lived episodes, this development proved to be permanent. Yet, there were still interferences. Louis' brother Lothar II had largely inherited the northern Frankish quarrels together with the capital Aachen. Soon, however, Lothar's rather unfortunate rule affected the Apennine peninsula more than anyone there would have liked, especially through the prolonged scandal of his divorce. The young king had repudiated and officially divorced his wife Theutberga in 857 in favour of his concubine Waldrada – this political and theological issue was to remain unresolved until Lothar's premature death in 869.[34] The first result of it in Italy was that Louis cautiously but officially married his own long-time concubine Angilberga in 860 and had the dotal charter predated to 851 in order to legitimate the two daughters who had already been born. Thereby, he finally broke off the betrothal to the Byzantine princess that had already been concluded in 842, no easy diplomatic decision. Soon, his brother's case was brought before the pope by Theutberga's supporters, among them the king of West Francia, Charles the Bald. Nicholas sided with Theutberga and nullified the divorce. Even worse: in due course, he excommunicated not only the archbishops of Cologne and Trier, but also two Italian bishops, John of Ravenna and Hagano of Bergamo. This prompted Louis II to besiege Rome in early 864. This attack did not change anything in north Alpine politics, but it weakened both the emperor and the pope. Louis could get his bishops reinstated and had a permanent imperial envoy created in the Lateran – Arsenius, bishop of Orte and uncle of Anastasius. He also obtained land in the Roman duchy, which he distributed among his followers. In the public opinion, the attack on Rome was detrimental for Louis' standing, however. The empress Angilberga, who had been essential in negotiating the peace between emperor and pope, rose to considerable importance in the government of the kingdom at this occasion. As Louis' wife was a Supponid, one of the influential families that had been installed in Italy by Lothar I, her elevated role was not received positively by everyone in Italy.[35]

In 865, Louis launched the largest and longest military campaign of his rule, again in southern Italy against the Saracens. With a sizeable, all-Italian army, he first ensured the support of all Christian southern potentates through persuasion or show of force and then launched an attack on the strongly fortified Emirate of Bari. In February 871, Bari finally fell, and Louis took its last emir, Sawdan, captive. The biggest part

---

[34] Heidecker, *The Divorce of Lothar II*.
[35] Gantner, 'Louis II and Rome'; Buc, 'Text and ritual'.

of Apulia was under the emperor's control at this point as well, so that the Frankish troops went on to besiege the last Saracen stronghold on this side of the peninsula, the important harbour of Taranto. Louis II was at the pinnacle of his reign, controlling the entire Italian peninsula, except for parts of Calabria.[36]

Not all had gone smoothly during the campaign, however, as we learn from a letter Louis sent in spring 871 to the Byzantine emperor Basil I (867–887). After personally murdering his predecessor Michael III, Basil had directly sought an alliance with the West. His envoys had ended the dispute around the now deposed patriarch Photios by accepting all judgments by Pope Hadrian II (867–872). Basil also directly sought an alliance with Louis II. Both emperors agreed on a marriage alliance, with Louis' daughter Ermengard being betrothed to a son of Basil. All seemed to be concluded in 870, and the Byzantine fleet was sent in order to help the Franks take Bari, but somehow, everything ended in quarrels, with Basil officially declining to address Louis as emperor and Louis not giving his daughter into marriage to Byzantium. The letter to Basil is a bitter one, fiercely reiterating the emperor's position in the dispute – while still trying to make good on the military alliance. It also contains a very eloquent description of Carolingian imperial ethos and thought as opposed to Byzantine views.[37]

Whether or not the expedition would or could have been prolonged after this we cannot know, because Louis suffered his biggest personal defeat in August of the same year. The southern Lombards under the lead of Prince Adelchis justifiably feared that the emperor intended to get the whole south permanently under his control. Hence, they rebelled and took Louis prisoner in Benevento, together with his wife and Ermengard. After about forty days, the emperor was set free, but had to swear never to return south. Louis was swiftly cleared of his oath by Pope Hadrian II, who also re-crowned him emperor in 872.[38]

In the south, too, the situation was volatile: only weeks after Louis' release from captivity, a sizeable army coming from Africa had started to besiege Salerno. Only with the help of new Frankish troops could the city be saved.[39] Capua was also soon taken by Louis and largely controlled by Angilberga from 872 onwards. Louis was possibly considering to re-start his southern project when he died unexpectedly on 12 August 875 at the age of about fifty. He had spent a lot of time during his final years trying

---

[36] Kreutz, *Before the Normans*, pp. 36–57.
[37] Louis II, ep. to Basil I, ed. Henze, *MGH EE* 7, pp. 386–94.
[38] Granier, 'La captivité de l'empereur Louis II'.
[39] Kreutz, *Before the Normans*, pp. 55–7.

to negotiate his succession – given that he had only one surviving daughter at the time, who could not succeed him in his office. Louis was very much inclined to give his *regnum* and probably the imperial office to one of the sons of his uncle Louis the German. John VIII, pope since 872 and a supporter of Louis in principle, was far more inclined to crown Louis' younger uncle, Charles the Bald. Ironically, both uncles had prevented Louis from inheriting his brother Lothar's kingdom (Lothar had died in 869 without legitimate heirs). Instead, the two uncles had split up that kingdom between themselves in the treaty of Meersen in 870, much to the dismay of Pope Hadrian II, who had even threatened both of them with excommunication. Still, after his southern triumph and disaster, Louis followed the traditional policy his father had already defined – and supported the east Frankish line.[40]

Epilogue of Carolingian Italy: Years of Chaos and Carolingian Heirs

Upon Louis' death, however, things turned around quickly: John VIII swiftly travelled to Charles the Bald, invited him to Italy and crowned him as emperor and king of Italy in Rome in 876. The east Frankish relatives were slower to act, but seem to have been able to command stronger forces. Charles left Italy in a hurry after his second visit in 877, before Carloman of Bavaria, his nephew, arrived with a sizeable army. A war for Italy was prevented by Charles' demise on the way back to Gaul. Carloman was elected king of Italy by the Italian Frankish nobles accordingly, but then died in 879.[41] His heir was his youngest brother, Charles the Fat, who even succeeded briefly in unifying the Carolingian kingdoms between 885 and 887, when he was ousted by his illegitimate nephew Arnulf. Until 899, Italian rule changed frequently between Berengar, margrave of Friuli and Carolingian through his mother's side, the Guidones Guy III and Lambert II (both numbers as dukes of Spoleto) and Arnulf.[42] In 899, it seemed at first as if Berengar would finally get Italy under his control, but Louis III, the young grandson of Louis II of Italy through his mother Ermengarde and heir of the kingdom of Burgundy through his father's side, intervened and was crowned emperor. Louis only fell into Berengar's hands through treason in Verona in 905, was blinded and sent back to Burgundy.[43] Berengar continued to have difficulties ruling Italy. After all, during the rather chaotic thirty years since Louis II's death, the potentates on the peninsula

---

[40] Bougard, 'Ludovico II'.   [41] Arnold, *Johannes VIII*.   [42] RI 1,3,2, ed. Zielinski.
[43] Zielinski, 'Ludwig der Blinde'.

had largely followed their own interests. Hence, Berengar was only crowned emperor in 915 and practically lost his kingdom in 923 when he was beaten by Rudolf II of Upper Burgundy. Berengar was murdered in spring 924 in his last loyal city of Verona. With his death, the western empire also ceased to exist for four decades, until it was renewed for Otto I in 962.[44]

Carolingian control in Italy, established in the final decades of the eighth century, faded irretrievably after 875, as many sources of the time let us know. One of the most drastic assessments was made by an anonymous author from northern Italy around the year 900, who wrote the so-called *Libellus de imperatoria potestate in urbe Roma*:

> From this day on, the sublime rights of royal majesty have neither been claimed by an emperor, nor by a king, either because the power to do so was lacking, or because knowledge of it has been lost in the numerous fights and relentless partitions of the kingdom. Because ever since, battles, slander and pillage have shaped the realm.[45]

Carolingian Italy had an afterlife until the deposition of Berengar II of Ivrea in 961 – indeed every ruler between 888 and 961 could claim descent from the Carolingians in some sense.[46] The kingdom had changed faster, however. It was soon far from being well organized as it had been in the 860s and 870s. Carolingian influence still prevailed in the *regnum* for some time. Carolingian legislation was copied and used, just as a few products pertaining to the Carolingian *correctio* were still copied and used. This did not change in Ottonian times either, which is no wonder, as this dynasty was in many ways heir to the preceding one. In the sense of political order and social impact, however, Carolingian Italy had not outlived the ninth century.

---

[44] Arnaldi, 'Berengario I,'.
[45] *Libellus de imperatoria potestate in urbe Roma*', ed. Zucchetti, pp. 209–10.
[46] Buc, 'Italian hussies and German matrons'.

Section I

Was There a Carolingian Italy?

3   Talking about the Carolingians in Eighth- and Ninth-Century Italy

Thomas F. X. Noble

Faced with the intellectual feast promised by the Vienna conference, my appetite proved too ambitious. I originally thought I would try to talk about 'What Was Carolingian about "Carolingian" Italy?' For a start, the very term 'Carolingian' needs a good deal of explanation. And no single definition could ever be offered. One could talk about Carolingian ideological domination, supposing for the moment that one could satisfactorily define a Carolingian ideology.[1] One could talk about political, legal, or institutional influence. This would involve sifting narrative sources as well as capitularies and charters; a daunting task. Stefano Gasparri has argued that relatively few Franks and other northerners followed Charlemagne to Italy,[2] whereas Paolo Delogu believes that the Lombard ruling class was gradually replaced by Frankish, Alemannian, and Burgundian nobles.[3] It seems to me possible that more northerners followed Lothar in the 830s than Charlemagne in the 770s. In any case, we must follow up on the prosopographical researches launched more than a half-century ago by Eduard Hlawitschka.[4] Did the appearance of the bipartite estate represent a Carolingian imposition on the Italian rural scene or was it a local, home-grown innovation?[5] One could talk about cultural issues ranging from the introduction of Carolingian-style school reforms to the spread of Caroline minuscule.[6] But there would be ironies and paradoxes involved in studying the cultural impact of the Carolingians on Italy. The Italian poets, grammarians, and theologians who joined Charlemagne's court were deeply influential.[7] John Mitchell

---

[1] The most recent account with a good discussion of the methodological problems is Kramer, 'Great expectations', esp. pp. 25–74.
[2] Gasparri, 'The aristocracy', pp. 72–5.
[3] Delogu, 'Lombard and Carolingian Italy', pp. 305–8.
[4] Hlawitschka, *Franken, Alemannen, Bayern und Burgunder in Oberitalien 774–962*.
[5] Wickham, 'Rural economy and society', esp. pp. 129–31.
[6] Everett, *Literacy in Lombard Italy*; Mitchell, 'Literacy displayed'.
[7] See, e.g., Godman, *Poetry of the Carolingian Renaissance*, pp. 4–33; Chiesa (ed.), *Paolino d'Aquileia*; Chiesa (ed.), *Paolo Diacono*.

has wondered whether much of what we typically call Carolingian art was not in fact Italian.[8] My point is that I could as well be asking how Italian were the Carolingians! It would indeed be foolish, in light of the chapters that will accompany this one as well as the magnitude of the topic, to suppose that I could answer all the questions I just posed – and many more that I could have posed.

For Sherlock Holmes, the first principle of good detection was to begin with the obvious. It seems to me that an obvious place to start is by asking how writers in Italy talked about the Carolingians between 774 and 875, that is, between Charlemagne's conquest of the Lombard kingdom and the death of Louis II. How, when, and why did writers in Italy discuss the Carolingians? Did they do so with warmth or with hostility? What kinds of things do *we* know which *they* passed over in silence? Despite Pippin's campaigns in 755 and 756, there was no decisive Carolingian impact on Italy before the fall of Desiderius in 774. After 875 every region of Italy fragmented so dramatically that while one might be able to speak of Carolingian legacies, any talk of direct and continuing Carolingian influence would be of questionable validity.

Several years ago in a conference at Durham University on 'England and the Continent in the Tenth Century', an obvious homage to Wilhelm Levison's famous book about the eighth century, I assembled a group of tenth-century narrative historians from various parts of Europe and adopted the conceit that they were my reporters and I was the news bureau chief.[9] I then reported on what my various 'journalists' told me. Today I wish to do the same thing with a series of Italian writers. I will focus on the *History of the Lombards* in the Gotha Codex, the history of Andreas of Bergamo, the Roman *Liber Pontificalis*, Agnellus of Ravenna's *Book of Pontiffs*, the *Chronicle* of Benedict of Monte Cassino, and the *History of the Lombards of Benevento* by Erchempert. Alert readers may wonder about the absence of the Salerno chronicle from this list. Although it is delightful and informative, I omitted it because it was written in the last decades of the tenth century. I asked each author two basic questions: *When* did you talk about the Carolingians and *how* did you talk about them? The first question gets to how interested various Italian writers were in the Carolingians and what they thought was important about them and their activities. The second question gets to the matter of attitudes. To put things into perspective, I will also mention

---

[8] Many of his studies could be cited. I choose only: Mitchell, 'L'arte nell'Italia longobarda e nell'Europa carolingia'; 'Artistic patronage and cultural strategies in Lombard Italy'; 'Karl der Große, Rom und das Vermächtnis der Langobarden'.

[9] Noble, 'The interests of historians in the tenth century'.

some things that Italian writers did not talk about. If my topic were the Carolingians in Italy, I could have added the Italian capitularies, whether issued in or for Italy, but these sources fundamentally reflect the Carolingians talking to and about themselves.[10] Likewise, the major Carolingian annals – say the *Royal Frankish Annals*, the *Annals of St-Bertin*, or the *Annals of Fulda* regularly shed clear light on Italian situations but these are Carolingian, not Italian, sources. Clearly, a history of Carolingian Italy would demand attention to these sources, and to others as well, but that is not my intention here.

Another obvious point is that Italy is a spectacularly complicated place. It has been so from Roman times until today. Talking about Carolingian Italy inevitably involves asking what parts of Italy one might imagine the Carolingians as having ruled or seriously influenced. In the end, one is reduced to speaking confidently only about the Po basin, about Lombardy – or Lombardia – more or less. The Carolingians influenced Benevento but never controlled it. Carolingian influence in Campania, Calabria, Apulia, and Basilicata was negligible.[11] Paolo Delogu argued, quite rightly it seems to me, that Friuli, Tuscany, and Spoleto were effectively marches.[12] So if we ask about how Carolingian Italy was we must admit that our question is bounded by both thematic and geographical considerations.

Turning then to when Italian writers talked about the Carolingians invites me to split the question: When did Italian writers talk about Carolingians in Italy itself and when did those writers notice developments in the wider Carolingian world? In fact, my writers devoted about equal amounts of attention to both subjects. Where Italy itself is concerned, the Italian writers provide extremely disjointed accounts. They give us brief notices that do not add up to anything like a narrative. Where the wider Carolingian world is concerned, the writers reveal general interest but are often confused about basic details.

The era of Charlemagne receives some attention in several of the sources. Prior to Charlemagne's reign, the Franks appear only in very

---

[10] See especially Azzara and Moro (eds.), *I capitolari italici*, which contains excellent historical commentary and editions of the capitularies which improve somewhat on the standard Boretius-Krause edition in the *MGH*.

[11] There is no point in providing here a bibliography on early medieval Italy. I cite a few basic works and some that have particularly influenced my thinking. The classic narrative remains Hartmann, *Geschichte Italiens*, vol. III. More recent is Fumagalli, *Il Regno italia*. Delogu, 'Lombard and Carolingian Italy' is solid. The essays in La Rocca (ed.), *Italy in the Early Middle Ages* are wide-ranging and authoritative. Comprehensive and excellent remains Wickham, *Early Medieval Italy*, esp. for present purposes pp. 28–79. On the south, Kreutz, *Before the Normans*, pp. 1–54 and Brown, 'Byzantine Italy'.

[12] Delogu, 'Lombard and Carolingian Italy', p. 305.

brief references to marriages between the Lombard and Merovingian royal families.[13] Perhaps the intent was merely to establish some antecedent connections between the two peoples. The Gotha Codex and Andreas speak very briefly about Charlemagne's Italian campaign of 773–4.[14] The former says Charles came to defend St Peter while the latter offers only the rather odd statement that Desiderius gave his daughter to Charles, but discord arose because Charles had an evil brother. Charles, Andreas says, forgot the good things that Desiderius did for him.[15] He does not inform us about what those good things might have been. The Gotha Codex adds that Charles permitted the Lombards to keep their own laws.[16] Andreas says that it was Pope Leo who, having been harassed by the Lombards, went to Metz for three years and invited Charles to come to Italy – an obvious misstatement. And he adds that because the pope judged the Franks astute, he encouraged them to come to Italy and conquer the Lombards – something they had already done.[17] Agnellus adds the otherwise unattested assertion that Archbishop Leo of Ravenna invited Charles to Italy and showed him the way and claims that Charles plundered the Lombard kingdom and took his father-in-law Desiderius away as a hostage.[18] This may be how things were remembered around 840 when Agnellus was writing. Andreas, writing forty years later, says that Rotcaud and Gaido rebelled because of the devastation. He also says that the Lombards defeated the Franks at Livenza but subsequently were themselves defeated and submitted with some of the vanquished being permitted to retain their offices.[19] No Frankish source corroborates this statement. The Gotha Codex, written probably between 806 and 810,[20] seems to have something like this in mind when it says that Charles elected to forget the wrongdoings of those who rebelled.[21] The *Liber Pontificalis* contains a detailed and largely accurate portrayal of events in Italy from 768 to 774 but focuses on Rome and says nothing about Charles having devastated Italy. The *Liber Pontificalis* does not mention Rotcaud's rebellion. No Italian narrative explicitly mentions Charlemagne's visits to Italy in 781 and 787, although Erchempert says

[13] *Historia Langobardorum codicis Gothani*, cc. 4, 5, p. 284.
[14] *Historia Langobardorum codicis Gothani*, c. 9, pp. 286–8; Andreas, *Historia*, c. 3, p. 223–4.
[15] Andreas, *Historia*, c. 5, p. 224.
[16] *Historia Langobardorum codicis Gothani*, c. 9, pp. 286–8.
[17] Andreas, *Historia*, c. 4, p. 224.
[18] Agnellus, *Liber Pontificalis ecclesiae Ravennatis*, c. 160, p. 338. Andreas also says that there was great desolation in Italy: Andreas, *Historia*, c. 4, p. 224.
[19] Andreas, *Historia*, c. 6, p. 225.
[20] Pohl, 'Memory, identity and power in Lombard Italy', p. 21; Berto, 'Remembering old and new rulers', p. 28.
[21] *Historia Langobardorum codicis Gothani*, c. 9, p. 286–8.

that Charlemagne was always attacking Benevento and that God, who supported the Beneventans, spread plague among the Franks who had to turn back.[22] Andreas says that Charles departed from Italy and left it in the hands of his son Pippin. Charles also, Andreas says, took nobles and first-borns as hostages.[23] This is a garbled account of Charles' visit to Rome in 781, when Pope Hadrian crowned and anointed Pippin, and his visit to Benevento in 787, when he took Grimoald and others hostage. He adds that Charlemagne built a palace in Rome, something he did not in fact do.[24] With no sense of chronological order, the Gotha Codex says that Pippin defeated the Avars, liberated Corsica, and punished the Beneventans for breaking their oaths.[25] Erchempert says that Pippin wished to subject Grimoald to himself, as Arichis had once been subject to Desiderius. He goes on to say that Grimoald married a niece of the emperor – Charlemagne was not yet emperor – but eventually rejected her because all the Franks were opposing him; he could not control the 'barbarous Franks'. The Franks 'gnawed' at Italy like locusts, Erchempert says.[26] These statements are more or less true but not very helpful in building up a picture of Carolingian activities in Italy. Charlemagne's imperial coronation is virtually ignored except by the Gotha Codex, which says he became emperor to defend St Peter,[27] and by the *Liber Pontificalis*, whose account, as is well known, does not square with the Frankish sources.[28] On the whole, ninth-century writers do not seem to have known very much about Carolingian activity in Italy or to have been very interested in what the Carolingians did in this early period when, as the Gotha Codex puts it, the Lombard kingdom ended and the Kingdom of Italy began.[29] In so far as the Gotha Codex does not develop this point and no other source mentions it, I think it would be an exaggeration to see in this simple, albeit true, statement a dawning sense of Italian identity – not that anyone has done so.

---

[22] Erchempert, *Historia*, c. 6, p. 236.   [23] Andreas, *Historia*, c. 5, p. 224.

[24] See, in general, Noble, *Republic of St. Peter*, pp. 153–81. The hostage-taking was real enough and perhaps remained in memory in the south: *Annales regni Francorum*, anno 787, ed. Kurze, p. 74. Charles may in 781 have renovated some quarters near St Peter's for himself and for Frankish officials visiting Rome: Brühl, 'Die Kaiserpfalz bei St. Peter' and 'Neues zur Kaiserpfalz bei St. Peter'.

[25] *Historia Langobardorum codicis Gothani*, c. 9, pp. 286–8.

[26] Erchempert, *Historia*, cc. 2, 6, pp. 235, 236–7.

[27] *Historia Langobardorum codicis Gothani*, c. 9, pp. 286–8.

[28] The basic details are in Noble, *Republic of St. Peter*, pp. 291–9. Perhaps the fullest account remains Heldmann, *Das Kaisertum Karls des Großen*. See also: Wolf (ed.), *Zum Kaisertum Karls des Großen* and Folz, *The Coronation of Charlemagne*. The most recent and sprightly account are Fried, *Charlemagne*, pp. 373–430, and Nelson, *King and Emperor*, pp. 367–86.

[29] *Historia Langobardorum codicis Gothani*, c. 5, p. 284.

Moving on to the era of Louis the Pious and Lothar, the sources have
more to say, but, once again, what they say is often wrong and rarely
helpful. Andreas notes the death of Pippin and Charlemagne's conferral
of the kingdom on Pippin's son Bernard. He says that Francia was left to
Louis 'who began to be called emperor'. He adds, without clarifying
details, that Italy enjoyed prestige and abundance. He then makes the
remarkable statement that Louis' wife Ermengard hated Bernard and
had him blinded without Louis' knowledge. Andreas also says that Louis
was 'prudent, learned, merciful and peaceful' and that there was peace
everywhere. This is a marked contrast to the desolation he ascribed to
Charlemagne's era. And yet Andreas, like other Italian writers as we shall
see, was confused about the Carolingian family. He says that Louis had
two sons with Ermengarde, Lothar and Louis, and one with Judith,
Charles. He missed Ermengarde's son Pippin.[30] Andreas adds only one
other detail from the era of Louis. He says that the Lombards had been
suffering attacks by the Slavs until the emperor made Eberhard duke of
Friuli.[31] Agnellus mentions the deaths of Charlemagne's sons Pippin and
Charles and the succession of Louis, but he provides very few useful
details.[32] The *Liber Pontificalis* is astonishingly silent about the era of
Louis the Pious. The life of Stephen IV mentions briefly the pope's
journey to Francia and says that he got everything he asked for.[33] What
he in fact got was the *Pactum Ludovicianum*, the more or less definitive
Carolingian settlement of the papal lands in Italy.[34] This document was
confirmed under Stephen's successor Paschal but his vita does not say a
word about it. No Italian source mentions that Stephen crowned Louis at
Reims in 816. Agnellus merely confirms that Pope Stephen got whatever
was asked from Louis while he was in Francia, but it is hard to know what
he had in mind.[35] The life of Paschal is utterly silent about the murder-
ous strife in Rome in the 820s and does not mention the *Constitutio
Romana* of 824 that put Franco-papal relations on a firmer legal
footing.[36] A faint echo of Paschal's troubles is found in the life of his
successor Eugenius, where we read that the officials held hostage in
Francia were repatriated.[37] Lothar's imperial coronation in Rome is
mentioned in no Italian source and we receive no reports about his
activity in Italy. Andreas says that Louis made Lothar emperor,

[30] Andreas, *Historia*, cc. 5, 6, 7, pp. 224–6.
[31] But his sense of chronology here is seriously awry: Andreas, *Historia*, c. 8, p. 226.
[32] Agnellus, *Liber Pontificalis ecclesiae Ravennatis*, c. 168, p. 349.
[33] *LP* II, Life 99, p. 49.   [34] Noble, *Republic of St Peter*, pp. 148–83.
[35] Agnellus, *Liber Pontificalis ecclesiae Ravennatis*, c. 170, p. 350.
[36] Noble, *Republic of St. Peter*, pp. 308–22.   [37] *LP* II, Life 101, p. 69.

presumably a reference to the *Ordinatio Imperii* of 817[38] and he also says, incorrectly, that Louis gave Italy to Lothar's son Louis.[39] Andreas takes one plunge into Frankish politics in the era of Louis and he adds an Italian twist to the story. He says that some evil men persuaded Lothar to take his father's wife Judith away to Italy, whereas Erchempert says only that Lothar captured Louis and his wife but was subsequently forced by Louis' nobles to free the imperial pair.[40] This did happen in the rebellion of 830. But Andreas adds that Archbishop Angilbert of Milan along with some noble supporters stirred up Lothar in the first place. Lothar sent Angilbert to his father to win back his good graces. Angilbert allegedly threatened Louis with eternal damnation if he did not pardon his son.[41] No Frankish source mentions Angilbert. Agnellus adds the otherwise unattested detail that Archbishop George of Ravenna wished to curry favour with Lothar by taking his daughter Rotruda from the baptismal font.[42] The second rebellion in 833 is passed over in silence in the Italian sources as is Lothar's destructive sojourn in Italy beginning in 834. Pope Gregory IV's ill-starred trip to Francia in 833 is ignored. Once again, Italian writers seem neither interested in nor well informed about Frankish rule in Italy or wider developments in the Carolingian world.

Beginning around 840, the situation changes pretty dramatically. We begin to get more details about affairs in both Italy and Francia. Several writers note the death of Louis the Pious and the succession of his sons. Agnellus says the empire was divided, but Erchempert says the 'Kingdom of the Franks' was divided.[43] Agnellus says that Lothar got the greatest part, Pippin got Aquitaine, and Louis got Bavaria. These were, he notes, the sons of Ermengard. Charles got the 'best' part, but he does not say what it was. He also adds the detail that Louis' daughter Gisela married Eberhard who, as noted above, was mentioned by Andreas for helping the Italians against the Slavs.[44] To the best of my recollection, Eberhard is the only non-royal or imperial Frank mentioned so far by an Italian chronicler. He must have made a mark in north-eastern Italy.[45] Erchempert says that Lothar got Italy and Aachen, Louis

---

[38] But the *Ordinatio Imperii* did not assign Italy to Lothar and Lothar was not crowned in Rome until 823, so it is a bit difficult to discern what Andreas was thinking about. See Boshof, *Ludwig der Fromme*, pp. 129–34, 158–62 for basic details.

[39] Andreas, *Historia*, c. 6, p. 225.

[40] Andreas, *Historia*, c. 6 p. 225; Erchempert, *Historia*, c. 10, pp. 238–9.

[41] Andreas, *Historia*, c. 7, p. 225.

[42] Agnellus, *Liber Pontificalis ecclesiae Ravennatis*, c. 171, p. 351.

[43] Agnellus, *Liber Pontificalis ecclesiae Ravennatis*, c. 172, p. 352; Erchempert, *Historia*, c. 11, p. 239.

[44] Agnellus, *Liber Pontificalis ecclesiae Ravennatis*, c. 172, p. 352.

[45] See Schmidinger, 'Eberhard, Markgraf von Friaul'.

got Bavaria, and Charles, of another mother, got Aquitaine.[46] He does not mention Louis' son Pippin who died in 838 and left his realm of Aquitaine to his like-named son. Aquitaine was contested between Charles and Pippin II for many years and, as I shall tell just below, Agnellus knew that Charles succeeded to the West Frankish kingdom, so perhaps that is what he meant by 'best'. Andreas does not discuss the succession to Louis but instead describes the family of Lothar. Lothar ruled with his son Louis in Italy, Lothar II in Francia, and Charles in Provence.[47] He ignored Lothar's brothers. Events surrounding the fierce struggle among the sons of Louis the Pious were widely noticed albeit in ways that are incomplete and confusing. Agnellus offers a plangent assessment of the troubles in the Frankish world:

Before the world can be consumed according to the Gospel, there will be pestilence and hunger and terrors from heaven, angers, quarrels, dissensions and strife. Nation will be raised against nation, and kingdom will rage against kingdom, and the youth will outrank the old man, and the younger generation will render no honor to their elders, but sons will despise their fathers, and will not only deride them, but even subjugate them.[48]

Fair enough, but concretely what was his point with respect to Italy? Andreas says that instead of fighting pagans, presumably Vikings, the Franks turned to fighting each other. Andreas mentions the Battle of Fontenoy in 841 and says, oddly, that so many Aquitanians died that the Northmen got free rein in Francia.[49] Agnellus says that Lothar was fighting against Charles. He adds that Archbishop George of Ravenna asked Lothar to permit him to travel to Francia with papal envoys. He did travel to Francia with a huge and costly retinue, supposedly to attempt to make peace among the brothers but actually to urge the emperor to help him escape from the authority of the pope.[50] It is not my story here, but Agnellus took a very dim view of Archbishop George, which probably explains why he offered more details about this Frankish démarche than he usually did. In fact, as the St-Bertin annalist says, George had been sent to Francia by Pope Gregory IV, but Lothar did not permit him to consult with his brothers. George was captured at Fontenoy and sent home 'honourably', presumably by Charles and Louis, a fact that Gregory's vita does not mention.[51] So the lengthy harangue of George

---

[46] Erchempert, *Historia*, c. 11, p. 239.   [47] Andreas, *Historia*, c. 7, p. 226.
[48] Agnellus, *Liber Pontificalis ecclesiae Ravennatis*, c. 68, pp. 237–8, trans. Deliyannis, p. 183. Oddly, Agnellus inserts these words, which bear on the last years of his life (he died around 846), into his account of Bishop Victor (538–545).
[49] Andreas, *Historia*, c. 7, p. 226.
[50] *Liber Pontificalis ecclesiae Ravennatis*, cc. 173, 174, pp. 352–3.   [51] *AB* (841), p. 38.

delivered by Charles and reported in detail by Agnellus probably did not take place.[52] The various treaties beginning with Verdun in 843 that carved up the Frankish world are passed over in silence. None of the Italian writers seems to have noticed that the strife among the Franks had important implications for Italy.

The *Liber Pontificalis* has a fair amount to say about Louis II after being virtually silent about the Carolingians for some twenty years. The vita of Sergius II (844–847) says that news of the election reached the 'unconquered Augustus', that is Lothar, who sent Drogo (Louis the Pious' half-brother and the archbishop of Metz) and Louis to Rome. Frankish troops and clerics entered Bologna and perpetrated 'slaughter and butchery, indeed tyrannical cruelty, savage wickedness, ferocious purpose and atrocious intent'. None of this mayhem is mentioned by the St-Bertin annals, which, moreover, say that Lothar sent his envoys to Rome to assure that no future pope would be elected except on the emperor's orders and in the presence of his representatives.[53] The *Liber Pontificalis* omits these details. Nevertheless, the pope sent envoys out nine miles to 'gloriously welcome' the king. Although Louis assured the pope that he had no evil intentions, his troops devastated the suburbs. Still the pope crowned and anointed him and made him king of the Lombards. Drogo allegedly stirred up trouble in Rome for the pope while the Franks asked the pope to get the leading Lombards to swear an oath of loyalty to Louis. It is difficult to say which Lombards are meant here but, as we shall see just below, the Lombards of the south considered themselves to be *the* Lombards. Siconulf of Benevento came to Rome with many soldiers to meet Louis. In fact, as Erchempert reports, Siconulf had bribed Guy of Spoleto 50,000 gold coins to get Louis to recognize his claims in the south.[54] Were not Erchempert so ambivalent about Louis II and hostile to Guy, it might be possible to take this statement as a grudging recognition of Louis' authority in the south. Louis returned to Pavia and the Romans were delighted to be delivered from 'the plague and yoke of tyrannical frightfulness'. The last part of Sergius' vita recounts the Saracen attack on Rome in August of 846 and has a vague reference to the Frankish *schola* but no further reference to the Carolingians.[55] Benedict of Monte Cassino says that a Frankish army chased the Saracen attackers to Gaeta where it was defeated, further details which

---

[52] *Liber Pontificalis ecclesiae Ravennatis*, c. 174, pp. 354–5.   [53] *AB* (844), pp. 45–6.

[54] Erchempert, *Historia*, c. 18, p. 241. The *scholae* were more or less permanent settlements for foreigners located in the *borgo* between St Peter's and the Tiber. They are not very well attested: Reekmans, 'Le développement topographique de la region du Vatican'.

[55] *LP* II, Life 104, pp. 87–99.

the *Liber Pontificalis* omits.[56] The vita of Leo IV (847–855), perhaps understandably, concentrates on the pope's construction activity, especially the erection of the Leonine City. Still, it is odd that the text does not mention Louis II's imperial coronation in 850. The *Liber Pontificalis* does say that Leo called a council (in 853) on the advice of the 'serene emperors'.[57] Leo's vita ends with a curious story. An obscure Daniel, tagged as 'evil', went to Louis II with false claims that the Magister Militum Gratian had said that the Franks were of no use and that, accordingly, Rome should make a treaty with the Greeks and expel the Franks from 'our kingdom' – whatever that is supposed to mean. Louis was angry and headed for Rome, where the pope received him honourably. Pope and emperor held court to investigate Daniel's claims against Gratian, but the Romans called Daniel a liar. Daniel was condemned by Roman law, but Louis pardoned him.[58] Neither Frankish nor other Italian sources mention these events.

Where news of the Carolingians is concerned, the vita of Benedict III (855–858) concentrates on the challenge mounted against Benedict by Anastasius. A to-and fro of envoys and messages between Rome and Louis II seems to have been marked by a good deal of both deceit and confusion. The emperor's envoys finally figured out that Anastasius' supporters had attempted to deceive them and that the Romans actually backed Benedict. Anastasius was dismissed from Rome.[59] The vita does also say that on the election of Benedict III, a decree was sent to Lothar to inform him 'as the old custom demands'.[60] We saw above that at the time of the election of Sergius II, Lothar insisted on his rights in the papal election process. Those rights were, of course, grounded in the *Constitutio Romana* of 824. When Leo IV was elected, the Romans proceeded to consecrate him immediately because of the dire Saracen threat to the city, but they acknowledged that they had not met their obligations to the emperor.[61] Turning to the vita of Nicholas I (858–867), we encounter two developments pertaining to the Carolingians. We learn that Nicholas was consecrated in the presence of Louis II and that the pope dined with the emperor and kissed him as his dearest son. Louis left Rome and after a short while the pope came out to meet him at Tor di'Quinto, where the emperor did groom service. Louis made generous gifts to St Peter's.[62] The wider Frankish world

[56] Benedict of Monte Cassino, *Chronica*, c. 6, p. 472.   [57] *LP* II, Life 105, p. 129.
[58] Ibid., p. 134.
[59] *LP* II, Life 106, pp. 141–2. These developments have not been comprehensively studied since 1920: Perels, *Papst Nikolaus I und Anastasius Bibliothecarius*.
[60] *LP* II, Life 106, p. 141.   [61] *LP* II, Life 105, p. 107.
[62] *LP* II, Life 107, 151–2, 159.

comes up in the vita in connection with the long-running divorce case of Lothar II and his wife, Theutberga, and with the struggle between Hincmar of Reims and Bishop Rothad of Soissons. Although one has to turn to the papal correspondence and to Frankish sources for a full account of these issues, the report about these Frankish causes célèbres is the fullest one in the *Liber Pontificalis*.[63] The vita of Hadrian II (867–872) reports only that Duke Lambert of Spoleto entered Rome as a tyrant, and that he plundered houses, spared no monasteries, and gave girls to his followers for ravishing. The text does not mention Louis' recoronation in 872.[64]

It would exhaust my space to try to narrate the extraordinarily complicated politics of southern Italy from the 830s to the death of Louis II in 875. Although their accounts are anything but clear and complete, Andreas and Erchempert, and to a lesser degree Benedict of Monte Cassino, reveal the basic issues. Three points seem reasonably clear. First, Louis II wished to exert real control in the south but failed to do so. Second, aristocratic factionalism arose repeatedly and caused Benevento, Salerno, Capua, Naples, and Amalfi to battle each other constantly, with one group or another requesting aid from Louis II. Third, various leaders hired Saracen mercenaries to advance their own political projects only to lose control of those mercenaries at the very time when Saracen bands captured Bari and Taranto.[65]

The Italian chroniclers make seemingly random reference to the Carolingians, primarily to Louis II and Guy of Spoleto, in the years between 844 and 852, and then they go almost quiet about the Franks until Louis spent five continuous years in the south from 866 to 871. Even during those years, however, the sources do not permit a coherent narrative. The driving force in the south was a virtual civil war in Benevento complicated by independent Saracen incursions and strife occasioned by Saracen mercenaries hired by Benevento and Salerno. Saracens captured Bari in 847 and from that base were attacking widely. According to Erchempert there were numerous appeals to Louis to come to the aid of the threatened locals. Erchempert says there was real fear that Louis would not come south.[66] Benedict of Monte Cassino adds some revealing details. He says that the 'Lombards' sent envoys to Louis in 'Francia' to request help from Louis. He also says, apparently with reference to the year 852, that Abbot Bassacius went to 'Francia' to seek help from Louis. And he says that after Louis had campaigned in

---

[63] Ibid., pp. 159–63. For the details see Noble, 'Pope Nicholas I and the Franks'.
[64] *LP* II, Life 108, p. 177.   [65] See the works cited in n. 11 above.
[66] Erchempert, *Historia*, c. 20, p. 242.

Benevento he returned to 'Francia'.[67] Francia here can only mean northern Italy, so in Benedict's view the real Lombards were in Benevento and
northern Italy was effectively Frankish. Erchempert says that Louis took
hostages from the Calabrians and sent them to 'Langobardia'.[68] Note
that what Benedict calls Francia, Erchempert calls Lombardy. This is as
close as any of these authors comes to a statement that reveals something
about identity. Louis did come to Italy in 847 and he attacked Bari
without success. In the next year or two, apparently having tired of
constant strife in Benevento, he divided the region into two autonomous
principalities.[69] Louis' efforts seem to have been preceded by those of
Guy of Spoleto, who cashed in again on the quarrels of the Beneventans.
In 844 he had taken money to help Siconulf (who was his son-in-law) but
in, probably, 848 he took 70,000 gold coins from Radelgis to persuade
Siconulf not to attack him.[70] Anyway, Louis assigned Benevento to
Radelgis and Salerno to Siconulf. This solution proved only marginally
successful, and at the same time factional squabbling in Capua proceeded apace.[71]

Albeit with differing emphases and amounts of information, the Italian
writers all pay some attention to the five years (866–871) Louis II spent
in the south. Benedict gives a remarkably detailed account of Louis'
military muster in 865.[72] Benedict simply had to have seen the document
and one wishes he had been similarly forthcoming on other events.
Although Louis visited many parts of the south and attempted to introduce his authority everywhere, the main events were Louis' capture of
Bari and its emir, Sawdan,[73] and then Louis' capture and brief detention
by the Beneventans.[74] A minor theme running through the sources is the
complicated relationship between Louis II and Capua.[75] Andreas attributes Louis' capture to evil Beneventans who, chafing under Frankish
domination, also rounded up numerous Franks. Erchempert, who ought

[67] Benedict of Monte Cassino, *Chronica*, cc. 2, 12, pp. 469, 474.
[68] Erchempert, *Historia*, c. 35, p. 248.
[69] Erchempert, *Historia*, c. 19, p. 242. On the *division* see Kreutz, *Before the Normans*,
    pp. 32–5.
[70] Erchempert, *Historia*, c. 17, p. 241.
[71] Erchempert, *Historia*, cc. 21–32, pp. 242–6 passim.
[72] Benedict of Monte Cassino, *Chronica*, c. 3, pp. 469–70. For the actual document see
    I capitolari italici, no. 45, pp. 210–4.
[73] Andreas, *Historia*, c. 14, p. 228; Erchempert, *Historia*, c. 33, p. 247. It is surprising that
    Benedict of Monte Cassino does not mention this important historical fact.
[74] Andreas, *Historia*, c. 16, pp. 228–9; Erchempert, *Historia*, c. 38, p. 249. *La cronaca della
    dinastia capuana*, c. 1, p. 300. Once again, Benedict passes over this event in silence.
[75] Benedict, *Chronica*, cc. 14, 19, pp. 475–6, 477–8; Erchempert, *Historia*, c. 32, p. 246–7;
    La cronica della dinastia capuana, c. 1, pp. 298–300. For basic details see Kreutz, *Before
    the Normans*, pp. 69–70.

to have known better, says Louis was captured because he had failed in Rome. He means that Louis had failed to get Pope Hadrian II to reconcile the two Frankish bishops who had been censured for approving the divorce of Lothar II from his wife Theutberga. He also says that Louis was detained because he refused to kill Sawdan, the emir of Bari. Nevertheless, and paradoxically, he calls Louis the 'saviour of the province of Benevento'. There might be something to the latter claim, but the former is ridiculous. Erchempert obviously knew something about Lothar II's marital problems and says that he came to Italy to see his brother. From Frankish sources we know that Lothar did attempt unsuccessfully to get his brother Louis II to prevail upon the pope to grant him a divorce.[76] It is not clear to me why Andreas chose to speak about this case or why Erchempert connected it with Benevento. Indeed, Lothar II died in 869 while Louis was besieging Benevento, so any 'failure' in Rome would have been irrelevant to Louis' capture in 871. Perhaps the Italian writers feared that Louis II had been distracted by his brother's troubles and proffered a garbled account of the basic details and chronology.

Be that as it may, after the fall of Bari and the capture and release of Louis II, Italian writers lost interest in Carolingian activities in the south of Italy. Andreas alone adds a few rather random additional details pertaining to events in the north. He notes the rebellion in Burgundy of Hubert, Theutberga's brother, and its suppression by Conrad. Then he discusses the death of Louis II (875) and his burial in Brescia on the orders of Bishop Antonius. Right away, Archbishop Anspertus of Milan demanded Louis' body and went to Brescia to fetch it. Andreas tells us that he accompanied the body part of the way to Milan. Finally, Andreas says that the nobles and Engelberga, Louis' widow, gathered in Pavia and asked Louis' uncles Charles and Louis to come as kings and compose the situation. In fact, very complicated Carolingian family politics ensued, but Charles (the Bald) did come to Italy and was crowned emperor in Rome in 875.[77] Interest in the Carolingians ends here for the sources I have been following.

Lothar I, who spent a considerable part of his reign in Italy, is strangely absent from these narratives. Louis II gets a good deal more attention. But he sort of pops up in the stories when someone needed his help against political foes or Muslim marauders. The *Liber Pontificalis* relates that Louis II provided some funds for the construction of the Leonine

---

[76] *AF* (868), pp. 66–7; *AB* (869), pp. 153-6. The latter is by far the fuller account. The Fulda annalist telescoped events from 866 to 869 into a few lines.

[77] *Historia Langobardorum codicis Gothani*, cc. 9, 18, 19, pp. 226–7, 229–30.

City, twice did groom service for Nicholas I, and the successive vitae take some pains to show how the popes and the Romans lived up to the terms of the *Constitutio Romana* without, however, referring explicitly to that document. These few details, alongside Benedict's substantial account of Louis' military muster in 865, are all we have to go on in terms of institutional details, even though Louis reigned in Italy for thirty-five years (840–875). If Charlemagne's defeat of Desiderius in 774 inaugurated the 'Kingdom of Italy', one would be hard pressed to discern the existence of the kingdom from the Italian narrative sources.

Let me turn now to how the Italian sources talk about the Carolingians. I am going to focus on three issues: First, what kinds of titles did the Italian writers give the Carolingians? Second, what kinds of positive things did these writers say about the Carolingians? Third, what kinds of negative sentiments were expressed?

Not one of my sources uses a title exactly like the ones found in Frankish diplomatic materials. But they often come close. The Gotha Codex speaks of 'the most glorious Charles, King of the Franks'.[78] Note that the author does not add king of the Lombards and does not mention the imperial title. Neither Andreas nor Agnellus offers anything that looks remotely like a title. In the vita of Hadrian I, the *Liber Pontificalis* offers 'His excellency the God-protected King Charles the Great'.[79] This, incidentally, constitutes the first time any source calls Charles 'Great', attached *Magnus* to *Carolus*. Otherwise, Charles is 'most Christian' or 'most excellent'.[80] Charles the 'Great' reappears in the life of Leo III, where he is otherwise the 'Lord King Charles' or rather more expansively 'king of the Franks and of the Lombards and patrician of the Romans'.[81] Under Stephen IV we read of the 'Pious, Serene Lord Emperor Louis'.[82] The life of Sergius II offers 'the unconquered augustus emperor Lothar'.[83] Under Leo IV we find 'his beloved spiritual son Lord Lothar augustus' and 'most pious and serene Caesar'.[84] The life of Hadrian II provides 'the Christian emperor Louis (II)'.[85] Bearing in mind the steady flow of correspondence between the popes and the Carolingians, it is not surprising that the *Liber Pontificalis* approximates official Carolingian titulature. Erchempert offers 'Caesar Louis' who ruled in succession to 'Augustus Charles'.[86] Benedict offers 'Lord

---

[78] *Historia Langobardorum codici Gothani*, c. 1, p. 282.
[79] *LP* I, Life 97, pp. 494, 495. A bit later (p. 497) Charles is not only *magnus* but also 'a Deo institutus patricius Romanorum'.
[80] Ibid., pp. 494, 495, 496, 497.   [81] *LP* II, Life 98, pp. 5, 6.   [82] *LP* II, Life 99, p. 49.
[83] *LP* II, Life 104, p. 87.   [84] *LP* II, Life 105, p. 123.   [85] *LP* II, Life 108, p. 175.
[86] Erchempert, *Historia*, c. 10, p. 239.

Emperor Louis Augustus'.[87] The dynastic chronicle of Capua refers to 'emperor Louis'.[88] On the whole it seems fair to say that the Italian writers did not put much stress on the imperial dimension of Carolingian rule, but neither did they routinely call them 'Kings of the Lombards' or 'Kings of Italy', and only the *Liber Pontificalis* called them 'Patricians of the Romans'.

Those writers could, however, lay on the praise. For the author of the Gotha Codex, Charles was 'good, pious, merciful and compassionate'. The author adds, 'Though he might have destroyed everything he became clement and indulgent'. Charles' son Pippin was 'great and glorious'.[89] For Andreas the Franks were 'astute and noble'. Louis the Pious was 'very wise, prudent in counsel, merciful and a lover of peace'. He says that Louis II was 'moved by compassion and sorrow' to aid the Calabrians. And God protected Louis when the Beneventans captured him.[90] Agnellus says that Louis was kind, while his father was mighty.[91] The *Liber Pontificalis* uses various iterations of great, mild, gentle, merciful, Christian, truly Christian, orthodox, pious, serene, and peaceful.[92] Erchempert and Benedict, however, are stingy with praise. Erchempert almost grudgingly says that Louis was a great man and the saviour of Benevento – from the Bari Muslims, of course.[93] Benedict calls Louis II's wife Engelberga 'glorious' but skips the adjectives when talking about Louis himself.[94] I am inclined to argue that the positive things that these writers say are mainly boilerplate. They are not descriptions that differentiate one person from another, and they provide the historian with almost no help in interpreting the actions of the Carolingian rulers in Italy or the attitudes of Italian writers to them. I have in mind Clemens Gantner's fine book *Freunde Roms*, which shows how papal discourse constructed others, indeed otherness, in the eighth and ninth centuries. I find no such discourse in my Italian writers.

Or perhaps it could be argued that if there is no consistent positive construction of the Franks there is a consistent and relentlessly negative one. Andreas says that although Charles invaded Italy by divine will, his appearance was accompanied by great desolation and that people were

[87] Benedict of Monte Cassino, *Chronica*, c. 4, p. 471.
[88] *La cronaca della dinastia capuana*, c. 1, p. 298.
[89] *Historia Langobardorum codici Gothani*, c. 9, pp. 286–8.
[90] Andreas, *Historia* cc. 6, 14, 18, pp. 225, 227, 229.
[91] *Liber Pontificalis ecclesiae Ravennatis*, *Versiculi* ll. 25–6, p. 139.
[92] Representative examples: *LP* I, Life 98, pp. 494, 497, 498; *LP* II, Lives 98, 99, 105, pp. 5–6, 49, 129.
[93] Erchempert, *Historia*, c. 34, p. 247.
[94] Benedict of Monte Cassino, *Chronica*, c. 4, p. 471.

killed by the sword, by hunger, and by animals. When Lothar II visited Italy, Andreas says, he wreaked devastation and harassed poor people.[95] Agnellus speaks of 'fierce Lothar the war-bringer' – he means Lothar I.[96] He also tells two tales that seem to me to have a negative tinge. He mentions how Charlemagne took away from Ravenna the statue of Theodoric and he mentions some beautiful jewelled gifts that Justinian had sent to Ravenna but that Charles could not afford to buy.[97] The *Liber Pontificalis* is generally positive, but in the life of Sergius II the author goes on a rant about Lothar II's devastating progress through Italy and in particular the 'slaughter, butchery, cruelty, savage wickedness, ferocious purpose and atrocious intent' visited upon Bologna. A bit later, the same vita says that the Franks oppressed Rome's suburbs with 'pestilential devastation'. When Louis II left Rome, the Romans were glad to be delivered from the 'enormous plague and yoke of tyrannical frightfulness'. In the time of Leo IV, the magister militum Gratian apparently claimed that the Franks were of no use to Rome; at any rate, a shady character named Daniel told Louis that Gratian had so expressed himself. In the time of Hadrian II, Lambert of Spoleto plundered Rome.[98] With Erchempert things heat up even a bit. He praises Duke Arichis as 'a most Christian man, greatly distinguished and energetic in war'. He goes on to say that Arichis tried to secure the passages into Benevento against 'Frankish trickery' and that the Franks 'gnawed away like locusts'. Arichis, he avers, removed all fear of the Franks. Grimoald wished to marry a niece of the emperor but all the Franks opposed him, and he was unable to calm the 'barbarous Franks'. Interestingly, in discussing Charlemagne, Erchempert accords him no titles and uses no adjectives about him and says simply that he was always attacking Benevento and was driven away because of plague, with God looking after the Beneventans. But recall that Andreas says that God protected Louis II from the Beneventans. A bit later, Erchempert says that Siconulf was driven by a lust for money 'to which the race of the Franks is greatly enslaved' – he had been talking about the skilled extortionist Guy of Spoleto. In the time of Louis II, the Franks 'gravely persecuted and cruelly distressed' the Beneventans.[99]

What conclusions might flow from the preceding discussion? Walter Pohl has said that the image of the Franks in Italian sources is

---

[95] Andreas, *Historia*, cc. 4, 7, pp. 224, 226.
[96] *Liber Pontificalis ecclesiae Ravennatis, Versiculi* ll. 26–7, p. 139.
[97] Ibid., cc. 94, 143, pp. 259–60, 321–2.
[98] *LP* II, Lives, 104, 105, 107, pp. 87, 88, 91, 134, 177.
[99] Erchempert, *Historia*, cc. 2, 3, 5, 6, 17, 34, pp. 235, 236, 241, 247.

ambiguous.[100] I do not disagree, but I would suggest that the ambiguity is not very deep. Italian writers do not seem to me to have evinced much interest in the Carolingians, whether cisalpine or transalpine. They often seem to have had poor information. When they praise Carolingians, they do so in ways that were conventional and only weakly informative. They criticize the Carolingians as tricky and as plunderers. I think that the balance of the evidence suggests that the prevailing view was negative.

Paolo Delogu has argued that there was no strong sense of Lombard identity, that personal and local interests were stronger.[101] That is basically true based on the texts that I have discussed, but there are those intriguing suggestions in Erchempert and Benedict that 'real' Lombards were Beneventans and that the original Lombard kingdom had somehow turned into 'Francia'. The Franks were always foreigners. The evidence is very slim, and I would not press it further.

Erchempert begins by saying that history is written to accumulate glory. I do not think he was referring to his own glory. As for the Lombards, he does begin with a sorry tale of how no one has recently – he means after Paul the Deacon – said anything positive about them.[102] And yet his tale hardly accumulates glory for the Lombards of Benevento, or indeed for any of the southern Italian principalities, and certainly not for a 'Kingdom of Italy'.

So let me offer a deliberately provocative conclusion: 'Carolingian' Italy simply did not exist for ninth-century Italian writers. It is a comparatively modern construct grounded in chronological and dynastic considerations more than in historical and cultural ones.

---

[100] Pohl, 'Invasions and ethnic identity', p. 29.
[101] Delogu, 'Lombard and Carolingian Italy', pp. 301–3.
[102] Erchempert, *Historia*, c. 1, pp. 234–5.

4   The Name of the Kingdom

Paolo Delogu

Since the earliest times following the conquest of Italy, the Langobard kings endeavoured to build an identity for their kingdom, aiming to go beyond the tribal organization of the people towards the creation of a lasting state structure. For this purpose, they made use of various cultural references, which accompanied a resolute politics of affirmation of royal power, both inside and outside the kingdom.

In the eighth century, these tendencies attained a high degree of maturity and complexity; kings like Liutprand, Ahistulf and Desiderius expressed an idea of the Langobard kingdom that can be summarized as follows: sovereignty belongs to the *gens Langobardorum*, which has a collective identity based on ancestral traditions and on the Catholic faith. The king rules in accordance with the kingdom's body politic, which is formed by all the freemen who share the Langobard identity, not necessarily coincident with the whole population of the kingdom. The king's rule is intended to secure the *salvatio* of the *gens*, both in the political and the religious and moral field. The name of the kingdom, as well as the title of the king derive from the sovereign people, and are, respectively, *regnum* and *rex Langobardorum*.[1]

The country over which the Langobards dominated had little relevance for the identity of the state; it was generically referred to as a *provincia*:[2] a term probably derived from the late antique official language, which came to the Langobards through ways that are difficult to ascertain. More usually, royal laws and deeds make reference to the kingdom as being formed of four regions that had a certain political or administrative identity: Austria, Neustria, Tuscia and Spoleto. In the eighth century, the kings strove to further extend their domination over other parts of the Italian peninsula, such as the Langobard duchy of

---

[1] A summary of these aspects in Delogu, 'Ritorno ai Longobardi'.
[2] *Leges Langobardorum*, ed. Beyerle: Rothari, cc. 3, p. 18; 4, p. 18; 193, p. 52; 256, p. 67; 264, p. 69; 273, p. 71; Liutprand, cc. 11, p. 103; 18, p. 108; 48, p. 122; 49, p. 122; 80, p. 137; 84, p. 139; 85, p. 140.

Beneventum, traditionally independent of the royal power, as well as the central and southern regions still under the rule of the Byzantine empire. In those years, the whole Italian peninsula seems to have become the would-be space of the Langobard kingdom; probably in that period a legend concerning Authari, one of the first Langobard kings in Italy, gained significance: according to the story, the king had reached in arms the farthest limits of Calabria to fix there the future boundaries of the Langobard kingdom.[3] Nonetheless, the tendency to make the kingdom coincident with the Italian peninsula left no trace in the official denomination of the kingdom, which continued to be named after the titular people of sovereignty.

After the Frankish conquest, these concepts were progressively abandoned; the Langobard identity was rejected, but no other equally coherent and meaningful concept took its place to express a new identity of the kingdom. This failure might be illustrated with reference to the political and institutional vicissitudes, but it can also be described through the history of the name of the kingdom, if it is considered as a reflection of political ideas and programs. A hypothesis that was formulated more than a hundred years ago, but still deserves attention, suggested that the Carolingian rulers deliberately replaced the term, as well as the concept, of *regnum Langobardorum* with that of a *regnum Italiae*, as an efficient means of effacing the ethnic tradition and of giving the kingdom a new identity, taken from geography. The new name would have lasted for long time, even until after the end of the Carolingian domination.[4]

This reconstruction brings to light an interesting problem, but the solution it gives does not seem to be decisive. In fact, the Frankish rulers failed the purpose of totally effacing the Langobard stamp of the kingdom; on the other hand, the very concept of *Italia* was far from offering a satisfying qualification for the kingdom.

Already in the Langobard period *Italia* was a multi-faceted term. In a learned context, it designated the whole Italian peninsula. Paul the Deacon, in his *Historia Langobardorum*, uses the word precisely in this sense when he gives the catalogue of the provinces into which Italy was divided; but he takes the list, together with the names, from ancient sources, not from current usage. Other names used equally by him for the peninsula, such as *Ausonia* or *Latium*, were also taken from the classical antiquity.[5] *Ausonia* instead of *Italia* is also found in other aulic

---

[3] Paul the Deacon, *Historia Langobardorum*, III, 32, ed. Bethmann and Waitz, p. 112.
[4] Leicht, 'Dal Regnum Langobardorum al Regnum Italiae'.
[5] Paul the Deacon, *Historia Langobardorum*, II, 24, ed. Bethmann and Waitz, p. 86.

or encomiastic texts of the Langobard period.[6] But in other contexts, *Italia* only designated the northern regions of the peninsula. So for instance in King Rothari's laws (636), a chronological note reckons the years passed since the entrance of the Langobards into the 'provincia Italiae': a term that seems to refer to one late-imperial province, perhaps the *Italia annonaria*, rather than to the entire Italian peninsula. Later on, *provincia* without any determination was used by the same Rothari and by other Langobard kings to designate the whole kingdom.[7] An eighth-century text that mentions Milan as 'Italiae metropolis' probably refers either to the ecclesiastical province of Milan, or to the northern regions of Italy, given that Milan never was the ecclesiastical metropolis of all Italy.[8] Another document, a private charter from Lucca, for all its ambiguity seems to distinguish *Etalia* from another constitutional dimension, called *provincia*, when it underlines that the same juridical usages were in force in both areas.[9] If the interpretation of the document is correct, the author seems to think that Lucca did not lie in *Etalia*, but in the *provincia*, that is, in the kingdom, of which *Etalia* was only a part.

In the Frankish-Merovingian texts, *Italia* is rarely found, for the most part only when they record military expeditions of the Frankish kings against the Langobards. In those cases, it has only a general, geographic meaning, and is used without any special determination.[10] Also, the early Carolingian annals use *Italia* when reporting King Pippin's expeditions against the Langobard king Ahistulf, but some of them also use *Langobardia* as an equivalent term.[11] This fact suggests that the redactors of the annals, also when they spoke of *Italia*, were thinking of the Langobard part of the peninsula, whatever extension it had in their minds. Subsequently, reporting Charlemagne's conquest, the same annals show a preference for *Italia*, probably in order to avoid the

---

[6] For instance: *Versus de Verona*, ll. 88–90, pp. 152–4: ... *Iam laudanda non est tibi / urbis in Ausonia // splendens pollens et redolens / a sanctorum corpora // opulenta inter centum/sola in Italia* ...

[7] *Leges Langobardorum*, ed. Beyerle, Rothari, Proem, p. 16. Leicht, 'Dal Regnum Langobardorum', suggests the possible remembrance of the *Vicariatus Italiae*, with the province *Italia annonaria*.

[8] *De Liutprando rege*, ed. Waitz, p. 11.

[9] *Codice Diplomatico Longobardo* II, ed. Schiaparelli, nr. 287, p. 419: ... *et nonnulli liceat nolle quod semel voluit, sed sicut pater iudicat, in eo moderamen persistat eo quod scriptum est quod partibus Etaliae usus capeat, non solum Etaliae sed omnis provincie. Et nullus de filii mei contra hanc meo iudicio aliquando agi presumat* ...

[10] *Liber historiae Francorum*, c. 26, 35, ed. Krusch, pp. 284, 301.

[11] *Italia* in *Annales sancti Amandi, continuatio*, y. 755, ed. Pertz, p. 10; *Annales Laurissenses minores*, cc. 18, 20, ed. Pertz, p. 116. *Langobardia* in *Annales Laureshamenses*, y. 754, 756, ed. Pertz, p. 28; y. 770, p. 30; *Annales Petaviani*, y. 754, 756, ed. Pertz, p. 11; cf. *Chronicon Moissiacense*, ed. Pertz, p. 293: *fines Langobardorum*.

reference to the Langobard identity of the kingdom, though *Langobardia* does not disappear in their language, and occasionally it is also used in the official vocabulary of the Frankish Chancery.[12] When *Italia* occurs, it rather sounds as if it was being used as a generic reference to the country, rather than as the official name of the kingdom. So, for instance, when the Royal Annals remember the early unction of Charlemagne's children as kings, they say that the two princes were consecrated by the pope respectively as kings *in Italia* and *in Aquitania*; these two territories are mentioned as spheres of domination rather than as structured kingdoms, although the kingdom, in Italy, had long since existed.[13] Other annals also registered the anointing of Charlemagne's children as kings not *of* Italy, or *of* Aquitania, but *super Italiam* and *super Aquitaniam*.[14] In the same manner, the first official documents of Charlemagne and his son Pippin, who was installed in the Italian kingdom as subordinated king, mention *Italia* generically as the ambit of the Frankish domination, even avoiding the institutional term *regnum*, let alone any reference to its Langobard tradition.[15]

The reasons for this reticence might depend on the consciousness that *Italia* was an ambiguous term, which designated either the entire Italian peninsula or a part of it. This last is the case of the *Divisio regnorum* of 806, the document in which Charlemagne predisposed the partition of the empire among his three sons, to be done after his death. Some

---

[12] The *Continuatio* of the *Annales Alamannici*, as well as the *Annales Guelferbitani* and the *Annales Nazariani*, use *Langobardia* for Charlemagne's expedition in 773 (*Annales Lauresham enses, Alamannici, Guelferbytani et Nazariani*, ed. Pertz, p. 40). In the year 776, the *Annales Alamannici* have *Karolus rex in Italiam*, whilst the two others have *Karolus rex in Langobardia* (*Annales Lauresham enses*, ed. Pertz, p. 40). A diploma of Charlemagne of the year 775 says: ... *infra regna quem adquaesivimus Deo propitio Italiae qui dicitur Langobardia vel Valle Tellina* ... (*Diplomata Caroli Magni*, nr. 94, ed. Mühlbacher, p. 136). The diploma is preserved in original. *Longobardia* also in the diplomas nr. 89, y. 775, p. 129; nr. 200, y. 803, p. 269.

[13] *Annales regni Francorum*, y. 781: ... *duo filii suprascripti domini Karoli regis inuncti sunt a supradicto pontifice* ... *domnus Pippinus rex in Italia et domnus Hlodowicus rex in Aquitania* (*Quellen zur karolingischen Reichsgeschichte*, I, ed. Rau, p. 40).

[14] *Annales Lauresham enses*, y. 781, ed. Pertz, pp. 31–2; *Annales Laurissenses minores*, c. 14, ed. Pertz, p. 118.

[15] *MGH Capit.*, I, nr. 91, p. 191 (Pippin, ys. 782–787): ... *Qualiter complacuit nobis Pippino* ..., *cum adessent nobis cum singulis episcopis, abbatibus et comitibus seu et reliqui fideles nostros Francos et Langobardos qui nobiscum sunt vel in Italia commorantur* ...; *MGH Capit.*, I, nr. 94, c. 5, p. 199 (Pippin, y. 787): ... *Stetit nobis de illos homines qui hic intra Italia eorum seniores dimittunt* ...; *MGH Capit.*, I, nr. 95, c. 4, p. 201 (Pippin, ys. 787–788): ... *de diversis generationibus hominum qui in Italia commanent* ...; *MGH Capit.*, I, nr. 98, p. 204 (Charlemagne, y. 801): ... *Karolus Dei gratia, etc.* ... *omnibus ducibus, comitibus, gastaldiis seu cunctis rei publicae per provincias Italiae a nostra mansuetudine praepositis* ...; ibid., c. 8, p. 206: *De servis fugacibus. Ubicumque intra Italiam* ... *servus fugitivus inventus fuerit* ...

dispositions concerning 'Italiam vero quae et Langobardiam dicitur' seem to use the term *Italia* only for the territories of Langobard tradition.[16] A decade later, the redactor of the Royal Annals, in the version traditionally attributed to Eginhard, remembered that in 786 Charlemagne engaged in an expedition against the Beneventan Langobards, with the aim of conquering that 'part of Italy' which was the 'residua portio' of a kingdom whose king he had captured and whose larger part, consisting precisely in *Langobardia*, he already possessed.[17] In this text, the identification of *Italia* and *Langobardia* drops down, because the latter is considered to be a part of *Italia*; it does not even include all the Langobard territories, given that Beneventum remained outside of it. In this case, *Italia* recovers its classical, peninsular dimension, which was not coincident with the Frankish kingdom in Italy. Not by chance, the same redactor modifies the passage of the Royal Annals concerning Pippin's royal anointing in 781 and says, ' ... Pippinus in Langobardia [not *in Italia*, as the Annals say] ... Hlodewicus in Aquitania rex est constitutus'.[18]

The precise meaning of *Italia* and *Langobardia* was also problematic for the natives. Private charters use these terms when they reckon the regnal years of the Carolingian kings in Italy, but regional usages differ substantially. The charters drawn up in the northern region reckon the years from the beginning of the Frankish domination *in Italia*, sometimes stating precisely *hic in Italia*, thus giving the term *Italia* a local dimension. Conversely, the Tuscan deeds almost regularly make their chronological computation begin with the Frankish conquest of *Langubardia*, as if the scribes did not consider *Italia* inclusive of the whole complex of the Langobard territories, especially Tuscany.[19] In fact, later documents,

---

[16] *MGH Capit.*, I, nr. 45, c. 2, p. 127.

[17] *Annales qui dicuntur Einhardi*, y. 786, ed. Pertz, p. 169: *Rex ... statuit Romam proficisci et partem Italiae quae nunc Beneventus vocatur, adgredi conveniens esse arbitratus, ut illius regni residuam portionem suae potestati subiceret, cuius caput in capto Desiderio rege maioremque partem in Langobardia iam subacta tenebat ...*

[18] *Annales qui dicuntur Einhardi*, y. 781, ed. Pertz, p. 161. Other passages also suggest that pseudo-Eginhard used *Italia* as a mere locative term. See for instance y. 776, p. 155; y. 800, p. 189; y. 806, p. 193.

[19] For northern Italy see, for brevity's sake, the collection of charters in *Codex diplomaticus Langobardiae*, ed. Porro-Lambertenghi, passim; dates with the clause *hic in Italia*: nr. 90, p. 169; 152, p. 262; 157, p. 270. For Tuscany see *Memorie e documenti*, for instance nr. 151, p. 87: *regnante domno nostro Carulo rege Francorum et Langobardorum anno regni eius quo cepit Langubardiam primo ...*; so also in nrs. 155, 156, 159, 163, and, almost regularly, in many others until the death of Charlemagne. That *Langubardia* was meant including all the Langobard territories is made probable by some rarer dating formulas that reckon: ... *anno regni eius [of Charlemagne] in gente Langobardorum ...* (*Memorie e documenti*, nr. 162, p. 93; 224, p. 131). A couple of Tuscan documents that mention Italia instead of Langubardia make a precise reference to the conquest of Pavia: *Memorie*

also of an official nature, openly distinguish *Italia* from *Tuscia*, probably as a lasting heritage of the separate identity that the region already boasted in Langobard times.[20] Nonetheless, *Langobardia* could also be used in a sense close to that of *Italia* to designate only the northern Italian regions distinct from *Tuscia*.[21]

So, both *Italia* and *Langobardia* were concepts that swung back and forth in the first decades of the Carolingian domination in Italy, and as such they were little apt to become the official denomination of the kingdom. Moreover, it seems that for a long period there was no certainty concerning the destiny of the Frankish domination in Italy, a fact that belittled the interest for the kingdom's identity. In the *Divisio regnorum*, *Italia/Langobardia* designated only a province in a future large aggregation which had also to include *Bavaria*, a part of *Alamannia* as well as several *pagi* of *Burgundia*; together, these countries were to form a new kingdom for Pippin after his father's death.[22] It is not clear in that context whether Charlemagne meant that the duchies of *Tuscia* and Spoleto were also part of *Italia/Langobardia*, or if the disposition concerned only the northern regions of Italy. In any case, the ancient Langobard kingdom would have lost its distinct identity in the new organization of the Frankish lands to become a part of a larger kingdom, extended on both sides of the Alps. In the same document Charlemagne ordered that – should Pippin die before his brothers – the 'regnum quod ipse habuit', a kingdom still unnamed, was to be divided between the survivors, along a line that approximately followed the watercourse of the river Po and subsequently the ridge of the Apennines to the papal territories in Emilia and Lazio; in this case, the duchies of *Tuscia* and Spoleto were expressly included in the partition as distinct entities. In both cases, the regulations would have led to the disintegration of the old Langobard kingdom.

---

e documenti, nr. 200, p. 116: *regnante domno nostro Carulo et Pippino figlio eius regibus Francorum et Langobardorum ac patricio Romanorum in Etalia postquam Papia civitate ingressus est anno undecimo et quarto*; the same formula in nrs. 247, 270, 334.

[20] *Italia* referred only to the northern regions of the kingdom in a *placitum* concerning real estates possessed by Louis II *in finibus Italie, Tussie, Spoleti et Romanie* (*I Placiti del regnum Italiae*, ed. Manaresi, nr. 65, p. 235); *exercitus Italiae* distinguished from the Tuscan army in *Constitutio de expeditione Beneventana facienda* (*MGH Capit.*, II, nr. 218, p. 96). For the role of Tuscany in the Langobard kingdom see Kurze, 'La Toscana come parte del regno longobardo'.

[21] *Langobardia* distinguished from *Tuscia*, as well as from *Beneventum* and *Romania*, in a diploma of Louis II from year 861 (*Diplomata Ludovici II*, nr. 32, ed. Wanner, p. 132); *Langobardia* in private documents also of northern Italy: *Carte Cremonesi*, ed. Falconi, nr. 7, y. 841, p. 21: *Scio et bene memoro quando domnus Karolus rex istam patriam Langobardiam adquisivit ...*, where *patria* seems to refer to the author's region.

[22] *MGH Capit.*, I, nr. 45, p. 127.

Eventually, things took a different course. Charlemagne preserved the unity and the autonomy of the kingdom in Italy, where, after the death of his son Pippin, he installed his grandson Bernhard as king. It is not clear why Charlemagne and after him his successor Louis the Pious, who also hesitated about the subject, finally decided to keep the kingdom alive as a distinct political structure. One can guess that they considered the kingdom as a suitable tool for keeping all the Langobard territories, including Tuscany and the duchy of Spoleto, under strict Frankish control. Moreover, the Italian *regnum* had a border position in the peninsula, facing Rome and the papal territories, as well as the Langobard Beneventum, definitely evading control from Frankish domination. Even the Byzantine empire was still active in southern Italy and in the Venetian lagoons. The kingdom could fulfil this function better in a unified state, which might be a sound bulwark of the Carolingian empire facing the Mediterranean world.

The kingdom thus preserved its organic, separate structure; actually the term *regnum Italiae* gained ground, as noted in the previously quoted old essay. Probably there were political milieus, not necessarily spokesmen of the Frankish dominators, which seriously considered the possibility of creating a new identity for the kingdom, even a patriotism around the name of *Italia*. The *Historia Langobardorum* preserved in the *Codex Gothanus* repeatedly uses *regnum Italiae* and *rex Italiae* for Pippin, and concludes the narration of his deeds by saying that thanks to his rule 'splenduit Italia, sicut fecit antiquissimis diebus'.[23] Nonetheless, the two terms did not become official titles of the Carolingian domination in Italy. In Charlemagne's charters that mention 'regna nostra Francia et Italia', *Italia* has the same generic meaning of *Francia*.[24]

The difficulty of giving a new name, representative of a new identity, to the Frankish kingdom in Italy appears also in the fact that the official title of the king remained *rex Langobardorum*. Charlemagne joined it to *rex Francorum* and kept both of them in use even after the assumption of the imperial title. He gave the same title to Pippin and Bernhard when he appointed them as kings in Italy. One can wonder why the ethnic title of the king was kept alive whilst the political line aimed at suppressing the Langobard identity of the kingdom. One possibility is that both the political mentality and the chancery practice were not yet ready to accept

---

[23] *Historia Langobardorum codicis Gothani*, c. 9, ed. Waitz, p. 11. On this source see L. A. Berto, 'Remembering old and new rulers'.

[24] *Diplomata Caroli Magni*, nr. 93, y. 775, p. 134; nr. 125, y. 779, p. 175. The same generic meaning is probable in the diplomas nr. 132, p. 182; nr. 187, p. 251, where a *regnum a Deo nobis concessum Italiae* is mentioned.

the idea of a royal title referring to a country instead of a people.[25] Perhaps different ideological implications were associated with the two terms 'king' and 'kingdom'. *Rex Langobardorum* proclaimed the domination of the Frankish king over the Langobards, whilst *regnum Langobardorum* implicitly admitted that the Langobards remained the titular body politic of the kingdom; it is not by chance that this term never occurs in Carolingian sources, except when they speak of the past.[26] Nonetheless, the preserved mention of the Langobards in the royal title shows how difficult it was to find a new synthetic representation of a body politic which was now composed of Franks, Langobards and other ethnic groups, who lived side by side in the kingdom and jointly took part in the political activity.[27]

Uncertainties and difficulties concerning the name of the kingdom seem to fade when Louis the Pious came to power. In the *Ordinatio imperii* of 817, by which the new emperor disposed the future government of the imperial lands after his death, the term *regnum Italiae* occurs for the first time in an official document; subsequent documents confirm that the term had gained a technical meaning. For instance, it is found in a *capitulare* of Lothar, addressed 'omnibus sanctae Dei ecclesiae et nostris fidelibus in regno Italiae consistentibus', and later on, in the agreement between the same Lothar and his stepbrother Charles (the Bald) for the partition of the imperial provinces.[28] The adoption of this term in the conceptual repertory of the Chancery brings to completion the process of official de-nationalization of the kingdom, with the complete effacement of any remembrance of the Langobard kingdom. *Langobardia* continued to be used both in private and in public deeds, but only to designate the

---

[25] Also in the new kingdom of Aquitania, Louis the Pious bears the title *rex Aquitanorum*: cf. Wolfram, *Intitulatio. I.*, pp. 221–2.

[26] *Chronicon Moissiacense*, ed. Pertz, p. 295: *[Desiderius] ... qui per donationem Pippini regis Francorum regnum tenebat Langobardorum ...; ... porro gloriosus rex Karolus cuncta Italia sibi subiugata vel ordinata ... in Francia reversus est. Sic regnum Langobardorum finivit.*

[27] *MGH Capit.*, I, nr. 91, p. 191 (Pippin, ys. 782–787): *... qualiter complacuit nobis Pippino excellentissimo regi gentis Langobardorum, cum adessent nobis cum singulis episcopis, abbatibus et comitibus seu et reliqui fideles nostros Francos et Langobardos qui nobiscum sunt vel in Italia commorantur*; ibid., nr. 95, c. 4, p. 201 (Pippin, ys. 787–788): *De diversis generationibus hominum qui in Italia commanent.* Cf. also *Annalium Alamannicorum continuatio Murbacensis*, a. 796, in *Annales Laureshamenses, Alamannici, Guelferbytani et Nazariani*, ed. Pertz, p. 48: *Pippinus rex Langobardorum cum ipsis Langobardis et Baguariis perrexit in regionem Wandalorum*; *Chronicon Moissiacense*, a. 797, ed. Pertz, p. 302: *Aestatis tempore transmisit rex Carolus Pippinum filium suum cum suis quos in Italia habebat, Francos, Langobardos et Bagoarios cum aliqua parte Alamannorum in finibus Avarorum.* Cf. also *Annalium Alamannicorum Continuatio*, y. 797, ed. Pertz, p. 48: *Ericus [marquis of Friaul] cum quibusdam Francis et Langobardis in Wandalis prelium commisit.*

[28] *MGH Capit.*, II, nr. 201, c. 14, p. 62; *Annales Bertiniani*, a. 839 (*Quellen zur karolingischen Reichsgeschichte*, II, ed. Rau), pp. 44–5. See also *MGH Capit.*, II, nr. 200, p. 58.

northern Italian regions, mostly in the sense of modern *Lombardia*, without any institutional meaning.[29]

The problem of the royal title seems to have been solved with the accession of Louis the Pious to power. It is well known that the emperor suppressed the ethnic titles in his imperial *intitulatio* and pursued the ideal of an *imperium christianum* in which ethnic distinctions were deprived of any relevance. Essentially the concept of *regnum Italiae* denied the existence of a titular people of sovereignty; the political foundation of the kingdom rested on the knot of the churches and the sovereign's *fideles*. However, the consolidation of the concept of *regnum Italiae* did not involve the official adoption of the corresponding title *rex Italiae*. Louis the Pious seems to have conceived the government of the kingdom as the projection of the imperial office, rather than the task of a delegated king. Actually, in the *Ordinatio imperii* he foresaw that the government of the kingdom was destined for his son Lothar, who on the same occasion was associated with the father's imperial dignity;[30] the system of *Unterkönigtum* practiced by Charlemagne was so driven to an end, and the destiny of Bernhard, the *rex Langobardorum* in charge, became extremely uncertain and ended tragically.

Lothar ruled the kingdom bearing the imperial title in the ten years or so in which he acted in concordance with his father, as well as after his rebellion, when he was formally bereaved of the imperial title, confined in Italy and prohibited from leaving. Possibly his forced exile strengthened the autonomy of the kingdom,[31] but the ruler's title remained the imperial one, because Lothar in Italy continued to exhibit the title of emperor, even suppressing his father's name in public acts, though the scribes of private charters continued to reckon the regnal years of both sovereigns. The kingdom was confirmed in its autonomy, but remained devoid of a titular king because the imperial title was by its very nature universal and had no possible limitation to any particular people or country.

Nonetheless, eventually Lothar restored the separate government of the kingdom, when, after Louis the Pious' death, he recovered the complete imperial dignity, together with the rule over a large complex of transalpine provinces, where he moved, returning to Italy only once.[32] He appointed his son Louis as king, but the title was not *rex Italiae*, but,

---

[29] See the documents quoted above, n. 19.
[30] *MGH Capit.*, I, nr. 136, c. 17, p. 273: *Regnum vero Italiae eo modo praedicto filio nostro, si Deus voluerit ut successor noster existat, per omnia subiectum sit sicut et patri nostro fuit et nobis Deo volente praesenti tempore subiectum manet.*
[31] Jarnut, 'Ludwig der Fromme', pp. 350–62.
[32] An isolated stay of Lothar in Pavia has been detected by Zielinski, 'Ein unbeachteter Italienzug Kaiser Lothars I. im Jahre 847'.

again, *rex Langobardorum*. The ideological work previously done to give the kingdom a new identity seems here to have been forgotten.

Possibly the choice depended on problems of international relations. The *Liber Pontificalis* reports that when pope Sergius II was elected, Lothar sent Louis, already king in Italy, to Rome to check the regularity of the election.[33] In an atmosphere of suspicion and tension, an agreement was finally reached: Sergius II's election was legitimized; in his turn. the pope crowned Louis as 'king of the Langobards' in a ceremony that had no precedent. But when the Frankish counsellors of the king required that the pope and the Romans swore fidelity to Louis, Sergius II and the Roman nobility rejected the pretention, saying that the Romans' oath was only due to the emperor, not to the king of the Frankish kingdom in Italy. The distinction put an end to the confusion created by the union of the two functions in Lothar's person. In this context, Louis' royal title might also have been discussed. For the Papacy, *rex Langobardorum* was the only acceptable title, because of its roots in the traditional world of kingdoms, but above all because it clearly limited the Frankish royal sovereignty in Italy to the territories of the ancient Langobard kingdom, leaving out the papal provinces. In addition, *Italia* remained an ambiguous concept for both parties. The popes used to distinguish between *Italia* and *Tuscia*, apparently ignoring the peninsular extension of the term.[34] Inside the kingdom, *Italia* was also employed to designate only the northern regions, and could still be replaced with *Langobardia* not only in private charters but also in official documents.[35] For this reason, the term was progressively abandoned, both in the name of the kingdom and in the royal title, to be replaced by the more neutral term *regnum Italicum*, whose use finally prevailed.[36]

Contrary to the papal auspices, Louis II's political activity had a decided peninsular scope, but it was carried out thanks to the imperial dignity, which Louis received a few years after his coronation as king of the Langobards. Otherwise, it would have been difficult to legitimize his action in Ravenna as well as his repeated interference in the election of the popes and even his military enterprises in southern Italy, aimed not to

---

[33] *Liber Pontificalis*, Sergius II, 483–488 (vol. II, pp. 87ff.); Louis was already king in Italy before 844: *Regesta imperii*, ed. Zielinski, 27, p. 12.

[34] Letter of Hadrian I to Charlemagne of 790–791: *Immo de consecrationis vitio, quod partibus Italiae, Tusciae heresis simoniaca fieri multisque locis non sinitur* ... (*Codex Carolinus*, no. 94, ed. Gundlach, p. 634).

[35] Documents already quoted at n. 21.

[36] For instance: *MGH Capit.*, II, nr. 214, y. 855, p. 88: ... *duo capitula infra regnum nostrum Italicum populo commoranti in legem dare praevidimus* ...; ibid., nr. 219, c. 2, p. 97: ... *providimus de Iudeis ut nullus infra regnum Italicum ultra kalendas Octobris maneat* ... Cf. also *Diplomata Ludovici II*, nr. 52, ed. Wanner, p. 168.

enlarge the kingdom's territory but to fight against the enemies of the faith and their Langobard supporters.[37] Not by chance, as soon as he was associated with his father's imperial dignity, Louis let the royal title drop and, after his father's death, vindicated his right to succeed him in the government of the transalpine provinces, precisely because of his imperial dignity. The political situation compelled Louis to restrict his activities within the limits of the Italian territory, but he always considered himself as emperor in the full extension of this dignity.

Nonetheless, the kingdom remained a distinct identity, to which he dedicated much more attention than his predecessors had. He endeavoured after the reformation of moral customs, the re-organization of the church, the administration of justice, the public duties of the freemen in the courts of justice and in the army. Resolutions taken for the welfare of the kingdom were motivated with the care for peace, the *salus* and *salvatio* of the people, this last being a concept which had already occurred in the political proclamations of the Langobard kings.[38] But neither the people of the kingdom nor the kingdom itself was given a distinctive name. Besides, Louis II proudly proclaimed his Frankish origin, even against the Byzantine emperor, maintaining that it was no obstacle to his being a true Roman emperor. Similarly, the two main powers in non-Carolingian Italy, that is, the Papacy and the southern Langobards, regarded him as a Frank, the latter even as a racial enemy.[39] On the other hand, the Franks

---

[37] Delogu, 'Strutture politiche e ideologia nel regno di Ludovico II'; Hees, *Studien zur Geschichte Kaiser Ludwigs II*; Zielinski, 'Ludwig II. von Italien'; Bougard, 'Ludovico II re d'Italia, imperatore'; Bougard, 'La cour et le gouvernement de Louis II, 840–875'.

[38] *MGH Capit.*, II, nr. 215, y. 856: *dum ... non solum aecclesiasticam utilitatem et populi pacem vel salvationem, sed etiam totius regni statum perquirere studeremus ...*; ibid., nr. 216, y. 865: *... cum domnus et magnificentissimus Hludowicus augustus ... in augustali aula resideret tractaturus de statu sanctae matris ecclesiae et pace divina dispositione sibi commissi imperii ac generali totius populi salute ...*

[39] Origin and Frankish identity of Louis II underlined in his letter to the Byzantine basileus Basil I, in *Chronicon Salernitanum*, ed. Westerbergh, c. 107, pp. 106–21. *Franci* in *Liber Pontificalis*, Sergius II, 483: *[Lothar] ... Drogonem ... cum excellentissimo Ludovico filio suo magnoque cum Francorum exercitum Romam direxit ...* (II, p. 87); *Franci* also ibid., 484, p. 88; 486, p. 89; 488, p. 90. See also *Liber Pontificalis*, Leo IV, 554–555, (II, p. 134) with the episode of the Roman *superista* Gratian who had been charged that *... nimium super Francos murmurans, dixit secrete quia Franci nobis nichil boni faciunt ...* The immediate intervention of Louis II promoted a judiciary assembly *... omnibus Romanis proceribus pariter et optimis Francis ... sedentibus ...* As regards the Langobard South: *Franci/Galli* in Erchempert, *Historia Langobardorum Beneventanorum*, c. 29, ed. Pertz and Waitz, p. 245: *Gallorum exercitus*; c. 29, p. 245: *[the Saracen Saugdan] ... super Beneventanos et Francos se iniecit*; c. 34, p. 247: *... coeperunt Galli graviter Beneventanos persequi ...* At c. 35, p. 248 Erchempert designates Louis' kingdom as *Langobardia*. The *Chronica sancti Benedicti Casinensis* repeatedly uses the term *Francia*: so at c. 2, ed. Pertz, p. 469: *[the Beneventans] ... nimium afflicti necessitatemque compulsi Franciam legatos dirigunt atque gloriosi imperatoris Hludowici implorant augusti clementiam*; cf. also c. 12, p. 474: *... per*

never qualified their domination over Italy as a *regnum Francorum*, even less as a Frankish empire.[40]

The difficulty of giving the kingdom a proper name, also in relation to the complex figure of Louis II king-emperor, comes to light in the epitaph that was composed for his grave in Sant'Ambrogio's basilica in Milan. According to this text, Louis had received the *sceptra Hesperiae* from his grandfather Louis the Pious at his very birth; he had ruled over *Hesperia* since his childhood with a strong and peaceful mind. Here the concept of *Esperia* occurs once more after the Langobard period, probably because it was felt to be more appropriate than *Italia* to designate Louis' sphere of domination, though *Italia* perfectly fitted into the metrical scheme. But the celebration of Louis hinges on the title of *caesar*, and his relations with Rome and the empire: Rome, *Latium* and *Gallia* mourn over his untimely death.[41] *Italia* does not appear, and neither do the Langobards, in spite of their mention in the royal title. In sum, under Louis II there was a kingdom ruled by a Roman emperor of Frankish stock; the body politic had no definite identity, although the kingdom was a coherent institutional structure, whose ruling class was well rooted in its system and nourished the firm purpose of keeping it alive.[42]

Few possibilities present themselves for perceiving how this complex situation was interpreted by the kingdom's subjects. Only the short history composed by Andreas of Bergamo sheds some light on the subject.[43] The basic idea is the continuity of the kingdom notwithstanding the shift of domination from the Langobards to the Franks, a continuity guaranteed by the fact that the kingdom never ceased to have its own kings. Charlemagne is remembered as the conqueror of the kingdom, not as its king. According to the writer, after having 'subiugata et ordinata Italia', he went back to *Frantia*, leaving the kingdom to his son Pippin, who in his turn left it to his son Bernhard, who is remembered as *rex Langobardorum*. When Bernhard died, the emperor Louis the Pious gave the kingdom to his grandson Louis (II). For all its falsity, this last information reveals that the purpose was to credit an uninterrupted series of local kings, which was deemed to be the basic requisite for the

---

idem tempus Bassacius abbas … adiit Franciam, qui obsecrans gloriosum imperatorem Hludowicum …; cf. also ibid., c.6, p. 472; c. 8, p. 473; c. 13, p. 475.

[40] Seals and bulls of Louis II show the legenda DECUS IMPERII, without any reference to the Frankish basis of the power; cf. *Diplomata Ludovici II, Einleitung*, ed. Wanner, p. 28f.

[41] The epitaph in *MGH Poet.*, III, ed. Traube, p. 405.

[42] Absence of 'identité culturelle' in the government of Louis II remarked also by Bougard, 'La cour et le gouvernement', p. 267.

[43] On this author see Berto, 'Remembering old and new rulers', pp. 29–50.

subsistence of the kingdom. Lothar, like Charlemagne, is excluded from the series, probably because he was considered a transient sovereign.

Nonetheless, the body politic appears to be fragmented also in Andreas' History. The Langobards have a distinct identity and are remembered in various occurrences separate from the Franks, with a role of their own.[44] Furthermore, the author's decision to put a short summary of Paul the Deacon's History before the narration of more recent vicissitudes bears witness to Andreas' intent to underline the continuity of the kingdom, as well as to remember the past Langobard tradition, which he probably shared.[45] Nevertheless, there is no doubt that in Andreas' view the power was in the Franks' hands, and the Langobards could only have a role in the kingdom if they accepted a peaceful and loyal relation with them.[46] This awareness does not give rise to complaints or vindications, but it influences the general idea of the kingdom, its structure and identity. The cohesion of the body politic is seen in the person of the sovereign. The solidarity of the various ethnic groups living in the kingdom is based on the sovereign's person, rather than on their integration. The king, then, becomes the essential reference for the political unity of the inhabitants of the kingdom. An episode in the History clearly illustrates this principle. When the Franks invaded the kingdom, the resilience of the Friauler Langobards faded when they were made aware that there was no more a *caput* for them – that is, a pole of reference and cohesion – because the king in whom their *confortatio* lay had already been defeated.[47] The ethnic principle is not deemed a sufficient reason for resistance. On the other hand, the relevance of Louis II in Andreas' narration mainly depends on the Christian dimension of his action, culminating in the war against the Saracens, in which both Langobards and Franks found a common purpose. Quite consequently,

---

[44] Andreas of Bergamo, *Historia*, c. 8, ed. Waitz, p. 226: ... *Multa fatigatio Langobardi et opressio a Sclavorum gens sustinuit* ...; c. 12, p. 227: ... *Reliqui [Sarraceni] in castro qui dicitur Bari se fortiter munierunt, ubi domnus imperator per 5 ann. eas cum Franci et Langobardi et ceteris nacionum suorum fidelium possidens* ...; c. 15, p. 228: ... *[Louis II] statim mittens principibus suis, id est Hunroch, Agefrid et Boso, cum electa manus Francorum et Langobardorum vel ceterorum nationes* ...

[45] Andreas of Bergamo, *Historia*, c. 1, ed. Waitz, p. 223: *Haec autem superscripta summationem cui incredibile aparet, relegat tota historia Langubardorum; omnia hec veraciter invenit, in quantum hic scripta sunt; et plures multa illuc invenitur, nobilitatem eorum vel victoriae et bella quas gesserunt.*

[46] Carolingians ruling over Italy: Andreas of Bergamo, *Historia*, c. 5, ed. Waitz, p. 224; c.6, p. 225; c. 7, p. 226. Prestige of the Franks: ibid., c. 5, p. 225: ... *per eum [Charlemagne] nomen Francorum longe lateque percrebuit usque ad hodiernum diem*: Date of an event: ibid., c. 17, p. 229: ... *complete sunt ann. centesimo ex co Francorum gens Italia ingressi sunt. Fidelitas* towards the Franks: ibid. c. 4, p. 224: ... *eamus; eorum fidelitate bene nobis erit.*

[47] Andreas of Bergamo, *Historia*, c. 4, ed. Waitz, p. 224.

the interruption of the royal succession after Louis II's death was deemed by Andreas, who was writing close to the event, as the source of deep troubles.[48]

These conceptions were probably shared by the leading groups of the kingdom. Another episode told by Andreas confirms the intent to build a political tradition based on the memory of the local kings. After Louis II's death, Archbishop Anspert of Milan ordered that the emperor's body, which had been buried in Brescia, be removed and transferred to Milan, to be buried in Sant'Ambrogio, where was the tomb of King Pippin, and possibly some forms of commemoration of King Bernhard.[49] Archbishop Anspert seems to have aimed at creating a centre of royal devotion in Milan, whose guardian he planned to become.

In this context, giving the kingdom a name representative of its identity remained a difficult task. In Andreas of Bergamo's History, there is the same superposition of disparate elements that has been noticed elsewhere. *Italia* occurs several times, mainly as a geographical indication, whose extent is difficult to guess. Perhaps Andreas used the term to designate only the northern regions of Italy, around the Po Plain where he lived; if this was the case, it was ill suited to represent the entire kingdom. *Regnum Italiae* occurs only once, apparently as current phraseology more than having a technical purpose.[50] As regards the royal title, it is still *rex Langobardorum*, when referred to Bernhard.

The uncertain definition of the kingdom and the inadequacy of the name *Italia* to represent it come again to the forefront in the unhappy adventure of Charles the Bald in Italy. It is not clear whether the Frankish king really intended to succeed his nephew Louis II in the kingdom. At any rate, after having been consecrated emperor by pope John VIII, Charles was received by an assembly of ecclesiastic and lay magnates of the kingdom, which took place in Pavia in February 876. Girolamo Arnaldi has convincingly argued that on that occasion Charles was not elected king of the Italian kingdom; rather, the magnates, who presented themselves as the *optimates* of the *regnum Italicum*, acknowledged Charles' imperial dignity and hailed him as their 'protector, lord and

---

[48] Andreas of Bergamo, *Historia*, c. 19, ed. Waitz, p. 229: ... *Post cuius obitum magna tribulatio in Italia advenit* ... It is worth noting that neither Charles the Bald nor Karlman is considered an Italic king by Andreas, who refers the royal title of Charles to his reign in *Frantia*, whilst he does not give Karlman any title.

[49] Andreas of Bergamo, *Historia*, c. 18, ed. Waitz, p. 229. Memory of king Bernhard: Malfatti, *Bernardo re d'Italia*, pp. 46–51, 60–63.

[50] Andreas of Bergamo, *Historia*, c. 19, ed. Waitz, p. 230: *Carlomannus vero regnum Italiae disponens post non multum tempus ad patrem in Baioaria reversus est.* In this passage Karlman is not yet king. *Regnum Italiae* does not appear in Karlman's diplomas, which use instead *regnum Italicum*, whilst the royal title is undetermined.

defensor', to which they promised obedience and loyalty 'as to their *senior*'.[51] The deliberation partly derived from the de facto coincidence of the imperial and the royal function, as established with the experiences of Lothar and Louis II; but it retained many elements of ambiguity, because on that occasion there was no proper royal election or acclamation. It was rather a matter of a voluntary adhesion to the emperor, from a group of magnates, but not from all those living in the kingdom, who also signed, one after the other, a document that recorded their engagement. The deliberation did not settle the government of the kingdom definitely, above all because Charles did not intend to stay in Italy for very long. Instead, he decided to appoint a representative in the person of the Provençal count Boso, who for that purpose received the title of duke together with a ducal crown.[52]

A duke ruling over a kingdom that had always had its own kings would have been a very strange affair, difficult to accept even for the magnates who adhered to Charles the Bald. But it is possible to explain the confused situation if one links the appointment of the duke to the term *ducatus Italiae*, which occurs not in that context, but a little later, in a group of deeds issued by Charles III (the Fat), who in the meantime had become in his turn emperor and king.[53]

Ducatus Italiae has been considered, and probably was, an elusive institutional term; nonetheless, it might precisely refer to the effort of giving the new situation of the kingdom a political settlement, if one assumes that the name *Italia* designated not the whole kingdom, but the territories in the Po Plain and in Emilia, from whence Charles' electors came.[54] There was no intent of lowering the kingdom to the level of a duchy; rather, a structure was put in place that was deemed apt for co-ordinating, and possibly ruling, the area where the consensus to Charles was more solid. The term *Italia*, which had already been used to refer to the northern regions of Italy, became the official name of an institutional

---

[51] Arnaldi, 'La tradizione degli atti dell'assemblea pavese del febbraio 876'. Arnaldi's argument is based on the examination of the textual tradition of the acts. As it was already noted by the editor of the document, in *MGH Capit.*, II, nr. 220, pp. 98–100, the clause concerning the royal election is missing in two manuscripts whose preeminent authority is demonstrated by Arnaldi. One can add that Andreas of Bergamo did not know of a royal election of Charles the Bald.

[52] *Annales Bertiniani*, a. 876: ... *Bosone, uxoris sui fratre, duce ipsius terrae constituto, et corona ducali ornato, cum collegis suis, quos idem dux expetiit, in eodem regno relictis ... (Quellen zur karolingischen Reichsgeschichte, II*, ed. Rau, p. 238).

[53] The deeds quoted below, n. 56.

[54] In the Election document of Charles the Bald, the subscriptions of the dukes of Friaul, Tuscia and Spoleto are missing. Probably other magnates belonging to the same areas did not take part in the assembly. Also, the bishops who signed the document come from northern Italian dioceses, with the exception of the bishop of Florence.

structure of regional width, and so definitely ceased to represent the entire kingdom. In fact, it is quite unlikely that the duchies of Tuscia and Spoleto, whose dukes did not take part in Charles the Bald's election, adhered to this order. The ironical result of the situation was a kingdom without a king, subject in theory to a distant emperor, who was locally represented by a *missus* whose power extended over only a part of the territory.

The lasting difficulty of defining the kingdom's identity finally becomes evident in a set of four deeds issued by Charles the Fat in Ravenna, on February 14 and 15, 882, in a large assembly of bishops and *fideles* that gathered when the emperor met pope John VIII in that town. Charles the Fat had taken royal power over Italy in the year 879, seemingly with an action that was ratified *post eventum* by an assembly of bishops, counts, 'seu reliquos primores ex Italia' who were summoned by him in Ravenna instead of Pavia, namely, outside the kingdom.[55] In Charles III's documents issued in his first years of reign, the kingdom is always referred to as *regnum Italicum*, whilst the dates reckon the regnal years *in Italia*, side by side to those *in Frantia*, namely, with a mere locative sense. The royal title bears no specification. This is a general occurrence after Louis II's death: the royal title exhibited by subsequent kings loses every reference to *Italia* or to the Langobards, and remains as a pure title of function, without any determination. The four deeds from Ravenna were issued after the imperial coronation and probably show the effects of a larger vision of the Italian situation, all the more so because they were issued on a solemn occasion, again in an international context, in the pope's presence. They granted or confirmed estates and rights to several churches of northern Italy and imposed the perpetual observance of the provisions in all the institutional ambits subject to the imperial authority. These are listed with the same words in each of the four documents: 'per totius nostri imperii fines in toto regno Romanorum et Langobardorum et ducatus Italiae, Spoleti et Tuscie'.[56] The formula reveals how the Italian political geography was seen by the imperial Chancery. There were two distinct areas of sovereignty, two *regna*, subject under different titles to the imperial authority: the *regnum Romanorum* and the *regnum Langobardorum*. The first probably consisted of the territories of the Roman church, at least those in Romagna, where the emperor resided at the moment; the second was the Italian kingdom, which could not be designated any better than by its ancient ethnic name.

---

[55] *Regesta Imperii*, ed. Zielinski, 600, p. 239.
[56] *Diplomata Karoli III*, nr. 49, ed. Kehr, p. 83; nr. 50, p. 84; nr. 51, p. 86; nr. 52, p. 88. The diplomas nr. 50 and 51 are preserved in original.

The reasons for this choice are as complex as they are meaningful. From the imperial Chancery's perspective, *regnum Italicum* appeared devoid of real qualifying value; *regnum Italiae*, already rarely used, was even less useful, given that *Italia* had become, also for the Chancery, the name of a duchy that embraced only the northern regions of Italy, as is evident by its juxtaposition to the two duchies of Tuscia and Spoleto. As things were, the Chancery did not find any better means to define the kingdom in its entirety than its ancient ethnic definition, which the Carolingian domination had striven to cancel during the course of a century.[57]

A different question is whether the name of the kingdom involved the re-qualification of the body politic, that is, whether the Langobards were once more considered as the titular people of the kingdom. In Charles III's deeds there are references to the ancient term of *arimanni* for the freemen; a deed of 883 for the church of Bergamo has an unexpected recollection of episodes concerning the Langobard kings Grimoald and Cunincpert, as precedents of the new dispositions.[58] Nonetheless, there are no hints that allow us to believe that the Langobards were again considered the essential component of the body politic of the kingdom, which continued to be for the most part named *regnum Italicum*. But from outside the kingdom, in the Carolingian regions beyond the Alps, the redactors of annals began again to use the terms *Langobardia*, *Langobardi* when they spoke of Italian affairs.[59] This use was consolidated in the tenth century. Regino of Prüm regularly uses *Langobardia*, *Langobardorum fines* and *Langobardi* when reporting events concerning Italy. Flodoard of Rheims in his Annals calls the two Berengars *Langobardorum reges* and considers the political agents in the kingdom to be of Langobard stock.[60] Later on, and from a different point of view, the Roman chronicler Benedetto of Sant'Andrea del Soratte repeatedly uses *rex, regnum* and *gens Langobardorum* when he narrates northern

---

[57] *Italia*, but not *regnum*, or *rex Italiae*, occurs in the dates of Charles III's diplomas, which reckon his regnal years *in Frantia* and *in Italia* separately. Both terms seem to refer to generic areas of domination, where the years had different numbers, rather than being the names of the kingdoms.

[58] *Regesta Imperii*, ed. Zielinski, 721, pp. 292–3.

[59] *Annales Bertiniani*, y. 879: *Karolus ... in Longobardiam perrexit et ipsum regnum obtinuit ...*; y. 880: *... Karolus autem a Longobardia rediens ...* (*Quellen zur karolingischen Reichsgeschichte*, II, ed. Rau, pp. 278, 280); *Annales Fuldenses*, y. 879: *... sed quoniam in divisione regni Langobardorum iuramentum suum irritum duxit, Hlodowicum procul dubio a suo iuramento reddidit immune ...*; y. 882: *... [Charles III] ... post haec praeparatis copiis ex omni regno suo, Longobardis, Alamannis Francisque secum assumptis ...* (*Quellen zur karolingischen Reichsgeschichte*, III, ed. Rau, p. 110, 132).

[60] *Reginonis Chronicon*, ys. 877, 881, 882, 894, 896, 901 (*Quellen zur karolingischen Reichsgeschichte*, III, ed. Rau, pp. 252, 260, 262, 300, 304, 310). *Flodoardi Annales*, ed. Lauer, y. 922, p. 7; y. 924, p. 22 s.; y. 951, p. 132.

Italian events.[61] When the direct Carolingian rule over Italy came to an end, a synthetic definition of the kingdom's identity probably became easier for foreign observers, and they found it in the local Langobard tradition, which had never completely disappeared and now seemed to be a suitable connotation for the generality of the kingdom. Conversely, from inside the kingdom reference to a given people, let alone the Langobards, never appears. Like the last Carolingians, the local kings who succeeded them bore a royal title without any determination, changing it to the imperial title when they had the opportunity to obtain it.[62] The royal title, for which they fiercely fought against one another, was meant as a personal qualification without any reference to a titular people of the sovereignty. When the kingdom was named, it was still a *regnum Italicum*, whilst the regnal years were reckoned 'in Italia', but *Italia* was not reinstated as the name of the kingdom. Nonetheless, towards the middle of the tenth century some charters from the Spoleto region are dated with the years of the Christian Incarnation, 'seu regnantibus domno Hugone et Hlothario filio eius regibus Langobardorum in Hitalia', or even with the regnal years 'domni Hugonis regis gentis nostrae Langobardorum'.[63] They bear witness to a spontaneous process that was then under way, which sought to rebuild the collective identity of the inhabitants of the kingdom under the Langobard name. This process becomes clear a little afterwards in the works of Bishop Liutprand of Cremona. In the presence of the Basileus of Constantinople, who was believed to abase him by saying 'You are not Romans, but Langobards', Liutprand vindicated the merits of Louis II 'emperor of the Langobards and the Franks', and proudly extolled his own Langobard identity.[64]

---

[61] *Il Chronicon di Benedetto*, ed. Zucchetti, p. 155 and passim.

[62] Zimmermann, 'Imperatores Italiae', pp. 394–5.

[63] *Regesto di Farfa*, III, nr. 348, p. 50; nr. 350, p. 51. A date mentioning Berengar II and his son Adalbert as kings of the Langobards also ibid., III, nr. 361, p. 65. The dating formulas should not depend on the indirect tradition of the documents, because the redactor of the *Regesto* normally uses different expressions.

[64] Liutprand of Cremona, *Relatio de legatione Constantinopolitana*, c. 7, ed. Becker, p. 179: ... *tenuerunt illam [terram, i.e. Apulia] potestative Langobardi, quam et Lodovicus Langobardorum et Francorum imperator de manu Saracenorum multitudine prostrata liberavit*; c. 12, pp. 182–3: ... *quos [Romanos] nos, Langobardi scilicet, Saxones, Franci, Lotharingi, Bagoarii, Suevi, Burgundiones, tanto dedignamur, ut inimicos nostros concitati nil aliud contumeliarum nisi 'Romane' dicamus* ...

5   Was There a Carolingian Italy?
Politics, Institutions and Book Culture

François Bougard

'The Carolingians in Italy' is a literary myth. In order to account for the installation of the Franks on the Italian peninsula, our manuals have clung to a received vulgate. They assert that Pippin the Short and then Charlemagne allied themselves with the papacy, at the pope's request, in order to stave off the Lombard threat against the exarchate of Ravenna and defend the interests of the Holy See. But at the end of the tenth century, south of Rome, the story included other elements. An anonymous chronicler in Salerno said that around 770 relations were cordial between the Franks and the Lombards, who were united by marriage. But the Lombards quarrelled among themselves and certain of their *proceres*, sent ambassadors to Charles inviting him to take possession of Italy and chase away King Desiderius. Charles came, accompanied by Franks, Alemans, Burgundians and Saxons, and met with great success.[1] In other words, the responsibility for the Carolingian 'liberation' of Italy is credited to the Lombards themselves, regardless of the fact that in the mouth of Arechis, prince of Salerno, the expression *nefandus Karolus*[2] is an echo of and riposte to the *nefandi Langobardi* in the papal lexicon. At about the same moment, a monk at S. Vincenzo al Volturno wrote an enthusiastic account of the supposed visit by 'Emperor Charles' to his monastery.[3]

Two centuries after the conquest, there was no doubt about the existence of a 'Carolingian Italy'. It was an incontestable fact, a fact that neither needed to be idealized nor against which one could invent lively stories of moral or military resistance. Italy had been Carolingian. And so what? That the kingdom of Italy was 'Carolingian' was obvious to everyone in the ninth century. Prayers for the king or the emperor and for the

I thank Patricia Stirnemann for the translation of this chapter and the exchange of stimulating remarks that accompanied it. I would also like to thank Winfried Rudolf, Giacomo Vignodelli and Giorgia Vocino for their critical reading.
[1] *Chronicon Salernitanum*, 9, ed. Westerbergh, p. 11.
[2] *Chronicon Salernitanum*, 10, ed. Westerbergh, p. 14.   [3] Braga, *Il Frammento Sabbatini.*

salvation of the kingdom or the empire were said, or should have been said, every day in all of its monasteries.[4] All the notaries allude to it when dating acts to the years of the reigning Carolingian sovereign, whose name and, sometimes, portrait were also inscribed on the coins in circulation. Anyone seeking a favour, to be endorsed by a written document, made a request to the king or emperor; these diplomas did not therefore shower down by virtue of the pre-established wishes of the prince or because of some governmental 'strategy', and instead reflect demands coming from below. Simultaneously, the generosity of the king could take the same form for everyone, thus creating a sense of belonging to the same world. What monastery, large or small, did not ask for and obtain immunity from the encroachments of government agents, just like establishments north of the Alps?

The question posed by the organizers of this volume – 'Was there a Carolingian Italy?' – is thus surprising, as are others that it implies: How 'Carolingian' was Carolingian Italy after Charlemagne? How was it governed by the Carolingian sovereigns? How different were the aspirations from reality? Such queries seem to presuppose the existence of a 'model' reality north of the Alps. But this remains to be demonstrated at a moment when historiography insists on permanent makeshift solutions, on fluidity, porosity or any equivalent term, and more precisely on the fact that disparity between aspirations and reality existed throughout the empire. In this sense, Italy, which is understood in the following text as the area of the *regnum,* was just one experimental political and institutional laboratory among others, be it Aix-la-Chapelle or any of the territories governed by the Franks. One must be wary of the habitual Franco-centrism that considers it impossible to think of Italy as a distinct reality, standing apart from its enveloping political construction called the empire.[5] Because of its geographic position, it is seen as a border province (in the face of the Avars and the Slavs, Byzantium, *Langobardia minor* and occasionally the Saracens) within a sort of aggregate all too readily perceived as conforming to a layout with a centre and peripheries. The approaches ought to be bilateral and focus more on reciprocal acculturation than on colonial borrowings and influences, as in 'newer' lands like Saxony or, to some extent, Bavaria. They should also account for the regional diversity within the different realms.

Keeping in mind these caveats, I will take on the challenge with regard to the categories of politics, institutions and culture, fully aware that one can barely scratch the surface.

[4] Choy, *Intercessory Prayer.*
[5] With the notable exception of J. R. Davis, *Charlemagne's Practice of Empire.*

Political Integration

From a bird's eye view of the Carolingian century, we can take the pulse of the kingdom, as though we were drawing a curve of Italian 'Carolingianity'.

It must be remembered from the outset that Italy was not like the other territories. It was a kingdom, and the only one that was conquered by the Franks. Not that there were no other *regna*, but the others were Merovingian and were thus more easily integrated into the larger Frankish assemblage. Charlemagne could have rescinded Italy's status as a kingdom, but he decided instead to appropriate for himself the title of king of the Lombards. In the absence of possible *comparanda*, it is useless to wonder whether it would have been the same elsewhere. Within the Carolingian political construction, Italy was different from the moment of its birth and was perceived as an entity apart. Furthermore, Italy was synonymous with the papacy, regardless of the latter's claims to territorial autonomy. When Charlemagne delegated the kingship to Pippin (781), another experiment began in what historians call a 'sub-royal' regime. This saw namely a country governed by a king with limited powers, whose filial relationship with the man soon to become emperor affected the condition of the region placed under his authority.

The years of Pippin's reign (781–810) were those of the *baiuli*, well-trained administrators like Adalhard of Corbie, who built the foundations of a Carolingian regime. On Pippin's death, their work was continued by the *missi* until 813, when Bernard took office. Officials outside the kingdom played a major role between 818 and 822, when, after the revolt of Bernard, Italy found itself without a sovereign.

The arrival of Lothar signalled the momentary end of kingship in Italy, because the man sent to govern already held an imperial title (817) and did not need that of king of the Lombards to assure his legitimacy. Whence the fact that historiography, including that of the time, lacked the figure of a sovereign to whom one could link the territory in an emotional manner, as had been the case with Pippin and Bernard. Lothar's posterity suffered as a result: he was forgotten for the most part, except by Agnellus of Ravenna. With him the realm seems to distance itself a bit from Francia, not because of hostility or any lack of fidelity to the regime, but rather a relative indifference, which in the end was more beneficial to Louis the Pious than to his son and competitor.[6]

---

[6] Bougard, 'Italia infirma'.

This did not prevent certain factions from taking part in the internal disputes of the empire. Archbishop Angilbert of Milan (824–859), for example, had a hand in the coup d'état of 833. It is especially during the period 820 to 840 that signs of a greater integration into the empire begin to show. After years of interruption, capitularies begin to appear regularly in Italy, and the territory provides benefices for men of standing residing north of the Alps and vice versa. Eginhard controls S. Giovanni Domnarum in Pavia; the patriarch of Grado has his hands on Moyenmoutier; loyalists of Lothar who were installed alongside him in 833 are provided for in the kingdom. The link between the queen and S. Salvatore in Brescia is confirmed. A mixed aristocracy arising from marriages between the conquerors and the conquered slowly finds its place, as exemplified by the count of Parma, Adelgis, who was the son of the Swabian count Suppo I and his Lombard wife.[7] As the emperor is only occasionally present, those who wish to obtain diplomas must come in person or make their request by procuration at Aix-la-Chapelle, Frankfurt or Compiègne. But the increasing mobility forced upon the elites by the absence of the ruler highlights the link between the kingdom and the central heartbeat of the empire.

Under Louis II, there is a very different relationship. Italy once again has a king, who is physically present from 840 at the latest. The *Liber Pontificalis* describes his coronation (844) and resurrects the title of king of the Lombards.[8] Louis became emperor in 850 and the alliance between empire and kingdom was made manifest in his marriage to a member of the Italian aristocracy, if one accepts the idea that his wife, Engelberga, daughter of the aforesaid Adelgis, was partly of Lombard origin.[9] He is remembered as the man who unified the lords behind his military enterprise in the south and momentarily saved Benevento from the Saracens, and also as an emperor who was firm with Byzantium and governed in peace.[10] But there is a flip side to the coin. For the first time, here was an emperor totally devoted to Italy, but he was enclosed on the peninsula and incapable of thinking about the fate of the empire, except for trying belatedly to arrange his succession, although his wishes would not be respected. Must he be considered a prisoner of his surroundings? In reality, the handicapped situation of Louis II was simply another consequence of the Treaty of Verdun. His uncles Charles the Bald and

---

[7] Bougard, 'Supponides', pp. 384–6.   [8] *LP* Sergius II, ed. Duchesne II, p. 89.

[9] Bougard, 'Supponides', pp. 388–9.

[10] *sanctissimus vir, salvator scilicet Beneventanae provinciae*: Erchempert, *Historia Langobardorum Beneventanorum*, c. 34, ed. Pertz and Waitz, p. 247; *suo autem tempore magnam pacem, quia unusquisque gaudebat de bonis suis*: *Catalogus regum Langobardorum et Italicorum Brixiensis et Nonantulanus*, ed. Waitz, p. 502.

Louis the German were no more able to leave their own regions, except for minor territorial gains at the expense of *Francia Media*. Italy is, in this sense, neither more nor less 'Carolingian' than Western and Eastern Francia.

Following Louis II's death (875), the kingdom became the object of the ambitions of several candidates for the throne, some of Carolingian blood, others not or only partially; some were already head of a *regnum*, others were not. These years of competition show how important the stakes were. Hincmar would, of course, write that Louis II 'is called the emperor of Italy', an expression that seems to underline the incongruity between the title and the territory, but which should not be over-interpreted, to judge by the way Florus of Lyon describes the destiny of the imperial dignity, then in the hands of Lothar, after 843.[11] The fact remains that, at the announcement of Louis' death, Charles the Bald hastened to Italy to obtain the supreme dignity, fulfilling a desire already aroused in 871, when he heard the rumour of the death of the emperor, then held captive in Benevento. It is true that the king of Western Francia assumed the imperial crown before being recognized as the 'protector' of Italy by the nobles assembled in Pavia. But one might suppose that he would not have failed to have had himself designated as sovereign of the realm when he first came to the capital, if he had been sure of a consensus, which was then not yet the case, at a moment when the troops of his nephew and competitor, the son of Louis the German, had advanced as far as Milan. The same observation holds for Arnulf's brief passage through Pavia in 896.

Once more, the indissoluble link between the peninsula and the Carolingians was made manifest, for without Italy they would be deprived of access to Rome, which over time had become the necessary precondition for any large project. In the early 810s an imperial coronation was still imaginable outside Italy. After the *Ordinatio imperii* of 817, and especially after the Treaty of Verdun, such an eventuality was inconceivable, except in territories that escaped the influence of Frankish

---

[11] *Annales Bertiniani*, ed. Grat, Vielliard and Clémencet, a. 856 (p. 73), 863 (p. 96: *Italiae vocatus imperator*), 864 (p. 115: *imperator Italiae nominatus*). Before Hincmar, Prudence of Troyes adopted more neutral formulations, where geographic precision does not seem mixed with acrimony or sarcasm: *rex Italiae* (a. 853, p. 68, after referring to his uncle Louis as *Germaniae rex*), *imperator Italiae* (a. 856, p. 73, before describing his brother Lothar as *rex Franciae*), *rex* (a. 858, p. 78), *Italorum rex* (a. 859, p. 82). After these first mentions for the years 863–864, Hincmar simply uses *imperator* or *imperator Italiae*. Cf. Zimmermann, '*Imperatores Italiae*'. — Florus, *[Querela de divisione imperii]* 75–76, ed. Dümmler, p. 561: *Induperator ibi prorsus iam nemo putatur, / Pro rege est regulus, pro regno fragmina regni.*

power, like Christian Spain (Asturia–León) or England.[12] Since the emperor, like the kings, mastered only one *regnum*, it was necessary to embrace the universalism of the Church of Rome, which now held the balance of power, in order to give meaning to his title.[13] Indeed, the *Ordinatio imperii* was confirmed by the papacy, and the written oaths of the Treaty of Verdun were sent to the Holy See, confirmed by the synod and preserved in the pontifical archives.[14]

Men and Institutions

The change in political dominion in 774 led to the substitution of numerous members of the elite laity, as has been studied many times over. The rhythm and speed of these replacements are open to discussion, but by the 810s, one generation after the conquest, the ruling counts were now Franks and Alemans. In the 830s, the same phenomenon can be observed in relation to the viscounts, who replaced the Lombard gastalds both in title and as an 'ethnic' group, while the supporters of Lothar in Italy swelled the ranks of the immigrant administrators. Given that they maintained patrimonial and family links with the area north of the Alps, most of them had their sights set more on the horizon of the empire than on that of the kingdom. This forestalled the risk of regional particularism, at least until the last third of the ninth century.[15] Concerning the relative impact of these institutions, historiography in the late 1960s was torn between two opinions: that of Paolo Delogu, for whom the count held only weak control over his territory, and that of Vito Fumagalli, who, conversely, saw all the signs of a spreading influence of the power of the counts and their representatives.[16] Maybe, we need not choose one side or the other, considering that the situation probably varied between different parts of the kingdom; for example, the county of Piacenza was different from Tuscany, where the strong position of the duke eclipsed that of the counts, about whom we are not well informed. The situation in the duchy of Spoleto was different again. Not that the county of Piacenza was 'more Carolingian'

---

[12] Sirantoine, *Imperator Hispaniae*; Kleinschmidt, 'Die Titulaturen'.

[13] Zimmermann, 'Imperatores Italiae', p. 398.

[14] *Ordinatio imperii*: Agobard, *epp.* 15–16, ed. Dümmler, pp. 225, 227. — Treaty of Verdun: Hadrian II, *Epp.* 21, ed. Perels, p. 724; John VIII, *Fragmenta Registri* 41, ed. Caspar, p. 297.

[15] Bougard, 'Laien'.

[16] Delogu, 'L'istituzione' (against which reacted Keller in *Quellen und Forschungen aus italienischen Archiven und Bibliotheken*, 79 (1968), 554–6); Fumagalli, 'L'amministrazione'.

for all that, for while it may correspond well with the ideal type, nothing tells us that all the northern territories reflected the model in like manner.

The replacement of the ecclesiastical elite cannot be considered in the same light. The pace of change was much slower, where it occurred, because while the king controlled the appointment of lay administrators, it was only when a bishop died that he might be replaced with one who perhaps better met the sovereign's expectations. It was also less systematic. Some cities, like Verona [with the Alemans Egino until 799, and his successors Ratoldus (†840) and Bilongus (†860)], had non-Lombard bishops early on, but Tuscany was quietly sheltered from the phenomenon. It must also be noted that Italy was more attached than other realms to the 'free' election of the bishop by the local clergy.[17] Bishops and abbots coming from the north were nonetheless effective instruments for binding the kingdom to the empire. The bishops of Verona assured the link with Alemania and Bavaria, with Reichenau and Freising. The career of a man like Waldo, who was a monk at St Gall, abbot of Reichenau, bishop of Pavia and Basel, and finally abbot of Saint-Denis – which, like Saint-Martin of Tours, received Alpine valleys from Charlemagne in 774 – is one of those that forged links between the regions. Joseph, the Austrasian bishop of Ivrea from the 820s onwards, was also the ephemeral abbot of Fontenelle, and managed both the see of Maurienne and, latterly, the abbey of Novalesa, thus wielding authority on both sides of the Alps.[18] Furthermore, the see of Chur in Raetia was annexed to the ecclesiastical province of Milan – under the Frankish archbishop Angilbert – until the 840s.

What should be noted is the role of the bishops in the political and institutional life of the kingdom, namely their decisive integration into the power structure instead of the separate, parallel existence they maintained under the former regime.[19] Although the evolution was already under way in the eighth century, especially during the reign of Liutprand, the association of prelates with the government can indeed be credited as one of the profound 'Carolingian' changes in Italy. But this affirmation is mitigated by two observations: first, this was merely a continuation of the preceding Merovingian tradition; second, the participation of the Italian bishops in the ecclesiastical reform advocated by the Franks seems to have been distant, at least at first, to judge, for example, by the absence of

---

[17] Fischer, *Königtum*, pp. 52–7; see also the diploma 157 (anno 819) of Louis the Pious for the church of Piacenza and the introduction to its edition: *Diplomata Ludovici Pii*, ed. Kölzer, pp. 390–3.

[18] Gavinelli, 'Il vescovo Giuseppe di Ivrea'.

[19] Bertolini, 'I vescovi'; Tabacco, 'Il volto ecclesiastico'.

any episcopal capitularies such as those found north of the Alps during the reign of Charlemagne. It is not until the episcopacy of Joseph at Ivrea that we find an isolated instance of such legislation around 840–850.[20]

In any case, this association was reflected in the flowering and composition of the assemblies 'of the kingdom', and in the formulation and content of the texts that they produced. Even if the kingdom of Italy produced its own capitularies, their tone is no less 'Carolingian' than the general capitularies for the empire, which were well distributed in the *regnum*, to judge by their manuscript tradition.[21] It should be recalled that it is in Lombard Italy that the word *capitulare* first seems to appear with regard to legislation, being used in the prologue of the laws of Aistulf from 750, whereas in the Frankish world it is not found until the end of the eighth century, when it is applied to the capitulary *de villis*. Nothing can be deduced from this chronology, however, given the fact that the word *capitulare* was already part of the lexicon of Gregory of Tours, who uses it for tax-rolls.[22] Furthermore, as of the eighth century, the word is used in liturgy (*capitulare lectionum*) and Frankish texts are explicitly organized in *capitula*. Nevertheless, this little detail of vocabulary reminds us that Italy, when it came to creating norms, was not virgin territory and may even have been a source of inspiration.

The 'culture of the assembly' in the early Middle Ages,[23] echoed both in the capitularies and in the regular additions to the laws of the Lombards, which were promulgated by the king *cum iudicibus nostris et fidelibus*, went hand in hand with the meetings of the courts (*placita*), which saw justice being exercised in the name of the king and applied to free men. Nothing could be more incorrect than to call this institution a 'Carolingian innovation'. It is rather an ever-evolving creation, springing sometimes from a Merovingian base, sometimes from a Lombard one, with the contributions mixing and crisscrossing. To read a judicial report written in the mid-ninth century in Francia or in Italy gives the impression that the two are easily interchangeable; it is impossible to say whether one is more Carolingian than the other, or whether they do not belong to a common 'Carolingianization'. The appearance of professional judges (*scabini*) in Italy in the 780s was indeed a novelty, but the same had occurred in Gaul only a few years earlier; it was therefore a shared novelty, rather than a question of northern influence. The

---

[20] *Capitula Episcoporum* IV, ed. Pokorny, pp. 11–12; Davis, *Charlemagne's Practice of Empire*, pp. 211–15. For Joseph of Ivrea, see *Capitula Episcoporum* III, ed. Pokorny, pp. 235–42.
[21] Bougard, *La justice*, pp. 36–9; Mordek, *Bibliotheca capitularium*. For the current state of research on Italian capitularies, see Davis, *Charlemagne's Practice of Empire*, pp. 278–89.
[22] Gregory of Tours, *Decem libri historiarum*, IX, 30, ed. Krusch and Levison, p. 449.
[23] Wickham, 'Public court practice'; Wickham, 'Consensus'.

inquisitio, which developed during the ninth century, is likely to be an Italian contribution, however, or was at least based on a common late-antique matrix.[24]

As for the vocabulary and the formulary, the Frankish contribution is evident (witness the very word *placitum*, the lexicon of investiture, etc.). By the 810s, the Lombard judges and notaries from Pavia had assimilated what had been transmitted to them by personalities like Adalhard of Corbie.[25] But at the end of the ninth century, the invention of new formularies – offering four or five possibilities for writing procedures, as opposed to only one formerly available – was purely internal to Italy. Thanks to these new developments in the production of documents, the kingdom distanced itself emphatically from practice north of the Alps. It is the result of an internal evolution, which cannot be judged in terms of the flawed application of or deviation from a supposed Carolingian model. Indeed, the traditional view was arguably mistaken as to which of the two models was the more Carolingian. Charlemagne wanted to create a centralized public notarial profession, controlled by the *missi*, which would rapidly become a lay profession, thus encouraging the formation of a group of writing professionals. Whereas his reform was successfully applied in the kingdom of Italy, which offered a cultural terrain ready to receive it, it did not take hold north of the Alps, where the notaries, in the absence of qualified professionals, remained ensconced in the Church. In the 'discrepancy between aspirations and reality', Gaul finds itself on the negative side, and as a consequence Italy had at its disposal two types of writing – one documentary and deriving from the new 'Lombard' cursive, the other a book hand and Caroline – whereas north of the Alps they had to make do with only one.[26] Anyone looking through Italian private charters of the ninth century spots at a glance subscriptions and other documents written by clerics, where they were unable to use the type of script, whether the new cursive or Caroline, that was usual for the given type of source. An example is offered by the four documents written between 854 and 875 in Caroline minuscule by the *clericus* Gumprandus concerning the rural church of Varsi in the diocese of Piacenza, which stand out among the 300 others written in cursive by lay notaries.[27] The adoption of Caroline script for documents obviously happened at a different pace depending on the region, the generational turnover of scribes and their practice of

---

[24] Davis, *Charlemagne's Practice of Empire*, pp. 259–78; Esders, 'Die römischen Wurzeln'.
[25] Bougard, *La justice*, pp. 133–7; Bougard, '*Tempore barbarici?*', p. 339.
[26] Bougard, 'Notaires'; Witt, *Two Latin Cultures*, pp. 61f.
[27] *ChLA*[2], LXVIII, no. 40; LXIX, nos. 2, 4, 11.

writing, whether frequent or occasional – or is late, partial, hybrid and not slavishly based on models.[28] Italian notaries also adopted without any difficulty the routine of drafting rental contracts (*livellum*), while north of the Alps only oral agreements existed.

The most visible phenomena, which it is tempting to read as signs of particularism, can thus, in contrast, be considered as evidence of a more complete integration, where the student surpasses the master. Other examples, however, testify to a common path. The obligation of the tithe, decreed at Herstal in 779, aroused universal resistance and encouraged 'territorialization' throughout the whole Carolingian world during the ninth century. The creation of canonical chapters is yet another example. Intended for the entire empire in 816, it took hold in Italy belatedly, with a time-lag of two or three generations, depending upon the city. One could probably blame the slow pace with which prelates of the Lombard tradition were replaced. Even so, this reform did not excite the debates that took place north of the Alps. It is in the library of Nonantola that one finds the oldest manuscript of the *Institutio canonicorum* (816), which was copied around 825 and which testifies to a marked interest in that 'invention'.[29] Many other institutions could be invoked for which Italy offered a common experimental ground, or a welcome mat, such as the *beneficium*. Sometimes Italy provided the source of inspiration for institutions and traditions that were later returned to her, rethought and transformed by adaptations made in and for the Frankish world, such as the Roman liturgy.[30] The manorial system (demesne, tenure, work services) had existed since the sixth century in Ravenna and since the eighth or even before in Lombard lands, but it appears that it experienced an unequalled degree of rationalization during the Carolingian century.[31] The social consequences resulting from the expansion of the system, traditionally analysed on the basis of the contracts of *livellum*, are still open to discussion.[32]

At the end of the period, one last example shows that Carolingian allusions could still give legitimacy in an uncertain political context. Assemblies that produced capitularies lasted namely in Italy until 898,

---

[28] Among many other titles: Ferrari, 'La biblioteca', 82–3; Santoni, 'Scrivere'; De Angelis, *Poteri cittadini*, pp. 47–8; Marrocchi, *Monaci scritori*, ch. 1.

[29] Roma, Bibl. Naz. Centrale, Vitt. Em. 1348; Kurdziel, *Chanoines*.

[30] Albiero, '*Secundum Romanam consuetudinem*'.

[31] Toubert, *L'Europe*, pp. 152–5; Wickham, *Framing*, pp. 278–9 (concerning Italian papyrus 3, ed. J. O. Tjäder, in *ChLA*, XX, no. 709, which provides the same type of information on land, men and fees that one would find in a Carolingian polyptych).

[32] Fumagalli, 'Le modificazioni'; Sigoillot, 'Destins'; Bougard, '*Tempore barbarici*', pp. 349–50.

some fifteen years longer than north of the Alps. They were convoked by Wido of Spoleto and after him by his son Lambert, men who had no link with the family of Charlemagne. Better yet, and perhaps because of the latter fact, the content of their legislation is resolutely anchored in the Frankish tradition, just like the programmatic inscription *Renovatio imperii Francorum* on their imperial seal, as if nothing had changed since the opening years of the ninth century, or as if it was necessary to return to this already ideal past. Facing Wido and Lambert, Berengar, who could vaunt his descent from Louis the Pious through his mother, took no similar initiative, even after his accession to the imperial throne in 915, when at last he could govern unopposed.

It remains true that institutions more readily invite generalizations, but these do not exhaust the field of possibilities. Rather than consider in what manner Italy is or is not Carolingian, it is more pertinent to affirm a) that on many points Lombard Italy is not different, because the 'Carolingian world' which took centre stage is founded on a shared *koinè*; b) that the *regnum* sometimes offered more advanced solutions, or put theory or imperial injunctions into practice in an unforeseen manner; c) that, like the rest of the empire, Italy is not uniform, and there exist realities on both sides of the Alps that are more or less close to the 'model'.

Intellectual Production and Reception

Concerning all the themes discussed up to now, one can argue for or against the view that Italy is only one element among many in a shared Carolingian construction. By contrast, the area of culture offers a prime locus for illustrating the limits of Italy's integration into the empire.

The numbers speak for themselves. Of the 7,650 manuscripts attributed to the ninth century and catalogued in summary form by Bernhard Bischoff, a little under 9 per cent are of certain or presumed Italian origin; or, to put it differently, not even one book in ten during that period was copied on the peninsula.[33] This is a very weak contribution

---

[33] Bischoff, *Katalog der festländischen Handschriften*; manuscripts in private collections are not taken into account. The estimate of 9 per cent is very optimistic, because it is based on the systematic attribution to Italy of all items for which an Italian origin is mooted, regardless of the alternative provenances proposed or the measure of reasonable doubt expressed by Bischoff with a well-nuanced palette of terms (question mark, 'wohl', 'vielleicht', 'vermutlich', 'möglicherweise', 'scheint möglich', 'ist Oberitalien möglich?', 'wahrscheinlich', 'nicht ausgeschlossen'). On the other hand, we must restore to Italy the manuscript Bern, Burgerbibl. 363, from Milan, which Bischoff attributed to St Gall, cf. Gavinelli, 'Per un'enciclopedia carolingia'; a few discoveries can also be added, such as

when one realizes that Italy furnished 20 per cent of the western manuscripts surviving from the seventh and eighth centuries and nearly 90 per
cent of those preserved from the fifth and sixth. The decline, already
perceptible in the eighth century, only accelerated sharply thereafter.[34]
As for the authors represented, one in ten, regardless of where he was
working, is Italian.[35] It is always possible to question the dating and
origin of this or that manuscript, or to invoke the vagaries of conservation
and the incompleteness of the survey, especially for the fragments, but
these factors would only change things marginally.

The gap could be explained in part by the inflationary production of
the newly founded Carolingian centres and the rise of other European
libraries; in part, too, by the fact that Italy was smaller and not as rich and
had fewer large monasteries. In short, there was less demand, even if
Italy, and particularly the kingdom, did not lack great centres of writing,
with chapters and monasteries at Verona, Ivrea, Vercelli, Novara,
Nonantola, Bobbio, Milan and Monza. I confess that a comparison
would perhaps be more appropriate between Italy and regions like
Aquitania or Bavaria. But the divide was not just quantitative, and it
would be risky to think in terms of 'per capita production'.[36]
Furthermore, we could also have compared the production of private
charters in the ninth century, an area in which the pre-eminence of Italy –
with the exception of St Gall – is absolute.

The texts that were copied remained traditional: the Bible, patristic
literature, liturgy and law, as well as medicine, grammar, poetry, glossaries and miscellanea for teaching. There were a fair number of classical
works, but, apart from Flavius Josephus and Ps. Hegesippus, who are
part of the Christian canon and widely diffused,[37] they were copied less

---

Intra (Verbania), Arch. Cap. 12 (10) and 14 (12), cf. Gavinelli., 'Testi agiografici',
pp. 53–8; see also below, nos. 74 and 77, and the Appendix.

[34] Lowe, *Codices Latini antiquiores*; 'Addenda' by Bischoff, Brown and John. A list of
manuscripts and a bibliography can be consulted on the regularly updated *Earlier Latin
Manuscripts* site: ed. Stansbury and Kelly, https://elmss.nuigalway.ie

[35] According to the tally in Valtorta, *Clavis Scriptorum*. I do not distinguish between the
place of composition, for example, in the case of the *History of the Lombards* and *The Book
of the Bishops of Metz* by Paul the Deacon, one written at Monte Cassino, the other
during his stay at the Frankish court at the request of Archbishop Angilramn.

[36] Buringh, *Medieval Manuscript Production*.

[37] Flavius Josephus: Bamberg, Staatsbibl., Class. 78 (Bischoff, 'wohl'); Basel, UB, N I 3
no. 11; Cologny, Bibl. Bodmeriana, 98 and 99 (from Nonantola); Kassel,
Gesamthochschulbibl., 2° theol. 285 (Bischoff, '?'); Monza, Bibl. Capitolare, b 20/136;
Weissenburg in Bayern, Stadtarchiv, 806 (Bischoff, 'wahrsch. Oberit.'). — Hegesippus:
Cherbourg, Bibl. municipal, 51 (from Verona); Karlsruhe, Badische Landesbibl., Aug.
perg. 101 (Bischoff, 'wahrsch. Oberit.').

intensively than north of the Alps.[38] Not that classical works were lacking in the libraries, even if many fifth- to seventh-century manuscripts of these texts had been taken north. The list of titles in the manuscript Berlin, Staatsbibl. Diez B Sant. 66, which is linked to Verona or Bobbio, is sufficiently long and varied to illustrate this point, and includes many rare texts.[39] But apart for those needed for teaching or found in thematic miscellanies, e.g. extracts from Pliny the Elder in computistical manuscripts,[40] they were not Italy's main interest or, to say it in a different manner, the need for such books was less urgent here than it was in the north.

The type of intellectual production in Italy was different from that found elsewhere. After the contribution furnished by the generation of the *grammatici*, who came to the court of Charlemagne to lay the foundations of the programme of education in Gaul, the genres considered as 'typically' Carolingian – the exegetical commentaries whose breadth is still being discovered,[41], the mirrors of princes, the theological and doctrinal treatises – are decidedly not the work of Italy, or of Italians.

Exegesis: during his sojourn at the court of Charlemagne, Peter of Pisa abridged the commentary of Jerome on the Book of Daniel, his work surviving only in a manuscript copied for the king.[42] But in the ninth century, Italian exegesis was the work of personalities coming from the north, whose intellectual formation was already complete: the Visigoth Claudius (†827/8), who was sent to Turin by Louis the Pious in 816, and the Frank Hildemar of Corbie (†c. 850), who wrote a commentary on the Gospel of Luke, of which only a small fragment remains.

Specula principum: Paulinus of Aquileia (†812) composed a *Liber exhortationis* for his protector and friend Erich, Duke of Friuli. After this *speculum*, the only moralizing literature one can cite is the treatise by

---

[38] Witt, *Two Latin Cultures*, p. 53. See Bischoff's catalogue (including south-Italian mss) for Cato Minor (no. 2630), Celsus (nos. 1238, 6927), Cicero (nos. 968, 1164, 3815, 6416–17, 6866, 7232; Glossae, no. 80), Dares (nos. 208, 1236), Horace (no. 2651), Hyginus (no. 3088), Justin (nos. 1235, 2333, 7014), Juvenal (nos. 1236, 1987), Livy (nos. 208 [Florus], 209, 1232), Lucan (no. 5115), Lucretius (no. 1984), Quintilian (nos. 213, 2633), Seneca (nos. 680, 5313, 6581, 6781), Virgil (no. 3352; Servius, nos. 988, 1201, 6150).

[39] Villa, 'Die Horazüberlieferung'; Licht, 'Additional note'; McKitterick, *Charlemagne*, pp. 365–8.

[40] Ferrari, 'La trasmissione', pp. 305–7, 309, 314; Ferrari, 'La biblioteca' del monastero di S. Ambrogio', pp. 84–97 (*excerpta* of Pliny the Elder in the mss Milan, S. Ambrogio, Arch. Capitolare, M 15 and Montecassino, Arch. dell'Abbazia, 3; see also Lucca, Bibl. Capitolare, 490); Paris, BnF, lat. 7900A (Terence, Horace, Lucan, Juvenal, Martianus Capella); Bern, Burgerbibl., 363 (Horace, *excerpta* of Ovid).

[41] Guglielmetti, 'Un'esegesi incontenibile'.   [42] Gorman, 'Peter of Pisa'.

Hildemar *De octo vitiis principalibus*, which is known only from a late manuscript.

Liturgy: after his return to Italy in 786, Paul the Deacon impressively accomplished the mission to which Charlemagne had entrusted him concerning the liturgy by composing the *Homiliarium*, which was adopted throughout the Carolingian world for the readings of the nocturnal office. Thereafter, the only work attributable to a specific author that one can cite is the 'sermon' on the Assumption ascribed to Bishop John of Arezzo (†900), which is an assemblage of Greek sources without any direct practical aim.

Theological and doctrinal treatises: it was again Paulinus of Aquileia that spearheaded the battle against adoptionism with his *Contra Felicem*. His successor Maxentius (†837) wrote a response to the questionnaire that Charlemagne sent to several bishops in the empire concerning baptism. Yet another response to the same questionnaire was endorsed by Archbishop Odilbertus of Milan (†812).[43] Thereafter, the only debate that would have any impact concerned the iconoclastic position of Claudius of Turin and its consequences. It was broached by Eldradus (†840), abbot of Novalesa in the diocese of Turin, but only a few lines of his text have survived, and its original length is unknown.[44] The affair was treated especially in the *Responsa* of Dungal (flor. 825) 'against the perverse assertions' of Claudius, a work composed in 827 at the request of Louis the Pious and Lothar. But it would be hard to make this Irishman, who had recently arrived in Pavia from the abbey of Saint-Denis, a representative of Italian culture.

Italy seems to have been fertile ground for the partisans of predestination. The ideas of Gottschalk, who was present at the court of Duke Eberhard of Friuli (†864/6) in the 840s and corresponded with a bishop named Lupus, perhaps of Chieti, spread far enough that they caused some concern at the council at Pavia in 850 and are reflected in two passages of the Milanese *Expositio missae canonicae*.[45] But the debate itself seems absent, perhaps being left to the northerners. Bishop Noting of Verona (†863) consulted Hrabanus Maurus (†856) for arguments necessary to refute the heterodoxy, and when the archdeacon Pacificus (†844) was interrogated on the question by one of his students, he went to Hildemar to seek help in providing an answer.[46] Everything leads us to

[43] Keefe, *Water and the World*, II, pp. 154–70, 462–6.
[44] *Monumenta Novaliciensia vetustioria*, ed. Cipolla, I, p. 403.
[45] Brovelli, 'La Expositio missae canonicae', pp. 137–41.
[46] Hrabanus Maurus, *Epistolae* no. 22 (a. 840), ed. Dümmler, p. 428; *Epistolae Variorum* no. 33, ed. Dümmler, pp. 355–7 (a. 841–846 ca). Kershaw, 'Eberhard of Friuli', pp. 91–7; Gillis, *Heresy*, pp. 90–106; Pezé, *Le virus*, pp. 51–4, 443–7.

believe that Pacificus, the Lombard specialist in computus, was not at ease with this type of theological discussion, although he quoted several passages on predestination in two manuscripts. Was this a clever man-oeuvre in order to remain neutral on a sensitive subject, or is it that a distinction should be drawn between the intellectual preparation and the appetency for 'public debate'?

Hagiography: little was produced in the Lombard period, in striking contrast to the Merovingian logorrhoea in the field. Conversely, the Carolingian period marks an 'explosion' of hagiographical writing in Italy. The importance of the genre for political competition was well perceived by ecclesiastical elites in the kingdom. Yet the production remained quantitatively limited, with some thirty entries in the *Bibliotheca hagiographica latina* for the ninth century from northern Italy, Tuscany and Umbria.[47] Several dozen texts were composed north of the Alps during the same period. Italy was also the land where northerners came to collect relics, but it received very little in return. This might explain the delay in compiling passionaries (with the notable exception of Verona, Bibl. Capitolare, XCV), again in contrast with Northern initia-tives, where greater care was taken to gather materials about saints whose relics have been brought from many different places.[48]

Nor was **contemporary historiography** overabundant in Italy. After the works of Paul the Deacon and the brief anonymous history of the Lombards probably written between 806 and 810,[49] one has to wait until the late 870s for the composition of Andrea of Bergamo's *Historia*. The most significant contribution comes from the fringes of the kingdom: the *Liber Pontificalis* by Agnellus of Ravenna, conceived as a pendant to that of the Roman popes. One searches in vain for annals in the Frankish mode. As regards monastic chronicles, if we except the *Chronicae Sancti Benedicti Casinensis*, which was written outside of the kingdom, only the *Constructio Farfensis* can be cited.[50]

In short, as literary historians have long noted, the 'unfurling wave' of the Carolingian renewal was but a ripple in Italy.[51] One must admit that

---

[47] Vocino, 'Santi'; Vocino, 'Under the aegis'. Syntheses on northern and central Italian hagiography are to be published in volumes 7 and 8 of *Hagiographies: Histoire internationale de la littérature hagiographique latine et vernaculaire en Occident des origines à 1550* (Turnhout).

[48] Dolbeau, 'Naissance', p. 32.

[49] *Historia Langobardorum codicis Gothani* [Erfurt, Universitäts- und Forschungsbibliothek Erfurt/Gotha, Memb. I 84, fols 335r–337v], ed. Waitz; ed. and trans. Berto, *Testi storici e poetici dell'Italia carolingia*, pp. 1–19.

[50] *Chronicae Sancti Benedicti Casinensis*, ed. and trans. Berto; *Constructio monasterii Farfensis*, ristampa anastatica with foreword by U. Longo.

[51] Brunhölzl, *Histoire*, p. 246.

Italy (the *regnum*) did not participate in whole sectors of culture classified as 'Carolingian'. It was not until the 910s that the panegyric of Berengar I gave a wake-up call to literary production, to which Atto of Vercelli, Ratherius of Verona, Liudprand of Cremona, Gezo of Tortona, Stephen of Novara and Gunzo responded during the course of the tenth century. If authors like Stephen of Novara and Gunzo remain quite 'Italian' in their works (poetry, grammar), one also notes a timid thematic renewal with the treatise of Gezo on the Eucharist and the commentary of Atto on the Epistles of Paul, the first 'Italian' contribution to biblical exegesis since Hildemar and Claudius of Turin (to whom Atto owes so much).

Patronage is surely a key factor. Many books were produced in the north at the behest of Frankish rulers or within the context of related intellectual circles. Peter of Pisa, Paul the Deacon and Dungal wrote at the request of Charlemagne, Louis the Pious and Lothar. The court of Pippin can be credited with a short history of the Lombards and the celebration in verse of the victory over the Avars.[52] The only Frankish king who was durably attached to the kingdom after Pippin, Louis II, also preferred military adventure to religious and theological debates. But apart from a panegyric that has recently resurfaced, and which confirms the relative strength of the Italian laudatory poetry, a 'discipline' anchored in the schools of late antiquity, he did not particularly inspire creative activity.[53] As elsewhere, Italian literary production owed something to demand emanating from political circles, but in the kingdom it was quite limited and restricted to certain genres. Creativity and diversity found refuge in the Beneventan and Neapolitan south, with history (Erchempert), hagiography and translations from Greek, and at the papal court in Rome (Anastasius Bibliothecarius, Iohannes Diaconus). An abbot of Monte Cassino, Bertharius, composed verses for Empress Engelberga when she came to the monastery in 866. The *Rhytmus de captivitate Hludovici* (872?), only partially preserved in a manuscript copied in Verona at the end of the ninth century, was also a Beneventan work, which was perhaps presented to Louis II, if one accepts the idea that it was not written to mock the misadventures of the emperor in southern Italy.[54]

If Italy was not producing much, was it very receptive to what was going on elsewhere? Judging from the ninth-century manuscripts of supposed or certain Italian origin and the inventories and lists of books

---

[52] *De Pippini regis victoria avarica* [Berlin, Staatsbibl., Diez B Sant. 66, pp. 127–8], ed. Dümmler; *Testi storici e poetici dell'Italia carolingia*, ed. and trans. Berto, pp. 67–71.

[53] Orth, 'Fragment einer historischen Dichtung'.

[54] *Rhythmus de captivitate Lhuduici imperatoris* [Verona, Bibl. Capitolare, XC (85), fols 76r–7v], ed. Traube, pp. 404–5; ed. and trans. Berto, *Testi storici e poetici dell'Italia carolingia*, pp. 73–7, with introduction pp. XXXIV–VII. See Granier, 'La captivité'.

surviving from before the early eleventh century (see appendix), about ten Carolingian authors were known south of the Alps. Among them, Alcuin (†804) – who was hugely popular in northern libraries (Reichenau, St Gall, Lorsch, Murbach, Fulda), where his works were arranged into separate sections like those of the Church Fathers – enjoyed an incontestably good transmission, especially if one thinks of the two Italian manuscripts copied very early on: Rome, Bibl. Casanatense, 641 and, more notably, Verona, Bibl. Capitolare, LXVII; the manuscript from Verona was already taken to Freising in the early ninth century, however. One notes the association in Italian *miscellanea* of the *De fide sanctae et individuae Trinitatis*, the *Quaestiones de Trinitate*, the *De anima* and computistical texts, works which all belonged to the same textual tradition.[55] Texts for grammatical and moral teaching are also well represented (*De dialectica, De rhetorica, Ars grammatica*). Not surprisingly, the library of Eberhard of Friuli contains the *De virtutibus et vitiis*, suitable for the moral instruction of the great laymen.

After Alcuin, who belongs to the generation of Charlemagne,[56] come Smaragdus (†830 ca) and Hrabanus Maurus. Smaragdus is represented by his liturgical vademecum (*Expositio libri Comitis*) and grammar (*Liber in partibus Donati*), but does not seem to have had much immediate success with his commentary on the Rule of St Benedict or the *Diadema monachorum*, except perhaps with Frankish readers, if the volume bequeathed by Eberhard of Friuli to his son Rodulfus, abbot of Saint-Bertin, Saint-Vaast and Cysoing (†892), was one of these two texts. The *Diadema* was present at Novalesa and S. Liberatore alla Maiella in the eleventh century and, perhaps, in Friuli in the tenth. One might also suggest that the other Smaragdus work bequeathed by Eberhard, this time to Berengar, was the *Via regia*. Hrabanus, the other Carolingian Father in the eyes of the northern librarians, seems somewhat under-represented, given the prolific nature of his work, with the exception of the library of Farfa and that of the church of Arezzo, whose bishop John was probably trained at Farfa and brought a copy of the *Commentarius in genesim* to his town from France.

The reception of other authors is less certain, when it can be reconstructed at all. One of the two preserved copies of the *Collectanea* on the Pauline Epistles of Florus of Lyon († c. 860) was copied in Milan, probably during Florus' lifetime.[57] The treatise of Paschasius Radbertus (†865) on the Eucharist, that reflection on the real presence, is transmitted by only one ninth-century manuscript south of the Alps. Similarly Haimo of Halberstadt is represented by only one manuscript. Eginhard (†840)

---

[55] See Appendix. Ferrari, 'La biblioteca del monastero di S. Ambrogio', pp. 103–4.
[56] Jullien, 'Alcuin et l'Italie'.   [57] Below, n. 81.

is – remarkably – represented at Vercelli and Bobbio by his *Libellus de psalmis*, whereas the *Vita Karoli*, which was probably sent to Rome, is not attested in the kingdom until the end of the tenth century.[58] This indifference to contemporary history extended, moreover, to earlier works relating to the Franks. Paul the Deacon did bring Gregory of Tours' *Ten Books of History* to Monte Cassino – the manuscript, which preserved the original version of the work, was recopied under Abbot Desiderius around 1086–7[59] – but apart from the '*Gesta Francorum*' owned by Eberhard of Friuli, which was possibly also a copy of the *Ten Books*, there is only one other ninth-century manuscript of Gregory[60]. Fredegarius is also known through only one manuscript.[61] Similarly, Bede was sought after not for his *Ecclesiastical History*,[62] but for his computistical and exegetical works.

It is always difficult to draw definitive conclusions from the number of early manuscripts surviving – *teste* the *History of the Lombards* by Paul the Deacon, which is preserved in only three copies of Italian origin, despite the local interest that the work undoubtedly generated.[63] Nonetheless, it is unlikely that the evidence discussed above does not reflect contemporary transmission patterns to a certain extent. Indeed, in some cases the reception of Carolingian authors seems to be quite late: it is only in the early eleventh century that the works of Amalarius, Haimo of Auxerre (†875/878 ca), Hrabanus Maurus and Remigius of Auxerre appear on the shelves of the library at Nonantola.[64] Similarly, the library of Farfa was not badly supplied with Carolingian authors according to a list of the early eleventh century: Alcuin, Hrabanus, Haimo, Remigius of Auxerre and, perhaps, Benedict of Aniane with his *Concordia regularum* were all represented, which should come as no surprise given the monastery's links with the Frankish world, although it is not known when these works actually entered the collection[65]. It seems likely that the library of Fonte

---

[58] Licht, 'Einharts *Libellus de psalmis*'; Tischler, *Einharts* Vita Karoli, pp. 436f.

[59] Bourgain, 'Gregorius Turonensis ep.', p. 154; ms. Montecassino, Arch. dell'Abbazia, 275 (Inguanez, *Catalogi codicum Casinensium antiqui*, p. 7).

[60] Bruxelles, KBR, 9403.   [61] Milan, S. Ambrogio, Arch. Capitolare, M 13 (ca s. ix$^{3/3}$).

[62] The *Historia ecclesiastica gentis Anglorum* is only transmitted in the following manuscripts: Roma, Bibl. Naz. Centrale, Vitt. Emm. 1452, from Nonantola; part of book I in Bern, Burgerbibl., 363. The history was used by Paul the Deacon for his *Historia Langobardorum*, and copied for S. Liberatore alla Maiella under prior Theobaldus about 1010: Carusi, 'Intorno al *Commemoratorium*', p. 185. It was also at Vercelli in the tenth century (Bibl. Capitolare, Fragm. 50; see Rudolf 'A tenth-century booklist'; I thank R. W. for sharing his paper before publication) and perhaps at Novalesa at the beginning of the eleventh: *Cronaca di Novalesa*, ed. and trans. Alessio, pp. LVII–VIII (entry entitled *Regum Anglorum*).

[63] Pani, 'La trasmissione'.

[64] Gullotta, *Gli antichi cataloghi*, p. 6 = Branchi, *Lo scriptorium*, p. 387: acquired under Abbot Rodulfus (1002-1035). See also the entry '*Haimo*' at Monte Amiata, s. xi^{in}: Gorman, 'Codici manoscritti', p. 39.

[65] Brugnoli, 'La biblioteca', 10–1.

Avellana, the foundation of Peter Damian, drew from the Farfa holdings during its constitution[66]. Not infrequently, importation was due to external forces, such as the arrival of laymen like Eberhard of Friuli or monks from abroad. In the early tenth century, Bobbio would not have received any Carolingian works without the bequests of Dungal and others like Theodorus, Adelbertus and Peter, or of great prelates such as Liutward. Liutward came from a different cultural space: formerly a monk at Reichenau, he was sent to Vercelli in 880 by Charles the Fat, whom he served as arch-chancellor, and was then briefly abbot of Bobbio (885–886). Notker the Stammerer dedicated his *Gesta Karoli* to him, but this did not guarantee the diffusion of the work in Italy.

Reception depends on those who order books or have them copied, or on the men who write them. Without a personality like that of Bishop Joseph of Ivrea, the library of the chapter would not have had Alcuin or the liturgical and juridical works coming from Saint-Amand, southern Francia and Lyon, books that still exist today.[67] Thanks to Archbishop Angilbert of Milan inviting Hildemar of Corbie to his see, the library at SS. Faustino e Giovita in Brescia boasted two of his works ('*Dicta*') in the tenth century.[68] In Verona, Pacificus not only imported books from Luxeuil,[69] he also made copies of the works of Alcuin (the aforesaid *De dialectica* and *De rhetorica*) and of Hrabanus' commentary on the Books of Judith and Esther.

As regards the liturgy, the *Homiliarium* of Paul the Deacon is not alone. If Amalarius had only a modest echo in Italy, the Franco-Carolingian sacramentary was adopted very soon at Verona, and there are also several copies of sacramentaries with the masses composed by Alcuin.[70] The *romanum carmen* encountered resistance of the so-called *cantus ambrosianus* in the kingdom. According to a legend that may be partially true,

---

[66] Pierucci, 'Inventari', pp. 163–4 (Remigius, Amalarius, Haimo, Paschasius, in a list dated 1045–50).

[67] Ferrari, 'Libri e testi prima del Mille', pp. 517–25; Gavinelli, 'Il vescovo Giuseppe di Ivrea'.

[68] Bischoff, 'Das Güterverzeichnis', pp. 57–8. The library of the chapter of Vercelli also had a *Liber Ildemari* in the tenth century (Rudolf 'A tenth-century booklist').

[69] Verona, Bibl. Capitolare, XL (38), *CLA* IV.497-499, Bischoff 7038c (Gregory, *Moralia*, on the palimpsest of Virgil, Livy, Euclid).

[70] Verona, Bibl. Capitolare, XCI (86) (s. ix$^{1/4}$), linked to Pacificus. — Firenze, Bibl. Med. Laur., Aedil. 121 (s. ix$^{3/3}$); London, BL, Add. 16605 (s. ix$^{4/4}$); Verona, Bibl. Capitolare, LXXXVI (81) (s. ix$^{2/3}$). At least four Gregorian sacramentaries copied in France also arrived in Italy: Modena, Bibl. Capitolare, O.II.7 (ca. s. ix$^{2/4}$), Monza, Duomo, 89, now in the Bibl. Capitolare (ca s. ix$^{3/4}$, donated by King Berengar, who perhaps inherited it from Eberhard of Friuli) and Padova, Bibl. Capitolare, D 47 (s. ix^{med}). Deshusses, *Le sacramentaire grégorien*, pp. 35–43 for a listing of the mss; Ferrari, 'Libri liturgici', pp. 265–79. See also the "Nonantola sacramentary" (Saint-Denis, c. 875) offered to the monastery by John Bishop of Arezzo: Paris, BnF, lat. 2292.

Paulinus of Aquileia submitted two *pueri* to an ordeal in order to obtain God's judgment – hence the supposed diffusion of the Franco-Roman practice to the *plebs Itala*.[71] There are also less famous, but no less important, contributions that show a reception of Carolingian catechetical works and interests. These include commentaries on the mass, such as the *exposition missae 'Primum in ordine'*, and, moreover, the *Expositio missae canonicae*, which bears witness to efforts to adapt local uses to the Romano-Carolingian reform, while managing to safeguard particularism.[72]

On a more mundane level, materials for teaching coming from the north provided a stronger stimulus to Italian scholarship. The need to educate led to the making of compendia that mix elements of computus and astronomy, theology and exegesis, chronology and history, creating a potpourri that not only provides a mixture of extracts from classical texts and contemporary pieces but also makes visible a working method. Without being different from what was done in the north, the practice was here taken to extremes.[73] As regards alphabetic encyclopaedias, Italy played a crucial role in the direct textual transmission of the ancient *Liber glossarum*, and many other glossaries were copied in the ninth century.[74] The arrival of the *Liber glossarum* in Italy may have been even more precocious that the earliest surviving Italian witness, if we note that the *baiuli* of Pippin, Waldo of Reichenau, Adalhard of Corbie and Angilbert of Saint-Riquier, were abbots of monasteries that each had a copy.[75]

Legal texts are also well represented: at Novara, Brescia and Verona; at Ivrea, thanks to Bishop Joseph; at Vercelli, thanks to Liutward; at

---

[71] Montecassino, Arch. dell'Abbazia, 318 (s. xi$^{2/2}$), pp. 244–5; Rusconi, 'L'ordalia'; Winkelmüller, 'Politische Unifikationsbestrebungen'.

[72] Mazzuconi, 'La diffusione'; Brovelli, 'La Expositio missae canonicae'.

[73] Milan, S. Ambrogio, Arch. Capitolare, M 15 (above, n. 40); Monza, Bibl. Capitolare, c 9/69 (s. x, a copy of a ms. reflecting Dungal's teaching: Ferrari, 'La trasmissione dei testi', pp. 306–7).

[74] *Liber glossarum* (http://liber-glossarum.huma-num.fr/): Milan, Bibl. Ambrosiana, B 36 inf. [Milan?, s. ix$^{2/4}$]; Monza, Bibl. Capitolare, h 9/164 [s. ix$^{4/4}$]; Vercelli, Bibl. Capitolare, 2 (LXII) [s. ix$^{4/4}$ or x^{in}, from Bishop Atto]; another fragment is in Udine, Arch. di Stato, 132 [late ninth c.], and two others unknown to Bischoff are in Bazzano-Bologna and Modena, cf. Barbero, '*Credo sit Papias integer*', p. 325. Another fragment from the early tenth c. is in Cremona (Arch. di Stato, Notarile, G. 1), and comes from a volume given by Bishop Odelricus to the cathedral in 984 (Becker, *Catalogi bibliothecarum antiqui*, p. 81 no. 72; Tirelli, 'Gli inventari', pp. 48–50). — Other glossaries: Milan, B. Ambr., B 31 sup., C 243 inf., Montecassino, Arch. dell'Abbazia, 316, Montserrat, Bibl. del Monastero, 1038; Munich, Bayerische Staatsbibl., Clm 29670/2; Vatican, BAV, Vat. lat. 3320, 6018.

[75] Grondeux, 'Introduction', p. 6.

Bobbio, thanks to Abbot Agilulf (†896).[76] Both ancient and contemporary legislation was copied. As well as Roman law (*Epitome Iuliani, Breviarium Alarici*)[77] we find the 'national' laws so necessary in a country where individuals professed widely varying laws. Capitularies, whether like those made for the Frankish assemblies of 813 and 816 or gathered in collections, were also transcribed, although without going as far as to copy compilations like that of Ansegisus, which would enjoy a later reception.[78] With around fifty manuscripts, there is no lack of canon law. The *Dacheriana* arrived from the south of France, which was its centre of diffusion. But the Decretals of Pseudo-Isidore were also successful, and the nine copies made in Italy – which represent nearly half the ninth-century manuscript tradition – competed on equal footing with the *Dionysio-Hadriana*. It is in the area of law, where rare works, both new and ancient, were keenly sought out (such as the acts of the eighth ecumenical council of 869–870, the *Collatio legum Mosaicarum et Romanarum* or *Lex Dei*, and the *Liber Diurnus*),[79] that Italy finally produced original works of its own. Among these are the *Lex romana canonice compta*, the *Dionysiana Bobiensis*, the *Excerpta Bobiensia* and, at the end of the ninth century, the *Anselmo dedicata*. Excerpts of the *Anselmo dedicata* are to be found in a contemporary manuscript copied in Reims, which also contains Florus' brief and polemical compilation on the treatment of episcopal jurisdiction in the Sirmondian Constitutions.[80] This manuscript ended up in Milan, though admittedly

---

[76] Ferrari, 'Libri e testi prima del Mille', pp. 522–5; Gavinelli, 'Il vescovo Giuseppe di Ivrea'; Gavinelli, 'Transiti di manoscritti'; Gavinelli, 'Una raccolta canonica'; Gavinelli, 'Modelli librari', pp. 114–6; Pantarotto, 'La (ri)costruzione'.

[77] *Epitome Iuliani*: Guttaring, Pfarrarchiv; Milan, Bibl. Trivulziana, 688; Paris, BnF, lat. 4568; Vienna, ÖNB, lat. 2160; see also the *Institutiones*, Verona, Bibl. Cap., CLXXIII A + Bibl. Civica, 3035 + New Haven, Yale Univ., Beinecke 744 {Beinecke 744 is not listed in Bischoff's catalogue; see Radding and Ciaralli, *The* Corpus Iuris Civilis, p. 51}. — *Brev. Alarici*: Klagenfurt, Bibl. des Kärntner Geschichtsvereins, 10/2, from Nonantola. There are also two copies of the *Breviarium Alarici* from southern France at Ivrea: Bibl. Capitolare, XXXV (17) and XXXVI (18). F. Patetta; 'Il Breviario alariciano'.

[78] Canons of 813: Novara, Bibl. Capitolare LXXI (18). — 816: Geneva, BPU, lat. 28, from Aosta; Roma, Bibl. Naz. Centrale, Vitt. Em. 1348, from Nonantola (see n. 29). — Ansegisus: Vercelli, Bibl. Capitolare, CLXXIV (15) and the remarks of Bougard, *La justice*, pp. 41–2. — For a recent hypothesis regarding the personal law-book of Joseph of Ivrea (Wolfenbüttel, Herzog August Bibliothek, Blankenburg. 130), Esders, 'Deux *libri legum*'.

[79] *Collatio*; Zadar, Državni Arhiv, Misc. CLXXVI Poz. b. z. — *Liber diurnus*: Egmond, Klosterbibl., G. II; Milan, Bibl. Ambrosiana, I 2 sup. (Bobbio, bequeathed by the priest Theodorus); Vatican, ASV, Arm. XI. 19. — Eighth ecumenical council: Vat. lat. 5749; Palma, 'Antigrafo/apografo'.

[80] Milan, Bibl. Ambrosiana, A 46 inf., fols. 51r–2v; Zechiel-Eckes, 'Florus Polemik gegen Modoin'.

at an undetermined date. Might it have been a gift, like the Hrabanus Maurus commentary sent by Hincmar to Liutward of Vercelli?

Philology, a powerful vector for the circulation of books and texts, also had a notable impact. Pacificus was engaged in a lively exchange with Lyon, as illustrated by notes in his hand alongside those of Florus in an Italian copy of Origen's commentary on the Psalms.[81] Eldradus of Novalesa sent Florus his copy of Jerome's version of the Hebraic Psalter, asking him to correct it for his abbey.[82] These endeavours went well beyond the *emendatio* of the *libri catholici* requested of priests in the *Admonitio generalis*. Among the contemporary authors whose activities were known in Italy, it was Florus, who was geographically close to the kingdom, who excited the most interest. His transmission also helps reveal the channels that linked the Po Plain and St Gall; the Milanese manuscript of the *Collectanea* on the Pauline Epistles testifies to the existence of a 'textual reservoir' close to St Gall, where another copy of the work was preserved (Stiftsbibl., 279–81).[83] We have already seen that the ecclesiastical province of Milan had long since turned its gaze towards the Alps.[84] One could also cite the books that Liutward of Vercelli received from St Gall, among them the *Liber sequentiarum* of Notker the Stammerer and the bilingual (Latin–Greek) Pauline Epistles, and the influence that the style of St Gall exercised on the decoration of manuscripts made in Vercelli.[85]

The example of philology shows that, in the field of erudition, one searches in vain to establish who influences whom. One must speak rather of a community of intellectuals, who played across borders in a zone linking the centres along the Po River with St Gall, Reichenau and Lyon, and stretching even further north to Auxerre and Reims in the second half of the ninth century. The teaching of grammar and law involved the same actors and triggered the same mobility, as shown by the investigation into the anonymous poet of the *Gesta Berengarii imperatoris*. He was probably a disciple of Remigius of Auxerre, and was educated in Verona and in the Lombard schools, but drew most of his material from north of the Alps, especially for the glosses that accompany his text.[86] Both grammar and law share with liturgy and

---

[81] Lyon, Bibl. municipale, 483 (13); *CLA* VI.779, Bischoff 2564a.

[82] *Cronaca di Novalesa* IV, fragm. 6, p. 198–217 [= *Epistolae Variorum*, no. 26, ed. Dümmler, pp. 340–3].

[83] Gavinelli, 'Tradizioni testuali carolinge', pp. 278–80.   [84] Above, p. 60.

[85] Gavinelli, 'Tradizioni testuali carolinge', pp. 275–7. Liuward also received a copy of the *Vitae patrum* and the *Epistles* of Jerome. He may have been the recipient of the ms. of Eginhard's *Libellus de psalmis* (Vercelli, Bibl. Capitolare, CXLIX), which according to Licht, Einharts *Libellus de psalmis*' presents some characteristics of the late St Gall style, but we do not know precisely when the ms. arrived at Vercelli.

[86] Duplessis, 'Réseaux intellectuels'.

medicine[87] the concrete side of applied science, something which, in contrast, is not present in the oeuvre of the great authors, except for certain works devoted to these disciplines that met with a certain success in Italy, such as those of Alcuin and Smaragdus.

It is because – I insist – the culture of the kingdom of Italy was *different*. It was a culture that was practical, juridical and educational. It had a strong secular stamp, which distinguished it from that of all the others.[88] In spite of the relatively high number of prelates from the north of the Alps, Italy lacked the output of the churchmen, who were so numerous in the northern regions, so it remained attached to its traditional specialities linked with the liberal arts. It bears repeating that if Italy made its own personal contribution to the Carolingian renewal and provided many of the foundations that this 'renaissance' did not formerly possess – as is true of so many architectural, artistic and graphic[89] forms – it took little back. To be more precise, it took only what served its direct interests, which were inherited from a system that had been well established during the Lombard period. Indeed, the originality of Italy lies in this cultural generosity or, to put it in a more detached manner, in this 'asymmetry'.[90] The kingdom was seen as a storehouse for correct texts from the past and for technical resources, books one could go to and consult, copy or take across the Alps, either individually (to answer a specific learned question) or in batches (as happened after the capture of Pavia and the Lombard treasure in 774).[91] Even if this was a long-term phenomenon – from the sixth to the eleventh century – Italy's singularity became all the more pronounced in the ninth century, when innovative texts proliferated in the north without convincing the south that they were worth reading and copying. This element of imbalance obliges us to reject any idea of complementarity between 'regions', each with a different genius but supposedly harmoniously integrated into the heart of the same empire. Hence Florus of Lyon hated the Treaty of Verdun: because of the cultural fragmentation implied by political compartmentalization.[92]

---

[87] On medicine, Ferrari, 'Manoscritti e cultura', pp. 255–6; Bischoff, *Katalog*, nos. 224, 1238, 1239, 1650, 2116, 2525, 2796, 2805.

[88] Witt, *Two Latin Cultures*. This observation would no doubt have been reinforced had the documentation from Pavia survived. Almost nothing has come down to us.

[89] Supino Martini, 'Aspetti della cultura grafica'; De Rubeis, 'Sillogi epigrafiche'; De Rubeis, 'La capitale damasiana a Tours'.

[90] Chiesa, 'Le vie della cultura', p. 20.

[91] Jullien, 'Alcuin et l'Italie'; Villa, 'La produzione libraria'; Bischoff, 'Italienische Handschriften'.

[92] Florus, *[Querela de divisione imperii]* 49–50, ed. Dümmler, p. 561: *Discebant iuvenes divina volumina passim / Litteras artes puerorum corda bibebant.*

This, indeed, justifies our asking whether there was, after all, a Carolingian Italy.

Appendix: A provisional list of contemporary northern authors copied or received in Italy during the ninth century (with dating and original provenance according to Bischoff) or mentioned in book inventories up to the beginning of the eleventh century. [For the *Liber glossarum* see note 74.]

Alcuinus (†804)

- Ivrea, Bibl. Capitolare, XXX (16) ('Frankreich', ca. s. ix^{med}): *De psalmis poenentialibus, De fide s. et individuae Trinitatis, De virtutibus et vitiis.*
- Milan, Bibl. Ambrosiana, M 1 sup. ('wohl Oberitalien', ca. s. ix$^{3/4}$): *ep.* 143 (*computus*).
- Milan, Bibl. Ambrosiana, O 95 sup. ('Frankreich?' ca s. ix$^{3/3}$): *Ars grammatical*; in Italy in the tenth c.
- Milan, S. Ambrogio, Arch. Capitolare, M 15 ('Oberitalien', s. ix$^{3/3}$): *De Trinitate, Quaest. de Trinitate, carm.* 85,3.
- Montecassino, Arch. dell'Abbazia, 3 (Montecassino, 874–92 [879?]): *De fide s. et individuae Trinitatis, Quaestiones de Trinitate, De anima, carm.* 85,3 + computus.
- Munich, BSB, Clm 6407 (Verona, s. ix^{in}; marg. of Pacificus): *De rhetorica, De dialectica, ep.* 134 (*de baptismate*).
- Paris, BnF, lat. 2849A (fols. 1–23: 'Frankreich?, Italien?', ca. s. ix$^{3/4}$; fols. 24–76: '[wohl südl.] Frankr. Italien?' ca. s. ix$^{4/4}$): *De fide s. et individuae Trinitatis, Quaestiones de Trinitate, De anima.*
- Rome, B. Casanatense, 641 (Montecassino, 811–2): *De fide s. et individuae Trinitatis, Quaestiones de Trinitate, De anima, carm.* 85,3 + computus.
- Rome, B. Naz. Centrale, Sess. 71 (1349) (Nonantola, s. ix/x): *De psalmorum usu.*
- Vatican, BAV, Vat. lat. 3850 ('Italien', ca. s. ix$^{4/4}$): *De dialectica, De rhetorica.*
- Verona, B. Cap., LXVII (64) (Verona, s. viii/ix): *De fide s. et individuae Trinitate, De anima.*
- Libraries:
    - Eberhard of Friuli, 863/4: *De virtutibus et vitiis* (bequeathed to his daughter Judith [Becker 12.47]).

- Bobbio, s. ix/x: *In Genesim*; *In Iohannem* (from Dungal [Becker 32.492, 493]); versus (from Dungal [Becker 32.526]); *De fide s. et individuae Trinitatis* (from the priest Theodorus [Becker 32.569]); *De rhetorica* (two copies, one from the priest Theodorus [Becker 32.587], one from the monk Peter [Becker 32.610]).
- Farfa, s. xi^{in}: '*alcuinum de trinitate*'.
- Vercelli, s. x$^{2/2}$: '*Liber domni Alcuini*'; '*Quaterni d<e Fra>nco et Saxon*' (= *De grammatica*) [Rudolf 'A tenth-century booklist'].
- Cremona, Bishop Odelricus, 984: *De dialectica* (bequeathed to the cathedral, 983).
- For the masses, see above, note 70.

Amalarius Mettensis chorep. (†850)
- Libraries:
  - Vercelli, s. x$^{2/2}$: '*Liber officiorum*' [Rudolf 'A tenth-century booklist']; if the title relates to Amalarius, the ms. in question is Vercelli, Bibl. Capitolare, CCXLVI (s. x), but it could also be Ambrosius or Isidorus.
  - Odelricus, bishop of Cremona, 984: '*Libri officiorum Amesarii*' [Becker 36.93].
  - Nonantola, s. xi^{in}: '*Amellarius*' = Roma, BNC, Sess. 30 (1570) (s. 11) [Branchi, *Nonantola*, pp. 208, 387].

Benedictus Anianensis (†821)
- Library:
  - Farfa, s. xi^{in}: '*concordia regularum*'.

Eginhardus (†840)
- Vercelli, Bibl. Capitolare, CXLIX (136) ('Eichstätt? St Gallen?' s. ix/x) [Licht, 'Einharts *Libellus de psalmis*", but with some uncertainty concerning the date of the arrival of the ms. at Vercelli].
- Library of Bobbio, s. ix/x: *Libellus de psalmis* (2 copies, one from the priest Benedictus, one from the priest Peter [Becker 32.600]).

Florus Lugdunensis diac. (†860 ca)
- Brescia, Bibl. Civ. Queriniana, G.III.2 ('Milan?' s. ix$^{3/3}$): *Collectanea in epistulas Pauli*.
- Milan, Bibl. Ambrosiana, A 46 inf. (Reims, s. ix$^{3/3}$), fols. 51r–2v: *Collectio 'Ex synodo Lugdunensis Ecclesiae'*; poss. at S. Dionigi in Milan in the xvth c.

- Bischoff also considers the ms. BAV, Reg. lat. 240, a copy of Florus' *Liber adversus Iohannem Scotum*, to be Italian, but the ms. is rather from France or from Fulda: K. Zechiel-Eckes, *CCCM* 260, pp. XXXIII–V.

Haimo Autissiodorensis mon. (†875/878 ca)

- Budapest, UB, U.Fr.l.m.2 (fragm., 'Oberit.? Nonantola?', ca. s. ix/x): *Annotatio libri Isaiae Prophetae*.
- Libraries:
    - Cremona, Cathedral and Bishop Odelricus, 984: *Homiliarium*, 2 vol. [Becker 81.61, 68; Tirelli, 'Gli inventari della biblioteca della cattedrale di Cremona', 66–67 nos. 69, 76].
    - Farfa, s. xi^{in}: '*super genesim*; *super esaiam*; *super epistulas pauli*; *super apocalypsin*'.
    - Nonantola, s. xi^{in}: *Expositio in Isaiam* = Roma, BNC, Sess. 36 (1270) (s. xi); *Homiliarium* [Branchi, *Nonantola*, pp. 209, 387).
    - Monte Amiata, s. xi^{in}: '*Aimo*', i.e. *Expositio in s. Pauli epistolas*? [Gorman, 'Codici manoscritti della Badia amiatina', p. 39].

Haimo Halberstadensis ep. († 853)

- Arezzo, Arch. di Stato, framm. 2.24, 2.27 (s. ix): *Homiliae* [Magiorami, *Frammenti*].

Halitgarius Cameracensis ep. (†830 ca)

- Milan, Bibl. Ambrosiana, L 28 sup. ('Oberit.?' s. ix$^{2/2}$): *Liber paenitentialis*.
- Novara, Bibl. Cap., LXXI (18) ('Oberit.', s. ix$^{3/3}$): *Liber paenitentialis*.
- Library of Bobbio, s. ix/x: '*canones*' (two copies, one from the priest Benedictus [Becker 32.538], one from the monk Adalbertus [Becker 32.556]).

Hrabanus Maurus (†856)

- Arezzo, Arch. di Stato, framm. I. 24a, I.24b (France, s. ix2/4): *Commentarius in Genesim*; brought by Bishop John, for the canonical school?) [Tristano, 'Un nuovo testimone'].
- Karlsruhe, Badische Landesbibl., Aug. perg. 115 ('Oberit.?' s. ix$^{3/4}$): *Commentarius in librum Numerorum*. Hrabanus' text is preceded by verses sent to Dungal by Donatus Scottus.
- Milan, Bibl. Ambrosiana, I 35 inf. (Bobbio, s. x^{in}): *Commentarius in Genesim*; = copy from the priest Benedictus?

- Vercelli, Bibl. Cap., CLIII (151) (Reims, s. ix$^{3/3}$):
  Commentarius in Deuteronomium (bequeathed by Hincmar to
  Liutward of Vercelli).
- Verona, Bibl. Cap., LXVIII (65) (Verona, s. ix$^{1/2}$):
  Commentarius in libros Iudith et Hester.
- Libraries:
  • Eberhard of Friuli, 863/4: *De laudibus sanctae crucis* =
    Torino, BNU, K II 20 (Fulda, s. ix$^{1/2}$); cf. *MGH Epp.*
    V, no. 42, p. 481.
  • Bobbio, s. ix/x: *In Genesim* (from the priest Benedictus
    [Becker 32.605]).
  • Farfa, s. xi^{in}: '*super psalmos;suoer ecclesiasticum; in treniis
    hieremiae; super regum; super xxcim prophetas;exposition in
    machabeorum librorum*'.
  • Montecassino, sub Theobaldo abate (1022–6; 1023): *De
    rerum natura* (Inguanez, *Catalogi codicum Casinensium
    antiqui*, pp. 5–6; ms. Montecassino, Arch. dell'Abbazia,
    132, from a Carolingian copy, but we do not know when
    it entered the library).
  • Nonantola, s. xi^{in}: '*Liber Rabani*' = Roma, BNC, Sess. 44
    (1473) (s. xi) [Branchi, *Nonantola*, pp. 210, 387].

Notkerus Balbulus (†912)

- Library of Odelricus, bishop of Cremona, 984: '*Sequentiarum
  libelli volumen unum*' [Becker 81.80] could be Notker's *Liber
  sequentiarum*, as hypothesized by Tirelli, "Gli inventari... di
  Cremona" (see *supra* Haimo Autissiodorensis), p. 68. Notker
  dedicated the work to Liutward of Vercelli (884).

Paschasius Radbertus (†865)

- Vatican, BAV, Vat. lat. 5767 ('Oberit.', s. ix$^{4/4}$?): *De corpore et
  sanguine domini* (bequeathed by the priest Theodorus; the ms.
  was used by Ratherius and Gezo).

Remigius Autissiodorensis mon. (†908)

- Libraries:
  • Farfa, s. xi^{in}: '*super ecclesiasticum*'.
  • Odelricus, bishop of Cremona, 984: *In Donatum* [Becker
    36.79].
  • Nonantola, s. xi^{in}: *Homiliae* = Roma, BNC, Sess. 45
    (1364) (s. xi) [Branchi, *Nonantola*, pp. 212, 387).

Smaragdus Sancti Michaelis abbas (†830 ca)
- Fulda, Hessische Landesbibl., Fragm., with other fragments in New York, PML and Stuttgart, Württ. LB (Bischoff 1335; 'Oberit.', s. ix/x): *Expositio libri Comitis.*
- Heidelberg, Universitätsbibl., Heidelb. 3965 with other fragments in Karlsruhe, Bad. LB (Bischoff 1511; 'Oberit.?' s. ix$^{3/3}$): *Expositio libri Comitis.*
- Karlsruhe, Badische Landesbibl., Aug. perg. 241 ('Oberit.?' s. ix$^{3/3}$): *Liber in partibus Donati* (exc.).
- Monza, Bibl. Cap., c 3/63 ('Oberit.', s. ix$^{2/3}$): *Expositio libri Comitis.*
- Munich, Bayer. Staatsbibl., Clm 3234, 3235, 3245 (fragm.; 'vermutlich Oberit.', s. ix$^{2/3}$): *Expositio libri Comitis.*
- Munich, Bayer. Staatsbibl., Clm 6214 ('Oberit.', s. ix$^{2/3}$): *Expositio libri Comitis.*
- Libraries:
  - Eberhard of Friuli, 863/4: '*Smaragdum*' (bequeathed to his son Rodulfus [Becker 12.33]).
  - Cremona, Cathedral, 984: '*Smaragdi volumen unum*' [Becker 36.52].
  - Andreas Bishop of Tortona, 934: '<S>maragdum unum' [Chartarium Dertonense, n° 60].
  - A Friulian monastic library (Sesto al Reghena?), s. x^{med}: '*L(iber) Smaragdo*' [Scalon, *Produzione*, p. 137 n° 6; perhaps the *Diadema monachorum*].
  - Novalesa, s. xi^{in}: '*Diadema*' [*Cronaca di Novalesa*, p. VII].
  - S. Liberatore alla Maiella, 1014/19: *Diadema monachorum* (written on the order of Prior Theobaldus [Carusi, 'Intorno al *Commemoratorium*', p. 185]).

Section II

Organizing Italy

6   The Government of a Peripheral Area
The Carolingians and North-Eastern Italy

Stefano Gasparri

This chapter presents the results of research into the political strategies employed by the Carolingians in governing north-eastern Italy (Friuli and Veneto), an area divided between Lombard and Byzantine traditions. This was a region that had acquired considerable political importance in the late Lombard period, when two dukes of Friuli, Ratchis and Aistulf, became kings and the local aristocracy represented the strongest military grouping within the kingdom, accustomed as they were to fighting against Avars and Slavs along the eastern border.[1]

The arrival of the Carolingians did not cause any major changes to the existing situation, and the era proved, with some interruptions, to be essentially one of continuity. The importance of north-eastern Italy in the Carolingian period is confirmed by a long series of public documents concerning the area: I am referring to the *Notitia Italica*, the plea of Rižana, the pact of Ravenna, the synod of Mantua, the *Pactum Lotharii* and the plea of Cremona of 851. Taken together, these documents clearly reveal the Carolingians' unfaltering interest in the governance of this vast area of the kingdom, which was of great strategic and commercial value.

The Friulian aristocracy was, nonetheless, the only one to put up armed resistance against the Frankish armies. The revolt of Hrodgaud is carefully documented in the Frankish sources and also by the Italian historian Andreas of Bergamo.[2] The different versions do not overlap, however, and although there are no doubts as to the final outcome described in the *Annales regni Francorum* – that is, the defeat and death of Hrodgaud – it is likely that Andrew preserved a stronger memory of an earlier period, in which Charlemagne had striven to reach an agreement with Hrodgaud and his allies, the dukes of Treviso and Vicenza.[3]

---

[1] On the reigns of Ratchis and Aistulf, see Gasparri, *Italia longobarda*, pp. 100–7.
[2] Borri, 'Troubled times'.
[3] On the Lombard memory after the defeat in 774, see Gasparri, 'The fall of the Lombard Kingdom'.

Moreover, according to Einhard's version of the annals, Charlemagne began by installing Hrodgaud as duke of Friuli. Rather than making a new appointment, he may, however, have been merely confirming Hrodgard's existing status, as he would do three years later when he confirmed Hildeprand in the office of duke of Spoleto.[4]

Unlike in Spoleto, however, the agreement in Friuli did not last long, and after defeating Hrodgaud, Charlemagne ultimately *disposuit omnes per Francos*, placing Frankish *comites* in the rebellious cities.[5] This was the first Frankish initiative in the north-east of the kingdom. In a famous passage, Andreas of Bergamo describes the sufferings that followed in the wake of the Franks' arrival in Italy – *alii gladio interempti, alii fame perculsi, aliis bestiis occisi, ut vix pauci remanerent in vicos vel in civitates* – and links them to the suppression of Hrodgaud's revolt. Although his words may derive in part from a similar passage by Marius of Avenches describing the Lombard invasion two centuries earlier, they should not be underestimated.[6]

Harsh, repressive measures were taken against anyone aligning themselves with Hrodgaud. Confiscations are attested very early on and continued for a long time. In June 776, Paulinus of Aquileia received the property of a certain Waldand, a follower of Hrodgaud; further confiscations are mentioned in 799 and 811.[7] Everything points to Friuli having undergone a heavy military occupation. The goods confiscated belonged to men on Hrodgaud's side who had been killed in battle. The only exception was Aio, who had fled to the Avars before being captured by King Pippin, who proceeded to pardon him, return his goods and make him a count (probably of Friuli).[8]

Some years after the revolt of Friuli, the so-called *Notitia Italica* paints a very similar picture to that described by Andreas – although it uses less apocalyptic terms.[9] The *Notitia* is the first known capitulary promulgated by Charlemagne in Italy, and almost certainly dates to 20 February

---

[4] *ARF*, s.a. 776, ed. Kurze, p. 43. In the other version of the Annals (*ARF*, s.a. 775, ed. Kurze, p. 42) it is written that Hrodgaud *fraudavit fidem suam*. Hildeprand's story is narrated in *LP* 1, Life 97 Hadrianus, pp. 495–6.

[5] *ARF*, s.a. 776, ed. Kurze, p. 44.

[6] Andreas of Bergamo, *Historia*, 4, ed. Pertz, p. 224; Marius of Avenches, *Chronica*, s. a. 569, ed. Mommsen, p. 238: *Alboenus rex Langobardorum [...] Italiam occupavit, ibique allii morbo, alii fame, nonnulli gladio interempti sunt*.

[7] *DD Pippini, Carlomanni et Caroli Magni*, 112, ed. Mühlbacher, pp. 158–9, and ibid. 214, pp. 285–7. In general, on Hrodgaud's revolt: Krahwinkler, *Friaul im Frühmittelalter*, pp. 119–43; Gasparri, 'Istituzioni e poteri', pp. 115–18.

[8] *DD Pippini, Carlomanni et Caroli Magni*, 187, ed. Mühlbacher, pp. 251–2; Gasparri, 'Istituzioni e poteri', pp. 118–19.

[9] *Notitia Italica*, 88, ed. Boretius, pp. 187–8.

781.[10] The capitulary annulled numerous *cartulae obligationis*, which had seen entire families going freely into servitude; numerous sales that were unfavourable to the sellers, because drawn up at a moment of dire need (*tempore necessitate famis*), as well as donations that had received insufficient *launegild*, again because the donor had been *strictus necessitate famis*, were also annulled; even donations to the Church were to be carefully evaluated by a synod before being confirmed. Charlemagne clearly states that only contracts drawn up in areas affected by his recent war – *ubi nos aut nostra hostis fuerimus* – were to be reviewed. Contracts dating to the reign of Desiderius, even though they may also have been drafted *per districtionem famis*, would therefore remain valid. This means that the *Notitia Italica* was clearly written primarily – if not exclusively – with north-eastern Italy in mind, the only area to have put up armed resistance and, therefore, that with the heaviest concentration of Frankish troops. This resistance possibly predated the revolt of Hrodgaud, given that already during the campaign of 773–774 Adelchis had fled to Verona.[11] While the Pavian area was undoubtedly caught up in the conflict, the consequences in the north-east were far more devastating.

The *Notitia* represents the Carolingians' first attempt to impose order on this vast area of the kingdom and also addresses the severe social hardships that followed in the wake of the Frankish armies.[12] Bernard's revolt of 817 may also have had consequences in the north-east, suggesting that the region had yet to be fully pacified.[13] In fact, after 817 we know of at least one case of land being confiscated from an *infidelis*; it is mentioned in a donation made by Louis the Pious to the monastery of Santa Maria in Valle in Cividale in 819, and clearly belonged to one of Bernard's men.[14]

The great importance attributed to the governance of the north-east by the Carolingians was primarily motivated by military reasons, given that the duchy of Friuli bordered the territory of the Avars and the Slavs. In a diploma drawn up for Paulinus of Aquileia in 792, in which Charlemagne grants an exemption from certain tributes and the free election of the patriarch, the king also added an *elemosina* involving the

---

[10] The new date, different from the traditional (776), is proposed convincingly by Mordek, 'Die Anfänge', in particular pp. 17–27.

[11] Mordek, 'Die Anfänge', pp. 17–27, links die *Notitia* to the anointing of Pippin als *rex Langobardorum* and underlines its validity for the entire kingdom of Italy. On Adelchis, *LP* 1, Life 97 Hadrianus, p. 495.

[12] Mordek, 'Die Anfänge', p. 23: 'Die *Notitia* ist Karls erstaunlich entgegenkommende Antwort auf die negativen Folgen seiner Eroberungspolitik.'

[13] Depreux, 'Das Königtum Bernhards von Italien'.

[14] *Diplomi inediti attinenti al Patriarcato di Aquileia dal 799 al 1082*, n.4, ed. Joppi and Mühlbacher.

exemption of the *homines* of the church of Aquileia from the obligations of *mansionaticum* and *fodrum*, specifying that this right would not apply if Charlemagne or Pippin should need to travel to Friuli or to the territory of Treviso *propter impedimenta inimicorum*.[15] The presence of the royal army would therefore nullify the exemption of the church of Aquileia. This document was drawn up at a time when Pippin and Eric, duke of Friuli, were organizing major expeditions against the Avars.[16]

The defence of the frontier was therefore a primary concern, forcing the Carolingians to introduce measures regarding the march of Friuli and its counts, dukes or margraves – depending on the titles currently in use.[17] Indeed, it was this consideration that led to the appointment of a man of the stature of Eberhard – described as *miles Christi* and *murus ecclesiae* in the sources – as duke of Friuli in 828, an office he would hold for around thirty years. As this subject has been well covered elsewhere, there is no need to dwell on it here.[18]

The construction of a political base in the region was not limited to building alliances with those local families whose loyalty might be swayed. The Carolingian power also relied heavily on the church of Aquileia, while their links to Grado were limited to those with Patriarch Fortunatus, on whom Charlemagne and Pippin pinned their hopes of an extension of Carolingian influence over Venice and Istria. The diplomas that Fortunatus obtained from Charlemagne – immunity and exemption from taxes for four ships of the church – were only valid during his lifetime, however.[19] Moreover, during the 827 synod of Mantua, Lothar made a decision that clearly favoured Aquileia and reduced Grado to the status of a mere diocese dependent upon Aquileia.[20] The synod was an attempt to impose order in the region, this time in the ecclesiastical sphere, with the ultimate aim of laying claim to the area of Istria. At the same time, however, such a decision was also politically hostile to the duchy of Venice.

Carolingian interests in Istria predate the synod of Mantua, as is revealed by the 804 plea of Rižana.[21] I have underlined elsewhere the importance of this plea in reconstructing the oldest political and social framework of Venice.[22] Here I would like to draw attention to the efforts made by Charlemagne's envoys to include the Istrian province within the

[15] *DD Pippini, Carlomanni et Caroli Magni*, 174, ed. Mühlbacher, pp. 233–4.
[16] Gasparri, 'Istituzioni e poteri', pp. 119–21.
[17] On the meaning of these titles, see Werner, 'Missus – Marchio – Comes', pp. 211–18.
[18] Gasparri, 'Istituzioni e poteri', pp. 124–5.   [19] See above, n. 14.
[20] *Concilium Mantuanum*, 47, ed. Werminghoff, pp. 583–9.
[21] Krahwinkler, ... *in loco qui dicitur Riziano*; on the plea: Borri, 'Gli Istriani e i loro parenti'.
[22] Gasparri, 'Venezia fra i secoli VIII e IX'.

Carolingian state without altering the underlying local political and social structure. One of these envoys was Count Aio of Friuli, the other was Cadolah, who was also probably a count or duke of Friuli. The local aristocracy, represented by 172 *capitanei*, presented complaints against Patriarch Fortunatus and his bishops, which stemmed from the Istrian churches often exercising their rights violently and asking for more tributes than due.

The most difficult part of the Frankish envoys' mission concerned the abuses by Count John, the local representative of Carolingian power, who kept the tributes paid by the Istrian aristocrats, or tribunes, for himself instead of giving them to the *palatium*. The count attempted to place the Istrian tribunes under his rule, imposing corvées, seizing their horses and even taking their sons hostage.

John's attempt to impose a seigneurial rule caused the tribunes to report his abuses. Charlemagne's *missi* opposed the patriarch and his bishops, and above all John, and re-established the ancient local privileges and customs in order to avoid violence on the part of the tribunes. The desperation of the latter had reached such a pitch that they declared that if Charlemagne refused to come to their aid *melius est nobis mori, quam vivere*. The resolutions passed in Rižana were confirmed by Louis the Pious ten or fifteen years later with the explicit aim of maintaining the internal political balance, avoiding abuses by the *potentiores* and winning the loyalty of the latter along with that of the entire Istrian people.[23] The eastern regions were always at the forefront of Carolingian interests, even after the Peace of Aachen in 812.

This celebrated treaty also had consequences for north-eastern Italy, where it took six years to reach an agreement. The peace process began in 807 with a truce entered into by Pippin and the Byzantine admiral Nicetas, before being interrupted by a brief outbreak of hostilities. Between 810 and 812 it drew to its definitive conclusion when the treaty was also ratified by the Byzantine emperor, Michael I. We know neither anything of its contents nor whether it involved the complete organization of the various spheres of influence, however. With regard to the topics of interest to us here, the annals only make specific reference to the return of Venice, occupied by Pippin in 810, to the Byzantines.[24]

The most important aspect of the peace process, as far as the kingdom of Italy was concerned, was the pact of 807, which was expressly mentioned in the subsequent agreement drawn up between Lothar and the

---

[23] *DD Ludovici Pii*, 82, ed. Kölzer, pp. 200–2.
[24] *ARF*, s.a. 807, 809, 810, 812, ed. Kurze, pp. 124, 127, 130, 132–3, 136. See Borri, 'L'Adriatico tra Bizantini, Longobardi e Franchi.'

Venetians in 840. The latter also informs us in its second chapter that the earlier pact had been entered into at Ravenna.[25] This pact, which must have referred to the exchange of prisoners and handing-over of fugitives, remained in force even after the brief period of war that culminated with the temporary occupation of Venice by Pippin. It must also have contained clauses protecting Venetian property in the kingdom of Italy. In fact, in the diploma of 841 that integrated his agreement of the previous year, the emperor confirmed his protection, mentioning the *decretum cum Grecis sanccitum* – clearly a reference to the Pact of Ravenna.[26] This protection was important, because it involved, for example, properties like that of Duke Giustiniano Particiaco in the territory of Treviso, as revealed by his will of 829.[27] Moreover, the intermediary between Lothar and the duke of Venice, Pietro Tradonico, was none other than Duke Eberhard of Friuli – further evidence of the importance of this diploma of confirmation.[28]

The lack of a broad agreement clearly defining the boundaries and spheres of influence of the kingdom of Italy meant, however, that relations between areas within and outside the kingdom remained fluid. For example, a Venetian source (the Chronicle of John the Deacon) tells us that, around 830, when Duke Giovanni Particiaco was forced to flee because of a severe political crisis within the Venetian duchy, he sought refuge in Frankish territory; his flight could be seen as evidence that Venice maintained close relations with the Carolingian empire even after the Peace of Aachen.[29]

These reflections are intended to show that it is misleading to present the Venetian duchy as being a totally separate entity from the kingdom of Italy after 812; on the contrary, it should be considered an appendix to the kingdom.[30] The *Pactum Lotharii* of 840 mentioned earlier is an important document concerning the duchy and should not be considered in terms of an agreement between two completely separate political entities; in fact, it contains important clauses that reveal the profound link between the kingdom and the duchy. As far as the kingdom was concerned, it meant settling all relations between the peoples in the north-eastern Adriatic area and those of the duchy: it makes explicit reference to the inhabitants of the communities of the Veneto, Friuli, Istria, the Exarchate and the Pentapolis, who all reached an agreement

---

[25] *Pactum Lotharii*, ch. 2, ed. Boretius and Krause, p. 131.
[26] *DD Lotharii I. et Lotharii II.*, 62, ed. Schieffer, p. 170.
[27] *Ss. Ilario e Benedetto e S. Gregorio*, 2, ed. Lanfranchi and Strina, pp. 17–24.
[28] On Eberhard, Gasparri, 'Istituzioni e poteri', pp. 124–5.
[29] John the Deacon, *Istoria Veneticorum*, II, 44 ed. Berto, p. 120.
[30] Gasparri, 'Venezia fra l'Italia bizantina e il regno italico'; see also above, n. 22.

with the lagoon communities on issues such as the grazing rights of livestock – to avoid seizure of livestock unlawfully occupying pasture land – and rights with regard to the cutting and transport of wood. The agreement reiterated regulations concerning fugitives, including slaves, and prisoners.[31]

Given that this agreement makes no mention of Byzantium, it has traditionally been interpreted within Venetian historiography as evidence of the definitive recognition of Venetian independence: an agreement in which Lothar and the Venetian duke, Pietro Tradonico, were two independent parties on equal footing seeking to resolve all outstanding matters between them.[32] The author of the *Istoria Veneticorum*, John the Deacon, who was writing in the period of Duke Pietro II Orseolo (circa 1000) and is the oldest chronicler of Venice, makes no mention of the agreement, however. And yet we know that John, who was a close collaborator of the duke and probably had some charge at the ducal palace, was familiar with this document, because he quotes sections of it in his account, albeit distorting their meaning.[33] John's silence on the matter impinges drastically on the importance attributable to the agreement, and we can safely exclude that it sanctioned the independence of the duchy. We are therefore dealing with a mistaken and anachronistic interpretation.

Let us return to our analysis of the agreement. It was issued by Lothar *suggerente et supplicante Petro, gloriosissimo duce Veneticorum*, and its purpose was merely to regulate relations between the two groups of communities, both of which were under the supreme authority of Lothar; proof of this lies in the fact that his *iudices* were entitled to exercise their judicial functions – at least in theory – within the confines of the duchy.[34] As part of his endeavour to establish order, Lothar also refers to various agreements drawn up in the past: those stipulated under Liutprand and Aistulf, the Ravenna agreement as well as old customs, which were in turn based on old pacts.[35] This long tradition of pacts and agreements on the eastern borders is a sign of the constant need – for the Lombards, just as for the Carolingians – to maintain close links between the areas inside and outside the kingdom. This is also revealed by section 17, which establishes that tolls on rivers must be exacted *secundum antiquam consuetudinem*: the custom referred to here is undoubtedly the old agreement

---

[31] Above, n. 25.
[32] This was for example the opinion of an historian of Venice as famous as Roberto Cessi: see Ortalli, 'Venezia dalle origini a Pietro II Orseolo', pp. 390–1.
[33] Gasparri, 'The first dukes and the origins of Venice'.
[34] *Pactum Lotharii*, ch. 10, 11, 12, 19, ed. Boretius and Krause, pp. 132–3.
[35] *Pactum Lotharii*, ch. 2, 26, 28, ed. Boretius and Krause, pp. 131, 135.

drawn up between Liutprand and the inhabitants of the Comacchio in 715, which was by now held to be valid for all merchants in the eastern Po Valley.[36]

And now we come to the second reason why this area of the kingdom was of such strategic importance for the Carolingians: its commercial traffic. Carolingian rulers took measures in relation to trade on numerous occasions. In 781, Charlemagne confirmed the old agreement with the inhabitants of Comacchio, who were the first merchants to ply their trade in north-eastern Italy, protecting them from malfeasance by public officers and restating the applicable regulations for their journey by boat from the Adriatic along the rivers of the Po Valley, with halts in the ports of Mantua, Parma, Piacenza and Cremona. This diploma reinforced a tradition dating back to the Lombard period.[37] For its part, the church of Cremona was the subject of a series of diplomas of a different type enacted by Lothar. The first dates to 841 – significantly, the years of the *pactum* and diploma for the Venetians – followed by a further seven diplomas ending with one drawn up by Charles the Fat. To this series we must add a *placitum* of Louis II dating to 851 or 852.[38]

These diplomas and plea transferred to the church of Cremona the right to exact tolls for commercial river traffic according to the rules originally laid down for the inhabitants of the Comacchio and now extended to merchants in general. The decision was made on the basis of a lost diploma drawn up by Charlemagne, which had conferred these public rights on the bishopric of Cremona. Around 800, Rotchild, the regent of the kingdom of Italy during the minority of Pippin, had recovered these rights, making it necessary for the Carolingians to implement a long series of measures to deal with the matter.[39]

The volume of diplomas issued confirms that the Carolingians attached great importance to regulating the commercial traffic travelling upriver from the Adriatic. It should also be mentioned that in the plea of 851/52, a group of local citizens who were obviously merchants had taken the initiative to go to Louis II to protest against the church of Cremona. Their protest was unprecedented and would remain the only instance for a long time: there are no further examples of autonomous political actions by the *cives* in cities in the kingdom of Italy during the Carolingian period.[40] The source still suggests that commercial activity

---

[36] *Pactum Lotharii*, ch. 17, ed. Boretius and Krause, p. 133. The agreement of 715 is edited by Hartmann, *Zur Wirtschaftsgeschichte Italiens*, pp. 123–4.

[37] *DD Pippini, Carlomanni, Caroli Magni*, 132, ed. Mühlbacher, pp. 182–3.

[38] Gasparri, 'Venezia fra i secoli VIII e IX', pp. 9–13. On the plea of 851/52: Gasparri, 'Italien in der Karolingerzeit', pp. 70–1.

[39] *I Placiti del 'Regnum Italiae'*, 56, ed. Manaresi, pp. 193–8.   [40] See above, n. 30.

in north-eastern Italy was already so far advanced that it could propel groups of merchants into the foreground as political actors. This dossier of sources makes explicit mention of the merchants from Comacchio, of Venetians and, finally, of merchants from Cremona. This is the reason why the Carolingians were so concerned with regulating this sector. All these measures can be better understood in the light of the above-mentioned section 17 of the *Pactum Lotharii*, which is proof of the existence of a series of provisions integrating each other, whether they concern the church of Cremona or the duchy of Venice.

The initiatives of the Carolingian kings and emperors drew upon a tradition dating back to the late Lombard period. They reveal a strong propensity to adapt to the particular problems affecting north-eastern Italy, a vast, extremely varied area extending from the Po Plain to the coast, the different parts of which were at the same time so deeply integrated as to necessitate measures that applied throughout the region, the existing borders, which were hardly impassable frontiers at that time, being thereby ignored.[41] Accordingly, Carolingian initiatives concerned both that part of the region located inside the kingdom and areas such as the duchy of Venice and, to some extent, Istria that lay beyond its borders.

The innovative nature of the measures implemented by the Carolingians – their incisiveness within the Italian situation – stemmed from the rulers' capacity to act effectively within a far wider and more complex context than their Lombard predecessors, and from their focus on the governance of the entire area. This was achieved by simultan-eously taking into account military, commercial, political and ecclesi-astical issues as well as problems between local communities. Their unswerving attention of the Carolingians to the north-east has no equal in the other areas of the Italic kingdom.

---

[41] Gasparri, 'La frontiera in Italia'; in general on this topic, see Pohl, Wood and Reimitz, *The Transformation of Frontiers*.

7   Vassals without Feudalism in Carolingian Italy

Giuseppe Albertoni

Early Medieval Vassals: 'Conceptual Black Holes'?

In recent decades, the study of vassals and fiefs has seen profound changes, to the extent that the very legitimacy of the concept of feudalism is now being questioned.[1] The two concepts were and, to a certain extent, continue to be at the centre of a lively historiographical debate, which really took off at the beginning of the 1990s, with the publication of Susan Reynolds' much-discussed *Fiefs and Vassals*.[2] This debate, however, has concentrated on the central thesis of Reynolds' book, which she herself summarized in a more recent article, where she presents an overview of how *Fiefs and Vassals* was received, challenged and debated by medievalists all over the world in the twelve years after its publication.[3] In this account she reaffirms that her main aim was not to do away with the entire concept of feudalism, but to point out the errors inherent in the legal-historical interpretation of feudalism, hitherto considered most 'acceptable' and 'objective'.[4]

The Belgian historian François Louis Ganshof had been the principal proponent of this meaning of feudalism, largely through his highly popular book, *Qu'est-ce que la féodalité?*, which postulates a 'Carolingian feudalism', from which the 'classical feudalism' later developed.[5] According to Reynolds, however, this 'Carolingian feudalism' never existed, and its 'inventor' committed a series of – largely conscious – epistemological errors, projecting back into the early Middle Ages juridical concepts which were, in fact, only developed from the twelfth century onwards by the Lombard lawyers who compiled the *Libri* or *Consuetudines feudorum*.[6]

I would like to thank Rachael Murphy for the translation of my text into English.

[1] For a quick historiographical update on the recent debate, see Patzold, *Das Lehnswesen* and Albertoni, *Vassalli, feudi, feudalesimo*, pp. 65–86.
[2] Reynolds, *Fiefs and Vassals*.   [3] Reynolds, 'Fiefs and vassals after twelve years'.
[4] Reynolds, 'Fiefs and vassals after twelve years', pp. 15–16.
[5] Ganshof, *Qu'est-ce que la féodalité?*; English translation: Ganshof, *Feudalism*.
[6] Reynolds, *Fiefs and Vassals*, pp. 3–14.

Until *Fiefs and Vassals*, it had been thought that this compilation just pertained to local juridical traditions and did not extend beyond Lombardy, or, at most, northern Italy: in other words, it expressed an exception to the rule, or, in Ganshof's words, an Italian *allure distinctive*.[7] It is greatly to Reynolds' credit that she revealed how the *Libri feudorum* had, in fact, quickly gained a wider significance: in the first decades of the thirteenth century, they were integrated into Justinian's *Corpus iuris civilis*, which meant that they were studied and commented upon in the leading universities of the time.[8] According to Reynolds, a succession of steps taken by the lawyers of the late Middle Ages and early modern era then led to the *Libri feudorum* being in a position 'to provide an account of the origin of fiefs that offered both a hypothesis to guide research into medieval history and a framework for discussing the constitutional relations of king and nobles in the historians' present'.[9] Consequently, 'neither the relationship that medieval historians call vassalage nor the kind of property that they call fiefs took their shape from the warrior society of the earlier Middle Ages'.[10]

Reynolds' hypothesis thus presented a radical challenge to a centuries-old scholarly tradition, a 'Kuhnian paradigm'[11] that had been, until then, widely shared, with the exception of a few important, but isolated, dissonant voices.[12] It is thus no surprise that the reactions to *Fiefs and Vassals* were numerous and, initially, sometimes fairly critical.[13] Nor is it surprising that most of the reactions focussed on Reynolds' 'central argument', and, therefore, on the part played by the Lombard *Libri feudorum* in the definition of a new European feudal legal system, subsequently codified by sixteenth- and seventeenth-century French and English legal historians. This is reflected in the themes of some of the important international conferences held in the past twenty years suggest.[14]

---

[7] Ganshof, *Qu'est-ce que la féodalité?*, p. 107.

[8] Reynolds,'Fiefs and vassals after twelve years', p. 16. See also, Reynolds, *Fiefs and Vassals*, pp. 215–30.

[9] Reynolds, *Fiefs and Vassals*, pp. 3–14 and, in particular, p. 5.

[10] Reynolds, 'Fiefs and vassals after twelve years', p. 16.

[11] See Kuhn, *The Structure of Scientific Revolutions*; Reynolds, 'Afterthoughts on *Fiefs and Vassals*', p. 2, now in Reynolds., *The Middle Ages without Feudalism*, pp. 1–15; Fried, 'Debate'.

[12] See Odegaard, *Vassi and Fideles in the Carolingian Empire* and Brancoli Busdraghi, *La formazione storica*.

[13] Among others, see Fried, 'Debate'.

[14] See for example Dendorfer and Deutinger, *Das Lehnswesen im Hochmittelalter* and Spieß, *Ausbildung und Verbreitung des Lehnswesens*.

Early medievalists have not responded to anything like the same extent to Reynolds' proposed historiographical revision, which strikes at the heart of Ganshof's 'Carolingian feudalism'.[15] It deals with a concept that directly – to quote Ganshof *de droit*[16] – linked, as early as the ninth century, vassalage with the concession of the *beneficium*, which were both important elements in the resistance to what he called the *dislocation de l'État*, the disintegration of the State.[17]

Although it has had many variants, connected to the different historiographical traditions,[18] this idea of feudalism had offered an interpretative model long shared by the majority of early medieval scholars, despite the fact that, as early as the 1940s, research was being published that emphasized – in different ways – the multidimensional figure of the vassal and his – fairly intermittent and non-essential – relationship with the *beneficium*.[19]

Nor should we forget that in challenging Ganshof's 'Carolingian feudalism' Reynolds had suggested an analysis that, rejecting the idea of the warrior society as the origin of the fief, shifted the focus of the investigation onto 'ideas of property' and the ecclesiastical *precaria* in particular, which were seen as a form of possession from which subsequent concessions *in beneficium* had derived.[20] Among these various concessions was the one to vassals, who, from this perspective, suddenly appear to assume the role of supporting actors. This drastic diminution of the role of the vassal in Carolingian society and its political institutions had initially led Reynolds to maintain that studying early medieval vassalage was a waste of time.[21] She held it to be 'too vacuous a concept to be useful', since its various reconstructions were no more than 'out-of-date rumours', in which the terms *vassal* and *vassalage* represented 'conceptual black holes that are liable to swallow up any historical scholarship that ventures into them'.[22]

The fact that most early medievalists have not (with some important exceptions[23]) gone on the defensive in the face of this 'negationist' stance is, at first glance, surprising. This is partly explained, however, by the fresh winds that have been blowing through the halls of early medieval scholarship in recent decades.[24] This new approach, thanks to an intense dialogue with the social sciences and anthropology, has actually rendered

---

[15] See Fried, 'Debate'.   [16] Ganshof, *Qu'est-ce que la féodalité?*, p. 73.
[17] Ibid., p. 73 and pp. 101–2.   [18] See Wickham, 'Le forme del feudalesimo'.
[19] See Odegaard, *Vassi and Fideles*; Brancoli Busdraghi, *La formazione storica*; Budriesi Trombetti, *Prime ricerche*; Kienast, *Die fränkische Vasallität*.
[20] Reynolds, *Fiefs and Vassals*, pp. 48–74.   [21] Reynolds, *Fiefs and Vassals*, pp. 17–48.
[22] Ibid., p. 17, p. 34 and p. 47.   [23] See for example Fried, 'Debate'.
[24] See Gasparri and La Rocca, *Tempi barbarici*, pp. 11–27.

Ganshof's idea of the State obsolete;[25] it has also identified, following in the footsteps of Marc Bloch and Georges Duby, the tenth and eleventh centuries as the period in which there was a decisive 'mutation' or 'feudal revolution', characterized by the parcelling out of powers at the local level and by the, important but not central, role of the vassals of the lords as seigneurial agents.[26]

This all meant that Reynolds' hypothesis found fertile soil for its development, which is reflected in the fact that not only has the definition of 'early medieval feudalism' disappeared in the most recent and authoritative studies of early medieval society, even references to vassals and their role are often hard to find.[27] Meanwhile, scholars wishing to study subjects that used to be considered feudal have taken the same line as Reynolds and focussed on the genesis of the *beneficium/feudum* from the ecclesiastic *precaria*, while only rarely addressing the question of vassalage specifically.[28]

Although Reynolds' criticism of those who used to see vassals under every bed, and who attributed to them a key role in both social and political terms, is undoubtedly well-founded, her definition of the idea of vassalage as a 'conceptual black hole', into which one was well advised not to venture, seems something of a surrender in the face of a problem that might possibly be resolved by trying to define the terms *vassus/vassallus* on a case-by-case basis and in individual *corpora* of sources – in individual discursive universes – without putting on one's 'feudal glasses', but also without failing to appreciate the specificity of the role of a 'vassal'.

Who Were the Carolingian Vassals?

Following criticism – particularly that of the German medievalist Johannes Fried – of her demolition of early medieval vassalage, Reynolds herself addressed this question.[29] She thereby largely abandoned her initial 'negationism' and went on to propose according the term *vassus* four distinct meanings, depending on the period being considered: the vassal 'in the Carolingian sense (a lay servant with military and governmental duties); in the vernacular French sense of the *chansons*

[25] See for example Smith, *Europe after Rome*; Airlie, Pohl and Reimitz (eds.), *Staat im frühen Mittelalter*; Jussen, *Die Franken*, pp. 84–6.
[26] See Duby, *Les trois ordres*; Poly and Bournazel, *La mutation féodal*; and the recent West, *Reframing the Feudal Revolution*.
[27] See for example Davis, Charlemagne's Practice, Smith, *Europe after Rome*, and Wickham, *Inheritance of Rome*.
[28] See for example Kasten, 'Aspekte des Lehnswesen', Kasten, 'Das Lehnswesen'.
[29] See Fried, 'Debate', and Reynolds, 'Susan Reynolds responds to Johannes Fried'.

de geste (a soldier or valiant man, with no implication of relationship or service); in the later legal sense derived from the *Libri feudorum* (the holder of a fief under that lord); or in the wider sense developed by nineteenth-century post-Romantic historians (a fief-holder bound to his lord by the strongest bond of medieval society)'.[30] Reynolds went on to examine the first 'figure' of the vassal – the Carolingian, our particular focus – in more depth in a study written in 1999; in it she returned to, and elaborated upon, the work of the American historian Charles E. Odegaard, written fifty years before.[31] Odegaard was a contemporary of Ganshof: the latter's *Qu'est-ce que la féodalité?* came out a year before Odegaard's book on Carolingian vassalage. The latter is still the only monograph published on the subject, but was never widely read, partly, perhaps, because the picture of vassalage that it painted was limited by the concept of feudalism and openly counter to the interpretative models then dominating Anglo-Saxon, German and French historiography.[32] In his book, Odegaard, having analyzed the textual occurrences of the term *vassus*, suggested that *fideles* and, more generally, *commendati* should be clearly distinguished from a vassal, whose function would have been 'to hold himself in readiness as a completely equipped man of arms who can go wherever the king wills and stay as long as is necessary, to act as a bodyguard, to aid the king in policing the realm, in manning garrisons, and in serving with all his equipment in the army'.[33]

Drawing on the figure of the Carolingian vassal described by Odegaard, Reynolds also tried to identify three general features of the group in her 'Fiefs and Vassals after Twelve Years': 'that Carolingian counts were not referred to as royal vassals in official records of the time; that vassalage was not a particularity close or affective bond; and that there is no evidence either that the Carolingians used it to bind counts more closely to them or that counts or other great men were normally, if ever, vassals of the king'[34]. A clear distinction thus emerged not only between the *fideles, commendati* and vassals but also between counts and vassals, in particular the king's vassals. The latter had been, in Odegaard's words, 'a particular group of faithful servants entrusted with a certain function, not all persons who were in his commendation', who 'ranked below counts in the king's service, not because they were

---

[30] Reynolds, *The Middle Ages without Feudalism*, p. XII.

[31] See Odegaard, *Vassi and Fideles*, and Reynolds, 'Carolingian elopements as a sidelight on counts and vassals', now in Reynolds, *The Middle Ages without Feudalism*, pp. 340–6.

[32] Odegaard, *Vassi and Fideles*.   [33] Ibid., pp. 70–1.

[34] Reynolds, 'Carolingian Elopements', p. 340.

necessarily of lower social origin, but because counts had more specific and often more responsible duties, in which they were helped by vassals'.[35]

If we accept this non-feudal approach to Carolingian vassalage and the existence of various different types of vassal within the wider structure of loyalty in the Carolingian world,[36] we have to recognize that, with regard to the eighth and ninth centuries, the term *vassus* does not suck us into a 'conceptual black hole', but actually allows us to identify a particular male social figure who always finds himself in a relationship of asymmetrical reciprocity with another man; this figure, even in the perception of his contemporaries, was distinguished from individuals in other forms of subordination, as also emerges from the numerous studies that have appeared on Carolingian vassalage in recent decades.[37] New definitions of the vassal thus become possible, which, as well as challenging 'Ganshof's paradigm', set out what we might describe as the 'Odegaard/Reynolds hypothesis'.

With the above in mind, I believe we can identify a number of distinct – although not necessarily contradictory – approaches, which have tended to dominate recent research in the field. On the one hand lies what might be termed an inclusive approach, which has attempted to put forward a general definition of the vassal that reflects the multifaceted nature of the textual evidence. Steffen Patzold is one proponent of this approach; in a recent work on feudalism he defined Carolingian vassals 'as people who served the king or another power; most of them were in military service, leading small contingents, but they could also fulfil other roles, including, for example, those of *missi* or envoys, people who did not necessarily receive a *beneficium* from their lord'.[38] Other scholars have taken a more selective approach, which focusses more on the royal/imperial vassals and emphasizes their role in connecting central government with the periphery. Janet Nelson, for example, stated in her important synthesis on royal government in the Carolingian period that the term *vassus* 'meaning boy ... was applied originally half-humorously perhaps, to the man vested with the authority of a royal agent'.[39] The same approach is followed by

---

[35] Ibid.   [36] See Rio, 'High and low'.

[37] Among others, see Kienast, *Die fränkische Vasallität*; Wolfram, 'Karl Martell und das fränkische Lehnswesen'; Depreux, 'Tassilon III et le roi des Francs'; Sergi, 'Vassalli a Milano'; Kerneis, 'Les premiers vassaux'; Barbero, 'Liberti, raccomandati, vassalli'; Deutinger, 'Seit wann gab es die Mehrfachvasallität?'; Magnou-Nortier, 'Quoi de neuf sur l'origine de la vassalité'; Deutinger, 'Beobachtungen zum Lehnswesen'; Castagnetti, 'I vassalli imperiali a Lucca'; Salten, *Vasallität und Benefizialwesen*. For a summary, see Patzold, *Das Lehnswesen*, pp. 25–53 and Albertoni, *Vassalli*, pp. 89–121.

[38] Patzold, *Das Lehnswesen*, p. 38.   [39] Nelson, 'Kingship and royal government', p. 412.

Marios Costambeys, Matthew Innes and Simon MacLean, who in *The Carolingian World* stated very forcefully that, although 'there is simply no foundation for the notion that vassalage emerged in this period as a new form of lordship, characterised by tightly linked service and conditional tenure',[40] it would also be a mistake to see the king's vassals as central to the functioning of the army or as privileged possessors of *beneficia*: they were men who had served the king and who, upon return to their places of origin, maintained their designation as *vassi dominici*, thus constituting a *trait-d'union* that served to 'prolong bonds formed in the royal household and to use them to project a direct relationship between the king and local landowning communities'.[41]

The definitions of vassalage proposed by Nelson, Innes, Costambeys and MacLean can, of course, be included within Patzold's more general categorization, but raise the problem of the existence of a specific royal service and, more generally, of a single model of vassalage. With regard to *servitium*, the question of the vassals' military service and how they were integrated within the Carolingian military organization is a central, and disputed, topic among today's scholars of the period. The question had, in fact, already been posed by Odegaard,[42] before being taken up more recently by, among others, another North American medievalist, Bernard S. Bachrach. While considering Ganshof to be his 'maestro',[43] the latter entered into constructive dialogue with the theses of Odegaard and Reynolds and, on a number of occasions, highlighted the military role of the vassals, quite apart from the different levels of social, and legal, status that various types of vassalage involved.[44] Bachrach considered the military activity of vassals to have played a key role, in that it gave people from the lower classes the opportunity to climb the social scale on the strength of the concession of a *beneficium* in the form of military land, which was used to provide for soldiers, particularly those stationed in recently conquered territories, according to a military tradition with roots stretching back into late antiquity.[45] Stressing this continuity and the gradual but eventually widespread acceptance of the *vassi dominici casati* under Charlemagne, Bachrach revived Ganshof's hypothesis of an early

---

[40] Costambeys, Innes and MacLean, *Carolingian World*, p. 318.
[41] Ibid., pp. 318–19; Innes, 'Charlemagne's government', pp. 78–9 and p. 83. On the role of vassals in the royal palace, see Bachrach, *Early Carolingian Warfare*, pp. 75–7; on their function as links between 'centre' and 'periphery' in the role of *missi*, see Hannig, '*Pauperiores vassi de infra palatio?*'.
[42] See Odegaard, *Vassi and Fideles*, p. 18.
[43] Bachrach dedicated *Early Carolingian Warfare* to the memory of Ganshof.
[44] Bachrach, *Early Carolingian Warfare*, p. 77 and p. 309.
[45] Ibid., p.76–7; Poly, 'Terra salica' and Magnou-Nortier, 'Quoi de neuf'.

structural unity between vassalage and the *beneficium*, but one based on factors linked to military organization and not on the history of the two institutions. At the same time, he clarified the role of the royal vassals in the Carolingian military organization system, of which, although not the backbone, they were nevertheless an important part, above all in relation to the defence of newly conquered territories. The French historians Jean-Pierre Poly and Elisabeth Magnou-Nortier also traced the vassalage system back to traditions of late antiquity such as the *limitanei* and the *dediticii*, although the direction and emphasis of their argument differed from that of Bachrach. Other scholars, like Soazik Kerneis, even proposed the idea of a continuity stretching back to the *ambacti*, the Gauls' armed 'clients'.[46]

The question of the service required of a vassal is thus still dependent on which definition is used; but maybe remembering this can help us to understand that, while accepting the general outline proposed by Patzold, it might be useful to at least maintain a distinction between two general types of vassal, as was suggested at the end of the 1990s by Alessandro Barbero.[47] Although he recognized Susan Reynolds' innovative impetus, Barbero did not share the 'excessive negationism' which had led her 'more to muddy the waters than to purify them', and he proposed an analysis of vassalage in the context of the various client relationships that existed in Carolingian society, which he considered to be highly complex and tightly interwoven.[48] As Odegaard before him, Barbero ran through all the most noteworthy occurrences of the term *vassus*, but reached conclusions which differed somewhat from those of the North American historian and of the other scholars mentioned above. He considered that it was crucial to pay careful attention to the domestic service of the vassals and the probability that, sooner or later, this (particularly if it was military) would be rewarded with a *beneficium*, which would mean leaving the 'home' of the *senior*, whether the latter was a king or just a member of the elite.[49] From this perspective, the vassals during Charlemagne's reign would not have been characterized so much by their military service as by the fact that the armed *clientelae* which they formed were the only ones recognized as legitimate; consequently, even when they were made up of 'private' individuals, they would have assumed a 'public' connotation.[50] One of the things that distinguished these vassals from the armed bands of the Merovingian

---

[46] See Poly, 'La corde au cou'; Poly, 'Terra salica'; Magnou-Nortier, 'Quoi de neuf'; Kerneis, 'Les premiers vassaux'.
[47] Barbero, 'Liberti'.   [48] Ibid., pp. 8–9.   [49] Barbero, 'Liberti', p. 53.
[50] See ibid., p. 56, and Kienast, *Die fränkische Vasallität*, p. 22.

period would have been the reciprocal relationships between them, with the passage from a horizontal structure to a sharply vertical and asymmetrical one, as had already been pointed out in the 1980s in an important article by Régine Le Jan.[51]

The research outlined above, carried out after *Fiefs and Vassals*, seems to indicate very clearly that there is no single, simple answer to the question, 'Who were the Carolingian vassals?' However, it does allow us to understand that the general characteristics of the figure of the vassal put forward by Patzold are a useful common frame within which we can attempt to sketch a more precise picture, one which allows us to understand the role, functions and political, social and military significance of the different types of vassal that emerge in particular historical contexts. We will embark upon this sketch shortly, starting with Italy under the Carolingians.

Why Study the Italian Vassals of the Carolingian period?

I feel that it is useful to reopen the *dossier* on Italian vassals in the Carolingian period, because it still contains many open questions about their role – particularly in the government of the then *regnum Langobardorum* – notwithstanding the existence of important studies (unfortunately undervalued by Reynolds in the chapters of *Fiefs and Vassals* on Italy) which had already, in the 1970s and 80s, begun to question the historiographical tradition, often dominated by a rigidly legal-historical approach.[52] This lack of consideration is undoubtedly one of the reasons why many Italian medievalists met Reynolds' book so coldly, or even ignored it completely, at least with regard to the early Middle Ages, notwithstanding its translation into Italian and the high praise it gained from Giovanni Tabacco, who thoroughly approved of Reynolds' revaluation of the *Libri feudorum* and her 'healthy insistence on the need to always identify, correct, and audaciously interpret, restoring

---

[51] See Le Jan, 'Satellites et bandes armées'.

[52] Among the studies published before 1994 to which Susan Reynolds pays little attention, see Tabacco, 'Il feudalesimo'; Gasparri, 'Strutture militari e legami'; Sergi, 'I rapporti vassallatico-beneficiari'; Tabacco, 'Vassalli, nobili e cavalieri'; Castagnetti, *Minoranze etniche dominanti e rapporti vassallatico–beneficiari*; Sergi, 'Feudalesimo senza sistema', now in Sergi, *Antidoti all'abuso della storia*, pp. 101–14. Some of this research has been inspired by important monographs by German historians, including Hlawitschka, *Franken* and Keller, *Adelsherrschaft und städtische Gesellschaft*, which Susan Reynolds also ignored. On the Italian historiographical tradition up until then, which was dominated by historians of law like Pier Silverio Leicht and Guido Carlo Mor, see Sergi, *Antidoti*, pp. 125–36.

an entire patrimony of ideas to its radical problematization'.[53] Reynolds, in the – revised and updated – Italian translation (2004) of her book,[54] perhaps partly due to her limited knowledge of Italian, did indeed ignore important research on the identification of vassals in the documentary sources, the recreation of their prosopography, 'carriers', ethnic and social origins, and military roles. This research – although encompassing a range of approaches and conclusions – highlighted (as have done other, more recent, studies[55]) how the status of royal or imperial vassal was an important tool for securing political and social access or success, often used by people of the highest social rank, like Abbot Adalard of Corbie, cousin of Charlemagne.[56] It has, furthermore, revealed the steady spread during the mid-ninth century of vassals who served counts, bishops and abbots, and who played important roles in legal disputes and the maintenance of public order, although they were never significant militarily.[57] Lastly, it has highlighted the role of the royal or seigneurial *domus* as the locus for the exchange of the loyalty intrinsic to vassalage.[58] This fidelity, even when those involved were of low social rank, would always have been perceived by contemporaries as different from other ties of loyalty. The question of the connection between vassalage and *beneficium* has not been investigated in any depth, however, and remains partially unanswered;[59] although this approach has challenged the existence of an early medieval 'feudal system', it has often taken for granted the existence of a continuous structural link between vassals and *beneficia*.

However, irrespective of this last point, the 'precocity' of the re-energized Italian historiography has meant that most scholars – believing the question of Carolingian vassalage to have been solved – have almost completely ignored it.[60] This evasion has been largely prompted by the – often justified – desire to avoid a topic that has often appeared to be too closely linked to an obsolete historiographical tradition. Nevertheless, given the huge changes that the historiography of the Carolingian period has undergone in the past twenty years, I believe that the time has now

---

[53] Reynolds, *Feudi e vassalli*. Her 'Afterthoughts' also appeared in Italian, entitled 'Ancora su feudi e vassalli'. For Tabacco's review, see Tabacco, *Medievistica del Novecento*, pp. 703–4.

[54] Reynolds, *Feudi e vassalli*.

[55] See, for example, Castagnetti, *Una famiglia di immigrati*; Castagnetti, 'Transalpini e vassalli in area milanese'; Castagnetti, 'Il conte Anselmo I'; Castagnetti, 'I vassalli imperiali'.

[56] See *I Placiti del 'Regnum Italiae'*, vol. I, n. 25, ed. Manaresi, pp. 78–80. On Adalard, see Kasten, *Adalhard von Corbie* and Bougard, 'Adalhard de Corbie'.

[57] See Gasparri, 'Strutture militari' and Gasparri, 'Les relations de fidélité'.

[58] See Brancoli Busdraghi, *La formazione storica*.   [59] See Leicht, 'Il feudo in Italia'.

[60] Significantly, it was not included in *Il feudalesimo nell'alto medioevo*, devoted to the tenth–twelfth centuries.

come to re-examine the role of Carolingian vassalage, particularly in recently conquered territories like the *regnum Langobardorum*, which, perhaps, can best allow us to understand Carolingian forms of government and social control.

This will be the subject of the second part of this chapter, in which I wish to propose an avenue of research that I hope can lead to further, more detailed, analysis of the topic. My current research is only preliminary, therefore, and focusses on the reconstruction of the meaning given to the term *vassus* in the capitularies. The latter, although they certainly cannot be considered a homogenous *genre*, do share certain characteristics and a specific, and coherent, political vocabulary.[61] I will look particularly closely at the so-called Italic capitularies,[62] going through the dispositions about vassals, in order, I hope, to enable us to better grasp the latter's particular characteristics and roles. I will attempt to clarify whether these capitularies can answer our questions about the public function of vassalage; its role in government; the social profile of the vassals; their ties to the *domus* of their lords; the connection between vassalage and the concession of *beneficia*; and, last but not least, the meaning of the terms *vassus* and *vassallus* in the political lexicon.

What Do the Capitularies Tell Us about Vassals and the Government of the Realm?

This brief, chronological, analysis of the occurrences in the Italic capitularies of the terms *vassus*, *vassallus* and *vassaticum* as indicators of a social position or rank begins in the time of Charlemagne and King Pippin; we will pay particular attention to the seven capitularies in which explicit reference is made to vassals or vassalage.[63] The broader question of the gradual introduction of new forms of government by the Carolingians and their grafting onto Lombard tradition – which, given the scope of the subject, we cannot deal with here – will provide the background to our investigation.[64]

---

[61] See Mordek, *Biblioteca capitularia regum Francorum manuscripta*; McKitterick, *Charlemagne*, pp. 233–45 and Patzold, 'Normen im Buch'; see also the site http:// capitularia.uni-koeln.de/; on Italy: Bougard, *La justice dans le Royaume d'Italie*, pp 17–54 and Azzara and Moro, eds., *I capitolari italici*.

[62] See Azzara, ed., *I capitolari dei Carolingi* and Mordek, 'Die Anfänge'.

[63] *MGH Capit.*, I: n. 20b, pp. 46–51; n. 90, pp. 190–1; n. 93, pp. 196–8; n. 94, pp. 198–200; n. 97, pp. 203–4; n. 99, pp. 206–7; n. 102, pp. 209–11.

[64] See Manacorda, *Ricerche*; Tabacco, 'L'avvento dei Carolingi in Italia'; Delogu, 'Lombard and Carolingian Italy'; Albertoni, *L'Italia*, pp. 15–32; Gasparri, *774*; Cammarosano, *Nobili e re*, pp. 97–138; Gasparri, 'Italien in der Karolingerzeit'; Gasparri, *Italia longobarda*, pp. 100–41.

Turning now to vassalage, we seem immediately to be faced with two different problems: on the one hand the rapid introduction of royal vassals intended to help the counts to control the territories of the kingdom – as happened, according to the Astronomer, in Aquitaine in 778[65] – and, on the other, the appeal of the *vassaticum* when compared to the existent forms of dependence in the kingdom. We will focus primarily on the first question.

The projection into Italy of what might be described as a system of government in which the royal vassals were an important instrument for 'overseeing royal rights across the kingdom',[66] can partly be glimpsed in the so-called *Karoli epistola in Italiam emissa*. This was dated to 790–800 and classified as one of the *Capitularia italica* in Alfred Boretius' *MGH* edition, but is today, largely thanks to the studies of Hubert Mordek, dated to the autumn of 780 and considered to be an *Epistula capitularis* that was generally valid, including in Italy.[67] The fact that Charlemagne came to Italy in late 780 in order to speed up the administrative reorganization of the kingdom before assigning responsibility for the administration to his son Carloman/Pippin lends considerable weight to this hypothesis.[68]

From our point of view, the particular interest of this capitulary lies in its *incipit*, in which the king, addressing his representatives in the area, lists them hierarchically, giving first place to the *comites seu iudices* and second to *vassi nostri*, followed by the *vicarii*, *centenarii* and all the *missi* and king's *agentes*.[69] This hierarchy notwithstanding, however, we must remember that these groups were all required to obey the bishops, particularly in regard to the appointment of clerics to the various churches and – of particular interest to us – in order to put a break on their *inproba cupiditas* when exacting the *nonae* and the *decimae*, or not renewing the *precariae*. This reference – specified by Charlemagne himself – is explained in the famous *Capitulare Haristallense* of 779 (in the so-called *forma langobardica*), which reminds all *homines seculares* who held ecclesiastical property in *beneficium per verbo domni regis* to always pay the *nonae*, the *decimae* and other *census* in cases where these had already been established.[70] Irrespective of when and where this *forma* of the Capitulary

---

[65] Astronomer, *Vita Hludowici imperatoris*, ed. Tremp, c. 3, p. 290.
[66] Innes, 'Charlemagne's government', p. 83.
[67] *MGH Capit.* I: n. 97, pp. 203–4. See Mordek, 'Die Anfänge', pp. 8–17 and Manacorda, *Ricerche*, pp. 43–50.
[68] See Mordek, 'Die Anfänge', p. 13, based on Hlawitschka, *Franken*, p. 13 and Manacorda, *Ricerche*, pp. 1–14. For an up-to-date summary, see Gasparri, *Italia longobarda*, pp. 130–9 and McKitterick, *Charlemagne*, pp. 245–50.
[69] *MGH Capit.* I: n. 97, p. 203.   [70] *MGH Capit.* I: n. 20b, p. 50, c. 14.

of Herstal was issued (in the early decades of the ninth century?),[71] the key point for us is the broad category – *homines seculares* – who were able to avail of a particular type of *beneficium*, the *precaria per verbo regis*, which was clearly not just attributed to the royal vassals.[72] The wide range of people who could obtain a *beneficium* is borne out by other – both contemporary and subsequent – capitularies, beginning with *Pippini capitulare italicum*, probably issued between 806 and 810,[73] in which the counts and all Charlemagne's *fideles* with *beneficia de rebus ecclesiae* were again called upon to pay the *nona* and the *decima*.[74]

Within this wide range of 'beneficiaries' and *fideles*, however, the royal vassals, since the first decades of the Carolingian government in Italy, seem to have had their own particular characteristics. Whether it actually existed, at least as far as Italy was concerned, the hierarchy of 'royal agents' invoked by the *Capitulare Haristallense* presupposed the existence of *vassi dominici*, whose *servitium* was specified in some dispositions which emphasized the close link between royal vassals and their sovereign: '*De vassis regalibus,* – declares Charlemagne's *Capitulare missorum italicum* of 806/10 – *ut honorem habeant et per se aut ad nos aut ad filium nostrum caput teneant*'.[75]

Within the densely interwoven network of relationships that connected the public and private spheres, the royal vassals scattered throughout the territory thus appeared to hold an *honor*, which meant that they were expected to answer – contemporaneously – to both Charlemagne and Pippin. It was intended to guarantee them full justice in the event of a dispute, and, at the same time, to permit them to judge those who required justice from them.[76] According to the *Pippini capitulare italicum* of 806/10, it had to apply both to the royal vassals present in the territory (almost always described as *vassi* in the Italic capitularies of Charlemagne's reign as well as in the charters, *placita* and other documents of the time[77]), and to those who had to 'serve' at the royal palace, who were sometimes described using the specific term *austaldi*.[78] This term appears in the *Pippini capitulare italicum*, and one other, later (825),

---

[71] I cannot go into the complex debate on the dating and validity of the *forma langobardica*. See Azzara, 'I capitolari', p. 37 and p. 44, n. 32 and Mordek, 'Die Anfänge', pp. 6–8.

[72] See Reynolds, *Fiefs and Vassals*, pp. 104–5.

[73] See Azzara and Moro, *I capitolari*, pp. 78–9.   [74] *MGH Capit.* I: n. 102, p. 210, c. 6.

[75] *MGH Capit.* I: n. 99, p. 207, c. 9.   [76] *MGH Capit.* I: n. 102, p. 210, c. 10.

[77] The expressions used are *vassi nostri, vassi regales* and *vassi dominici*. The expression *vassallus* is only used in one instance, which we will look at shortly. In the documents recorded by Budriesi Trombetti in *Prime ricerche*, pp. 6–13, throughout the Carolingian era the royal and imperial vassals operating in Italy were almost always described as *vassi*.

[78] A precise definition of *austaldi* is given in *MGH Capit.* I: n. 162, p. 325, c. 1: *Ut domnici vassalli qui austaldi sunt et in nostro palatio frequenter serviunt.*

capitulary, from Lothar I (but in no other extant documents from the
Carolingian era); it designated the royal vassals who worked at the court
(the 'house of the king', *Haus*, probably the origin of *austaldi*[79]) in close
contact with the king, confirming a bipartition among the Carolingian
royal vassals, depending on whether they worked in the *palatium* or
elsewhere in the realm.[80] This division did not, however, exclude numerous opportunities to meet, since the 'royal agents' – who operated
throughout the territory and, on their travels, were often able to engage
in corrupt behaviour – frequently visited the royal palace. The *Pippini
capitulare Papiense* of 787, for example, addresses a heartfelt plea to the
bishops, abbots, counts and '*vassis dominicis vel reliquis hominibus qui ad
palatium veniunt aut inde vadunt et ubicumque per regnum nostrum peragunt*'
that they not, on their journeys, appropriate to themselves the goods – or
fruits of the labour – of others.[81] The same capitulary, however, also
attempts to protect these *itinerantes* on their journeys, specifying that they
had a right to be given shelter in the winter and providing for a legal
safeguard if this hospitality were not forthcoming, namely the require-
ment that those who had refused it pay a *bannum regium*. This applied
tam seniores tam et vassalli.

It is difficult to know whether the term *vassallus*, which is used
nowhere else in the Italic capitularies of Charlemagne and Pippin and
is understood here in relation to a *senior*, refers to a type of vassalage
different – and of a lower social rank – to that of the royal or counts'
vassals, as documents from the period seem to suggest'.[82] What we do
know is that the first mention of the counts' vassals in the Italic capitularies dates to 813. We are given a grim picture of them: the *nonnulli
fortiores vassi comitum*, like the younger counts and other *ministri*, 'are
accustomed to expect, almost railing, compensation or harvests, some to
feed themselves, others even without the excuse [that they need] food',
and oppress the people.[83] They do not appear in other sources until the
following decade; we then find them referred to, particularly in the
placita, as 'squadrons' assisting the count in his judicial activities.[84]

Simultaneous with the evidence for the royal and counts' vassals, we
find in the earliest Italic capitularies a type of vassalage linked to private

---

[79] See Azzara and Moro, *I capitolari*, n. 21, p. 159.
[80] We will turn to this shortly. For an overview, see Gasparri, 'Strutture militari',
pp. 705–6, n. 116. The *austaldi* referred to here recall the *pueri vel vasalli* described in
Hincmar of Reims, *De ordine palatii*, ed. Gross and Schieffer, p. 82.
[81] *MGH Capit.* I: n. 94, pp. 198–9, c. 4, also on the following point.
[82] See Budriesi Trombetti, *Prime ricerche*, pp. 22–3 and p. 65.
[83] *MGH Capit.* I: n. 93, p. 197, c. 6.
[84] See Budriesi Trombetti, *Prime ricerche*, pp. 14 and 17.

clients, and with no connections to the control of the kingdom or the management of power, which, nevertheless, Charlemagne and Pippin made specific attempts to regulate. An early example of such regulation was that introduced by Charlemagne just after the conquest of the *regnum Langobardorum*, when the new Frankish *vassaticum* seemed both to offer many Lombards an unexpected opportunity for social mobility and to allow the aristocrats who had come to Italy with the Carolingians to strengthen their own client relationships.[85] Both these developments risked destabilizing the still fragile Carolingian political order, and so Charlemagne decided to intervene, stipulating that whoever wanted to take a *homo Langobardiscus* '*in vassatico vel in casa sua*' first had to check carefully '*unde sit vel quomodo natus est*'; if this was not done, a *bannum regium* would have to be paid.[86] This law was then followed through in the *Pippini Capitulare Papiense* of 787, where the question '*de illos homines qui hic intra Italia eorum seniores dimittunt*' in order to enter *in vassaticum* was again tackled.[87] In the capitulary, it was established that '*ille homo qui eum recipere voluerit*' had to present himself, and his aspiring vassal, to the king within forty days. It is here apparent that the king, in this period, wished to maintain control over the organization of *senior/vassus* relationships, even when these were in the private sphere: this law is unparalleled in the Carolingian legislation of the time, except, perhaps, for the prohibition on forming a *trustis* provided for in the *forma communis* of Herstal's Capitulary.[88]

Do these dispositions imply a public dimension to all forms of vassalage, as has sometimes been claimed in the past?[89] I do not believe so. Instead, I see them as signalling a desire to regulate a society undergoing rapid change, in which the Frankish occupation had fractured the established social and political framework. In this context, entry into vassalage or, on different levels, the commendation,[90] which both involved the acquisition of *beneficia* and *honores*, opened up previously unforeseen opportunities for many Lombards,[91] although we are dealing with a phenomenon that, unfortunately, is difficult to track consistently in the unforthcoming documentation of the period.[92] The fact, however, that it appeared urgent to regulate the entry of Lombard *homines* into the

---

[85] See the overview given in Gasparri, *Italia longobarda*, p. 140.
[86] *MGH Capit.* I: n. 90, p. 191, c. 11.   [87] *MGH Capit.* I: n. 94, p. 189, c. 5.
[88] *MGH Capit.* I: n. 20, c. 11, p. 191, c. 11.   [89] See, for example, Barbero, 'Liberti'.
[90] See *MGH Capit.* I: n. 94, p. 200, c. 13, where it is recorded that the free Lombards had the right to commend themselves freely, if they honoured their duties to their count.
[91] *MGH Capit.* I: n. 91, p. 192, c. 7, which talks about Frankish and Lombard counts, and of *Francus aut Langobardus habens beneficium*.
[92] See Budriesi Trombetti, *Prime ricerche*, p. 22.

vassaticum confirms that, in the time of Charlemagne and Pippin, there were also at least two forms of vassalage in Frankish Italy: one linked to the government of the realm, in particular the administration of justice, and represented by the royal/imperial vassals – throughout the territory or working in the *palatium* – and, at a lower social level, by the counts' vassals; the other linked to private, domestic senior/vassus relationships, which probably found fertile soil in the tradition of the Lombard *gasindiatus*.[93] Both forms of vassalage were further clarified in the capitularies issued by Charlemagne's successors.

Let us first consider the disposition on vassalage issued by Lothar I, in a political environment already very different from that of Charlemagne's reign, and characterized by violent, dramatic power struggles.[94] These are just a handful of laws, recorded in five capitularies, issued between 825 and 832.[95] Notwithstanding their small number, these laws are significant on account of their specification of the vassals' service, beginning with their role in the military structure, a role which, as we have seen, is not immediately obvious in the first three decades of Carolingian rule in Italy. We will focus on a famous capitulary, the *Capitulare de expeditione Corsicana*, issued by Lothar in 825, in which he called up the army for an expedition to Corsica, which had been for some time subject to Saracen attack.[96] In the capitulary, Lothar addressed himself directly to the counts, to whom the drafting of able men had been delegated, and explained when it was legitimate not to respond to the call to arms. His dispositions contained some original elements not found in the general capitularies previously issued by his father and grandfather.[97] Lothar clearly identified the three categories of men who were eligible to enlist: the *domnici vassalli* with their *commendati*; the bishops' and abbots' *homines*; all other free men. Each of these categories contained further internal divisions.

Let us first turn to the *domnici vassalli*, who were divided into three categories: the *austaldi*, whom we have already met; *qui in nostro palatio frequenter serviunt*, those who lived on their own lands; and those who had

---

[93] On the question of the relationship between *gasindiatus* and vassalage, see, for an overview, Sergi, 'Vassalli a Milano', pp. 272–84 and Gasparri, *Italia longobarda*, pp. 139–42.

[94] See Costambeys, Innes and MacLean, *The Carolingian World*, pp. 213–22; Ubl, *Die Karolinger*, pp. 63–86; on Italy, see Cammarosano, *Nobili e re*, pp. 139–49.

[95] *MGH Capit.* I: n. 162, pp. 324–5; n. 163, pp. 326–7; n. 168, pp. 335–7; *MGH Capit.* II: n. 201, pp. 59–63 and n. 202, pp. 63–5.

[96] *MGH Capit.* I: n. 162, pp. 324–5. See Gasparri, 'Strutture militari', pp. 705–7 and pp. 711–2.

[97] See Gasparri, 'Strutture militari', p. 705; on the general rules of mobilization, a reference to the main capitulary is found in Ganshof, 'L'armée sous les Carolingiens'.

a royal *beneficium* and *foris manent*, an expression which seems to refer to vassals who had a military *beneficium*.[98] Only the last had to respond to a call to arms without exception, confirming their specialized military role, which clearly distinguished them from the *austaldi*, who were exempt from military service. Nor did the *homines* who had previously 'commended' themselves to the *austaldi* – here defined, significantly, as *seniores* – have to serve. Different again was the situation of the vassals who lived on their own *allodium*, and whose obligation to enlist was considered on a case-by-case basis. The reasons for the exemption of the royal *austaldi* (usually of high rank) are easily hypothesized: they were close to the king and their absence could have imperilled him. Their particular status, attested by their classification as *seniores*, meant that the men (not necessarily vassals) who had been 'commended' to them were also entitled to avoid enlistment. The discourse around *qui beneficia nostra habent et foris manent* was different, however; as noted above, they seem to correspond – in military terms – to the vassals documented in Aquitaine and therefore had to give precedence to their military duties.[99]

The complex grouping of royal vassals, as we have said, was distinguished from that of the abbots' and bishops' *homines*, who were probably also linked to the category of vassal, although this was not explicitly stated. These *homines* were, indeed, also subdivided: between those who *foris manent* and the *austaldi*.[100] This distinction did not, in this case, mean exemption from enlistment for those who served in the *domus*, however: all, in fact, had to go to war, with the exception of two men from the first category and four *austaldi*, who – it was specified – had to be *liberi*, thereby implying the existence of servile *austaldi* who, as such, were not even taken into consideration.

Those who were neither *vassi dominici* nor *homines episcoporum seu abbatum* were members of the broad category of *ceteri liberi homines*, which was, in turn, divided into *bharigildi* and the free *secundi ordinis*.[101] The *bharigildi*, if they were strong and healthy, had to enlist; if they were not, they had to provide aid to a fellow free man, who was able, but poor. Among free men of the second rank, the system of the *adiutorium* was adopted in Italy too, controlled and arbitrated by the counts.[102] Like the bishops' and abbots' *homines qui foris manent*, those in the *secundi ordinis* – with the exception of four *austaldi* each, and of all the other free men (the

---

[98] *MGH Capit.* I: n. 162, p. 325, c. 1. On the meaning of *foris* in this context, see Gasparri, 'Strutture militari', n. 116, pp. 705–6.

[99] On this particular type of vassal, see Bachrach, *Early Carolingian Warfare*, pp. 75–80.

[100] *MGH Capit.* I: n. 162, p. 325, c. 2.   [101] *MGH Capit.* I: n. 162, p. 325, c. 3.

[102] On the introduction of the *adiutorium*, see Gasparri, 'Strutture militari'.

bharigildi) – could, in accordance with their wealth, organize themselves on the basis of the *adiutorium* and prevent the poorest among them from having to go to war.

The dispositions of the *Capitula de expeditione Corsicana* have been much studied; Stefano Gasparri's important analysis in the 1980s, in particular, clearly demonstrated the many elements of continuity with the laws of the Lombard period.[103] From our point of view, it is important to emphasize, however, how this document makes explicit that which had already emerged indirectly in the capitularies of Charlemagne's reign: a clear distinction between *domnici vassalli* and all the other categories of free men and, at the same time, further distinctions within the former group – between those who worked in the palace, those who operated outside it (but had no *beneficia*) and, lastly, the vassals with a *beneficium*, who were the only ones to have a specific military function in an army which was structured around the service of free men. Among the latter were certainly the vassals of the *seniores* and counts, although this group was rendered 'invisible' by laws that favoured the legal status of the free man over any other social or political status.

Characterized by their duty to respond to the call to arms, the *vassalli domnici* with *beneficium* seemed to escape from direct royal control in the years after the gathering of the army for the 825 Corsican expedition – of which we know nothing. It is in this light that we should interpret an article from a capitulary dated 832, in which Lothar told his *missi* to get information in the respective cities about the *beneficia* of the vassals (and clerics) who had been appointed by his predecessors, and about those in possession of the said *beneficia*.[104] At a time of great political uncertainty following the murder of Bernard and growing tensions between Louis the Pious and Lothar, the latter, in his disposition, indirectly admits what must have been a very distressing fact: the existence of imperial *vassi casati* who had taken *beneficia* from other sovereigns and escaped his direct control, with all that meant in terms of the military service he could no longer assume would be provided in times of necessity.

Other laws related to vassals in Lothar's capitulary reveal a contradictory situation. The first, recorded in the ecclesiastical capitulary of Olona from May 825, deals with the question of people who have shown themselves not to be particularly worried about episcopal excommunication.[105] This question from the religious sphere gives us an important clue to the hierarchical relationship between counts and royal vassals. If a royal vassal was excommunicated, he had to re-establish a relationship

[103] Gasparri, 'Strutture militari', pp. 706–7.   [104] *MGH Capit.* II: n. 202, p. 64, c. 8.
[105] *MGH Capit.* I: n. 163, p. 326, c. 1.

with the bishop through the mediation of a count. In the event of no reconciliation, the king had to be informed before the vassal was imprisoned. This disposition – which indicates the hierarchical subordination of the royal vassal to the count, but also the continued existence of a direct bond between the former and the king – again takes us into a situation very far from that outlined by Ganshof's legal–historical tradition. The same is true of another (contemporary) disposition by Lothar, which shows us that the imperial vassals could act against the bishops in order to secure the ecclesiastic *decimae*, as did the counts and other *fideles* of the sovereign.[106] Moreover, like the counts, or the churches, the royal vassals could also have servants who, if they refused to take a 'pure coin of the correct weight', were subject to sixty blows.[107]

The last of Lothar I's capitularies referring to vassals is dated 832, and we have to wait almost a decade before we find any further *capitula* on the subject in the Italic capitularies: they reappear in an episcopal capitulary from Pavia, dated to between 845 and 850, by which time Louis II had assumed power in the Italic kingdom. In this disposition, the bishops, who had assembled in Pavia, accused the counts and the *vassi dominici* of the illegal practice of not only gathering priests and other *clerici* around them – something which even bishops were not permitted to do – but also of making people celebrate mass 'all over the place', without episcopal permission; what was worse, there was sometimes even doubt as to whether these celebrants were baptized.[108]

But if the relationships between counts, royal vassals and bishops were not always easy, one of Louis II's capitularies, dated to the end of 850, reveals the role of the bishops' vassals in helping the counts to maintain the public order, in particular in connection with the protection of pilgrims travelling to Rome, who were often attacked by bandits (*latrones*).[109] Noting that many marauders attacked, wounded and even killed pilgrims, Louis II decreed that the bishops' vassals, when necessary, could unite with the counts and their *sculdasci* in order to investigate *studiosissime* and capture and punish the wrongdoers, thus guaranteeing the safety of those who – whether praying or doing business – placed themselves under the royal *fiducia*.

With regard to the question of the vassals' military service in the king's army, we again have an important capitulary, this time connected to an expedition that Louis II had wanted to embark upon in 866, officially in response to requests for help against the Saracens, which he had received from princes in southern Italy, but actually in order to increase his

---

[106] *MGH Capit.* I: n. 168, p. 336, c. 8.   [107] *MGH Capit.* II: n. 201, p. 64, c. 9.

[108] *MGH Capit.* II: n. 210, p. 81, c. 3.   [109] *MGH Capit.* II: n. 213, p. 86, c. 1.

control over the Duchy of Benevento.[110] This expedition was not successful, and, despite some significant victories over the Emir of Bari, ended with the temporary 'arrest' of Louis II by Adelchis, duke of Benevento. Notwithstanding its outcome, a great deal of effort had gone into the preparation of the expedition of 866, as we can see in the *Constitutio de expeditione beneventana*, a capitulary which refers explicitly to that of Lothar I (825), while further specifying who was obliged to go to war and who could claim exemption.[111] The text seems to suggest that the protected position of the royal vassals, in particular those who worked in the palace, had, in general, weakened: unlike Lothar, who had opened his capitulary with the exemptions for royal and ecclesiastical vassals, Louis II structured his whole capitulary around the duty of free men who were able to raise their own *guidrigildus* from their property (*quicumque de mobilibus widrigild suum habere potest*);[112] these men, in general, corresponded to the *bharigildi* of Lothar's capitulary.[113] It was decreed that free men who did not meet the requirements (to enlist) would participate in a complex system of *adiutorium*, in accordance with their economic condition. The king's and counts' vassals only appear in this system, which provided for the confiscation of property (by the royal *missi*) from those who failed to enlist; as free men they were required to follow the general disposition, with an increased sanction if they did not enlist. Like the counts who stayed at home, the royal vassals (*bassi nostri*) also lost their positions, with consequences for their vassals (*bassalli*), who then, in turn, lost their goods and benefits.[114] In fact, the only justifiable reason not to answer a call to arms, whether for counts, royal vassals or bishops, was illness, which, if it was 'uncertain', had to be attested to on oath.[115]

Conclusions

And now we reach our conclusion. Apart from two brief references in the *Capitulare papiense* of Charles the Bald to the fact that bishops had to love –'like a father' – the counts and royal *vassalli* of their dioceses, and that bishops and counts should stay in their own cities, with their vassals, without living in the house of a person poorer than themselves,[116] we have no extant dispositions on vassals for the last twenty years of Carolingian government in Italy. From other documents we know that

---

[110] See Gasparri, 'Strutture militari', pp. 716–18.
[111] See *MGH Capit.* I: n. 162, pp. 324–25 and *MGH Capit.* II: n. 218, pp. 94–6.
[112] *MGH Capit.* II: n. 218, p. 94, c. 1.   [113] *MGH Capit.* I: n. 162, p. 325, c. 3.
[114] *MGH Capit.* II: n. 218, p. 95, c. 3 and c. 4.   [115] *MGH Capit.* II: n. 218, p. 96, c. 5.
[116] *MGH Capit.* II: n. 221, p. 103, c. 12 and c. 13.

the royal vassals, and those of counts and bishops, continued to be active within the kingdom, particularly in the exercise of justice, but their activity does not at this point seem to have been linked with the kind of emergencies that are regulated through legal dispositions.[117] The royal vassals, and those of the counts, bishops, abbots and abbesses, thus now appear to be established figures within the Carolingian government of Italy, as other contemporary sources confirm, often attesting to them holding *beneficia*, a possession which, however, is never exclusively theirs.

Nor is service in the king's army ever exclusive to them; they are required to give it, first, as free men within the category of *bharigildi* and, second, if they have been conceded a *beneficium*.[118] This applied for at least as long as the royal vassals – the *austaldi* – were working in the *palatium*; their numbers, however, seem to have gradually decreased during the reigns of Louis II and his successors. The involvement of the highest social ranks in the royal vassalage also appears to have waned over this period, according to other contemporary sources. The 'common' vassals, however, are almost entirely ignored by these sources: once their entry into vassalage had been regulated in the dramatic years after the conquest of the *regnum Langobardorum*, it seems that they ceased to pose the sort of problems that required specific legislation.

The case of Italy revealed by the capitularies thus confirms a more general evolution, already clearly identified by Odegaard, and shows the Carolingian ability to transform a domestic service based on a particular loyalty into an instrument of government and territorial control. In fact, two forms of vassalage were thereby created, with a common vocabulary, concept of loyalty and – probably – ritual system, but very different functions. Carolingian vassalage – whether Italian or not – is thus clearly far from being a 'conceptual black hole', but nor was it merely a bulwark against the disintegration of the state, as hypothesized by Ganshof for the last decades of the Carolingian empire. This idea of a dissolution is quite rightly being re-examined today in the light of more careful analyses of the dynamics of Carolingian politics over the long term.[119] Vassalage was, in fact, a very flexible instrument, which could be adopted by the government in relation to 'agents' who supported the king/emperor, the counts and the bishops in their functions both in the various *palatia* and in the realm generally, where they could be, but were not necessarily,

---

[117] See Budriesi Trombetti, *Prime ricerche*, pp. 6–23.

[118] See, for example, *Hlotharii capitulare de expeditione contra Sarracenos facienda*, dated 847 (*MGH Capit.* II: n. 203, pp. 67–8, c. 13), in which groups of eminent persons, mentioned by name, were made up both of *qui in Italia beneficia habent*, and those who *nihil habent in Italia*.

[119] See Costambeys, Innes and MacLean, *The Carolingian World*, pp. 383–4.

provided with a *beneficium*. It could also be adopted by individual *seniores* for services related to their own *domus*. It was this double nature of vassalage, and its involvement of people of very varied social rank and type, that generated the ambiguities the attempted – not always coherent – overcoming of which the capitularies and other documents bear witness to, through their use of the term *vassus* principally for the vassals who were royal, episcopal or counts' 'agents', and the term *vassallus* for the others. And so there were two 'vassalages' in the Carolingian era: an awareness of this double nature should guide us in a new, much needed analysis of the political and social roles of the vassals of Carolingian Italy, based on sources that I have not been able to include in this chapter.

8   Shaping a Kingdom
The Sees of Parma and Arezzo between the Reigns of Louis II and Berengar

Igor Santos Salazar

> Old men forget; yet all shall be forgot,
>   but he'll remember, with advantages,
>   what feats he did that day...

W. Shakespeare, *Henry V*
Act IV, Scene III

Introduction

At the end of February 901, in the great lodge (*laubia magiore*) of the papal palace beside St Peter's basilica, Pope Benedict IV and Emperor Louis III, together with a large group of bishops, counts and *iudices*, were judging a case that involved some episcopal property in Lucca. According to the *placitum* recording the occasion, twelve bishops took part in the tribunal on that winter's day in Rome, including the bishops of Arezzo and Parma, Peter III and Elbuncus, respectively.[1] Like the other prelates present in the Eternal City at the time for the imperial coronation of Louis III – an event which had taken place on February 22, just a few days before the court hearing[2] – Peter III and Elbuncus were Italian *fideles* of the Provençal emperor.

Louis III had been called to Italy by a faction of the aristocracy hostile to Berengar, the marquis of Friuli, who, since the death of Charles the Fat (888) – the last of Charlemagne's direct male descendants – had been involved in a struggle for possession of the Italian crown.[3] This war had led to a rapid turnover of kings on the throne in Pavia: Berengar himself,

This chapter is a version of a paper I gave at the International Medieval Congress in Leeds in 2016. I would like to thank Clemens Gantner and Roberta Cimino for their kind invitation. I am indebted with Giuseppe Albertoni and Giacomo Vignodelli for their comments on earlier written drafts.

[1] Placiti, n. 111 (February 901).
[2] For the date of the imperial coronation, see Bertolini, 'Benedetto IV', pp. 347–52.
[3] Louis III was the son of Boso of Provence and Ermengard, the daughter of the Emperor Louis II (r. 844–875).

Arnulf of Carinthia and the marquises of Spoleto, Guy and his son Lambert.[4]

The coronation in Rome in 901 thus also served as a snapshot of the supporters in Italy upon whom Louis III could count: a *mise en scène* of the social networks upon which the power of the emperor was based.[5] The presence of six Tuscan bishops was no coincidence, since the tribunal was deciding a case related to the property of the bishop of the capital of the march of Tuscany.[6] Moreover, the Roman *placitum* is useful because it casts the spotlight on the political discourse of the marquis of Tuscany, Adalbert II, the new emperor's real strong man.[7] Lastly, like the diplomas granted by Louis III himself before and after his coronation, it served to identify those who – from Novara to Arezzo and from Parma to Brescia – had decided to turn their back on Berengar.[8] The memory of this day is thus a good place to begin our examination of the political behaviour of the Italian bishops in the period between the end of Louis II's reign and the imperial coronation of Berengar of Friuli (915).

Much has been written in the field of European historiography on the political, social and cultural roles of bishops during this period,[9] just as a great deal of attention has been paid in recent years to political communication – both symbolic and ritual – and its dangers throughout the Early Middle Ages.[10] New debates have arisen from this fresh appraisal of the documentary evidence: while scholars have always tended to spend considerable time and energy on the royal and imperial *placita* and

---

[4] On the political situation in the *regnum Italiae* before and after 888, Delogu, 'Vescovi', is still a key text. See also, MacLean, '*After His death*'.

[5] The reference is to the work of Althoff, *Inszenierte Herrschaft*.

[6] Schwarzmeier, *Lucca und das Reich*.   [7] Liutprand, *Antapodosis*, II, 36–37.

[8] The episcopal church of Arezzo and its bishop, Peter III, had already had the privilege of a diploma granted by Louis III, while he was still, in the autumn of 900, only a king. It is particularly noteworthy that the diploma was the second delivered by Louis after his coronation at Pavia, D L III, n. 2 (October 12 900). Adalbert of Tuscany appears as the mediator in three of the diplomas issued by Louis in 900 and 901 (D L III, nn. 2, 9, 12); the names of some of the bishops and counts present in Rome as intercessors and/or recipients of his diplomas are also contained in this edition (D L III, nn. 3, 7, 8, 10, 11). These account for eight of the fourteen still extant diplomas issued in that brief period.

[9] For an overview of the Carolingian *ordo episcopalis*, see Patzold, *Episcopus*. See also, among others, Bührer-Thierry, *Évêques*; Eldevik, 'Bishops', pp. 776–90 and Patzold, 'L'épiscopat'. On Italy, more specifically, see Tabacco, *Struggle* and Sergi, 'Poteri temporali', pp. 1–16. For a pan-European conception of the form and function of the bishop in the Early Middle Ages, see also Reuter, 'A Europe of bishops', pp. 17–38, with references.

[10] See, among others, Althoff, *Spielregeln der Politik*; Mostert (ed.), *New Approaches*; Garipzanov, *The Symbolic*; Jezierski, Hermanson, Oming and Småberg (eds.), *Rituals, Performatives and Political*. See also Buc, *Dangers of Ritual* and Koziol, 'The dangers of polemic'.

diplomas, the application of new methodologies has seen considerable advances in the field in recent years. Although diplomas have since the 1960s been studied in an attempt to understand royal political agency in the late ninth and tenth centuries,[11] in recent decades scholars have revisited these texts with the aim of sharpening their analysis of the socio-political relationships among the aristocracies (both lay and ecclesiastic) in the former Carolingian empire. Indeed, royal and imperial diplomas provide an angle from which to examine the governance of the territory, mapping the ability to create (or to prevent) patronage networks between kings, queens, royal widows, abbots, bishops, canons, counts and their *fideles*.[12] As Geoffrey Koziol has recently argued, diplomas were performative, so they must be studied *not only* in their administrative and legal meanings but also as instruments of political communication used to establish new relationships.[13]

This chapter focusses particularly on the point of view of the recipients – the sees of Arezzo and Parma – in order to observe, at a local level, the political activities of some leading figures in Italy at the turn of the tenth century.[14] We will also be examining the judicial proceedings (*placita*) in which the bishops of Arezzo and Parma would have participated as members of the panel of judges, or, indeed, on occasion, as parties to a case. The reading of these legal documents, when conducted in conjunction with a survey of the data found through a chronological study of the entire body of diplomas, does indeed give us greater insight into the situations in which political alliances progressively came to be formed in a general context of shifting loyalties.[15] In other words, this chapter sets out to analyse, using the diplomas as evidence, the constant tension and continuous search for balance between different political forces within the Italian kingdom of the period.

---

[11] Fichtenau, *Das Urkundenwesen* and Bautier, 'Le règne d'Eudes (888–898)'; Keller, 'Zur Struktur'.

[12] Wolfram, 'Political theory', with references to his previous works; Koziol, *Begging Pardon and Favor*; Rosenwein, 'Family politics' and Rosenwein, 'Friends and family'; Mersiowsky, 'Towards a reappraisal'; Huschner, *Transalpine Kommunikation im Mittelalter*; Bougard, 'Du centre à la périphérie'.

[13] Koziol, *The Politics*, ch. 1 and Koziol, 'Is Robert I in Hell?'. On the theoretical implications of performativity, see the critical note in Moeglin, '"Performative turn"'. Royal/imperial diplomas must therefore be read, above all, as political narratives, both written and oral. See also Balzaretti, 'Narratives of success', p. 189.

[14] See also, Huschner, 'L'idea della cancelleria imperiale'; Vignodelli, *The King and the Cathedral Canons*. I am grateful to the author for letting me use his unpublished studies.

[15] The importance of legal documents in the analysis of early medieval society, particularly in Italy, has often been pointed out. See, for example, Keller, 'I Placiti'; Bougard, *La justice*; Wickham, 'Land disputes'; Bougard, 'Diplômes et notices de plaid'.

The chapter's particular focus on these bishops reflects the centrality of their political role. Unlike the lineages of counts and marquises, the greatest wealth of written sources documenting the political and economic action of bishops justifies this choice. But why Parma and Arezzo? First of all, because this period is relatively well-documented for both cities, in comparison with most of the contemporary Italian *civitates*. The Diocesan Archive of Arezzo[16] and various archives in Parma (the State Archive, the *Archivio Vescovile* and, above all, the *Archivio del Capitolo* of the cathedral)[17] preserve single-sheet parchments dating to between the middle of the ninth and the first decades of the tenth centuries, which contain numerous 'private' and 'public'[18] charters produced by, or directed to, laymen and laywomen, *presbiteri*, canons or bishops, all of them active in both *territoria civitatis*. Second, the bishops of Arezzo and Parma were leading figures who were deeply involved in Carolingian politics well before, and after, the year 888. Last, the two cities represent different types of *arena* within the kingdom: Parma, located in a strategic position in the Po Valley, along the Via Emilia, was a centre of strong lay power – that of the Supponid family;[19] Arezzo, located in a peripheral zone (relatively close to Rome, but rather far from Pavia), was governed by weak comital power and forced into complex dialogue with the marquis of Tuscany, thus offering a very interesting counterpoint to Parma in an analysis of early medieval Italian forms of political communication.[20]

---

[16] The charters held in Arezzo were recently published in *CDA*. Only those ninth-century charters conserved on their original parchments had been included in *ChLA²*, XC. Royal diplomas and judicial proceedings were published earlier in separate collections, such as the *Placiti*, as well as in the series of royal diplomas delivered by 'Italian' kings, edited in the first half of the last century by Schiaparelli, in D G – L; D B I and D L III – D R II.

[17] As in the case of Arezzo, those ninth-century charters from Parma preserved on their original parchments were published in *ChLA²*, XCII. For ninth-century charters preserved as copies, see Bernassi (ed.), *Codice diplomatico parmense*; the latter include documents from the monastery of St Alexander (Parma) and from St Antoninus in Piacenza, both of which collections are held in the State Archive of Parma (now available in a new edition, *ChLA²*, XCIII). For the tenth-century written records preserved in the various archives in Parma (both originals and copies), see Drei (ed.), *Le carte*. As in the case of Arezzo, royal diplomas and judicial proceedings were published earlier in separate collections already mentioned.

[18] On the dangers of a rigid public–private distinction between charters, see Costambeys, 'Disputes and documents'.

[19] For a study of Parma in the ninth and tenth centuries, see Schumann, *Authority*; Provero, 'Chiese e Dinastie' and Albertoni, 'Il potere del vescovo'. For the Supponids, see Hlawitschka, *Franken*; Bougard, 'Les Supponides', pp. 381–400; Lazzari, 'Una mamma carolingia'

[20] A general picture of Arezzo's history between the ninth and tenth centuries is provided by Delumeau, *Arezzo, espace et societés* and Cherubini, Franceschi, Barlucchi and Firpo (eds.), *Arezzo nel Medioevo*.

Italian Politics before and after the Year 888: Bishops Wibod of Parma and John of Arezzo

During the last years of Emperor Louis II's government, two bishops stand out in the kingdom of Italy: Wibod of Parma (860–895/6) and John of Arezzo (c. 867–900). Both can be studied by tracing references to them in diplomas, judicial proceedings and papal letters preserved in different archives from Piacenza to Rome and Naples. Records of synods and narrative sources, both Italian and foreign, help us to build up a picture of the two men.

Wibod of Parma, whose origins are unknown,[21] is first documented in 860 as a judge working in the imperial courts.[22] He then appears in 870 and 872 as the imperial ambassador in the delicate affair of Lotharingia, in which Louis II recognized Karlmann as his successor in exchange for the latter's acceptance of Louis' rights over Lorraine.[23] Papal letters also mention Wibod's role as Adrianus II's legate at the courts of Charles the Bald and Louis the German, again negotiating on behalf of Emperor Louis II.[24] The first mentions of John of Arezzo, on the other hand, are less prominent, and more complicated.[25] We learn from a document preserved in the *Registrum Farfense* that he probably came from Rieti in what is today the region of Lazio.[26] Moreover, although John also appears to have belonged to the entourage of Louis II, the source – the *Libellus de imperatoria potestate in urbe Roma* – that suggests this proximity to the emperor is not straightforward. According to the *Libellus*, John of Arezzo was *archicancellarius et secretarius* to the emperor.[27] Both prelates, however, really only came to prominence

---

[21] There are no detailed studies of the bishop of Parma. See Hlawitschka, *Franken*; Keller, 'Zur Struktur', pp. 221 and ff.; MacLean, *Kingship and Politics*, pp. 92–5 and 183–5 and Provero, 'Chiese e Dinastie', pp. 52–6.

[22] In Placiti, n. 65 (860), Wibod appears as the head of a tribunal called to resolve a dispute between Ucpold, count of the sacred palace, and Count Ildebert, for control of fiscal goods. He also appears in the college of *iudices* convened to settle a dispute in the area of Piacenza in July 874, Manaresi n. 77 = *ChLA*², LXV, n. 18.

[23] *Annales Bertiniani* s.a., 870, p. 113; s.a. 872, ed. Waitz, p. 120. The summits were held at Aachen (with Louis the German) and Pontailler (with Charles the Bald). See also Goldberg, *Struggle for Empire*, 299.

[24] Hadrian II, *Epistolae*, 21–26, ed. Perels, pp. 724–32 (27 June 870).

[25] On Bishop John of Arezzo, see Licciardello, *Agiografia*, pp. 148–55 and Heil, 'Clerics', pp. 216 and ff. I am grateful to the author for letting me consult his unpublished studies.

[26] *Regesto di Farfa*, III, doc. n. 322.

[27] Zucchetti (ed.), *Libellus*, 203. The fact that the reference is to an *Iohannes diaconus*, however, would seem to contradict an identification of this person with the imperial *archicancellarius*. The *Libellus* was also written almost a generation after the events it recounts, Costambeys, *Power and Patronage*, p. 342.

during the struggle for the crown of Italy, which started after the death of Louis II (875).

John of Arezzo supported Charles II's candidacy for the royal succession;[28] this was the function he performed while acting as papal legate, as the *Registrum* of Pope John VIII and the *Annals of St Bertin* record.[29] His presence at a synod held in Pavia in 876, where a part of Italian aristocracy swore fidelity to the new king, is unlikely to have been coincidental.[30] An archive in Arezzo contains a number of documents that testify to the closeness between Bishop John and Charles II, just a few weeks after the death of Louis II. Between September 875 and September 876, three royal diplomas were granted – in Pavia, Vercelli and Cologne – in favour of John's church, all of them still preserved on their original parchment.[31] The royal diploma granted in September 876 is of particular significance: it bears the imperial *legimus* at the foot of the parchment (written in a reddish-purple ink, following the uses of the Byzantine imperial chancellery), thereby underlining the high political position of John at the emperor's court as Charles' proxy in Italy.[32] Moreover, the diploma, which concerned the donation to Arezzo of the imperial monastery of Sant'Antimo, which was already held as a *beneficium* by the see, allowed the new emperor to create an ideal dialogue with the past through the evocation of the figure of Charlemagne, his grandfather, founder of the empire, and of the Tuscan abbey.[33]

---

[28] Charles was crowned emperor on Christmas Day 875, Nelson, *Charles the Bald*, p. 19 and Arnaldi, *Natale 875*.

[29] John VIII, *Registrum*, 5–8, ed. Caspar, pp. 4–8 and *Annales Bertiniani*, s.a. 876, ed. Waitz, pp. 128–32.

[30] The Bishop of Arezzo appears high on the list of the signatories to the document, preceded only by Ansbert, archbishop of Milan, *MGH Capit. II*, no. 221, pp. 100–4. A textual critique of this synod can be found in Delogu, 'Vescovi', p. 22 and Hartmann, *Die Synoden*, pp. 346–7.

[31] *ChLA²*, XC, n. 13 = *CDA*, n. 24 (29 September 875); *ChLA²*, XC, n. 14 = *CDA*, n. 25 (1 March 876) and *ChLA²*, XC, n. 15 = *CDA*, n. 26 (September 876). Most of the diplomas were probably prepared in Arezzo by writers connected to the episcopal circle, however, and subsequently validated by Charles' imperial chancellery. On this question, see the presentation of each diploma accompanying the transcriptions in the *ChLA²* and the relevant bibliography.

[32] In fact, only seven diplomas issued by Charles II included this special clause, see Bougard, 'I vescovi di Arezzo', p. 65. As pointed out by Koziol, 'the *legimus* for Bishop John of Arezzo reveals Charles's distinctive attitude towards imperial display', *The Politics*, p. 201. See also Metzger, 'The *legimus* subscription', pp. 52–8, with further bibliography.

[33] On the ideal dialogue established between past and present through the diplomas of the Carolingian era, see Zimmermann, '*Sicut antiquus sanctium est*', pp. 27–56.

Wibod's loyalties, however, were different. Close to Emperor Louis II and his wife Engilberga,[34] the bishop was, in accordance with Louis' will, a supporter of Karlmann. Indeed, Charles II granted no diplomas to Wibod, whom he knew to support Karlmann in the struggle for the empire.[35] After the emperor's death (in October 877), however, the series of diplomas delivered by East Frankish rulers in favour of recipients in Parma began, with Wibod and his followers being the main beneficiaries.[36] I prefer not to go into detail here about the problems relating to the diploma issued by Karlmann in favour of the church of Parma – in which the king granted Wibod the *districtus* of the city – and its subsequent confirmations, all preserved in later copies and probably heavily amended, if not falsified.[37] Here I am more concerned with the role of Wibod as 'der einflussreichste Politiker' among the East Frankish sovereigns in Italy[38] and the simultaneous political exclusion of John of Arezzo, as the royal diplomas from the reign of Karlmann unambiguously show.

With the end of Karlmann's rule over Italy and the succession of his brother Charles the Fat (879) came what has been seen as the beginning of the latter's policy of conciliation after a period of tension between pope, archbishop of Milan and followers, such as John, of West Frankish rulers. This strategy aimed at establishing a consensus that would pave the way for his imperial coronation. By comparing the number and contents of the diplomas delivered in favour of recipients from Arezzo and Parma, we may be able to decode Charles the Fat's politics in action.

---

[34] Engilberga was a member of the Supponid family as daughter of Adelgis (d. 853). She was the sister of Suppo II (d. 882), count of Parma: Bougard, 'Engelberga'.

[35] An important letter records the attempts of Pope John VIII to persuade Charles the Bald to take Bishop Wibod back into his good graces, John VIII, *Registrum*, 28, ed. Caspar, pp. 26–7 (November 876).

[36] *ChLA*[2], XCII, n. 13 = D Kn n. 23 (11 May 878/9?) delivered in favour of Wibod's chaplain, Adalbert. The only evidence we have of donations from Karlmann to Wibod is found in some later diplomas, see D K III, n. 15 (8 January 880), an original parchment preserved in the State Archives in Naples and D Arn, 125 (17 April 894).

[37] D Kn, n. 24 (11 May 879?). The problems relating to this diploma deserve a monograph of their own. Suffice it to say here that any examination of the critical and interpretative problems posed by a whole series of diplomas in which public rights are conceded to the see of Parma must begin with the study of a diploma issued by Otto I (D O, n. 239). In the latter, the *districtus* and some important tax revenues are granted to the church of Parma. It is possible that Ubert, bishop of Parma and Otto's *archicancellarius*, presented the new emperor with a *dossier* of forged diplomas (from Karlmann to Hugh of Provence), 'created' in order to strengthen the case of the see of Parma, see Manaresi, 'Alle origini' and Guyotjeannin, 'Les pouvoirs publics'. Delogu, however, considered the contents of the diploma from Karlmann to be genuine, Delogu, 'Vescovi', pp. 13–14. On immunity in the late ninth and early tenth centuries, see Bougard, *La justice*, pp. 259–64.

[38] D K III, p. 22.

At least seven diplomas (excluding the suspected forgeries)[39] were delivered between 880 and 887, two in favour of the church of Parma[40] and four to the benefit of Wibod, either alone or with Vulgunda, his *consanguinea*.[41] The political centrality of Wibod can also be deduced from the fact that the political networks developed by him allowed certain laypeople from Parma to gain access to the emperor's court. This may be true of a man called Christophorus, who received a royal diploma. The presence of laypeople is interesting, since it is revealed in documents devoted almost entirely to the administrative and commemorative tasks of ecclesiastical institutions and conserved exclusively in ecclesiastical archives.[42]

Meanwhile, Arezzo was by no means neglected by Charles III. On 15 November 879 the king confirmed the privileges of the Tuscan see, with Bishop John acting as a petitioner on his church's behalf. Reading between the lines of the diploma, a certain discontinuity is nonetheless perceptible, if we compare its language to that of the diplomas delivered to Arezzo by Charles the Bald. The text of the 879 document records very precisely the ancient privileges of the Arezzo church presented by John to the king (*ostendens nobis immunitatum praecepta*): diplomas issued by Charlemagne, Louis the Pious and Lothar, all of which are still preserved in the Diocesan Archive in Arezzo.[43] Significantly, the only sovereign whose name is not mentioned in the diploma is Charles the Bald, despite the document referring to fiscal goods that had been conceded by him to the see of Arezzo.[44] The dictates of 'political

---

[39] D K III, n. 175 (8 January 880) and D K III, n. 115 (16 April 885).

[40] D K III, n. 32 (13 March 881), in which Charles granted Lugolo to the church through the intercession of the Supponids, and D K III, n. 33 (13 March 881), which gives the church of Mezzano Scotti to Parma and is preserved in its original parchment. The first diploma, copied in a *placitum* dated 906 and conserved in an eleventh-century copy, was considered by Manaresi to be a forgery created by Parma to strengthen the patrimonial rights of the church, *Placiti*, p. 437 (he argued that Lugolo was not granted to Parma until 935, during the reign of Hugh of Provence). Recently, Lazzari has supported Manaresi's point of view, 'Tra Ravenna e Regno'. I wish to thank Prof. Lazzari for letting me read her unpublished research.

[41] D K III, n. 15 (8 January 880); *ChLA²*, LXX, n. 7 (14 April 881) = D K III, n. 36; *ChLA²*, XCII, n. 16 (22 June 885) = D K III, n. 126; *ChLA²*, XCII, n. 17 (a. 887) = D K III, n. 171. On the centrality of the royal fisc to these donations, see MacLean, *Kingship and Politics*, pp. 94–5. On Vulgunda, see Rinaldi, 'A ovest di Ravenna' and Lazzari, 'Tra Ravenna e Regno'.

[42] *ChLA²*, XCII, n. 35 (23 October 880) = D K III, n. 95. See also Provero, 'Chiese e Dinastie', p. 55.

[43] The diploma also recalls a diploma *deperditum* (now lost) delivered by Louis II.

[44] *CDA*, n. 28 = D K III, n. 12. On the goods coming from the royal fisc (Colonaria, Turre and Arialta) referred to in a diploma issued by Charles the Bald just four years earlier (September 875), see *ChLA²*, XCII, n. 13. On the importance of the royal fisc in the

memory' led the East Frankish sovereigns to word their diplomas very cautiously. Sometimes, this type of memory actually impinged upon concrete reality, as in the case of Arezzo, where the *praecepta* of Charles the Bald were consigned to oblivion. The imperial coronation of Charles the Fat must have served – as has already been mentioned – to modify this attitude somewhat.

At the imperial court, presided over by the emperor, in March 881 John achieved a great victory in a long-running dispute with the episcopal see of Siena; it concerned control of some baptismal churches, which, although situated in the Sienese civil district, were, as the ruling makes clear, located *inside* the diocese of Arezzo.[45] The court, convoked in Siena, displayed, almost liturgically, the political unity of the northern and central Italian lay aristocracy around Charles III: Berengar of Friuli and Adalbert of Tuscany were present at the trial, as were the Supponids. This was particularly significant given that at the time Guy (the future king and emperor) was fomenting rebellion against imperial power from his strongholds in the march of Spoleto. While in Ravenna a year later (882) John of Arezzo received another diploma. This document, in which Wibod of Parma was addressed as *summo consiliario*, provided the church of Arezzo with the means to resist pressure from the marquis of Tuscany over the lands owned by the see and the *arimanni* (free landowners) living within the diocese.[46] I will return to this question later.

Parma and Arezzo between Guy, Louis III and Berengar

Neither the depositions nor the subsequent death of Charles III (887/ 888), which represented the end of the monopoly of Charlemagne's heirs on the imperial throne, brought any dramatic changes to the political structures of Italy. Nor did the wars of Guy and his son Lambert of Spoleto against Berengar of Friuli and Arnulf of Carinthia between 888 and 896. The courts kept on meeting, numerous diplomas were delivered and members of the aristocracy (both lay and ecclesiastic)

---

creation of political networks in the Early Middle Ages, see now, Lazzari, 'Dotari e beni fiscali'.

[45] *ChLA²*, XCII, n. 17 = Placiti, n. 93. The text of the *placitum* can be read at http://saame .it/fonte/placiti-toscani-toscana-17/. [Last viewed: 5 February 2017.] The struggle for control of the baptismal churches lasted from c. 650 to c. 1220, with the church of Arezzo almost always 'winning'. Tabacco, 'Arezzo, Siena', p. 163 and Delumeau, *Arezzo*, pp. 475–584.

[46] *ChLA²*, XCII, n. 18 (15 February 882) = D K III, n. 50. The diploma is one of a group of six charters traditionally known as the 'Ravenna Constitutions'. On the legal context (and the similarities with capitulary legislation) of the 'Constitutions', see MacLean, 'Legislation and politics', pp. 400–2 and 408–9.

continued to choose which king they would support or betray – often, in fact, doing both.[47] At this stage, though – and this is a difference worth noting – the Italian bishops found themselves acting within ever diminishing political spaces. The roles of Wibod and John as Europe-wide actors ended after Guy's failed political adventure at the heart of the Carolingian empire.

At the local level, however, some small but significant rifts can be observed. The number of documents at our disposal decreases, for example, and between 887 and 889 there is a complete break, with no sign of any 'public' writings, just at the time in which the aristocracy begins to compete seriously for control of Pavia and the royal crown. The protagonists were, on the one hand, Berengar of Friuli, the candidate of the Italian aristocracies, who was linked by family ties and politically close to the eastern Franks (remember his close alliance with Arnulf of Carinthia),[48] and, on the other, the marquis of Spoleto, Guy, supported by the marquis of Tuscany, Adalbert II, among others.[49] Guy had been defeated in France, but in Italy victory smiled upon him: first at Bergamo and then, above all, on the Trebbia (in January 899), where he defeated Berengar and won the iron crown of the *regnum Italiae*.[50]

At this point, Wibod saw fit to abandon his traditional support for eastern candidates (such as Berengar) and endorsed Guy. Delogu has suggested that this change in Wibod's long-established political behaviour may have been prompted by his fascination with the political programme of the house of Spoleto. In fact, Guy and his son Lambert were the last Italian kings to devote themselves to legislative activity of the type characterized by politics with an imperial flavour and an eye to horizons wider than those of Berengar.[51] More probably (and more prosaically), Wibod, aware of Berengar's military weakness and, above all, of how unappealing politically the marquis was, appears to have waited for the

---

[47] Santos Salazar, 'Crisis?', p. 5.

[48] Moreover, even a non-historiographical work like the epic poem *Gesta Berengarii Imperatoris* emphasizes both Berengar's close ties with the eastern Franks and the alliance between the marquis of Friuli and the Supponids, the family to which his wife, Bertilla, belonged. Bertilla's brothers would always have fought at Berengar's side. In their military role they are recalled by the poet as *tria fulmina belli*, *Gesta Berengarii Imperatoris*, lib. II, v. 77, ed. Stella. On *Gesta*, see Duplessis, 'Nam cuncta'. On Berengar and Bertilla, Arnaldi, 'Berengario' and Arnaldi, 'Bertilla'. On the Italian political context in 888, see Cammarosano, *Nobili e re* and MacLean, '"After His Death"'.

[49] Significantly, Adalbert was the intercessor in the earliest extant diploma issued by Guy, D G n. 1 (27 May, 889).

[50] The coronation took place in Pavia on 16 February 889. On Guy, see di Carpegna Falconieri, 'Guido di Spoleto', pp. 352–4.

[51] Delogu, 'Vescovi', 39.

response of the armies before deciding which side to ally himself with. Whatever the case, Wibod's fidelity to Spoleto is reflected in the archives: between 890 and 892 various diplomas reveal the new political environment. In April 890 Wibod interceded in a diploma addressed to the church of Fontana Broccola, situated in the Apennines near Parma.[52] Soon afterwards, Wibod received confirmation that the property of the abbey of Mezzano Scotti was to go to the church of Parma.[53] The collaboration between bishop and emperor did not end there, however. In February 891, shortly after Guy's imperial coronation, Wibod is listed as his *archicappellanus*, interceding before the emperor in the diplomas addressed by Guy to his consort, the Empress Ageltrude[54].

Meanwhile, the Supponids paid heavily for their support of Berengar, losing their title as counts of Parma, despite attempts made to strengthen the family's landholdings in the mountains of the county of Parma. In fact, Berengar granted a diploma to the Supponid Unroch, a move that can be interpreted as a response to Guy's diploma in favour of Fonta Broccola.[55] Moreover, in granting that diploma, Berengar was acting as sovereign in an area that, thanks to the bishop of Parma, could be considered loyal to his enemy (Guy). The diploma thus takes on an explicitly political tone: first, because Berengar still proudly accorded himself the title of king; second, because Unroch then presented *his* king with a whole series of previous royal and imperial diplomas (*ostendit nobis precepta antecessorum nostrorum*) from Louis II to Karlmann and Charles the Fat, thus initiating a dialogue with the past that again underlined a legitimacy that the aristocracies linked to the West Frankish kings, from Charles the Bald to Guy of Spoleto, could not claim; last but not least, because Berengar did not want to close the (metaphorical) gates to Rome – the traversal of the Apennines. All in all, however, Berengar's aspirations were little more than wishful thinking. Indeed, in his will (dated 892), Wibod describes his property as situated *seu in marchia Berengarii adque in toto regno Italie*,[56] a detail which showed both the reality of Berengar's limited power – he is described as a mere marquis –

---

[52] *ChLA²*, XCII, n. 19 (23 April 890) = D G n. 2.

[53] *ChLA²*, XCII, n. 26 (September–February 892/3?) = D. G. n. 19.

[54] Ageltrude is described as *consors imperii*, a uniquely Carolingian tradition. These diplomas are preserved – not by chance – in the archives in Parma, D G, n. 4–7. Guglielmotti, 'Ageltrude'.

[55] Berengar's diploma was issued less than three weeks after the 890 diploma, to the benefit of Fonta Broccola, see D B, n. 8 (12 May 890).

[56] A number of copies of the will will have been preserved, as Wibod wished, and it suggests a certain spread of the concept *marchia Berengarii* among the aristocracies of the kingdom ruled by Guy of Spoleto. For the text of the will, see *ChLA²*, XCII, n. 24 (5 July 892). See also the copy preserved in the archive at Piacenza in *ChLA²*, LXX, n. 37.

and the fragmentation of the *regnum*.[57] An informed reader would have picked up the reference to the equally limited power of the Spoletingi. Wibod's will thus demonstrates the considerable political acumen of the wise old bishop, honed and polished by thirty years of Italian politics.[58]

Arnulf of Carinthia quickly sought to take advantage of this unstable royal power. At the request of Pope Formoso, he invaded Italy and laid siege to Pavia, where he was crowned king in 894. Arnulf's brief and violent coup was followed by a change of alliances.[59] Wibod received a diploma from the new king (conserved in an amended eleventh-century copy).[60] Berengar was now a mere vassal of Arnulf, Guy had been defeated; Wibod had again chosen the king who emerged victorious from battle. The subsequent deaths of Guy (894) and the bishop of Parma (895/6) further clouded the general picture. In those days, Lambert, Berengar and Arnulf were all able to proclaim themselves king of Italy.

After Wibod's death, at the end of Arnulf's adventure a new bishop of Parma was appointed: Elbuncus, the former *archicancellarius* of Guy and Lambert. This choice was no coincidence: Elbuncus had worked at the courts of the lords of Spoleto, in close contact with Wibod, and must have been nominated by them as bishop of Parma.[61] Elbuncus' first appearance in the charters concerns the court case held in the bishopric of Florence on 4 March 897.[62] The court was presided over by Amadeus, count of the palace, and by Marquis Adalbert II. Elbuncus and the bishops of the Tuscan seats of Luni, Siena and Florence, among others, were sitting as assistants. Later, in the year 901, as mentioned before, the bishop of Parma is present in Rome, close to the new emperor, Louis III. Once again, the church of Parma had turned its back on Berengar, preferring a sovereign with a broader reach. Berengar would not have forgotten this slight.

Parma, in fact, was always a *lieu de mémoire* for the house of Spoleto. Guy had been buried, by Wibod, in the city's cathedral;[63] diplomas and other documents related to his widow, Ageltrude, were held in the

---

[57] Gasparri, 'L'identità', p. 71.

[58] A division of the kingdom of which Wibod was already acutely aware, well before the narrative sources of the time actually mention the *divisio* of the kingdom between Lambert and Berengar: *Annales Fuldenses*, a. 896, ed. Kurze, p. 129.

[59] Fuchs and Schmid, *Kaiser Arnolf*. One year before, Zwentibold, Arnulf's son, had made an unsuccessful attempt to occupy the capital of the kingdom.

[60] D Arn, n. 125.

[61] Bougard, 'Elbungo' and Bougard, 'Du centre à la périphérie', pp. 23–4.

[62] Placiti, n. 102, http://saame.it/fonte/placiti-toscani-toscana-20/. [Last viewed: 5 February 2017.]

[63] Majocchi, *Le sepolture regie*.

cathedral's archives, and the former empress lived in the monastery of Fontana Broccola, one of the dependencies of the church of Parma. And so, although Elbuncus includes presents from Berengar in his account (possibly received[64] upon recognition of the marquis of Friuli's sovereignty after the defeat of Louis III in 905), his church had not received any diplomas from Berengar.[65] One has to wait until 920 to find the first diploma delivered by the king in favour of the church of Parma;[66] it is not surprising that this delivery did not take place until after Elbuncus' death, since he had been an ally of Berengar's enemies.

The fact that no royal diplomas issued by Berengar in favour of the bishop of Parma survive cannot plausibly be put down to their disappearance or chance destruction, because many diplomas relative to Parma during the ninth century have come down to us on their original parchments.[67] Moreover, in the *dossier* of Parma's charters there are no incidental references to lost (*deperdita*) diplomas from Berengar, as there are for those of previous kings and emperors. It is therefore highly likely that Berengar did not issue diplomas in favour of Elbuncus for political reasons, although the bishop of Parma refers to Berengar twice as his *senior* in his will. Lambert's old *archicancellarius* had probably been too involved with Berengar's rivals, with the result that the king was inclined to keep him in a sort of political limbo for many years. Thus, he was denied the privileges that other *fideles* of Louis III, such as Bishop Garibaldus of Novara or Marquis Adalbert of Ivrea, son-in-law of Berengar, were granted, despite both men, like Elbuncus, only reprofessing their loyalty to the king after the blinding of Louis III.[68]

---

[64] *Filacterium quod senior meus domnus Berengarius piisimus rex mihi dedit.* Elbuncus also mentions in his will the golden spurs and precious stones which belonged to Lambert, however, *Le carte*, ed. Drei, n. 9 (a. 914).

[65] A *placitum* of 906, which records a *missus* of Berengar conducting a dispute within the territory of Parma and the bishop's receipt of goods from another enemy of the king, Adalbert of Tuscany, is probably a forgery 'created' in Parma circa 935: *Placiti*, n. 118 (May 906). The court was ruling on the possession of the fiscal court of Lugolo, supposedly given to Parma by Charles the Fat, D K III, n. 32 (13 March 881), a diploma considered by Manaresi to be a forgery, *Placiti*, p. 437. For the political and patrimonial contexts of the 'creation' of this false *dossier*, see Lazzari, 'Tra Ravenna e Regno' and Cimino, *Remembering Bertha*. The theory that the *placitum* and the diploma are forgeries seems to be strengthened by the fact that they suggest a relationship between Elbuncus, as bishop of Parma, and King Berengar that is not consistent with the known political context.

[66] D B, n. 130 (26 September 920). Barbara Rosenwein, too, considered Elbuncus to have been excluded from Berengar's gift networks, Rosenwein, 'Family politics', p. 250, n. 21.

[67] Charters relate that the city was visited by fire in the early years of the ninth century. See the diploma delivered by Berengar to Aicardus, Elbuncus' successor, D B, n. 130.

[68] Rosenwein, 'Family politics', pp. 267 and 274–5.

Let us now take a step back in time and focus on the case of Arezzo. In the Tuscan city, unlike in Parma, in the case of the Supponids, Adalbert II continued to play a key role throughout the entire period after the death of the last Carolingian sovereign. Although he was linked by family ties to the kings of the Spoleto household (Guy was his maternal uncle and Lambert his cousin), he was not always loyal to them. In August 898 he openly rebelled against Lambert, his former ally. After the death of the king, the marquis emerged as the most important 'king-maker' in Italy: at times supporting Arnulf, at times Berengar, then Lambert, finally Louis III.[69]

Meanwhile, the bishops of Arezzo received three diplomas between September 898 and March 901, which reveal that significant changes had occurred in the march's political patterns. The first diploma was granted to John of Arezzo by Lambert[70]. It confirmed the allocation of the court of Cacciano to the bishop, who was acting on behalf of the church of Arezzo. A clause states *ut nullus dux, comes, gastaldius aut quislibet publicus exactor* has the right to intervene on matters concerning the properties given: one can presume that the explicit reference to a *dux* refers to Adalbert II. The marquis was now a rebel. In fact, Lambert had captured Adalbert in Borgo San Donnino (modern Fidenza) in late summer 898.[71]

Lambert died only six weeks after the diploma was compiled, thus allowing Adalbert to enter Italian politics once again. Bishop John died two years later; he had acted at the highest diplomatic level in the empire during the second half of the ninth century, and now, with his death, Arezzo's autonomy against the marquis was over. Indeed, things changed rapidly after John's death: as early as October 900, Adalbert – one of Louis' main supporters[72] – was interceding before the new king in a diploma being granted to the new bishop of Arezzo, Peter III. Significantly, no mention of a *dux* is made in the parchment, although there are clauses stating that public authorities should not intervene.[73] Adalbert was here acting as the diploma's main intercessor and was doing so on behalf of the diocese of Arezzo, which – it is worth noting –

---

[69] Fasoli, *I re d'Italia* is still pertinent.   [70] DD L, n. 2 (2 September 898).

[71] Liutprand, *Antapodosis*, lib. I, 41. The quoted clause can also be understood as a simple formula, often included in the diplomas of Lambert's predecessors (see, for instance, Charles III's diplomas in *ChLA²*, XC, nn. 16 and 18). Its appearance at this particular time also suggests tensions between marquis (*dux*) and emperor, nonetheless, particularly if compared with the next diploma received by the church of Arezzo (October 900). See also Santos Salazar, 'Crisis?'.

[72] Louis III was the brother of Bertha, Adalbert's second wife, Cimino, *Remembering Bertha*.

[73] *ChLA²*, XC, n. 21 = D L III, n. 2, p. 113.

had until then remained clearly autonomous from the Tuscan marquises. This diploma therefore testifies to a sensational political reversal and reveals the person that was really driving political affairs.

In 905, Louis III's Italian adventure ended. Between then and 912, Berengar's sovereignty over the march would not be recognized.[74] Then, in 915, the death of Adalbert II changed political patterns once again: it is surely no coincidence that Berengar was crowned as emperor only months later, in December of that year.[75] Adalbert's death had cleared the road to Rome for the old king.

Now without rivals in Tuscany (Berengar also managed to detain Bertha, the widow of Adalbert II, and her son Guy, the new marquis, in Mantova[76]), the imperial coronation was the realization of a dream for which Berengar had been forced to wait far too long – almost thirty years. On returning from Rome, he was able to start exercising his power in places that had previously been 'forbidden'. He also appears to have taken advantage of this moment in symbolic terms. Thus, for the first diploma that he delivered in favour of the church of Arezzo, the emperor preferred not to stop in Arezzo itself, a traditional staging point on the journeys of kings and emperors to and from Rome.[77] He thereby achieved three objectives: two symbolic, displaying his new status as emperor to the Tuscans, while humiliating the bishop of Arezzo by obliging him to leave his city and meet the new emperor on the Apennines; one logistical, expressing his desire to spend as little time as possible in Tuscany, an area which had rarely been loyal to him, as soon as he got to Mugello.[78]

Only six months later in Ravenna,[79] Berengar granted Peter III all the possessions of the church of Arezzo located in the city itself as well as those in Città di Castello, Chiusi and Florence. Significantly, Adalbert's son Guy, the marquis of Tuscany, now at liberty, does not feature as an intercessor for the emperor. Indeed, the clause against the *dux* was again

---

[74] This aspect posits that Tuscan notaries (excluding those active in the charters of the abbey of St. Salvatore al Monte Amiata) shared 'une discipline collective et la conscience d'appartenir à une même zone de production documentaire', Bougard, 'Le royaume d'Italie', p. 499.

[75] Bougard, 'Le couronnement impérial'.

[76] Liutprand, *Antapodosis*, lib. II, 55. The central political role of Bertha in both Tuscany and Italy during the first decades of the tenth century is discussed in Gandino, 'Aspirare al regno', pp. 249–68 and Cammarosano, *Nobili e re*, pp. 232–6.

[77] D B I n. 109.

[78] Adalbert of Tuscany only sided with Berengar in 899/900, as in the case of the bishoprics of Lucca and Florence. In Tuscany, only Luni constituted a safe platform of power close to Berengar; in fact, its bishop, Odalbertus of Luni, was Berengar's *missus* in 900 and again in 910. See Tomei, 'Chiese, vassalli', pp. 4–6.

[79] D B I n. 111 (June 916).

included in the royal diploma. Berengar was attempting to safeguard the
possessions held by the church of Arezzo (as good emperors always did),
well aware that during the struggles for the Italian crown neither the
marquis nor Tuscany had supported him.

The 'political memory' of Berengar was destined to last a long time.

Conclusions

The political behaviour of the bishops, their quest for sources of legitimacy for their power (and for that of their kings), was a fascinating struggle,
played out at different levels, from the diocese to counties, marches and
kingdoms. Moreover, as we have seen, these contests cannot be interpreted merely by following, unquestioningly, the declared ties of loyalty
between the various actors referred to at a time of particular tension; the
diplomas and *placita* also demonstrate how opportunism, pragmatism
and the historical memory of each bishopric are key to any deconstruc-
tion of the strategies followed by the bishops – but also by many lay
members of the aristocracy – in the creation of their political networks.
Furthermore, these networks could take several different forms – often
conflicting, always negotiated. Much depended on the political capacities
of the individuals involved.

This world can be examined from two points of view. The first looks at
the spaces for political activity open to the kings and emperors between
870 and 915. The mechanism of rule was constantly being negotiated
with regional aristocracies (both lay and ecclesiastic). It could also be
profoundly affected by 'moments of oblivion', however, dictated by brief
episodes of war, revenge or long-lasting enmity, as can be seen in the
examples from the reigns of Charles the Bald and Karlmann cited above,
or during the government of Berengar, spurned in Tuscany from 905 to
912. This rejection was reflected in Berengar's behaviour towards the
sees of Arezzo and Parma, the latter never granted a diploma, the former
only after the death of Adalbert II. These 'political memories' were
obviously never unambiguous or agreed upon by all. Here we move to
the second point of view: the spaces open to bishops for political activity.
Prelates always needed to establish relationships with kings and emperors
in order to preserve their roles within the *ordo episcopalis* of the kingdom
(a crucial part of the ideological apparatus between the ninth and tenth
centuries) and to ensure the political and economic privileges of their
respective churches. Both Wibod's shifting loyalties and the choices of
Elbuncus and Peter III can probably be understood from this perspective, the latter seeming even more closely linked to the *Realpolitik* neces-
sities of the constantly mutating *regnum*. Arezzo, in particular, was

trapped between its traditional proximity to royal power and the political and military power of Adalbert II, with the result that its bishop was forced to spend longer cut off from the engines of royal power than ever before.[80]

So, if the old forget, – and everything is, in the end, forgotten – well, at least we have the diplomas and *placita* to bear witness to the complex web of political ties in the late ninth and early tenth centuries. The cases of Parma and Arezzo demonstrate how the complex and multiple political identities of each bishop were not in the gift of the central authorities, but rather a right to be recognized and negotiated in everyday politics; this dynamic changed very little after the year 888. This is not all, however. In a centre like Parma, particularly rich in historical documents, for example, Bishop Wibod would be remembered as one of Charlemagne's grandsons in an epigraph commissioned by the cathedral canons in the second half of the sixteenth century.[81] The manipulation of the 'feats' – and the political memory – of the bishops and emperors in Parma was thus destined to continue long after the Middle Ages were over.

---

[80] Arezzo's relentless pursuit of confirmation for its privileges in the forty years between 875 and 916 is stunning.

[81] The epigraph dates from 1567 and is found in the presbytery of the cathedral in Parma: *Vidiboldo Caroli Magni nepoti Ecclesiae Parmen Episcopo et comiti viro religiosissimo canonici Parmen. beneficii non immemores dignitatis eorum authori p. MDLXVII*; see Zarotti and Turchi, *Le epigrafi*, p. 179, n. 230.

Section III

Carolingian Rulers

9 Staying Lombard While Becoming Carolingian?

Italy under King Pippin

Marco Stoffella

This chapter will concentrate on certain aspects of the first stage of Carolingian rule over Italy. Broadly speaking, I will focus my attention on the three decades between 781 and 810,[1] which correspond to the period in which the young Carloman/Pippin was made co-ruler of the Carolingian kingdom of the Lombards.[2] I will consider not only some features of Pippin's co-rulership over the *regnum Langobardorum*, which his father Charlemagne had conquered during the campaign of 773–774,[3] but also certain major transformations that took place in different areas of the realm during their period of political control.[4] In the first part of this chapter, I will discuss some of the results of recent research carried out by scholars with diverse perspectives and interests.[5] In the second, I will focus on various new aspects. Finally, I will offer a number of new hypotheses, each of which may require further investigation in the coming years.

During the joint rule of Charles and Pippin, especially, many aspects of Carolingian government in Italy were characterized by both continuity and change. During Easter of 781, Carloman, one of the sons born to Charlemagne and Queen Hildegard, had, at the age of four, finally been baptized by Pope Hadrian I. Celebrations took place in Rome on 15 April and were attended by the royal Carolingian family. This

---

[1] Manacorda, *Ricerche sugli inizi*; Tabacco, 'La storia politica', pp. 73ff.; Tabacco, 'L'avvento dei Carolingi', pp. 443–79; Albertoni, *L'Italia carolingia*, pp. 26–32.

[2] Delogu, 'Il regno longobardo', pp.188–95; Delogu, 'Lombard and Carolingian Italy', pp. 300–4.

[3] Gasparri, 'Il passaggio', pp. 25–43; Gasparri, *774*; Gasparri, *Italia longobarda*, pp. 118–24; Pohl, '*Gens ipsa peribit*', pp. 67–78.

[4] Collavini, 'Duchi e società', pp. 125–66; Collavini, 'Des Lombards aux Carolingiens', pp. 263–300.

[5] Cammarosano, *Nobili e re*, pp. 74–96; Gasparri, *774*; Stoffella, 'Crisi e trasformazione'; Stoffella, 'Per una categorizzazione'; Stoffella, '*Lociservatores*'; Stoffella, 'Ecclesiastici in città'; Stoffella, 'Ufficiali pubblici'.

occasion also saw Carloman being bestowed with the weighty name of Pippin and the child king made co-ruler of Carolingian Italy. The pope anointed him *rex Langobardorum*, an official title Pippin continued to use throughout the nearly three decades of his joint kingship, and one which clearly had political resonance, due to its previous use by his father. Narrative sources are very precise regarding what happened in Italy during winter 780 and spring 781. The *Annales mettenses priores*, in particular, highlighted the multiple events that took place in the period (both in Rome and in Milan) in order to celebrate the royal family and, more precisely, the sons of Charlemagne and Hildegard.[6] They also stressed the importance of the co-rulerships involving Carloman/Pippin and his younger brother Louis that had been established in Italy and Aquitaine, respectively.[7]

Before moving on to other aspects, I will retain the focus on continuity and change in the period and discuss the long-standing issue of whether or not the Lombard ruling class in early Carolingian Italy was substituted by Charlemagne and his son Pippin. Due to the slow introduction of the mechanisms of Frankish government, this process was certainly not complete or rapid. If we consider the most important political institution of the period, the one of the counts, it is clear that many Lombard dukes who were in power before 774 were not replaced before the end of the eighth century. As a matter of fact, there is evidence of only thirteen counts in northern Italy before the death of Charlemagne.[8] This scant number should not be surprising: in 782, the year after Pippin's coronation, Italian capitularies mention Lombard counts (*Langubardisci comites*), who were supposed to administer the kingdom together with their Frankish counterparts (*comites*).[9]

The recording of the novelties in the administration of Carolingian Italy was not restricted to narrative sources written by biographers and intellectuals: lay and ecclesiastical writers of private documents also diligently registered changes after Easter 781, adding both the new co-ruler over the *regnum Langobardorum* and his newly given name to their dating formulae.[10] If, however, we take into account the few still-preserved documents that were written in the territories of the former

---

[6] *Annales Mettenses priores*, pp. 68–9; McKitterick, *Charlemagne*, p. 95. This travel had been planned some time before and postponed. Davis, *Charlemange's Practice*, pp. 416–17; Kasten, *Königssöhne*, p. 138.

[7] Kasten, *Königssöhne*, pp. 138–41; Offergeld, *Reges pueri*, pp. 308–13.

[8] Gasparri, *Italia longobarda*, p. 138.

[9] *I capitolari italici*, nr. 5, ed. Azzara and Moro, pp. 58–60; Mordek, 'Die Anfänge', p. 33.

[10] An exception is in *I placiti*, I, nr. 5, ed. Manaresi, pp. 10–14, Spoleto, July 781, where only Charlemagne's regnal years are mentioned.

Lombard kingdom immediately after Easter 781, we would have to conclude that a misperception as to what exactly happened in Rome during the celebrations of Easter 781 must have prevailed in some localities.[11] Indeed, although the first mention of both changes – Charlemagne no longer being the sole ruler over the *regnum Langobardorum* and the elevation of his son, now differently named – is to be found in documents issued in northern Tuscany in September 781,[12] Pippin was not yet acknowledged as king in Lucca in June 781.[13] This is all the more surprising when one considers that Lucca was at that time the most important city in Tuscany and deeply connected with the Carolingian court, not least through its bishops.[14] It seems, therefore, that it took time for all the political novelties to be absorbed in some localities.

Unfortunately, very few private charters issued in the years 781 and 782 are still preserved: it is therefore difficult to state how quickly the co-rulership of Pippin was received in the different regions of Carolingian Italy.[15] We can again look to Tuscany and consider another document: this time it was issued in the city and bishopric of Volterra on 25 May 782, one year and forty days after Pippin's coronation.[16] In this case, the year of Pippin's reign was surprisingly counted as his first, instead of his second.[17] We can, moreover, detect uncertainty among notaries in the following years regarding the exact date of Pippin's anointment. Indeed, a significant number of documents issued between Easter 781 and July 810, when Pippin died, are imprecise when it comes to the years of the co-rulership of Charlemagne and Pippin over Carolingian Italy. Another document issued in Tuscany provides an example: in Lucca in July 784, the year of Pippin's reign was wrongly indicated as his third by a notary and subdeacon named Gumperto.[18]

In contrast to his father, Charlemagne, who is recognized as *rex Langobardorum* in documents written in Italy at the time of the seizure of Pavia in April–June 774, Pippin was not immediately acknowledged as co-ruler in all localities. There must have been confusion about when

---

[11] Private and ecclesiastical archives have been discussed in Brown, Costambeys, Innes and Kosto (eds.), *Documentary Culture*.

[12] *ChLA*, XXXVII, nr. 1077, pp. 30–1, Lucca, before 1 September 781.

[13] Ibid., nr. 1076, pp. 28–9, Lucca, June 781.

[14] Stoffella, 'Crisi e trasformazione', pp. 26–7.

[15] Mersiowsky, *Die Urkunde in der Karolingerzeit*, I, pp. 360–3.

[16] *ChLA*, XXXVII, nr. 1081, pp. 44–6, Volterra, 25 May 782.

[17] Ibid., p. 44, ll. 1–4: *Regnantes domni nostri Carulo et Pipino filio eius veris excellentissimi reges Francorum seu et Langubardorum, anno regni eorum in Aetalia octabo et primo, sub die octabo kalendas iunias, indictione quinta.*

[18] *ChLA*, XXXVII, nr. 1093, pp. 91–3, Lucca, 11 July 784.

exactly the anointment in Rome had taken place (an event that narrative sources date precisely to Easter 781). This misperception did not extend to the new naming of Carloman, however. It is striking that his new name was never misrendered, despite this novelty having, according to the sources, been introduced at the same time as co-rulership in Easter 781. Did word of both developments perhaps reach the different localities and notaries via separate communication channels? How did such a communication system reach from the centre to outer areas? Indeed, in early Carolingian Italy notaries always used the name Pippin and never that of Carloman when they issued documents after Easter 781. It would seem that notaries had problems in correctly counting the years of reign, since sometimes they even miscalculated the concordance of the regnal years of father and son. In the majority of these cases, diplomatists have solved the problem by dating the documents after Charlemagne's regnal years only, without really taking into account the discordance with the entries for Pippin. Finally, during the last two decades of the eighth century, when the number of private documents preserved in Italian archives increases, we can state that notaries officially dated Pippin's elevation to the throne to 15 April 781. This date has also been assumed as a rule by diplomatists seeking to date incomplete or damaged documents from the same period.

As previously stated, Pippin was but a child of four in 781; he could only have ruled over the former Lombard kingdom with the help of some political and intellectual figures faithful to his father (such as the *primicerius palatii Angilbert*, who accompanied the young king to Italy) or of some *missi*. Among the latter were Adalhard (who had been brought up at the court of Charlemagne and who was very close to him[19]), and Abbot Waldo;[20] together with Rotchild, they are said to have been the *baiuli* of Pippin.[21] Official narrative sources constantly underline the political subjection of the young *rex Langobardorum* to his father's orders,[22] whereas his political autonomy would be recognized immediately after 800. In some annalistic sources, such as the *Annales alamannici* (which have a strong regional orientation and may reflect specific political interests[23]) and the *Annales mettenses priores*,[24] Pippin's military campaigns tend to be described as less inclined to fulfil his father's orders than is the case in the *Annales regni francorum*.[25] This same tendency can also be

---

[19] Kasten, *Adalhard*.   [20] Munding, *Abt-Bischof Waldo*.

[21] Bullough, 'Baiuli', pp. 625–37; Kasten, *Adalhard*, pp. 42–7, 68–84.

[22] Delogu, 'Lombard and Carolingian Italy', p. 304.

[23] *Annales alamannici*, s.a. 796, p. 48; Lendi, *Untersuchungen*, pp. 118–26, 170.

[24] Hen, 'The Annals of Metz', 186–7; McKitterick, 'Political ideology', pp. 166–7, 170–1.

[25] *Annales regni francorum*, s.a. 796, p. 801; McKitterick, *History and Memory*, pp. 84–119.

observed in the description of some political developments that go back to the last part of the eighth decade of the eighth century.[26] Moreover, certain key clerical figures very close to the young *rex Langobardorum* (as well as the ecclesiastical aspects associated with the governing of the kingdom) seem to have been of central importance, especially in the first phase of Pippin's rulership.

I have briefly discussed the situation in northern Italy; if we move southward, circumstances were slightly different, since it is only during the last phase of Pippin and Charlemagne's joint rule that Frankish counts – and transalpine immigrants in general – are mentioned in private documents.[27] Particularly in Tuscany, it has emerged that episcopal churches, together with lay officials, were asked to help in the administration of the kingdom and to use their own bureaucracy to support the rulers.[28] Recent research has shown how deeply diocesan organizations were able to reach not only the clergy and the inhabitants of the cities and their suburbs but also, especially through the rectors of baptismal churches and their local vicars, those living in small and remote villages.[29] Local priests received precise instructions and updated tools in order to correct and to instruct local society:[30] they were directly regulated by bishops, whose careful direction of the clergy had seen the efficacy of their control over local populations increase from the last decades of the eighth century onwards.[31]

Bishops and other influential members of dioceses – mostly, but not exclusively, archpriests and archdeacons, who were all members of wealthy, local elite families – started to take a role in governing, including as the chairs of *placita*.[32] The administration of justice was, of course, one of the most prominent of the innovations introduced to Carolingian Italy during the reign of Charlemagne and Pippin.[33] Even if we have earlier evidence of Tuscan bishops who seem to have been careful in administering justice, at least in the decade that preceded the Carolingian conquest,[34] bishops and abbots rarely collaborated officially with kings on an

---

[26] *Annales Mettenses priores*, pp. 74–6.   [27] Hlawitschka, *Franken*.
[28] Stoffella, 'In a periphery', pp. 325–7.
[29] Violante, 'Le strutture organizzative'; Patzold and van Rhijn, *Men in the Middle*.
[30] van Rhijn, 'Manuscripts', pp. 177–98.   [31] Stoffella, 'Local priests', pp. 98–124.
[32] Wickham, 'Land disputes', pp. 229–56; Padoa Schioppa, 'Giudici e giustizia', pp. 29–73; Stoffella, 'Condizionamenti politici', pp. 35–63.
[33] Keller, 'Der Gerichtsort'.
[34] *ChLA*, XXXIII, nr. 984, pp. 107–10, Lucca, December 764; XXXV, nr. 1023, pp. 57–61, Lucca, 26 June 771.

institutional basis before 774, despite also belonging to the high aristocracy.[35] An analysis of the many judgments reports still preserved from the
first years of Carolingian rule over Italy, however, indicates that the
collaboration of bishops and abbots in regard to justice quickly became
the norm.[36] Recent studies by Stefano Gasparri and Andrea Castagnetti
have shown that the thirty-one *notitiae placiti* from between 774 and 820
reveal bishops, abbots, priests, archpriests and deacons to have chaired
the court eighteen times, giving a total of 58 per cent in favour of
clerics.[37] Nearly one third of the surviving *notitiae placiti* relate to sittings
held in *Tuscia*, where the eleven *placita* were chaired seven times by
priests, archpriests, deacons, bishops or abbots, the share of clerics thus
increasing slightly to 63 per cent.[38]

These percentages clearly underline the importance of ecclesiastical
institutions to the functioning of the new rule, not only in central Italy
but also in the northern part of it. Obviously, there are some peculiarities
that distinguish Tuscany, for instance, from the northern part of the
peninsula. It is to just such areas, where the functioning of local society
and its social cohesion can be better comprehended, that we must first
turn our attention, nonetheless, if we wish to understand how changes
took place in the first Carolingian period in the Italian peninsula. Only
then will we be in a position to tackle the territories for which sources are
scarcer. I will therefore begin by summing up some aspects of Tuscany,
by far the best-documented region in Carolingian Italy, before going
back to northern Italy. Finally, I will close my chapter with some more
general observations.

After the Frankish conquest of 774, some Lombard bishops were
exiled, only to be later re-integrated into their offices: Bishop Peredeo
of Lucca, for instance, despite his loyalty to King Desiderius, returned to
his episcopal see after a period of about three years of detention in
Francia.[39] In the short space of time remaining before his death, the
Lombard cleric (whose career is by far the best documented in late
Lombard and early Carolingian Italy) was able to reshape his duties
and to begin to implement certain strategies resembling those that would
later come to be defined as typically Carolingian. These included a great
investment in the major ecclesiastical institutions, especially the cathedral church, with the clear aim of furthering his political ends. His

---

[35] Stoffella, 'In a periphery'; Gasparri, 'Nobiles er credentes omines liberi arimanni';
Castagnetti, 'Giustizia partecipata', pp. 3–6.
[36] *I placiti*, I, nn. 1–31, ed. Manaresi, pp. 1–98.
[37] Gasparri, *Italia longobarda*, p. 134; Castagnetti, 'Giustizia partecipata', pp. 1–40.
[38] *I placiti*, I, nn. 6, 7, 9, 11, 15, 16, 19, 20, 25, 26, 29, ed. Manaresi.
[39] A recent summary can be found in Stoffella, 'Peredeo', pp. 318–19.

successors, though they included those of local origins and members of Lombard aristocratic families, sustained the new political course with a style of leadership and diocesan restructuring that conformed to Carolingian models. They also helped to reshape the cultural milieu through the production of the famous Biblioteca Capitolare Codex 490 and of a number of hagiographical texts, as well as occasioning the transfer of certain relics to the cathedral church.[40]

Some new ways of exploiting ecclesiastical estates also emerged: the instrument of the *benificium*, which was used immediately after the conquest (especially where there was a military occupation), left traces even in areas where the military problems were probably less serious than in the northern part of Italy. Some years ago I discussed the involvement of a Bavarian aristocrat named Nibelung with the monastery of St Bartholomew in Pistoia,[41] an abbey founded by a courtier of King Liutprand's and transformed into a *beneficium* thanks to the direct aid of Rotchild, one the *baiuli* of King Pippin.[42] Coinciding with the first mention of Boniface in 812, the Bavarian *comes* of Lucca (who was preceded in the same office by the Lombard duke, Allo,[43] and by the Frankish *comes*, Wicheram[44]), this *beneficium* was dismantled to demonstrate that the political situation had returned to normal and that the rights of the abbot and of the founder's heirs could again be defended.[45] Around the year 800, Tuscan sources inform of another *beneficium* on the rich lands of the monastery of St Vincent and St Fridian of Lucca,[46] a house that had again been patronized by Tuscan aristocrats close to the sovereigns during the period of the independent Lombard kingdom.[47] References to *beneficia* as well as to royal and imperial vassals become more frequent in Tuscany after the year 800;[48] the beginnings of the full

---

[40] Petrucci, 'Il codice e i documenti', pp. 77–108; Petrucci, 'Il codice n. 490', pp. 159–75; Unfer Verre, 'Ancora sul manoscritto 490', pp. 49–63; McKitterick, *History and Memory*, p. 52, Stoffella, 'Società longobarda a Lucca', pp. 36–45; Gantner, 'The Lombard recension', pp. 87–9.

[41] *CDL*, II, nr. 203, pp. 205–12, Pistoia, 5 February 767.

[42] Bullough, 'Baiuli', pp. 625–37; Stoffella, 'Le relazioni', p. 75.

[43] *ChLA*, XXXVIII, nr. 1098, pp. 9–13, Lucca, August 785; Ghignoli, 'Su due famosi documenti', pp. 62–4.

[44] *ChLA*, XL, nr. 1156, pp. 2–3, in front of St Reparata of Lucca, 7 January 797; *ChLA²*, LXXII, nr. 5, pp. 26–9, Lucca, 27 July 800; LXXIII, nr. 36, pp. 120–3, *In loco Vetruniana*, 13 October 810; Hofmeister, 'Markgrafen', pp. 284–5; Castagnetti, 'I vassalli imperiali', pp. 213–14.

[45] Manaresi, *I placiti*, I, nr. 25, pp. 77–80, Pistoia, March 812.

[46] *ChLA²*, LXXII, nr. 7, pp. 34–5, Lucca, before 11 September 801.

[47] *CDL*, I, nr. 7, pp. 16–19. Lucca, 20 January 685; Belli Barsali, 'La topografia di Lucca', pp. 496–7; De Conno, 'L'insediamento longobardo', pp. 102–4.

[48] Castagnetti, 'I vassalli imperiali'.

implementation of the running mechanisms of Carolingian rule in Italy, and especially in *Tuscia*, can therefore be dated approximately to between the years 806 and 812, that is, between the *Divisio regnorum* and the Peace of Aachen.[49]

As already stated, the general evidence from Tuscany in the early Carolingian period demonstrates a progressive alignment with traditional Carolingian models, even if with some peculiarities. The first mention of *scabini*, the local officers that played a crucial role in administering justice, in *Tuscia*, for example, dates to the last years of the eighth century. The diffusion of this function and of this title in Tuscany is, however, tied in with the death of Charlemagne.[50] In preceding decades, Tuscan notaries often refer instead to *lociservatores*, who performed duties similar to the *scabini*. Indeed, a number of *lociservatores* (local officers that were later called *scabini*) can be identified in the sources.[51] Both lay people and clerics, they were members of the local elite that had already been politically active during the reign of King Desiderius at the latest. They regularly co-chaired or even chaired *placita*, especially in Lucca, but the function of a *lociservator* can be defined neither as typically Lombard nor Carolingian: it is documented during the thirty years of Pippin's government, especially in Tuscany, and encompassed a range of local governmental duties that were somehow broader than those performed later by the *scabini* themselves.[52] Andrea Castagnetti has recently suggested that this term and its use are due to a possible cultural connection with Byzantine Italy.[53]

Finally, the new mode of dating already discussed by Stefano Gasparri (which was predominantly used in Pisa and Lucca immediately after 774, and which made constant reference to the Lombard kingdom's conquest) completely disappeared after the deaths of King Pippin and of his father, Charlemagne.[54] Although the title of *rex Langobardorum* kept its political and formal importance in the dating formulae of private documents – in northern Italy, to the contrary, it seems to have played only a minor role[55] – the death of Charles saw the memory of the conquest completely lose its importance in favour of other historical or political events, as is clear from two Tuscan documents that go back,

---

[49] Gasparri, *Italia longobarda*, pp. 136–7. Stoffella, 'Pipino e la Divisio regnorum'.
[50] Keller, 'Der Gerichtsort', pp. 17–19; Keller, 'La marca di Tuscia', pp. 137–9.
[51] Bougard, *La justice*, pp. 140–4.
[52] Stoffella, '*Lociservatores*', pp. 345–82; Stoffella, 'In a periphery', pp. 329–34.
[53] Castagnetti, 'Giustizia partecipata', pp. 21–7, 30ff.   [54] Gasparri, 'The fall', pp. 60–1.
[55] Fainelli, 'Per l'edizione', pp. 47, 50.

respectively, to 814, in the reign of Bernard,[56] and to 816, in that of Louis the Pious and Bernard.[57] Tuscan notaries appear to have been well up to date on political events and thus able to record them reliably, not least when it came to registering the deaths of kings.

Narrative sources have fixed Pippin's premature death to 8 July 810: Tuscan scribes adhered to this dating, promptly and efficiently reacting to the development during the summer of 810, both in the northern and in the southern part of the region.[58] The death of the young King Pippin led, namely, to the revival of the practice of counting only the reign of Charlemagne in the dating formulae of documents, as had already been the case between 774 and 781. If we turn our attention to northern Italy, however, and to the Veneto and the area surrounding Verona, in particular, we find that notaries' reaction to Pippin's death was not as expeditious as in Tuscany. There are, actually, singularities in this regard that need to be briefly introduced and discussed. The first and more complicated one concerns an original document that was written in the middle of February 810 at Caprino,[59] only a few kilometres north-west of Verona. At that time, the city on the Adige river was a very important bishopric, hosted a famous *scriptorium* and even had a school supported by Charlemagne. It is therefore astonishing that in winter 810 the notary Galdipert completely ignored the name of Pippin in the dating formula he used, the co-ruler and *rex Langobardorum* receiving no mention after his father's name.[60]

The premature disappearance of a king from the documents' dating formulae before his death is difficult to explain, and recent editions of Carolingian documents written or preserved in Verona fail to discuss the issue.[61] This peculiarity is even more striking if we consider that by 810 Pippin had already ruled over Carolingian Italy for nearly thirty years. Moreover, Verona is traditionally considered to have hosted Pippin's court and to have been one of the most important Carolingian

---

[56] *ChLA²*, LXXIV, nr. 6, pp. 33–5, Lucca, 20 April 814, p. 32, ll. 1–2: *Regnante domno nostro Bernardo gratia Dei rex Langubardorum in Dei nomine, anno regni eius secundo, duodecimo Kalendas magias, indictione septima.*

[57] *ChLA²*, LXXIV, nr. 22, pp. 81–3, Lucca, 31 August 816, p. 82, ll. 1–4: *Regnante domno nostro Hludovuichus serenissimus augustus a Deo coronatus magnus et pacificus anno tertio, et domno nostro Bernardus rex Langobardorum in Dei nomine, postquam in Etalia reversus est, anno regni eius quarto, pridie kalendas septembris, indictione nona.*

[58] *ChLA²*, LXXIII, nr. 35, pp. 118–19, Into the church of St Ponziano of *Urbanula*, September 810; *ChLA²*, LXI, nr. 18, pp. 62–3, At the monastery of St Salvator at Monte Amiata, October 810.

[59] *ChLA²*, LIX, nr. 4, pp. 29–31, Caprino, 15 February 810.

[60] Ibid., p. 30, ll. 1–2: *In Christi nomine. Regnante domno nostro Carolo regem in Italia anno tregensimo octabo, sub die quintodecimo de me[n]se februario, per indictione tercia, feliciter.*

[61] *ChLA²*, LIX, nr. 4, pp. 29–31; *Le carte antiche*, ed. Ciaralli, p. LXXIII.

strongholds of northern Italy. Finally, during the months before he died, King Pippin was active militarily in the Veneto, fighting with his army against Venice. So why did the notary Galdipert ignore Pippin's name, though he was even running the risk of invalidating the relevant act?

There is here, of course, room for speculation: one might, for instance, suppose that Galdipert made a mistake, but this hypothesis is not fully convincing, since similar occurrences cannot be found, whether in the area of Verona or in other parts of Carolingian Italy. I have already considered how notaries might have had, and, in the end, did have, some difficulty in swiftly registering that a new king or a co-ruler had been anointed. This was the case with Pippin, and one could suppose that the anointment in 781 of his younger brother Louis as co-ruler and king of Aquitaine caused similar difficulties there. In the case of the document written at Verona in February 810, however, we really cannot assume that Galdipert was not informed about the joint co-rulership of Charlemagne and Pippin, seeing as he would have had not a few years but rather decades to be brought up to speed. Alternatively, we might suppose the same notary to have been well informed on the major political events that, between 809 and the beginning of 810, were taking place not far from Verona. In particular, he might have known about the military campaign that Pippin was leading against Venice and the Byzantines; he might have also been aware of the sickness that caused the death of the king on 8 July. Could he possibly have been wrongly convinced that Pippin had already died, that is, five months before his recorded date of death? It certainly seems highly unlikely that the authors of the narrative sources re-ordered events in order to postpone the official date of King Pippin's death. Indeed, a counterproof to this theory is provided by a document issued in April 810 in Varsi,[62] not far from Piacenza, which was still dated according to the regnal years of both Charles and Pippin.[63]

If we take into account more documents issued near Verona or Treviso during the reign of Pippin, we regularly find him mentioned; we cannot therefore even suppose that some sort of *damnatio memorie* applied in this area in the latter years of his life. A document preserved in Verona, but presumably issued in a locality between there and Bergamo at the beginning of 806,[64] actually shows the notary responsible for the belief that

---

[62] *ChLA²*, LXVIII, nr. 5, pp. 26–7, Varsi, April 810; see also the one issued near Parma in *ChLA²*, LXXIII, nr. 34, pp. 116–17, Medesano, 16 June 810.

[63] *ChLA²*, LXVIII, nr. 5, p. 26, ll. 1–2: *Regnante domni nostris Carolo et Peppino filio eius in Italia, annis pietatis rignis eorum trigesimo sexto, vigesimo nono, mense abrile, indictjo tertia.*

[64] *ChLA²*, LIX, nr. 3, pp. 23–7, *Platiano*, 15 January 806.

King Pippin was the author of the conquest of Lombard Italy in 774, together with his father, Charlemagne![65] At the time of the *Divisio regnorum* and of Pippin's campaign against Corsica, therefore, a northern Italian notary was convinced that King Pippin had been militarily successful even before he was born; he was also inclined to believe that in 806 the co-ruler over the former *regnum Langobardorum* played a central political role that was not diminished or weakened by his illustrious father. Even after Pippin's death, notaries seem to have been well informed about institutional developments. A document issued in spring 812, not far from Treviso, was correctly dated according to the regnal years of Charlemagne alone.[66] When an important exchange was recorded in Verona in June 814, the *cancellarius* of the cathedral church, Stadibertus, dated the document according to the regnal years of Louis the Pious and of Bernard.[67]

These last examples give us more of an impression of how Pippin was perceived by his contemporaries in different parts of Carolingian Italy. But how should we finally solve the problems posed by the document issued in the territory of Verona in February 810? In order to find a plausible answer, it may be that an investigation of the treatment of the enigmatic figure of King Pippin by modern historians and the editors of the relevant documents will prove to be more instructive than the contemporary perception of the Carolingian ruler. There is, namely, a unique practice originating in the last century, but observed even in recent editions of documents written in the Veneto, of Carolingian documents produced in Verona and Treviso being dated early; this scholarly tradition maintains that notaries did not start counting Charlemagne's regnal years after the fall of Pavia in May–June of 774 (as happened in all the other regions of Carolingian Italy), but in April 773, that is, before even the beginning of the Frankish military expedition.[68] This interpretation goes back a century, at least, to Vittorio Fainelli's preparatory studies for his edition of the *Codice diplomatico Veronese*,[69] and has more recently been endorsed by the editors of

---

[65] Ibid., p. 24, ll. 1–4: *Regnantibus domnis nostris Carolo et Pippino filio eius viris excellentissimis [regibus Francorum et] Langobardorum, cum cepissint Italia annos [regni eorum tri]g[isi]mo tertio et vigisimo quinto, die quintodecimo [intr]ante mense ianuario, indictione quartadecima.*

[66] *ChLA²*, LX, nr.18, pp. 83–5, Cornuda, middle April – 31 August 812.

[67] Ibid., nr. 19, pp. 86–90, [Verona], 20 June 814.

[68] Bertolini, *Roma di fronte a Bisanzio*, pp. 681–6; McKitterick, *Charlemagne*, pp. 107–8, 112–13; Zettler, 'Die Ablösung der langobardischen Herrschaft', p. 599. Delogu, 'Il regno longobardo', p. 190, places the gathering of the Frankish army in Geneva in spring 773. Stoffella, 'In Threatening Times'.

[69] *Codice diplomatico Veronese*, ed. Fainelli.

the *Chartae Latinae antiquiores*.[70] With some remarks and refinements, which included him pointing out that Charlemagne's military campaign started in summer and not in April 773, this tradition was also accepted by the editor of the charters of the church of St Peter *in Castello* in Verona.[71]

This explanatory tradition (which arguably contradicts the political and military events of 773–774, and does not take into account that Verona was captured by the Franks a few months before Pavia definitively fell[72]), has been adopted in order to harmonize the regnal years of Charlemagne and of Pippin as well as the cycle of indiction in documents produced in the Veneto.[73] Here is not the place to go into further details: I will leave the discussion on this point for another occasion, when many documents produced in Verona and Treviso between the end of the eighth century and the beginning of the ninth will be more deeply discussed. Here, rather, I will stress the fact that in their explanatory and harmonizing efforts, editors of documents written in Verona and neighbouring areas have focussed more on the figure of Charlemagne than that of Pippin, sometimes even ignoring the concordance between the regnal years of father and son. Furthermore, the 'April 773 theory' may have helped to explain the regnal years of Charlemagne, but, unfortunately, not those of Pippin. This is precisely the case with the document issued in Caprino on 15 February 810, which has been analyzed because of the problems relating to the concordance between the regnal years of Charlemagne and the indiction, but not because of the absence of Pippin's regnal years. The consequences are that, even if the thirty-eight regnal years of Charlemagne and the absence of Pippin should encourage the re-dating of this document to 811,[74] or even to 812 – depending on when one places the beginning of Charlemagne's rule over Verona – the document has, because of the concordance with the third indiction, been dated to 810.[75]

Further examples would show that in the majority of cases in which the dating of a document written in the area of Verona in the early Carolingian period is uncertain, the regnal years of Charlemagne or the indiction have been taken to offer a plausible solution, ignoring the regnal years of Pippin and, in the end, neglecting the figure of the young

---

[70] *ChLA²*, LIX, nr. 2, pp. 19–21, Treviso, April? – 31 August 804, p. 19.

[71] *Le carte antiche*, ed. Ciaralli, p. LXXII.

[72] Bertolini, *Roma di fronte a Bisanzio*, p. 685, dates the fall of Verona to after the end of September 773. See also Zettler, 'Die Ablösung der langobardischen Herrschaft', pp. 597–9; Delogu, 'Il regno longobardo', p. 190.

[73] *ChLA²*, LIX, nr. 2, p. 19.   [74] *Le carte antiche*, ed. Ciaralli, p. LXXIII.

[75] *ChLA²*, LIX, nr. 4, p. 29; *Le carte antiche*, ed. Ciaralli, p. LXXIII.

king. There are no easy answers to these problems, and new analysis of those controversial documents needs to be conducted. The questions that have arisen, especially in the last part of this chapter, have, however, gone some way to showing that even recent historiography has favoured explanations revolving around the central political figure of Charlemagne, often to the detriment of his less famous son Pippin. The increased attention now being paid to Pippin's co-rulership over early Carolingian Italy should, in the near future, help us to focus on the diverse aspects of his nearly three-decades-long political career in Italy.

10 Carolingian Fathers and Sons in Italy
Lothar I and Louis II's Successful Partnership

Elina Screen

For Sedulius Scottus, 'offspring of a noble character' were one of the 'consolations in the present' received by 'just and holy rulers'.[1] In theory, adult sons were valuable assets who could help a Carolingian ruler lead armies, administer justice, rule more distant regions such as Italy and bind aristocratic families to the dynasty through marriage alliances.[2] In practice, discontented and rebellious adult sons, especially sons with aristocratic supporters and a regional powerbase of their own, might pose a real threat to the ruler's own position, as Louis the Pious famously experienced in 833–834 when his sons Lothar, Pippin and Louis the German deposed him.[3] In an unusually frank aside, when describing Louis the German's response to a rebellion by his son Louis the Younger in 866, Hincmar of Reims referred to Louis' 'wisdom born of long experience in such situations'.[4] Managing the tricky relationship with adult sons was indeed one of the standard challenges facing medieval rulers.[5] Exploring the father and son partnership of Lothar I and Louis II offers a valuable perspective on the forces at work in the relationships between senior and junior rulers more widely, as well as the specific circumstances at play in ruling Italy from Francia.

Given the size of the Frankish empire and the existing well-defined identity of the kingdom of Italy, in principle it was a practical decision for

---

[1] Sedulius, *De rectoribus*, ed. and trans. Dyson, c. 20, p. 192, ... *justis et sanctis rectoribus multa in praesentia solatia ... praeclarum sobolis indolem* ..., trans. p. 193. Maria Schäpers', *Lothar I., (795–855) und das Frankenreich*, which includes many insights on the period covered here, appeared after the completion of this text.

[2] Kasten, *Königssöhne und Königsherrschaft*, pp. 272–377, explores sons' roles in this period in detail; see also pp. 249–57 on marriage.

[3] On Louis the Pious and his sons, see de Jong, *Penitential State*, pp. 14–58.

[4] *Annales Bertiniani*, ed. Grat, s.a. 866, p. 131: *Hludouuicus autem senior in talibus experientia prudens* ..., trans. Nelson, *Annals of St-Bertin*, p. 135. For Louis' rebellions against his father, see e.g. *Annales Bertiniani*, ed. Grat, s.a. 838–40, pp. 24–36; for his own sons' rebellions *Annales Fuldenses*, ed. Kurze, s.a. 861–3 (Karlmann), 866 (Louis), 871 (Louis and Charles), 873 (Charles).

[5] See e.g. Nelson, 'A tale of two princes'; Costambeys, Innes and MacLean, *Carolingian World*, p. 209.

rulers based north of the Alps to establish a son as king in Italy, though at times, for example, Louis the Pious opted for direct rule facilitated by *missi*.[6] Making this relationship work meant finding ways to bridge both the mental distance between the concerns and aspirations of the senior and the junior ruler, and the physical distance between the senior ruler in Francia and the junior king in Italy: approximately 870 km separated the Pavia/Milan area from Aachen, including the formidable barrier of the Alps.[7] Like his younger brother Louis the German, Lothar had ample first-hand experience of being a rebel son, and Italy became his key power base and place of refuge when his relationship with Louis the Pious broke down after 829.[8] As far as we can tell from the limited evidence, however, Lothar I and Louis II seem to have maintained a stable and productive relationship from 840 to Lothar's death in 855. A sense of partnership between father and son at key moments, Lothar's gradual delegation of power and the absence of key triggers for rebellion help account for this success. Setting Lothar I and Louis II's relationship in the context of the father–son relationships between Charlemagne and Pippin of Italy, and of Louis the Pious with Pippin's son Bernard and Lothar I himself, suggests that the same factors were at work in Carolingian father-son relationships more widely.

Because of their centrality to politics and the succession, Carolingian father-son relationships consistently interested contemporary authors such as the Astronomer, who reported in detail on Louis the Pious' difficult relationships with his sons.[9] Carolingian kingship in Italy has a substantial modern historiography, too: Jörg Jarnut, for example, explored the changing status of Lothar I in Italy, while Bernard's short reign and rebellion have attracted much attention.[10] Father-son relationships tend to be explored from either a personal or a 'constitutional' perspective, that is, either thinking about family dynamics,[11] or

---

[6] See Gantner, chapter 2 above, and Costambeys, Innes and MacLean, *Carolingian World*, for good accounts of the political history and challenges of ruling under Charlemagne, Louis the Pious and Lothar I. Garipzanov, *Symbolic Language*, pp. 24–5, discusses the impact of different 'horizons of expectations', with examples of Italian influence at pp. 123–5, 130–1; see also McKitterick, *Charlemagne*, pp. 245–50. Louis' direct rule of Italy: Jarnut, 'Ludwig der Fromme', pp. 351–2.

[7] See Gravel, *Distances, rencontres, communications*, pp. 312–14 on travel to Italy, and pp. 83–92 on speed of travel.

[8] On this period, see Jarnut, 'Ludwig der Fromme', pp. 356–62, de Jong, *Penitential State*, pp. 38–58, and Screen, 'Lothar I in Italy'.

[9] Astronomer, *Vita Hludowici imperatoris*, ed. Tremp, e.g. c. 55–63, pp. 506–50, on 834–40.

[10] Jarnut, 'Ludwig der Fromme'; Noble, 'Revolt of King Bernard', among many contributions.

[11] For example, Schieffer, 'Väter und Söhne', and Nelson, 'Charlemagne – pater optimus?'.

alternatively emphasising succession arrangements, changes in titles and status and the responsibilities of the junior king relative to the senior ruler in a tradition going back to Gustav Eiten's 1907 classic study, *Das Unterkönigtum im Reiche der Merovinger und Karolinger*. This chapter falls into the first tradition, and will leave debates over terms such as subkingship to one side, to focus on how a working partnership was achieved.[12] To resort to cliché, it took two to tango: a successful partnership between father and son depended on the input of both parties, and was best achieved with a supportive aristocracy in the background. Our primary sources, however, consistently emphasise the perspective of the father in Francia.

Broadly speaking, the main narrative sources for the ninth century were written within Francia, while we have more charters and legal sources from Italy. Some Frankish authors were better informed on Italian affairs, for example the *Annals of Bertin*.[13] Overall, annalists were most interested in the doings of the senior ruler of the kingdom; sons usually only became newsworthy when they were acting in positive ways at their father's request, or acting against their father in negative ways. For example, Louis II only registered in the Frankish narrative sources when being crowned king in 844 and then emperor in 850, and leading armies against the Saracens or Benevento in 847 and 852, respectively. Indeed, actions undertaken by the son might be associated with the father: for example, the *Annals of St Bertin* refer to 'Lothar's army' in 848, meaning the joint Italian/Frankish army led by Louis II.[14] Most of our narrative sources, therefore, firmly present father-son relationships from the perspective of the father, often leading to silence on the sons and Italy.

Two mental frameworks were important in shaping father-son relationships as we see them in our sources. The first and dominant framework was the patriarchal, Judaeo-Christian tradition that emphasised the authority of the father over the son. Biblical encounters between fathers

---

[12] On the historiography, including the term 'subking', see Kasten, *Königssöhne und Königsherrschaft*, pp. 1–8; Costambeys, Innes and MacLean, *Carolingian World*, pp. 208–13, discuss the concept of subkingship.

[13] See e.g. the good information on events in 846, and 868: *Annales Bertiniani*, ed. Grat, s. a. 846, pp. 52–3; s.a. 868, pp. 143–4.

[14] *Annales Bertiniani*, ed. Grat, s.a. 848, p. 55: *Exercitus Hlotharii contra Saracenos Beneuentum optinentes dimicans, uictor efficitur*. See Bougard, 'La cour et le gouvernement de Louis II' for his career; Louis II's activities are calendared in *Die Karolinger im Regnum Italiae*, ed. Böhmer, Mühlbacher and Zielinski, *Regesta Imperii*, 1.3.1.

and sons that emphasised the son's obedience and submission echo through Carolingian writings on sons and fathers.[15] Thegan and Einhard cited Deuteronomy (21, 18–21) to emphasise the rightful punishment owing to contumacious sons.[16] David's rebellious son Absalom, caught by his long hair and killed, offered a suitable warning to ambitious sons tempted to disregard the fifth commandment, while David's grief for Absalom despite his transgressions provided a model for long-suffering fatherhood.[17] These ideas had great strength and gave fathers considerable leverage over their sons: for example, in 830 Louis the Pious was apparently able to bring Lothar to heel by claiming his rights to obedience as a father.[18]

But running alongside this top-down narrative, there was also a more reciprocal aspect to father-son relationships. As well as sons' well-defined obligations of obedience and subordination, fathers had more nebulous responsibilities towards their sons. Biblical exemplars could be found for this side of the relationship, too: in particular, St Paul enjoined fathers not to provoke their children to anger.[19] The history of Saul and David offered a salutary exemplar of the divine and human problems Saul incurred when he pushed David (effectively his adopted son) away through envy.[20] Fathers were thus expected to heed their children's limits, and the supporters of Louis the Pious' sons emphasised these texts in their writings in the 830s.[21]

Alongside this element of mutual religious responsibility, father-son relationships were also firmly rooted in Carolingian expectations of reciprocity in relationships between *senior* and *fidelis*, and pragmatic considerations in the practice of politics.[22] In a world where the exercise of power rested on personal relationships, the ruler had to take into account the interests and reasonable expectations of the ruled, in particular of key figures in the realm, and to listen to the counsel offered by

---

[15] See Kasten *Königssöhne und Königsherrschaft*, pp. 199–216, for an excellent survey, and Nelson, 'A tale of two princes', for a detailed case study.

[16] Einhard, *Epistolae*, ed. Hampe, no. 11, pp. 114–15; Thegan, *Gesta Hludowici imperatoris*, ed. Tremp, c. 53, p. 246.

[17] 'Honour thy father and mother': Exodus 20, 12 and Deuteronomy, 5, 16. Absalom: 2 Samuel 18, 9–33; Astronomer, *Vita Hludowici imperatoris*, ed. Tremp, c. 55, p. 508; discussed by de Jong, *Penitential State*, p. 54.

[18] Astronomer, *Vita Hludowici imperatoris*, ed. Tremp, c. 45, pp. 462–4.

[19] Colossians 3:21: 'Fathers, provoke not your children to anger, lest they be discouraged'; see also Ephesians 6.4.

[20] See esp. 1 Samuel 16:14–23, 18:1–12, 24:1–22, and Sedulius, *De rectoribus christianis*, ed. Dyson, c. 3, p. 66, on Saul's loss of his life and kingdom for unfaithfulness to God.

[21] Kasten, *Königssöhne und Königsherrschaft*, p. 202.

[22] On reciprocity, see Nelson, 'Kingship and empire', pp. 66–9.

'important persons and the senior advisors of the realm'.[23] Adult sons and nephews such as Bernard were expected to attend assemblies when summoned, suggesting they were among the king's potential counsellors, though neither neither Sedulius in the *De rectoribus christianis* nor Hincmar in the *De ordine palatii* ever state this overtly;[24] the reference to Louis II and Lothar taking counsel together in 847, discussed below, is an unusually explicit reference to a son in this context.[25] Adult sons could and did wield considerable influence in practice. For example, successfully leading the army created connections with the elite for Charlemagne's son Pippin of Italy, while the surviving letters and poetry also reveal his prominence, and suggest that his court at Verona was a centre of learning as well as law-giving.[26]

But nevertheless, successfully negotiating the relationship with their father required care and thought on the adult sons' part. The Astronomer's description of the uncertainties in Louis the Pious' circle about how to approach the aging Charlemagne about the succession gives a rare and vivid glimpse of the concerns felt by sons and their supporters in dealing with the father and senior ruler.[27] These supporters were the vital third party in determining how relationships with the senior ruler unfolded: Nithard and the Astronomer both emphasise the role of Lothar's supporters in destabilising Frankish affairs in the late 820s and 830s, while the success of Pippin of Italy in creating a body of supporters enabled his son Bernard to succeed him and attempt to defend his position as king of Italy.[28]

---

[23] Hincmar, *De ordine palatii*, ed. Gross and Schieffer, c. 34, p. 90: *Proceres vero praedicti sive in hoc sive in illo praefato placito, qui et primi senatores regni ...*, trans. Dutton, *Carolingian Civilization*, p. 530.

[24] Sons and nephews attending court: Kasten, *Königssohne und Königsherrschaft*, pp. 259–71. It is striking that neither Sedulius nor Hincmar speak of adult sons in any detail, though both discuss the importance of good counsellors: Sedulius, *De rectoribus christianis*, ed. Dyson, c. 6, pp. 82–90; Hincmar, *De ordine palatii*, ed. Gross and Schieffer, c. 31, pp. 86–8. Perhaps this is linked to the relative youth of the kings who received the respective works.

[25] See below, pp. 158–9.

[26] See Stoffela, chapter 9, on Italy under Pippin, Hammer, 'Christmas Day 800', pp. 13–17 on Pippin's prominent position, Kasten, *Königssöhne und Königsherrschaft*, pp. 332–2 on his capitularies, and McKitterick, *Charlemagne*, pp. 365–8 for a possible manuscript from Pippin's court circle.

[27] Astronomer, ed. Tremp, *Vita Hludowici imperatoris*, c. 20, p. 342.

[28] Bernard's rebellion with the support of his followers: Astronomer, *Vita Hludowici imperatoris*, ed. Tremp, c. 29, pp. 382–4; Lothar's supporters urged him either to wage war or depart from his father: Astronomer, *Vita Hludowici imperatoris*, ed. Tremp, c. 45, p. 462; Hugh and Matfrid trigger Lothar's opposition to Louis' succession plans: Nithard, *Historiae*, ed. Lauer, I, 3, p. 8. Compare also Pippin I of Aquitaine, whose supporters set up his son and enabled him to mount a spirited defence of his position: Nithard, *Historiae*, ed. Lauer, I, 8, p. 32.

Thus, though all father-son relationships had an element of partnership or mutuality to them, this is masked to a degree by the biblical and patriarchal framework of our narrative sources: and sometimes, as in Louis II's and Lothar's case, also by our limited evidence for the son's perspective. A handful of references in the charters, capitularies and *placita* (dispute settlements) are particularly important for developing a better understanding of Louis II and Lothar's partnership, to which we shall now turn.

Lothar and Louis II have been discussed with great insight by François Bougard and Brigitte Kasten, among others.[29] The outlines of this father-son relationship are thus well known. Louis was born to Lothar and his wife Ermengard, daughter of Count Hugh of Tours, in around 825.[30] He was their eldest son; his brothers Lothar II and Charles of Provence were respectively some ten and twenty years younger. The ebb and flow of Lothar I's own political fortunes meant that Louis II spent most of his formative years in Italy, where Lothar was largely resident from 829 to 840. As part of Louis the Pious' reconciliation with Lothar in 839, Louis II was recognised as king of Italy by Louis the Pious, and was named as king in the dating clauses of private charters from 840.[31]

Louis probably remained in Italy throughout the Frankish Civil War of 840–843, though his entourage seems to have been small, at least to judge by the single chaplain who has been identified.[32] In 844, Louis II was sent to Rome with Archbishop Drogo of Metz and a substantial army, and crowned king. From this point onwards, Louis can be seen hearing court cases and despatching his own *missi*.[33] Lothar remained actively involved in Italian affairs up to 850, however: he retained the sole right to issue imperial diplomata and continued to receive regular visits from his Italian lay and clerical *fideles*.[34] Indeed, in spring 847, Lothar

---

[29] Bougard, 'La cour et le gouvernement de Louis II'; Kasten, *Königssöhne und Königsherrschaft*, pp. 394–427; Clemens Gantner is currently preparing a major study of Louis II.

[30] On Ermengard, see Schäpers, *Lothar I.*, pp. 89–94.

[31] Reconciliation: *Annales Bertiniani*, ed. Grat, s.a. 839, pp. 31–2, trans. Nelson, *Annals of St Bertin*, p. 45; Louis recognised as king: Eiten, *Unterkönigtum*, pp. 139–55; Bougard, 'La cour et le gouvernement de Louis II', p. 250.

[32] Kasten, *Königssöhne und Königsherrschaft*, pp. 394–5; Bougard, 'La cour et le gouvernement de Louis II', p. 251.

[33] See Gantner, chapter 11, and Bougard, 'La cour et le gouvernement de Louis II', p. 252.

[34] The charters of Lothar I are edited by Schieffer, *Diplomata Lotharii I. et Lotharii II. / Die Urkunden Lothars I. und Lothar II.*, hereafter cited as DLoI and charter number; the recipient is given before the date. Lothar's surviving charters for Italian recipients are: DLoI 91–2, pp. 223–8 (Novalesa, 13.6.845 and 10.10.845), 93, pp. 228–9 (Volterra, 30.12.845), 97, pp. 235–6 (Godebert, deacon of Pavia, 8.7.846), 101–2, pp. 240–3 (Irmingard and Gisela/San Salvatore Brescia, 16.3.848, 20.3.848), 115, pp. 265–6

himself visited Italy.[35] In 850, Louis II was crowned emperor. From 851, Louis II started to play a greater role in lawgiving and to issue his own diplomata, while Lothar ceased making grants to Italian recipients.[36] In the early 850s, therefore, Lothar seems to have stepped back from day-to-day Italian affairs, though he continued to pay close attention to Rome.[37] The changes in Louis' title and the gradual delegation of power to Louis II have been discussed extensively by others;[38] I shall focus here on the management of the partnership by the father and the son, beginning with the perspective of Lothar I, the father and senior ruler.

Although Lothar only made one known visit to Italy after 840, it is worth emphasising that unlike Louis the Pious in particular, who had not travelled south of the Alps since his youth,[39] Lothar had the advantage of knowing the Italian kingdom, its complex politics and its personalities well. Lothar had placed his own mark upon the kingdom after 834, when he established his exiled supporters in Italy and built up connections with the key churches and monasteries, bringing about a significant 'Frankicising' of Italy in the process.[40] The particular circumstances of this period of opposition to Louis the Pious helped create a very tight-knit group of key supporters around Lothar. After the Treaty of Verdun, while some supporters like Liutfrid (son of Hugh of Tours, and brother to Lothar's wife Irmingard) headed north to Francia, others retained their Italian connections, and continued to serve Lothar and Louis II in Italy. In particular, Eberhard of Friuli, marquis of Friuli since 828, continued to be an effective and loyal supporter, holding lands and influencing events both north and south of the Alps, including leading

---

(with Louis II) (Gisela/San Salvatore Brescia, 8.9.851), 116, pp. 267–8 (Cremona, 8.9.851). Further charters, now lost, may also have been issued in this period: DLoI 163–4, p. 339, 166–87, pp. 340–9.

[35] Zielinski, 'Ein unbeachteter Italienzug'.

[36] Louis' first charter was issued on 10 January 851: *Diplomata Ludovici II/Die Urkunden Ludwigs II.*, ed. Wanner, no. 1, pp. 67–9. Kasten, *Königssöhne und Königsherrschaft*, pp. 417–21, discusses Louis' capitularies. Lothar's last charters for Italy were DLoI 115–16 (8.9.851), pp. 265–8.

[37] See below, pp. 156–7.

[38] See in particular Bougard, 'La cour et le gouvernement de Louis II' and Kasten, *Königssöhne und Königsherrshaft*, pp. 394–427.

[39] In 781 and 792: Astronomer, *Vita Hludowici imperatoris*, ed. Tremp, c. 4, c. 6, pp. 292–4, 300. Louis the Pious issued no charters for Italian recipients after 1 April 831: *Diplomata Ludovici Pii/Die Urkunden Ludwigs des Frommen*, ed. Kölzer, no. 298 (San Vincenzo al Volturno) (hereafter cited DLdF and charter number).

[40] Screen, 'Lothar I in Italy'; 'Frankonisierungsprozess': see Jarnut, 'Ludwig der Fromme', pp. 359–60, 362.

one of the armies despatched against the Saracens in 848.[41] As François Bougard has noted, Eberhard and other members of this key group patronised the royal convent of San Salvatore, Brescia, in another expression of loyalty and identification with Lothar's branch of the Carolingian family.[42] This top stratum of the Frankish elite, many of whom held lands on both sides of the Alps, thus provided an important human connection between Lothar's court and that of Louis.[43]

In addition to the lay nobility, the bishops provided further important connective tissue between the kingdoms. Lothar seems to have relied in particular on Joseph, bishop of Ivrea, Noting, bishop of Verona, Amalric, bishop of Como and Peter, bishop of Arezzo.[44] Jennifer Davis has recently shown how important the bishops were for Charlemagne's successful control of Italy, and this was surely no different for Lothar and Louis II.[45] Under Lothar I, as Jörg Jarnut has pointed out, Franks were increasingly appointed to Italian bishoprics.[46] The existence of this group of lay and ecclesiastical supporters holding Italian and often Frankish lands and offices had two implications: first, Lothar was well informed about, and remained well connected with, Italy. For example, we find Joseph, bishop of Ivrea, present at Aachen in both 845 and in July 846, when he requested a grant for Godebert, a deacon of Pavia.[47] Second, this group had a vested interest in smooth relations between father and son, because of the potential impact on their wider landholdings.

Lothar's itinerary also suggests his interest in dealing with Italian matters. Clusters of charters suggest that at least twice Lothar headed towards the south of his kingdom to meet his key Italian bishops and counts at Gondreville and Remiremont.[48] In August 843 Amalric, bishop elect of Como, and Noting of Verona were present at

[41] See Hlawitschka, *Franken*, pp. 221–3 (Liutfrid), and 169–72 (Eberhard). For their activity under Louis II, see Bougard, 'La cour et le gouvernement de Louis II', pp. 251–9.

[42] Bougard, 'La cour et le gouvernement de Louis II', p. 258; Veronese, chapter 14, p. 239.

[43] On the strong transalpine connections of Lothar's magnates and bishops, see Jarnut, 'Ludwig der Fromme', pp. 359–60. On Louis II's magnates' connections to Francia, see Bougard, 'La cour et le gouvernement de Louis II', p. 257.

[44] Bougard, 'La cour et le gouvernement de Louis II', pp. 251–3.

[45] Davis, *Charlemagne's Practice of Empire*, pp. 206–38.

[46] Jarnut, 'Ludwig der Fromme', p. 359.

[47] DLoI 91, pp. 223–5 (13.6.845), 92, pp. 225–8 (10.10.845). See also Bougard, 'La cour et le gouvernement de Louis II', p. 252, for travellers in 843.

[48] Jennifer Davis observed the same phenomenon in Charlemagne's charters. 'Even when Italian grants were given in Francia they were often given in groups, suggesting some "clumping" in the handling of Italian affairs, at least when it came to giving grants': Davis, *Charlemagne's Practice of Empire*, p. 221. Some clusters are also to be found in Louis the Pious' charters, e.g. DLdF 176, p. 436 (Piacenza, 27.4.820) and 177–80, pp. 438–447 (Farfa, 28.4.820).

Gondreville, as was Count Eberhard of Friuli: he and Noting together requested a grant for Aquileia. Six days later it was Peter of Arezzo's turn to receive two charters for his own church at Remiremont.[49] In 851 Louis II came to Gondreville, as did the envoy of the bishop of Cremona.[50] We do not know where the council held 'in Francia' in late 846 or, more likely, spring 847 was held, but the many southern bishops included in the list of benefice holders at the end of the document, and the decision to send part of the armies of Burgundy and Provence as well as Francia to Italy, suggests this council too might have been held at one of the more southern palaces.[51] The need to maintain close contacts with Italy might also have contributed to Lothar's swift and decisive campaign in Provence in 845, when he restored the region to his control after a rebellion by Fulcrad of Arles and others.[52] Even putting to one side the exceptional events stimulated by the attack on Rome in 846, therefore, Lothar's itinerary suggests that Italian affairs helped shape Lothar's movements. Gradually, however, he did step back and allow Louis II more space, especially from 851.

Considering the partnership from Louis II's perspective, the relationship with Lothar imposed certain constraints on what Louis could and could not do as king of Italy. Lothar expected Louis to travel to Francia as necessary, and Louis duly visited in 847 and 851 at least.[53] In spring 847 Lothar himself turned up in Italy, a visit that in itself indicates co-operation between father and son: when Louis the Pious expressed his wish to visit Rome in 837, Lothar closed the Alpine passes against his father![54] Even after 850, Lothar remained involved in papal affairs in particular. Lothar's visible interventions ranged from issuing a mandate instructing Louis to assist the Saxon pilgrim

---

[49] Gondreville: DLoI 75–7, pp. 190–5 (22.8.843), for Ortin, vassal of Bishop Noting, the church of Aquileia and the monastery of Bobbio. Remirement: DLoI 78–9, pp. 195–8, for the church of Arezzo.

[50] DLoI 115, pp. 265–6 (8.9.851, for Gisela, Lothar I's daughter and Louis II's sister); 116, pp. 267–8 (8.9.851, Cremona).

[51] *Concilia aevi Karolini 843–859*, ed. Hartmann, no. 12, pp. 133–9, p. 138 (episcopal attestations and identifications). This important capitulary is being studied by Sören Kaschke and is discussed in Gantner, 'Saracen attack'; the most extensive published study remains Dupraz, 'Le capitulaire de Lothaire I'; see pp. 280–9 for his identifications of the bishops.

[52] *Annales Bertiniani*, ed. Grat, s.a. 845, p. 49 and p. 51; *Annales Fuldenses*, ed. Kurze, s. a. 845, p. 35. See the *Divisio regnorum*, MGH Capit. 1, ed. Boretius, no. 45, pp. 126–30, c. 3, p. 127, for awareness of the different routes into Italy and the need for access.

[53] See above.

[54] *Annales Bertiniani*, ed. Grat, s.a. 837, pp. 21–2; on the 847 visit, see Zielinski, 'Ein unbeachteter Italienzug'.

Waltbert (probably in 850),[55] to sending joint *missi* with Louis II to Rome in 853.[56] Lothar's close connections with the bishops and nobles of the realm, and the steady flow of loyal bishops and key *fideles* heading for Aachen with news of the latest Italian developments, would also have limited Louis II's actions, both directly and indirectly. Three areas in particular suggest that, despite these constraints, in other ways Louis II gained more from partnership with Lothar.

It is striking, first, that in ruling Italy after 850, Louis continued to draw on members of the group associated with Lothar I. When Louis II's chancery was established in 851, it seems likely that Lothar took a hand, as the key officials had close connections with Lothar. Dructemir, an imperial notary who had served Lothar himself in 835–839, and probably remained in Italy in 840, acted as Louis' chancellor from 851–860, and Bishop Joseph of Ivrea, whom we already met in Lothar's service, held the post of archchaplain from 850–853.[57] This continuity also applied to the lay nobility. When Louis II eventually married, his wife Angilberga was from the Supponid family, with kinship ties to the group of Lothar's supporters (and also to the family of Cunegund, Bernard of Italy's wife).[58] Louis' subsequent relationships with figures such as Lambert of Spoleto had their ups and downs, but one of the successes of this particular father-son partnership seems to have been a smooth transition of power. Louis II inherited a fully functioning set of political relationships, which by and large he opted to continue to exploit.[59]

Second, despite the constraints and tensions involved in having a back-seat driver in Lothar, there were good reasons for Louis II to acquiesce in this situation. Carolingian sons tended to rebel if their position was threatened, or their aspirations for the gradual transfer of power from father to son were thwarted: prominent examples include Pippin the Hunchback and Bernard of Italy in the former category, and Charles the Bald and Louis the German's sons in the 860s and 870s in

---

[55] DLoI 108, pp. 256–7; Lothar also issued DLoI 109–10, pp. 257–9 for Waltbert, directed to secular authorities and the pope.

[56] *Liber Pontificalis*, ed. Duchesne, Life of Leo IV, c. 90, II, p. 129: the bishops despatched were the 'usual suspects', namely, Joseph of Ivrea, Peter of Spoleto and Peter of Arezzo.

[57] Bougard, 'La cour et le gouvernement de Louis II', p. 255; Kasten, *Königssöhne und Königsherrschaft*, pp. 407–8; *Die Urkunden Ludwigs II.*, ed. Wanner, pp. 1–6.

[58] Bougard, 'La cour et le gouvernement de Louis II', p. 260. The date of Louis II's marriage to Angilberga is uncertain; an earlier informal relationship (hinted at in the Annals of St Bertin? See *Annales Bertiniani*, ed. Grat, s.a. 853, p. 67) was later formalised; see Cimino, 'Italian queens'.

[59] Problems with Lambert: *Annales Bertiniani*, ed. Grat, s.a. 871, pp. 183–4. See also Bougard, 'La cour et le gouvernement de Louis II', pp. 257–8.

the latter.[60] Louis' inheritance in Italy was never threatened at any point by his father or brothers. As we have seen, from 844 Louis' own emergent court becomes visible, and from 851 Louis issued his own charters and ruled as more-or-less independently as co-emperor in Italy. Lothar II only emerged as a potential competitor in the early 850s; and when Lothar I finally gave Lothar II land in January 855, this was unthreateningly in the far north, in Frisia.[61] The depth of the dispute between Louis II and Lothar II at their meeting in 856 suggests that Louis II may also have expected to inherit land north of the Alps: such expectations would have offered another reason not to rock the boat.[62] The hope of a gradual transfer of power and of an inheritance north of the Alps, allied to the actual delegation of responsibilities over time, surely added to the factors keeping Louis 'on message' in his partnership with his father.

Third, when Louis and Lothar did come together, Lothar seems to have taken care to express their unity and make appropriate public acknowledgement of his son's status. Honourable treatment was important to Carolingian sons, as Pippin I of Aquitaine's feelings of resentment towards Louis the Pious in the winter of 831–832 reveal, when Louis received his son less favourably at court because of his disobedience.[63] Participant in multiple humiliating submissions to Louis the Pious himself, gleefully depicted by Thegan and Nithard, and with over three decades' experience of the staging of Carolingian family gatherings, Lothar doubtless understood the power of the visible expression of unity and acknowledgement of partnership.[64] Three incidents suggest that Lothar and Louis II regularly used such visible expressions of harmony when they met.

In spring 847, Louis II visited Francia to attend the major council which decided on the collective Frankish response to the devastating Saracen raid Rome in August 846, and from which an important capitulary survives.[65] Louis is twice named prominently in the capitulary. The

---

[60] See Nelson, 'Opposition to Charlemagne'; Noble, 'The revolt of King Bernard' and Nelson, 'A tale of two princes'.

[61] *Annales Bertiniani*, ed. Grat, s.a. 855, p. 70.

[62] *Annales Bertiniani*, ed. Grat, s.a. 856, p. 73. I am grateful to the audience at the Leeds IMC in 2016 for drawing the implications of the 856 dispute to my attention.

[63] *Annales Bertiniani*, ed. Grat, s.a. 831, p. 5: *Pippinus … ad eum [Louis] uenit, quem domnus imperator propter inoboedientiam illius non tam benigne suscepit quam antea solitus fuerat*; 832, p. 5: *Indignatus Pippinus quod a patre non fuerat honorifice susceptus …*

[64] See Thegan, *Gesta Hludowici imperatoris*, ed. Tremp, c. 55, p. 250, emphasising the visibility of Lothar's 834 submission to the army, and Nithard, *Historiae*, ed. Lauer, I, 7, p. 30, for the 839 submission, echoing the prodigal son's return in Luke 15, 12. Lothar also submitted publicly to his father in 831: *Annales Bertiniani*, ed. Grat, s.a. 831, pp. 3–4.

[65] *Concilia aevi Karolini 843–859*, no. 12, pp. 133–9.

first clause of the capitulary carefully emphasised Louis II's part in the decisions, made when 'we and our most dear son' came together in 'common counsel'.[66] Louis was also assigned to lead the army into Benevento against the Saracens: this involved leading not only the entire Italian army but also contingents from the armies from Francia, Burgundy and Provence.[67] The campaign was reported in the *Annals of St-Bertin*,[68] and as Clemens Gantner has argued elsewhere, proved important in developing Louis II's authority in Italy.[69] Again, we see Louis able to take a visible role at the heart of events concerning Italy (and indeed having a prominent position in the affairs of the Middle Kingdom to the north of the Alps).

In May 847, Lothar visited Italy, as Herbert Zielinski demonstrated when he published a fourteenth-century copy of a *placitum* dated 12 May 847.[70] This document is of interest for reasons including its reference to Leo, the judge and *vassus* of both emperors, but in particular in this context because it shows that while Lothar was in Pavia, he and his son acted as judges together: a very visible expression of unity and the qualities of good rulership, which also recognised Louis' status as king and judge.[71]

The final moment occurred in 851. At Gondreville in 851, Lothar and Louis issued their only joint charter, for Gisela, Lothar's daughter and Louis' sister, who was in the convent of San Salvatore Brescia.[72] Louis had now been crowned emperor, and we see here Lothar and Louis managing family affairs and the important spiritual relationship with San Salvatore together. Lothar is naturally named first, but it is perhaps not too fanciful to see this act as a marker of Louis' new responsibility, as well as harmony between father and son. So, whatever the tensions there may have been behind the scenes, whenever our sources allow us to see Lothar and Louis together, on these public occasions at least, the 'mood

---

[66] *Concilia aevi Karolini 843–859*, no. 12, c. 1, p. 135: Quia divina pietas *nos et karissimum filium nostrum ad commune colloquium* pervenire concessit, prudentie devotionique vestre, de quibus hic tractavimus et definivimus, breviter intimavimus. (My emphasis)

[67] *Concilia aevi Karolini 843–859*, no. 12, c. 9, p. 137: Decretum quoque et confirmatum habemus, ut karissimus filius noster cum omni exercitu Italiae et parte ex Francia, Burgundia atque Provincia in Beneventum proficantur ...; a list of benefice holders and those in the three armies follows c. 13, pp. 138–9.

[68] *Annales Bertiniani* 848, ed. Grat, p. 55. On the campaign, see Kasten, *Königssöhne und Königsherrschaft*, pp. 398–9.

[69] Clemens Gantner, work in progress.   [70] Zielinski, 'Ein unbeachteter Italienzug'.

[71] Zielinski, 'Ein unbeachteter Italienzug', p. 6: ... ad aures domni piissimi Hlotharii augusti et Lodouicus precelentissimus filio eius rex Longuobardorum notescet ...

[72] D Lo I 115, pp. 265–6 (8.9.851). On San Salvatore, Brescia, see Fischer Drew, 'Italian monasteries'.

music' was of harmony and appropriate collaboration, with an honourable place assured for the son beside the father.

Lothar and Louis II's successful partnership was achieved through careful management, good staging and doubtless a degree of good luck, which helped remove the pinch points that were most likely to trigger rebellion. Factors including a tight-knit elite that spanned both courts added stability to the partnership. Lothar I continued to take an active interest in Italian affairs, indeed seeming to shape his itinerary at least twice to facilitate contacts with his close Italian advisors. These people, the bishops in particular, gave Lothar the means to keep an eye on events in Italy and check any undesirable initiatives by Louis. But Lothar also publicly affirmed Louis' status when they met and was willing to delegate power and eventually acknowledge Louis as his co-emperor and partner in rule, especially after 851. Thus Lothar made available a place in the realm that was substantial enough, and honourable enough, to satisfy Louis. In turn, Louis II never faced an acute threat to his inheritance or tensions introduced by rivalries with his brothers or the renegotiation of an inheritance. Once a son had married and developed a following, the interests of the group around him clearly played a very important part in decisions to rebel or not, as Lothar's own career had shown. As we have seen, Louis took over the ruling group associated with Lothar, who had a vested interest in loyalty to both father and son. Had Lothar I lived beyond 855, we might speculate that the partnership between father and son could have become more fraught, as Angilberga's influence came more strongly into the picture.[73] But in the shorter term, obedience gained visible results for Louis II, in the form of added status and independence of manoeuvre.

Overall, this suggests that Lothar and Louis II's partnership should be included among the more successful Carolingian father-son relationships. Certain themes present in Lothar and Louis' relationship can be linked to the success or failure of relationships between Carolingian fathers and Italian subkings more widely. These may be summed up as positive factors assisting the father's control, and negative factors prompting the son (or nephew) to rebel. The presence or absence of a threat to the status of the son or nephew (especially a married son with children), the character of the junior ruler's relationship with the senior ruler's leading men and with his own aristocratic supporters, the demonstration of appropriate respect towards the son's position, and the delegation of some responsibilities, or a reasonable hope of achieving this,

---

[73] For a discussion of Angilberga's role, see Bougard, 'La cour et le gouvernement de Louis II', pp. 260–5.

seem to have played a part in ensuring success or triggering problems in Pippin of Italy's relationship with Charlemagne, and Bernard of Italy's relationship with his uncle Louis respectively.

Thanks in part to Einhard, Charlemagne has generally had a good press as a father.[74] Of his adult sons, only Pippin the Hunchback, who was being managed out of the family, rebelled. Nevertheless, internal tensions needed careful management at times and were clearly felt strongly by Charlemagne's sons, while Charlemagne's control of his family was achieved at some personal cost to his daughters and perhaps Charles the Younger in particular.[75] Pippin of Italy's relationship with Charlemagne seems to have been more straightforward. Like Charles the Younger and Louis, he did receive public recognition of his status through his leadership of armies, role in ruling Italy and prominent place in depictions of the court, such as the poem on the war against the Avars.[76] While there were limits to Charlemagne's delegation of power (for example, Pippin issued no charters and struck no coins), Pippin did play a part in the exercise of justice, and his inheritance of Italy was acknowledged in the *Divisio regnorum*.[77] On Pippin's death in 811, Charlemagne subsequently acknowledged his grandson Bernard as king of Italy in 812. Charlemagne's close relationship with key Italian bishops and his prestige as the conqueror of Italy may have helped assure his position with the Italian nobility, too.

In contrast, Louis the Pious is not remembered for his successful family management. Perhaps as a result of the doubtful position in which he himself had been placed regarding his succession to Charlemagne in 811–813, Louis decided to offer his sons certainty early on. His *Ordinatio imperii* of 817 clarified the superior position of Lothar I as the eldest son, but had the potential to generate tensions between his three sons. Its exclusion of Bernard of Italy also represented an outright threat to Bernard and his children's position, and triggered Bernard's rebellion.[78]

---

[74] Einhard, *Vita Karoli*, ed. Pertz and Waitz, c. 18–19, pp. 21–5; see Davis, *Charlemagne's Practice of Empire*, pp. 415–23, for Charlemagne's hesitations when it came to the succession.

[75] Pippin's rebellion: Nelson, 'Opposition to Charlemagne'; tensions: Nelson, 'The siting of the council at Frankfort', p. 160; Astronomer, *Vita Hludowici imperatoris*, ed. Tremp, c. 20, p. 342; daughters: Nelson, 'Women at the court of Charlemagne'. Hammer, 'Christmas Day 800', assembles the evidence for Charles the Younger's activities and influence.

[76] *De Pippini regis victoria avarica*, ed. Dümmler; see also n. 26 above.

[77] *Divisio regnorum*, MGH Capit. I, ed. Boretius, no. 45, pp. 126–30, c. 2, p. 127, and c. 5, p. 128, providing for the inheritance of grandsons; on Pippin, see Stoffella, chapter 9, in this volume.

[78] *Ordinatio imperii*, MGH Capit. I., ed. Boretius, no. 136, pp. 270–3, c. 17, p. 273; on Bernard, see Noble, 'The revolt of King Bernard'; de Jong, *Penitential State*, pp. 28–9.

Although Italian bishops and abbots continued to travel regularly to Francia, Louis may have had problems in asserting his authority in Italy through his lesser knowledge of the political situation and key players. A late and partisan source, the *Epitaphium Arsenii*, implies that Lothar and Wala found the kingdom in some disarray in 822.[79] In the second half of the 820s, Louis chose to keep Lothar I at his side, apparently following Charlemagne's model with Charles the Younger. Louis' specific problems with Lothar from the later 820s seem to have been triggered by a combination of uncertainty about the succession situation among his adult sons (all now with sons of their own), and deep divisions among the aristocracy. Nithard's emphasis on Lothar's aristocratic supporters is a useful reminder of the role that the magnates might play. Sons, just like fathers, had to respond to the concerns of their key supporters. The result of the dismissal of Hugh and Matfrid in 828 after the disastrous Spanish March campaign, and the rise of Bernard of Septimania's party at Louis' court, seems to have meant an irreconcilable faction of the aristocracy was aligned with Lothar against Louis the Pious.[80] Though Louis the Pious regained much of his authority after the deposition of 833–834, he was never able to assert control within Italy as a result of this strongly divided aristocracy and perhaps also his own lack of deep roots in Italy:[81] after 834, Louis' key Italian supporters such as Bishop Ratold of Verona and Boniface of Tuscany remained in Francia.[82] In Louis' case the interests of the Frankish aristocracy also played an important part in stimulating division, as opposed to creating cohesion between the kingdom of Italy and the imperial centre.

Carolingian visions of successful rule under God placed fathers and sons working in harmony at the heart of the kingdom. In reality, Carolingian father-son relationships were hard work. At their best, they offered an effective means of rule and achieved the successful delegation of power, with tangible gains for both parties. At their worst, poor father-son relationships could hamstring a reign, as Louis the Pious found.

---

[79] Paschasius Radbertus, *Epitaphium Arsenii*, ed. Dümmler, I.26–28, pp. 55–9; Jarnut, 'Ludwig der Fromme', pp. 350–1, suggests the unsuccessful campaigns against Liudewit helped trigger both Louis' eventual despatch of Lothar and the claims of corruption and injustice.

[80] See de Jong, *Penitential State*, p. 39 on the impact of Hugh and Matfrid's 828 dismissal, and pp. 52–3 on Louis' 'strict handling of real enemies'.

[81] On Louis' last years, see Nelson, 'The last years' and de Jong, *Penitential State*, pp. 52–8. See Nithard, *Historiae*, ed. Lauer, I, 3, p. 32, 4, pp. 14–16, 5, pp. 20–4, 7, pp. 30–2, for recurring references to Lothar's supporters.

[82] Hlawitschka, *Franken*, p. 54.

A degree of luck and good management could help rulers avoid the main pitfalls. The presence of secular and ecclesiastic magnates who helped bridge the gap between the courts, and who were interested in retaining unity, the gradual delegation of power and the public display of mutual respect ensured that, as far as we can tell, in the period up to 855, Lothar and Louis II were that rare thing, a contented – or at any rate, a silently discontented – Carolingian father-son partnership.

11 A King in Training?

Louis II of Italy and His Expedition to Rome in 844

Clemens Gantner

This chapter is dedicated to the earliest years of the rule of Louis II, later sole Carolingian emperor from 855 onwards until his death in 875. Louis was the eldest son of Emperor Lothar I (817/840–855) and his wife, Ermengard. In 840, he was nominated king of Italy by his grandfather Louis the Pious, shortly before the latter's death led to years of chaos and civil war between his sons, which would be resolved in 843 by the Treaty of Verdun. Italy had long been Lothar's powerbase, but after 843 he left it more and more in Louis' hands.[1]

Louis was probably born around the year 825[2] and was thus still quite young when he became king, being in reality a sub-ruler under his father. As ruler of Italy and thereby representative-in-residence of the Carolingian family in this part of the empire, it was within his competence to deal with Rome and the pope.[3] The precedent for this had been set by his father and grandfather, respectively, in the early 820s, when Lothar had been tasked with dealing with severe unrest in Rome. A settlement was reached and the so-called *Constitutio Romana* promulgated in 824.[4]

This document lay at the heart of developments in the year 844. At the end of January, the long-time pope Gregory IV had died. He had been in office since 827, an exceptionally long and chequered pontificate. He had also at times been a close associate of Lothar I, but their relations had certainly suffered under the suspicion of Lothar having used the pope in his power play against his father in 834 at the standoff that became known as the 'Field of lies'.[5] Still, he had at least been a pope well acquainted with the Carolingians. His successor, the priest Sergius, was

---

[1] Bougard, 'Ludovico II'. See also Zielinski, 'Ludwig II. von Italien'. On Louis' early years, see also Chapter 10 in this volume.

[2] Bougard, 'Ludovico II': 'Nato tra l'822 e l'825.'

[3] I have written elsewhere about the later developments, especially Louis' policy vis-à-vis Popes Nicholas I (858–867) and Hadrian II (867–872): see soon Gantner, 'Louis II and Rome'.

[4] Noble, *Republic*, pp. 308–22.   [5] Scherer, *Der Pontifikat Gregors IV.*, esp. pp. 133–201.

not. He was also swiftly consecrated and enthroned without awaiting the approval of the emperor, required by the *Constitutio* of 824. The Romans thereby openly contravened the agreement with the emperor.[6] Lothar, who had been at the head of the Carolingian contingent at Rome twenty years earlier, chose to dispatch his still quite young son Louis there to set things right.[7] The young king was not sent alone, but rather together with high-ranking men from Lothar's entourage and with other family members. The most prominent person was certainly Louis' great-uncle Drogo, archbishop of Metz.

The Fellowship of the King

Drogo was an illegitimate son of Charlemagne, and half-brother of the late emperor Louis the Pious.[8] There are several reasons why his appointment as co-leader of the mission to Rome is remarkable, all linked to Drogo's history with Lothar. Drogo had supported his half-brother Louis the Pious against the various revolts of his sons. He had been on Louis' side in 830 and he had remained loyal even on the 'Field of lies' in 834. It is no coincidence that Louis' re-crowning as emperor in 835 took place at Drogo's see in Metz. Drogo is nonetheless seen as one of the main forces behind the reconciliation of Louis with *all* his sons, even with Lothar in 839. After Louis' death in 840, Drogo must have at first accepted Lothar's claim to supremacy. Even after Lothar's heavy defeat at Fontenoy in 841, Drogo seems to have stayed loyal to Lothar rather than joining one of his other nephews, unlike his brother Hugh, who chose to follow Charles the Bald instead. At some point in 842, however, Drogo also defected to Charles; while Lothar made donations to Drogo's own monastery of St Arnulf in Metz in 841, it was Charles who did so a year later.[9] Interestingly, however, after an agreement was reached soon thereafter and the Treaty of Verdun concluded in 843, Metz was firmly back in Lothar's middle kingdom and Drogo seems to have been on quite good terms with the emperor again. We get the impression that Drogo was a figure bearing considerable influence and

---

[6] Noble, *Republic*, pp. 308–24 on the *Constitutio*. See *LP*, Sergius II, trans. Davis 3, pp. 71–2.

[7] Pseudo-Liutprand, *Sergius II*, *PL*, vol. 129, col. 1244: 'Hence, a rumour of his consecration eventually reached the ears of the aforementioned emperor; he was infuriated by such arrogance and sent his son Louis and Drogo, bishop of Metz, to Rome with a sizable army.' (My translation)

[8] On his early career, see Depreux, *Prosopographie*, pp. 163–7.

[9] Glansdorff, 'Drogon'. On Charles' donation, see ibid., p. 968.

constantly furthering his own agenda. It is therefore somewhat surprising that of all the possible influential clerics from Lothar's realm it was Drogo who was chosen to accompany the young king to Rome.

Besides Drogo, Louis travelled with a remarkable entourage, as the *LP* informs us rather belatedly towards the end of its historical section. The delegation was co-led, it seems, by the archbishops of Milan and Ravenna and consisted of twenty more named bishops, all from the kingdom of Italy.[10] The *LP* expresses a quite high degree of consternation that these churchmen evidently acted against the interests of the Roman Church – but, as Raymond Davis has rightly pointed out alongside his translation of this section, all of them held office within the sphere of Carolingian influence and none of the bishops mentioned was from the diocese of Rome.[11] What is more, while technically the Roman bishops had always hoped to extend their influence into the diocese of Ravenna and onto Ravenna itself, as well as into the duchy of Spoleto, these claims still did not correspond with the reality on the ground.[12]

In addition to the northern Italian bishops, several laymen, all of them addressed as counts, are also mentioned and were certainly leaders of the army that accompanied Louis: Boso, Adelchis, John, Vuldo, Bernard, Wifrid and Maurinus. Of these, only Vuldo is unattested elsewhere, whereas all others have been tentatively identified.[13] Boso quite certainly came from the family known as the Bosonids, which was closely connected to the Carolingians. The family seems to have had their main strongholds in Upper Burgundy, including in the Jura area, but some were certainly active in Italy too.[14] The John mentioned was count of

---

[10] See *LP* ii, Sergius II, ed. Duchesne, pp. 89–90, trans. Davis 3, p. 80, with further comments on the location of some of the sees.

[11] *LP*, Sergius II, trans. Davis 3, p. 80, n. 24.

[12] The next test of just how far the jurisdiction of the Roman bishop could reach was only really undertaken by Pope Nicholas I two decades later; see Herbers, 'Papst Nikolaus I. mit Erzbischof Johannes VII', and Gantner, 'Louis II and Rome'.

[13] Hlawitschka, *Franken*, pp. 237 and 292, speculates that Vuldo could have been count in the area of Piedmont or Liguria, as we lack reliable sources from there.

[14] See Bouchard, 'Bosonids'. It is unclear whether this Boso is to be identified as Boso the Elder (active in the first half of the ninth century) or his son of the same name (d. 878). We may express a slight preference for the elder Boso (see Bouchard, 'Bosonids', p. 409, fig. 2 and pp. 416–17, with n. 31), however, mainly because he is mentioned first in the list, which could imply seniority among the rank of counts. The fact that the younger Boso operated mainly in Italy also makes him a possible candidate (Hlawitschka, *Franken*, pp. 158–62, sees the younger Boso at work). On the hierarchy in such endeavours, see Gantner, 'Saracen attack'. See also *Konzilien der karolingischen Teilreiche*, ed. Hartmann, no. 12, pp. 133–9 for the capitulary of 847 (there 846) and Zielinski, 'Reisegeschwindigkeit'.

Seprio and at times *comes palatii* of the Italian kingdom.[15] Count
Bernard, probably of Verona, will certainly have been the same officer
who in 855 took part in the spectacularly failed mission to install the
priest Anastasius as pope instead of the already elected Benedict III.[16]
Wifred was count of Piancenza.[17] The most interesting counts were,
however, the two remaining ones, who may have belonged to the same
family: Adelchis was the count of Parma, attested since the 830s;[18]
Maurinus possibly stemmed from the same clan and was the count
palatine of the same name.[19] Both men were the Italian proponents of
the Supponid family, which possessed large landholdings in the Po
Plain. Before Louis, they had already supported his father, Lothar, and
very probably also his grandfather Louis the Pious.[20] Adelchis was to
become Louis' father-in-law in 853/860 and the whole family
would remain a cornerstone of the ruler's policy.[21] Adelchis' son
Suppo (II) seems to have in turn married the daughter of count
Wifrid. We can thus see here an influential group of northern Italian
noblemen, a network that Louis II would be able to rely on throughout
his reign. With Boso as the possible exception, the rank of counts in our
LP list was again dominated by 'Italians', all of whom belonged to
important Frankish families and who were here, of course, to support
their king and to ingratiate themselves with the new ruler and heir
apparent to the imperial crown. Endeavours like this expedition were
always also exercises in social cohesion.[22] The entourage served not
only to ensure the glorious appearance of the Italian army, however.
There was also practical value to Lothar's staging of the event: these
officers from northern Italy, certainly among the most important proponents of Carolingian rule on the peninsula, were also prepared to lead the
Italian army into battle, if necessary, as we shall see towards the end of
this chapter.

---

[15] Hlawitschka, *Franken*, pp. 212–13: Johannes *comes*.

[16] Hlawitschka, *Franken*, pp. 148–51: Bernardus. On Anastasius and his family's
involvement with Louis II, see Gantner, 'Louis II and Rome', and Arnaldi, 'Anastasio
Bibliotecario', as well as Perels, *Papst Nikolaus I und Anastasius*.

[17] Hlawitschka, *Franken*, pp. 287–8.

[18] *LP*, Sergius II, trans. Davis 3, p. 80, n. 28. Hlawitschka, *Franken*, pp. 110–11: Adelgisus
I. Bougard, 'Supponides', esp. p. 384. See also Bougard, 'Engelberga'.

[19] Bougard, 'Supponides', p. 384. Hlawitschka, *Franken*, pp. 236–37.

[20] See Hlawitschka, *Franken*, esp. pp. 299–309, and Bougard, 'Supponides'.

[21] On this problematic marriage, see Gantner, 'Common enemies', and Gantner, 'Ludwig
II. und Byzanz'.

[22] This can be shown even more clearly for the next expedition staged in 848; see Gantner,
'Saracen attack'.

What Happened in 844? A Short Source-Critique

There are three main sources that provide us with information about Louis II's 844 'visit' to Rome. First and foremost, there is the *Liber Pontificalis* (*LP*), the entry for Pope Sergius II (844–847) to be exact. It contains by far the longest account, but gives suspiciously little detail on some issues or does not mention them at all. The author of the part relevant for the first year of Sergius' pontificate was an insider from the papal administration, whose objective it was to write a text favourable to the pope and the Roman mainstream of the time. Hence, we find therein many half-truths and lacunae that can be identified by virtue of other sources. Furthermore, Sergius' rule sparked strong resistance in the Eternal City towards the end, which is reflected in an alternative and possibly enlarged version of the Vita Sergii, which, albeit sadly lost, can be partly reconstructed. Nonetheless, the analysis below will largely follow the chronology provided by the anonymous Roman writer.

Luckily, we have two more sources that tell us about the main achievements of both parties. First, there is the so-called *Pseudo-Liutprand*, a text stemming from the eleventh century that has often been regarded as an epitome of *Liber Pontificalis*. It is, however, far more than that, combining several other sources of information with a text of the *LP* that was more complete in respect to the ninth century than the versions that have come down to us – true especially of the end of the entry for Sergius II.[23] The other well-informed source is the *Annals of St Bertin*, at this point written by Prudentius of Troyes;[24] his account is both contemporary and usually knowledgeable about Italian matters. But it was certainly written far away from the events and shows a West Frankish bias.

Arrival in Rome

According to the *LP*, as soon as the Frankish army entered the papal *res publica*, which our author lets begin as far north as Bologna,[25] it started to plunder and pillage.[26] The *LP* is prone to depict actions disadvantageous to the pope in the most negative way possible, but the mission to Rome

---

[23] This section does not really concern us here, see Gantner, 'Saracen attack', and Gantner, *Freunde Roms*, pp. 251–2 and 307, as well as Levison, 'Papstgeschichte des Pseudo-Liudprand', and Jasper, 'Papstgeschichte des Pseudo-Liudprand', pp. 54–73.

[24] *Annales Bertiniani*, ed. Grat, Viellard and Clémencet, trans. Nelson, *The Annals of St Bertin*.

[25] For a definition of the papal *res publica*, the area under direct papal control, see Noble, *Republic*, and Gantner, 'Romana urbs'.

[26] *LP* II, Sergius II, c. 8, ed. Duchesne, p. 87.

may still have given the impression of a punitive expedition, though, as we will see, this may not have been its sole purpose.[27] The *LP* does not obfuscate the reasons, clearly connecting the start of the expedition with Lothar being informed that the Romans had consecrated a new pope without his consent. Indeed, this convention had been adhered to by the Romans in 827/8, with the result that Gregory IV had had to wait several months for his consecration.[28] The Romans may have felt that the time was ripe in 844 for getting rid of this embarrassing custom by simply ignoring it, maybe thinking that after the civil war in the Frankish kingdoms between 841 and 843 the Carolingians would be less inclined to enforce the regulation. If so, they did not consider Lothar's special personal interest in Italian affairs in general and in the Roman legal situation in particular. The civil war may, however, have been part of the reason why the emperor did not go south himself – he will still have been engaged in organizing the remaining parts of his realm and will also have felt the need to re-consolidate his power north of the Alps. But there was more to it than that. His eldest son, Louis, was expected to earn his spurs through this mission, something which would, as we have seen, prove a difficult assignment. It resembled the task faced by Lothar himself in the 820s, when he was the young ruler of Italy. It may even have been chosen on account of this nice parallelism, something not uncommon for Carolingian rulers.[29]

Lothar will have known very well that if the Franks were to make concessions to the papacy at a point when Rome seemed to be in relative safety and a normal transition between popes could be expected, the Romans would take the consecration of Sergius as a precedent and try to diminish the emperor's influence in Rome even more. Hence, Louis II's expedition was certainly meant as a stern intervention to safeguard Carolingian interests.[30]

After the first infringements had been committed on papal territory, the *LP* reports that a thunderstorm hit the Carolingian camp. Advisors of Drogo are said to have been killed by lightning strike. The Franks, however, were not receptive to this clear sign from God and chose to approach the Eternal City with alacrity. There they were received with all the honours due a king of Italy; in fact, the *LP* goes to some length to assure the reader that all requirements were indeed met.[31]

---

[27] *RI*, Zielinski, nos. 21–23, p. 9.   [28] Bonaccorsi, 'Gregorio IV'.

[29] In 799, for example, Pippin, the young king of Italy, was sent to welcome Pope Leo III on his way north in nearly the same way as his father, Charlemagne, had been in 753, when Pope Stephen II was travelling north. See Nelson, 'Charlemagne – pater optimus?', and Gantner, 'The silence of the Popes'.

[30] *RI*, Zielinski, nos. 21–23, p. 9.   [31] *LP* II, Sergius II, ed. Duchesne, p. 88.

The author also tells us that 'King Louis, the moment he noticed those holy crosses and standards coming to meet him, became cheerful and mightily glad.'[32] This innocently formulated sentence is clearly designed to portray the young king as a positive figure and thus to separate him in a way from his own army and entourage, to whom the pillaging is attributed instead. It also serves the narrative to depict the young ruler as a little naïve – and to show Pope Sergius to be fully on top of the situation. All these insinuations from the papal side were conscious and probably unmerited. But that does not mean that the author's observation has to be untrue: both sides, the Carolingians *and* the papacy, had probably not planned for a military confrontation.

The *adventus* description in the *LP* has been scrutinized by researchers, who have shown it to be a near identical copy of the one given for the first arrival of Charlemagne in 774 in the very same source.[33] This fine show of Roman traditionalism was kept up until the Franks reached St Peter's, where they were received with all due honours by the pope, accompanied by the Roman clergy and delegations of the branches of the Roman militia. Just when Louis was about to enter the church, the *LP* recounts that 'one of the troops [*unus de exercitibus*], in the sight of all the Franks, was seized by a demon and much troubled'.[34] In reaction, the pope immediately ordered the silver doors of St Peter's[35] to be shut and gave a long speech:

If you have come here with pure purpose and sincere intent and for the safety of the State and of the whole City and of this church, enter these doors at my bidding. But if you have not, these doors will be opened to you neither by me nor by my licence.[36]

The section leaves out whether the man belonged to the Frankish *exercitus* or the Roman militia, even though research has so far assumed that the soldier having, as it seems, some form of fit, was part of the

---

[32] *LP*, Sergius II, trans. Davis 3, p. 78 (ed. Duchesne, p. 88).

[33] See the analysis in Hack, *Empfangszeremoniell*, pp. 359–61. There is one significant deviation, when the author of the chapter on Sergius describes the ritual as *mos ... imperatorem aut regem susicipendum* without comparing it to the advent of an exarch or patriarch; see ibid., p. 298. The account was thus in all probability abridged. See also Twyman, *Papal Ceremonial*, pp 74–5.

[34] *LP* II, Sergius II, ed. Duchesne, p. 88, trans. Davis 3, pp. 78–9.

[35] This obviously happened in the atrium of the church. The silver doors were the middle entrance to the basilica proper. To get a grasp of the 'geography', the foldout plan by Tiberio Alfarno included in McKitterick, *Old Saint Peter's* is invaluable: the silver doors can be found as number 130. On the plan, see ibid., pp. 18–20.

[36] *LP* II, Sergius II, ed. Duchesne, p. 88, trans. Davis 3, pp. 78–79.

Frankish contingent.[37] Granted, the Frankish army is called *exercitus* when Louis' expedition is first introduced, while the Roman troops are said to have been ordered according to the so-called *scholae* of the *militia* in c.9.[38] Apart from that, there exists no real clue in the text that would confirm that the unfortunate soldier was, in fact, part of the Frankish army. Indeed, the whole incident appears suspiciously well orchestrated, with people standing ready at the doors to shut them immediately and with the pope having prepared just the right statement. The context, with all the Franks explicitly identified as bystanders, seems rather to point to the Roman troops instead, which would certainly fit the outcome of the episode. Louis was caught off guard and had to assert immediately that 'he had come with no evil purpose or any perverseness or bad intention'.[39] The seizure of the unnamed soldier fitted the papal scheme so well that that the whole incident may very well have been staged to impress the young ruler.[40]

The Negotiations

This was a suboptimal start for the negotiations which were to ensue in Rome in the coming days. The *LP* interestingly puts Louis' eventual crowning *before* these negotiations, but our other two sources, one contemporary, the other likely based on contemporary information, give a different impression: both the *Annals of St Bertin*[41] and *Pseudo-Liutprand*[42] place the events in the order we would expect. It is intriguing too that the *LP* never tells us what was discussed in Rome on the days in question.

We can only gather the following information from our main source. First, it names and incriminates at this point Drogo of Metz and with him all the leaders of the Frankish expedition – that is, those we encountered in the list already analysed above. All of those mentioned here acted against the church and good customs in the eyes of the *LP* author. The *LP* tries to make this seem even more of a scandal by showing that all but one of the bishops named belonged to the Italian ecclesiastical province. As we have seen, this information is misleading, as all these bishops came

---

[37] See, for example, Hack, *Empfangszeremoniell*, p. 360, or *RI* I,3,1, ed. Zielinski, no. 24, p. 10.

[38] *LP* II, Sergius II, ed. Duchesne, p. 87. [39] *LP*, Sergius II, trans. Davis 3, p. 79.

[40] Haller, *Papsttum*, pp. 29–30, states that the stricken soldier was Frankish (without further discussing the point), but rightly asserts that Sergius used the situation to gain the upper hand. He downplays Louis' accomplishments too much, however.

[41] *AB* a. 844, ed. Grat, pp. 45–6, trans. Nelson, p. 57.

[42] Pseudo-Liutprand, *Sergius II*, *PL*, vol. 129, col. 1244.

from sees that were not under direct Roman rule. The *LP* is deliberately unclear here, a strategy frequently employed. There is only one person conspicuously missing from the list of people who acted against the Roman church – the young king himself. There are two possibilities here. It may be that this is a realistic account, and Louis was, indeed, largely excluded from actual dealings with the papal side. While this is possible, the fact that he was nominal leader of the expedition makes it appear unlikely. The other option would be that the *LP* consciously tried not to tarnish the king's image in the text. This is a strategy that was deployed several times with respect to Louis' career, which saw many a clash with the papacy after 844: especially in 855 (support for the anti-pope Anastasius), 861 (support for Archbishop John of Ravenna), 864 (siege of Rome) and 867, when Spoletan troops even entered Rome and spread chaos in the city.[43] In the reports on all these events, Louis was never directly blamed for any misbehaviour of the Franks, so it should not surprise us that the *LP* refrains from doing so. Rather, a precedent was being created.

The second piece of information the *LP* relates merely constitutes the papal view on the outcome of negotiations – in short, the pope 'won' hands down, convincing his adversaries with his salvific words.[44] Again, this story is realistic, but it probably leaves a lot out. The pope certainly won one crucial part of the diplomatic exchange: apparently, the Franks had tried to get the Romans to swear an oath not only to Emperor Lothar, to whom they had already sworn fealty anyway and which was compulsory according to the *Constitutio Romana*, but also to Louis II. Louis, however, was not co-emperor yet, which made this request very problematic for the Roman side. Louis was king of the Lombards, and Rome was certainly not part of the Lombard kingdom. By swearing to the Lombard king, Rome would have accepted a legal subordination to that kingdom – something the papacy had fought to avoid since the time of Gregory the Great, and more intensively throughout the eighth century.[45] It is also clear that the Frankish side was well aware of this. Therefore, the request of an enlarged oath was either meant as a punishment or it was simply used as a maximum demand and thus as a tool to extort other concessions instead. Both other sources on the negotiations also provide us with short but partly insightful information about what happened. The very brief entry for Sergius in Pseudo-Liutprand relates that:

[43] Gantner, 'Louis II and Rome'.   [44] *LP* II, Sergius II, ed. Duchesne, p. 90.
[45] See Gantner, *Freunde Roms*, esp. pp. 139–218. Pohl, 'Papsttum und Langobarden'.

[Louis and Drogo] made the same Romans swear fealty to the emperor and, after a long debate, confirmed the aforementioned Sergius in his see: he [in turn] anointed the aforementioned son of the emperor as King of the Lombards.[46]

The *Annals of St Bertin* in turn inform us that:

..., when the negotiations had been concluded, [Sergius] consecrated Louis king by anointing him, and invested him with a sword. Bishop Drogo was designated papal vicar in the regions of the Gauls and Germanies.[47]

What we gather from this is that the pontificate of Sergius, contrary to what the *LP* wants us to believe, was not a priori accepted by the Frankish delegation, even though the impressive display of ecclesiastical power at the reception and at St Peter's would certainly have favourably influenced its stance on the matter. To keep the consecrated pope in office was thus already the great achievement of the Roman side, together, of course, with the refusal to swear allegiance to a king of the Lombards. The Frankish side, on the other hand, also achieved its most important goals: obviously, Louis was either supposed to be crowned by the pope from the outset or it came to be deemed an appropriate measure during the harsh negotiations. Either way, even the *Annals of Saint-Bertin*, notoriously unsympathetic to this branch of the Carolingian family, recorded this as a success. As our only source on this point, it also relates that Drogo was appointed papal vicar in the Frankish empire north of the Alps, which also came with the missionary territories in the east and north. Although our only testimony comes from Prudentius, a northerner, we can safely assume that this role was indeed granted, given that it was a largely ceremonial honour. The *LP* author could not mention this appointment, because he had already established Drogo as arch-villain at this point in the narrative. The silence of the *LP* may in turn account for Pseudo-Liutprand not providing this information either. The latter source provides us with another bit of information, however: the terms in Rome were mostly dictated by the Carolingian side (Louis and Drogo *fecerunt* and *confirmaverunt*). Moreover, even though none of the sources says so explicitly, it is clear that the validity of the *Constitutio Romana* was no longer disputed by the Roman side – this is what Pseudo-Liutprand means, when he refers to a confirmation of Sergius only after a serious

---

[46] Pseudo-Liutprand, *Sergius II, PL*, col. 1244 (not translated part in brackets): (*Unde, cum ejus consecrationis rumor ad praedicti aures imperatoris pervenit; indignatus de hac praesumptione, filium suum Ludovicum et Drogonem Metensem episcopum cum magno exercitu Romam direxit. Qui post multa damna Romanis illata,*) *ipsos Romanos imperatori fidelitatem jurare fecerunt, et praedictum Sergium post multas contentiones in sede demum confirmaverunt: qui praedictum filium imperatoris in regem Longobardorum unxit.*

[47] Prudentius, *AB* 844, ed. Grat, p. 45ff., trans. Nelson, p. 57.

debate. Granted, the *Constitutio* was technically not even upheld at the next election early in 847, but this occurred in very difficult political circumstances, after the Saracen attack on Rome.[48] From then on, it was respected until Louis' death. Apart from these issues, the cases of the deposed archbishops Ebbo of Reims and Bartholomew of Nantes were also discussed, but the two prelates were only readmitted to lay communion. Ebbo's case would still occupy Nicholas I. What Lothar and/or Drogo's interest in these cases was, is hard to tell. It may be that the ruling was a confirmation of Drogo's judgment, as he had presided at the council that deposed Ebbo.[49]

After prolonged negotiations, Louis was, as we have abundantly heard, re-crowned king of the Lombards and anointed as well. This was a novelty for someone who was already king of the Lombards, but certainly not for a Carolingian, which may have been the prime factor in this case. The *Annals of St Bertin* also tell us that he was 'invested … with a sword'.[50] As far as we know, this is likewise without precedent, certainly for a Lombard king.[51] As a symbol of lay rule and military leadership, this novelty was far from trivial, however. It is hard to say how it was understood by the parties involved. The pope was probably not investing Louis with the secular power over Italy, as this would not have been acceptable to the Frankish party. Maybe the sword symbolized rather a sort of worldly overlordship over the papal republic. This sounds improbable at first, but for one, this suzerainty would have only followed the spirit of the *Constitutio Romana*. And for another, we get a hint in that direction from a far later section of the *Annals of St Bertin*: in 877 Louis the Stammerer, son of Charles the Bald, is handed the royal insignia, amongst which is the 'sword of St Peter', by Richildis, his father's widow, when he assumes the kingship.[52] As Charles had in turn received the insignia of the Italian *regnum* in 875,[53] it seems logical that this was the very sword used in 844, with the connection to St Peter. This once, the

---

[48] Herbers, *Leo IV.*, pp. 99–104. See also Gantner, 'Saracen attack'.

[49] Glansdorff, 'Drogon', pp. 956–58. See also *LP*, *Sergius II*, trans. Davis 3, p. 81, n. 31, who, however, thinks that Lothar took an interest in reinstating Ebbo – but had that been the case, would he really have sent Drogo?

[50] Prudentius, *AB* 844, ed. Grat, pp. 45ff., trans. Nelson, p. 57.

[51] Nithard, *Historiae*, ed. Lauer I, 6, tells us that Charles the Bald was 'invested with the weapons of manhood' by his father, Louis the Pious, in 838 at the age of 15. See Nelson, 'Reign of Charles the Bald', p. 2. A sword is also mentioned at the coronation of Otto I in 936; see Widukind of Corvey, *Deeds of the Saxons*, I.2, c.1, ed. Hirsch and Lohmann, p. 66. Otto is invested with it by archbishop Hildibert of Mainz.

[52] *AB* a. 877, ed. Grat, p. 218 (*spatam quae vocatur sancti Petri*); trans. Nelson, p. 203. Note that, at this point, the annals were being continued by Hincmar, archbishop of Reims.

[53] On the events, see Arnold, *Johannes VIII.*, esp. pp. 67–76, and Nelson, 'Reign of Charles the Bald', pp. 19–22.

LP basically provides the same information, adding the detail that Louis girded himself with the sword.[54]

The *LP* also dates the event to the second Sunday after Pentecost, which would be 15 June 844. We have seen that the chronology of the *LP* vita is not reliable, but it is still probable that the date is correct. The coronation section was rather purposefully put before the negotiations by our author in order to detach the ceremony from the negotiations, thereby depriving the Frankish side of *the* key achievement – again, quite typical of this source.

Overall, the Roman 'visit', more so a visitation, must have felt like a success to the Carolingians. The papal side could likewise feel like a partial winner – and went on to depict Sergius accordingly in their historiography.

An Homage from Salerno

Once the business between the Franks and the papacy was concluded after about a week, Louis II had another important matter to attend to: he received a delegation from the southern Lombard town of Salerno, co-capital of the principality of Benevento, then headed by Prince Siconulf. The background for this is the civil war that had started among the southern Lombards after the murder of Prince Sicard in 839. One of the conspirators, Radelchis (839–851), had taken the throne in Benevento, but a sizeable portion of Beneventan Lombards rallied to Siconulf, the murdered prince's brother (and former rival).[55] Radelchis was soon forced to enlist the help of Saracen mercenaries in order to defend his position, which in turn prompted Siconulf to recruit a rival Muslim group, possibly from Spain (*al-anadalus*).[56] This led to a stalemate in 844, which Siconulf tried to overcome by enlisting the help of his brother-in-law Guy, *dux* of Spoleto, a Frank and one of the most powerful officers in the Italian kingdom of the Carolingians. It says a lot that despite family relations, Guy obviously had to be bribed with a respectable sum to help.[57]

The *LP* tells us that Siconulf was received and his right to princedom was recognized by King Louis.[58] The southern Italian chronicler Erchempert at least insinuates that bribes again played a role on this

---

[54] *LP* II, Sergius II, ed. Duchesne, p. 89, trans. Davis 3, p. 79.
[55] See Kreutz, *Before the Normans*, pp. 24–35.
[56] Erchempert, *Historiola* c. 17, ed. Berto, pp. 114–15: *Agarenos … Libicos* and *Hismaelitas Hispanos*.
[57] Erchempert, *Historiola* c. 18, ed. Berto, pp. 116–17.
[58] *LP* II, Sergius II, ed. Duchesne, p. 90.

occasion – for the onlooker in Rome, it may have been difficult to make a distinction between inducements and presents given to the overlord of the principality, which Louis technically was.[59] The Montecassinese monk reports further that Siconulf filed an official lawsuit, no doubt against Radelchis, and that he swore an oath, in all probability of fealty to Louis and/or Emperor Lothar; unfortunately our source is too unspecific here, which makes sense in the context of the overall narrative: Erchempert has Siconulf leave in anger, having achieved nothing. This may, however, have been at best a deduction drawn from hindsight, as the *LP*'s version is backed up by the *Annals of St Bertin*. Prudentius informs us that 'Siginulf, duke of the Beneventans, made his submission to Lothar along with all his men, and as a self-imposed penalty gave him 100,000 gold pieces'.[60]

We thus learn that Siconulf indeed swore to Lothar and that a fee was paid, Prudentius giving it a perfectly legal appearance, which it will have had from the Frankish point of view. After all, the rightful heir to the Beneventan throne was supported and was finally recognizing the submission of his duchy to the kingdom. This was perceived quite differently in the south, however. We must also note in passing that Siconulf is still styled as a duke in the Frankish source – a clear sign that the Franks were far from recognizing a special status for Benevento, which was instead seen as enjoying the same rank as Spoleto, having only temporarily defected. Siconulf's visit was, of course, a planned event, the prince having been informed of Louis' impending arrival in Rome. Davis even speculates that he may have attended the coronation, but this is not backed up by the *LP*.

For our purposes, it is important to note that Guy of Spoleto clearly orchestrated this part of the Roman visit. Guy was an important man. He had been a supporter of Lothar from the 830s and fled to Italy with the younger emperor after the failure of the rebellion of 834. He had been awarded the duchy of Spoleto for his services in 842 and was one of the key political forces in the Italian kingdom. His heirs would even briefly occupy the imperial throne towards the end of the century.[61] His involvement in such an important political affair is certainly not as puzzling as that of Drogo, which we discussed earlier. It was another strategic move on the part of the Carolingians. Yet again, an experienced politician with ties to the region (he had married the deceased prince's sister) was

---

[59] The Carolingians had long tried to establish real control in the south, but had so far only achieved a form of nominal suzerainty. See Gantner, 'Our common enemies'.

[60] *AB* a. 844, ed. Grat, p. 46, trans. Nelson, p. 57.

[61] See Carpegna Falconieri, 'Guido', and Hlawitschka, 'Widonen'.

aligned with the young king in order to help with a task that again demanded a certain amount of diplomacy as well as caution. In contrast to Drogo, Guy was in this case also following his own agenda, which was not necessarily aimed at ending the civil war, but rather at strengthening his own position. For his purposes, a weak Lombard principality in the south was ideal, even if it came at the cost of Saracen influence in the region.

Objective: Benevento?

It is even possible that bringing the southern 'duchy' to heel was an objective of the expedition from the outset. There are several indicators, the first and most obvious one being the staged appearance of the meeting, which was certainly pre-negotiated. Louis, as we have seen, arrived at Rome not only with a whole synod full of bishops but also, it appears, with a real army. Hence the plundering on the way south – the troops had to sustain themselves, after all. The question is, What was this army intended for? Even the *LP* makes it very clear that the Franks had no intention of attacking the city of Rome. It was not to be expected that Sergius II would pick an actual fight, seeing as he was only seeking recognition of his position. The Roman militia could, of course, have resorted to hostilities, had the Franks chosen to depose the pope – but what chance would they have had? In 855, when Benedict III was deposed and the Frankish envoys installed Anastasius as anti-pope, there is no mention of an actual *exercitus* having been necessary.[62] Why then come with an army in 844, when no subversion was to be envisaged? Only to make clear that the Franks could take Rome, should they wish to do so? We should rather assume that the Frankish side wished to keep open the option of staging a limited military operation in the south, should the need arise.[63] But why should an intervention in Benevento have been contemplated? First, the Carolingians will have wished to finally subjugate the weakened principality. Second, there had been intensive negotiations with the Byzantine empire in 842, when Louis II was betrothed to a Greek princess and Lothar and Louis were clearly urged to intervene against the Saracens. From the Byzantine point of view, the Franks were probably supposed to weaken Taranto, which had been taken by Aghlabid forces that very year. This development had led to the endangerment of ships supporting Byzantine Sicily against Muslim

---

[62] *LP* II, Benedict III, cc. 7–20, ed. Duchesne, pp. 141–4.
[63] See Gantner, 'Our common enemies', and see Ohnsorge, 'Kaiserbündnis', pp. 126–7, with n. 139.

invaders, who had already been active for a number of years. Thereby, they would also have cleaned up their own back yard.[64] Seen in this light, the question could instead be framed, Why did Louis *refrain* from intervening in the south? In all probability, the change was brought about by Siconulf and perhaps also the interaction with Guy of Spoleto. Siconulf will have promised to take care of things himself and to dismiss his own mercenaries as soon as possible.[65] It is possible that Guy undertook to assist with his forces in ensuring that the imperial appointee would be installed as duke/prince of Benevento.[66] We know from Erchempert, however, that Guy used to switch sides quickly in the southern conflict (despite being related to Siconulf), and it may well have been this reliance on the duke of Spoleto that ultimately doomed to failure Siconulf's grasp for power.[67] Also, it was simply not in Siconulf's best interest to enlist Louis' personal help in the south. He knew very well that this could lead to Carolingian overlordship, at least in the medium term. It was certainly bad enough to have involved Guy, who was following his own agenda whilst also having Carolingian interests at the back of his mind. Siconulf was thus mainly looking for symbolic support, and maybe even actively trying to keep Louis out of the south. The thing Siconulf needed most in this situation was official recognition to back up his claim to the title.

Within a few years, everyone knew better. Siconulf had failed to claim Benevento, even though he seems to have gotten close at times. The Saracen fighters had not been dismissed on either side, and in the meantime a Saracen force had firmly established itself at Bari.[68] It was these factors that led Lothar to organize a significant expedition into the south in 848, although officially it was in response to the largely unrelated

---

[64] For more details, see Gantner, 'Our common enemies', and Gantner, 'Ludwig II. von Italien und Byzanz'.

[65] That was the impression Prudentius got in Western Francia. *AB*, a. 844, trans. Nelson, pp. 57ff.: 'The Beneventans, who had previously bestowed their loyalties elsewhere, when they found out about this accepted Siginulf and applied themselves to driving the remnants of the Saracens out of their territory.'

[66] Guy did once attack the city of Benevento, though we cannot tell when exactly. See *Chronicon Salernitanum*, c. 83, trans. Matarazzo, pp. 118–19. See also Kreutz, *Before the Normans*, p. 31.

[67] Erchempert, *Historiola* c.17 and 18, ed. Berto, pp. 114–17 (giving a different chronology, which perhaps we should not trust fully). See Kreutz, *Before the Normans*, pp. 24–35, who, however, uses an older chronology on some events, like the *Divisio* of the principality, which she puts in 849, whereas 848 is far more likely (see Gantner, 'Our common enemies').

[68] Musca, *L'emirato*, pp. 15–37. As Lorenzo Bondiolo has recently shown, Bari probably fell earlier than previously thought; see his forthcoming article on 'A Carolingian frontier? Louis II, Basil I and the Muslims of Bari (840–871)'.

Saracen attack on Rome. I have dealt with Lothar's extremely interesting mandate that has come down to us elsewhere.[69] It is clear that the army's main objective was to take Benevento and rid it of the Saracens, which was duly achieved. Benevento was besieged and taken by force and all the captured Muslim troops beheaded, including their leader, Massar.[70] This event brought to an end the civil war, which was finally resolved by a partition of the southern principality. Siconulf officially received half of the duchy with his capital in Salerno, nominally as a gift from Radelchis in the so-called *Divisio principatus Beneventani*.[71] The agreement also included a strong sense of imperial suzerainty. Louis had now finished the last outstanding business from his trip to Rome four years earlier, even though he had again failed to solve the Saracen problem in the area.

Conclusion – What Did the Expedition of 844 Mean for Louis and for the Italian Kingdom?

> When all this was completed, His Excellency King Louis returned in great gladness to Pavia, from which capital he ruled since the start of his princedom. Then all the senate and people of Rome with their wives and children, glad at their deliverance from the enormous plague and yoke of tyrannical frightfulness, revered the holy prelate Sergius as the author of their salvation and the restorer of peace.[72]

This is how the *LP* 'celebrates' the departure of the Carolingian army. Once more, we see that Louis is carefully singled out as a positive figure. The Franks, however, are in the same breath criticized heavily one last time. Sergius, in an impressive display of medieval historical revisionism, is depicted as a bringer of peace, despite the fact that it had been his election that had brought about the intervention from the north. The *LP* indulges in what can only be described as spin-doctoring. Still, the short extract above shows us that relations between papal Rome and the Carolingians were now strained. After all, the Franks *had* intervened in Rome and they *had* arrived with an army. The Carolingians, on the other hand, certainly felt that the Romans had tried to trick them and were

---

[69] See Gantner, 'Saracen attack', and Gantner, 'Our common enemies'. The mandate ordered a general penitence in the realm, a levy to finance a wall around the Vatican (i.e. the Leonine Wall) and the military expedition. The document was ordered in chapters, hence its modern title 'Capitulare de expeditione contra Saracenos facienda', see *Die Konzilien der karolingischen Teilreiche 843–850*, ed. Hartmann, no. 12: 'Francia, Oktober 846', pp. 133–9.

[70] Kreutz, *Before the Normans*, p. 32.   [71] *Divisio principatus Beneventani*, ed. Martin.

[72] *LP*, Sergius II, c. 14, trans. Davis 3, pp. 82–3.

being insincere. Both positions were logical, but distrust did not prevail for long: the Saracen attack on Rome only a little over two years later resulted in a temporary closing of ranks.[73]

The expedition to Rome had also been Louis II's first real outing in his capacity as king. In some respects, it foreshadowed his later career in Italy: Louis' reign was dominated by his struggle with the Romans and the papacy, a contest for power he did prevail in after the death of Nicholas I, but with little lasting effect.[74] The young king was certainly made aware from the very first contact that dealing with the popes was hard work. Although perhaps less obvious in 844, the fight against the Saracen groups in the south and – intertwined with this – the quest for Carolingian and northern Italian dominance in that region would also acquire major importance during his kingship. Louis is, in fact, mostly remembered for this feature of his reign in contemporary and modern historiography. This issue was already alive in 844, even though no military actions were yet to be carried out in the south. The young king did, however, receive the submission of the most important potentate from the south, the man who at that point looked destined to win the civil war. That matters could not be so easily solved was a lesson Louis learned in the following years.

What makes the events of 844 special in a way is that Louis seems to have been treated like a king-in-training. In his dealings with the pope, he was guided by Drogo of Metz – maybe an odd choice, but certainly a man who could combine ecclesiastical expertise with the undisputed ability to represent Carolingian interests. He could also rely, even though this is not stressed as much in the sources, on a group of Franco-Italian counts, who, as far as we can tell, were there to lead the army of the Lombard kingdom. Possibly of equal importance at the time, but again not afforded any great prominence in the available sources, were southern affairs, of which Guy of Spoleto was chosen as guardian of Frankish interests. He was the obvious choice, as a loyal supporter of Lothar for decades and the only Frank who possessed sufficient political influence in the south. It is thus clear that Louis had not been left to face his task alone. It is highly likely that from his father's point of view he had the best possible advisors with him.[75] The downside for the young king, possibly

---

[73] Herbers, *Leo IV.*, esp. pp. 208–14 and 227–9.

[74] This view is reflected in a source written around the year 900, called *Libellus de imperatoria* potestate *in urbe Roma*, ed. Zucchetti. See an introduction to the text ibid., lxvii–cx. See also Brühl, 'Libellus de imperatoria potestate in urbe Roma', and Wickham, *Medieval Rome*, pp. 377ff. See also Gantner, 'Louis II and Rome'.

[75] See Chapter 10 in this volume for more insights into this particular father-son relationship.

around nineteen years old, was that his father had not, at the same time, handed over a lot of power. Lothar, though absent, still kept a tight grip on Italian politics. Given the developments in Rome in respect to both sets of negotiations, this was probably a wise move. Louis would soon get the opportunity to be establish himself as a ruler. In 846, he fought to defend Rome at the head of an ad hoc force inferior to the attackers. He was unsuccessful from a military perspective, but may have prevented the situation in central Italy from getting totally out of hand. In 848, he was at the head of the army that would take Benevento to end the civil war and, by dividing the principality, he was responsible for the establishment of a new order in the region.[76] This does not mean that Louis was now in charge on his own. Guy, for example, yet again played an important role in that endeavour, which is not surprising, given that he had been entrusted with the leading role in southern affairs for some time now. It is generally hard to envisage a medieval ruler operating independently of his advisors. Our extant sources simply award Louis far more agency than was the case, while still styling him his father's representative in Italian affairs. Despite all merited source criticism, we can see a young king who grew into his office gradually. The events of 844 in and around Rome were the first big step in that direction.

---

[76] See Gantner, 'Saracen attack', and Gantner, 'Our common enemies'.

Section IV

Cities, Courts and Carolingians

12 A Byzantine Cuckoo in the Frankish Nest?
The Exarchate of Ravenna and the Kingdom of Italy in the Long Ninth Century

Tom Brown

The title of this chapter may appear facetious. However, the metaphor of the Exarchate of Ravenna as an alien 'cuckoo' in the relatively familiar nest of Carolingian Italy can be a useful starting point for tackling two important and interrelated problems concerning the former province of the Byzantine empire. This geographical term is used here as shorthand for the large, strategically and economically important area of north-eastern Italy, stretching from Rovigo and Gavello in the north to Gubbio and Urbino in the south, in which the archbishop was the dominant ecclesiastical and to a large extent political force.[1]

The first and most obvious question is whether this area is 'Byzantine' in any precise sense. To many popular writers, art historians and tourist boards this has appeared self-evident; the Exarchate is seen as a Byzantine outpost in the west and Ravenna a small-scale Constantinople.[2] However even during the period when Ravenna and its hinterland came under the authority of the eastern empire (540–751) the ties were often tenuous. Feelings of localism and separatism were strong and the degree of imperial control became steadily weaker.[3] Knowledge of Greek was limited and, unlike Rome, the Eastern monastic presence was very limited.[4] Immigrants from the East such as soldiers and officials became assimilated, and the effect of the 'protective umbrella' provided by Constantinople was more to preserve late Roman institutions than to introduce eastern versions.[5] The most venerated saints in Ravenna were not in general easterners, apart from military

---

[1] The term can also be used of the Byzantine province in Italy in general or the immediate hinterland of Ravenna, approximately the northern part of the present-day Romagna. It is used here to include the area to the south, officially known as the Pentapolis, dominated by the coastal cities of Rimini, Pesaro, Fano, Senigallia and Ancona, where the archbishops had extensive lands and authority. On the territorial boundaries see Guillou, *Régionalisme*.

[2] This is fully discussed in Brown, 'Ravenna – Constantinople of the West?'.

[3] Brown, *Gentlemen and Officers*, especially ch. 8.

[4] Brown, 'Ebrei ed orientali a Ravenna'; Sansterre, 'Monaci e monasteri greci a Ravenna'.

[5] Ibid.

saints such as George and Theodore. The most popular saints had associations with Rome, Milan or the local area, rather than with Constantinople, with the exception of St Andrew, whose relics Archbishop Maximian (546–556) unsuccessfully sought from Justinian in the capital, and St Euphemia, regarded as a symbol of orthodoxy because of her Chalcedonian origin.[6]

On the other hand, it has to be admitted that Ravenna possessed many topographical features modelled on those of Constantinople (generally going back to the Theodosian rulers of the fifth century), stunning 'Byzantine' monuments completed (but not necessarily initiated) in the reign of Justinian and a *palatium*, which hosted the court of the emperor's representative, the exarch.[7] Clearly Ravenna was by Western standards an extremely impressive city, which visitors could have seen as an accessible 'virtual' surrogate for Constantinople and which rulers and archbishops could present as a symbol of imperial tradition.

It is also true that Ravenna retained some links with Constantinople after its fall to the Lombards in 751. On one level, as in the arguably much more 'Byzantine' city of Rome, there continued to be nostalgia for all things eastern. Agnellus was still familiar with Constantinople and regarded travel there as unexceptional. He speaks of the deacon Maurus who went there thirty years earlier (around 810) and who identified the grave of the historian's ancestor Iohannicis 'at a church near the Golden Gate'.[8] Our author also regularly mentions trips to Constantinople in passages dealing with the pre-751 period, which suggest that this was not an occurrence of the distant past, but still a contemporary possibility. His work is also full of references to the liturgical treasures and ecclesiastical furnishings of Ravenna churches, reminiscent of the gifts to churches described in the Roman *Liber Pontificalis*, and it seems likely that, as in Rome, some of these were Eastern objects that had come to the West comparatively recently. In addition, Agnellus is well known for his familiarity with Greek technical terms.[9] Clearly, communications with Constantinople continued in the ninth century, but when Agnellus' text gives out after c. 846, the evidence comes mainly from archaeological finds and references to *negotiatores* and *solidi* in documents.[10]

Perhaps surprisingly there is little evidence that the eastern empire had much interest in Ravenna after 751. Clearly Constantine V was

[6] See Brown, 'The political use of the cult of saints in Early Medieval Ravenna'.
[7] For details see Brown, 'Ravenna – Constantinople of the West?'.
[8] Agnellus, *Liber Pontificalis ecclesiae Ravennatis*, c. 148.
[9] Lazard, 'De l'origine des hellenismes d'Agnello'.
[10] For details see Cirelli, *Ravenna*, ch. 5, and Vespignani, *La Romania italiana*, pp. 67, 184–90.

concerned to recover the city in the decades after its capture, and entered into communication with the papacy and king Pepin III, but in later reigns any such preoccupation diminished.[11] One of the rare expressions of eastern interest in Ravenna occurs when Photius of Constantinople wrote a letter to the anti-papal archbishop of Ravenna, John VIII.[12]

It is difficult to account for this lack of interest. Possibly the authorities in Constantinople were aware of the deep antagonism towards the Greeks in Ravenna, reflected in Agnellus' text, or of the extent to which the key figures, the archbishops, had quickly reached an advantageous accommodation with the new Frankish rulers. It is therefore possible that Ravenna was seen as a lost cause, and an Eastern empire beset by enemies closer to home decided to concentrate its energies on retaining Venice and the coastal cities of the eastern Adriatic.[13]

The other issue this chapter will address is whether the Exarchate was central or peripheral in the world of Carolingian Italy and the broader empire. This question can only be tackled by appreciating the relative neglect of the area by historians until recently. To some extent, this is a reflection of the evidence. Scholars working on the history of early medieval Ravenna have little difficulty with the well-documented periods of exarchal rule (from the late sixth century to 751) and of the Ottonian domination from the mid-tenth century, and this is reflected in the published scholarship.[14] However, they come across somewhat of a brick wall for much of the ninth- and early tenth-century period, because of its complexity and obscurity and relative lack of sources. No wonder Mario Pierpaolo called the period 846–898 in particular 'un mezzo secolo di

---

[11] Recovery of the Exarchate seems to have been a motive in Constantine's negotiations with the powerful Frankish king Pepin III: McCormick, 'Byzantium and the West, 700–900', pp. 360, 365; on relations with Stephen II and other popes, Gantner, *Freunde Roms*, pp. 86–7, 109, 113. It is likely that Ravenna was also mentioned in letters *de imperio* to Charlemagne referred to in the *Codex Carolinus* which have not survived: Hack, *Codex Carolinus*, p. 64.

[12] Grumel, *Les regestes*, pp. 102–3, no. 514. It is interesting that Byzantine circles appear to have been aware of the archbishop's conflict with Pope Nicholas and sought to obtain John's support in the 'Photian schism': Wieczinski, 'The anti-papal conspiracy'.

[13] It is possible, however, that some border areas were fluid in their allegiance. Thus, a *placitum* of 838 referring to Rovigo on the northern confines of the Exarchate adjoining the duchy of Venice mentions an emphyteutic grant dated by the regnal years of the Eastern emperors Michael III and Theophilus (829): Benericetti, *Le carte ravennati*, no. 11, p. 28.

[14] Among the many studies of the earlier period see Guillou, *Régionalisme*, Brown, *Gentlemen and Officers*, Deliyannis, *Ravenna in Late Antiquity* and Bougard, 'Les Francs à Venise'. For the Ottonian period see Brown, 'Culture and society in Ottonian Ravenna', with references and bibliography. The Ottonian period is also a major focus of Schoolman, *Rediscovering Sainthood in Italy*. There is also a great deal of material in the monumental *Storia di Ravenna*, ii/1–2, ed. Carile and iii, ed. Vasina.

burrasca'.[15] In fact, however, the problem at least for the early ninth century is more apparent than real, stemming to a large extent from the fact that the most important sources (or at least those most intensively studied by Carolingianists) have either a transalpine or Roman perspective and tend to mention Ravenna only incidentally. Only occasionally do outside sources offer a more detailed picture; perhaps the most helpful example is papal correspondence, especially the letters of Pope Hadrian I (772–795) to Charlemagne preserved in the *Codex Carolinus* and utilized in a masterly paper by Jinty Nelson to reconstruct papal and Frankish policy towards Ravenna in Charlemagne's reign.[16] Until recently the main local source, Agnellus' *Liber Pontificalis ecclesiae Ravennatis* (completed c. 846), has received little attention.[17] In fact, it offers revealing insights on specific episodes as well as an aggressively local clerical perspective, although some of the archiepiscopal lives are fragmentary or missing as a result of the corrupt state of the main manuscript.[18] Happily there is some compensation for the dearth of narrative sources in records of the *placita* and councils held in Ravenna,[19] and in the parchment documents mainly preserved in the Archivio Arcivescovile di Ravenna. Unfortunately, the mere forty-eight parchment documents surviving from the ninth century represent a low point compared with the extremely important papyri of the period 445–700 and the several hundred preserved from the tenth century.[20] Another sphere that promises to improve knowledge of Ravenna and the exarchate in our period is archaeological and art historical research, which has pointed to dynamic economic development and extensive activity in repairing and adapting the artistic and architectural patrimony of the area.[21]

There are also broader, more historiographical reasons for scholars' failure to regard Ravenna and the Exarchate as central to the Carolingian world. The two main political divisions of northern and central Italy in Carolingian Italy have been seen as the (formerly Lombard) kingdom of

---

[15] This is the title of chapter xxvii of Pierpaoli, *Storia di Ravenna*, pp. 221ff.

[16] Nelson, 'Charlemagne and Ravenna'.

[17] Agnellus, *Liber Pontificalis ecclesiae Ravennatis*, ed. Deliyannis.

[18] For some pointers, see Brown, '*Romanitas* and *Campanilismo*', and Brown, 'Louis the Pious and the papacy'.

[19] An illuminating example of the use that can be made of these is MacLean, 'Legislation and politics'.

[20] Benericetti, *Le carte ravennati*. For a full register Cavarra et al., 'Gli Archivi come fonti della storia di Ravenna'. Some ninth-century transactions are recorded in the register compiled (interestingly on papyrus) in the late tenth century and known as the *Codex Bavarus: Breviarium ecclesiae Ravennatis (Codice Bavaro)*, ed. Rabotti.

[21] Cirelli, *Ravenna*, ch. 5, and Cirelli, 'Material culture in Ravenna'; Verhoeven, *Early Christian Monuments*, esp. catalogue, pp. 245–93.

Italy with its capital at Pavia and the areas under papal authority from the late eighth century, the territories labelled the 'Republic of St Peter' by Tom Noble.[22] The papacy claimed authority over the Exarchate as well as the areas closer to Rome by virtue of the Donations of Pepin and Charlemagne. The precise nature and extent of the power exercised by the popes over the area of Ravenna has long been a subject of debate among historians. Noble saw it as a 'double dyarchy', whereby the pope and the Frankish king shared rule, while the pope and archbishop divided authority.[23] Nelson favoured a more triangular relationship, with Charlemagne at times promoting Ravenna as an imperial capital and its archbishop as a 'right-hand man', partly as a counterbalance to the papacy.[24]

The supposed peripheral 'otherness' of Ravenna and its hinterland has also traditionally been emphasized by scholars who saw the area as retaining alien 'Byzantine' institutions and close links to the eastern empire even after its conquest by the Lombards in 751. For a long time, the degree of attention that was paid to the city, and other areas loyal to the East Roman Empire, was limited or unsympathetic. Byzantine historians who looked at relations with the West saw the Exarchate as a largely Hellenized province in which eastern officials and troops were dominant; such was the line taken in the groundbreaking work of Charles Diehl, published in 1888.[25] Italian scholars, conscious of their country's domination by outside powers up to 1860, tended to buy into this view of the imperial areas as 'colonial' territories occupied by a 'foreign' state, and devoted more attention to the Lombard areas of the peninsula, which were rather paradoxically seen as more 'Italian'.[26]

Only gradually has there been a shift away from this portrayal of Ravenna and the Exarchate as an 'alien' entity and proper emphasis on the area as a distinct but essentially Roman enclave, which had a dynamic character and development of its own.[27] Important elements of the city's distinctive character were its role as one of the preeminent harbours on the Adriatic coast, and its continued importance in its post-Byzantine phase, even in the face of competing centres such as Venice.[28]

---

[22] Noble, *Republic.*   [23] Noble, *Republic*, pp. 171–2.
[24] Nelson, 'Charlemagne and Ravenna'. This is broadly the view I took in my 'Louis the Pious and the papacy' and a question to which I plan to return in future publications.
[25] Diehl, *Études*. A broadly similar approach was taken in the equally valuable work of L. M. Hartmann, published one year later: Hartmann, *Untersuchungen.*
[26] Cosentino, 'La percezione'; Arnaldi, *Italy,* chapter 3.
[27] Even as late as 1969, André Guillou could portray the Exarchate as a not untypical regional province of the Byzantine empire: Guillou, *Régionalisme.* For a different view, Brown, *Gentlemen and Officers.*
[28] Brown, 'Ravenna and other early rivals of Venice'.

In fact, in recent years there has been a welcome upsurge in interest in the various areas that had been under direct Byzantine rule until the eighth century. For all their divergences in development, Ravenna, Rome and Venice retained common traditions and distinctive institutions, as indeed did the coastal cities that maintained closer ties to Byzantium in southern Italy and Dalmatia.[29]

In the case of Ravenna, it is clear that the vast area controlled by the archbishops had quite distinctive social and political institutions from the 'Germanic' heartland of the old Lombard, and later Frankish, kingdom of Italy. This can be seen, for example, in the ranks and titles used, the system of personal names and the organization and nomenclature of its agrarian estates.[30] For centuries, and indeed up to today, contemporaries termed it *Romania* (i.e., Romagna) as opposed to *Longobardia*. The city of Ravenna itself remained rich and powerful, contrary to the views of earlier scholars, as the incisive work of the archaeologist Enrico Cirelli, for example, has demonstrated.[31] It still retained the buildings associated with its glorious imperial past, which Mariette Verhoeven has recently shown were continuously repaired and restored.[32]

For decades after the Lombard conquest of 751, the descendants of the old elite of military landowners retained their dominant social and economic position and remained attached to traditional titles such as *dux, magister militum, tribunus* and consul. Thus, a trawl of the documents from 751 to 1000 produces 34 *comites*, 72 *duces*, 16 *magistri militum* and a vast number of consuls.[33] Naming patterns remained 'Roman' or even Greek,[34] and the organization of estates revealed in the documents, based on quite traditional *fundi* and *massae* rented out by means of leases or emphyteutic grants, is quite different from the *curtes* found in Longobardia.[35] Naturally documents and legal practice followed

---

[29] See, for example, West-Harling, *Three Empires, Three Cities*. The detailed studies in Martin et al. (eds.), *L'Héritage byzantin en Italie* cover these areas and also the parts of the south that remained under more direct Byzantine authority after 751. There has also been increased study of the cities of the eastern Adriatic, which came to assume a 'hybrid' position between the Frankish and Western worlds: see *Adriatic Connections* and Ančić, Shepard and Vedriš, *Imperial Spheres and the Adriatic*. The two most recent studies of Ravenna are Herrin, *Ravenna* and West-Harling, *Rome, Ravenna and Venice*.

[30] Fot the nature and extent of this ecclesiastical lordship, Fasoli, 'Il dominio territoriale', and more recently Cosentino, 'Ricchezza'. On late Roman survivals, Brown, *Gentlemen and Officers*, passim. On the use of the term Romania/Romagna, Casadio, 'Romania e Romagna'.

[31] Among the copious works of Enrico Cirelli, see especially his *Ravenna, Archeologia di una città*.

[32] Verhoeven, *Early Christian Monuments*.   [33] Vespignani, *La Romania italiana*.

[34] Cosentino, 'Antroponomia'.

[35] Pasquali, *Agricoltura*; Pasquali, 'Una signoria rurale'; Mancassola, *L'azienda curtense*.

Roman traditions, and were quite distinctive from the Lombard area.[36] This attachment to traditional institutions and usages of the Roman past of course has its parallels in other coastal cities of the Adriatic and in cities nominally loyal to the Byzantine empire in the South such as Naples, Amalfi and the Gaeta. However, ties with the Byzantine empire were no longer as direct as in the case of Venice or the southern Italian or Dalmatian cities, and we do not find in Ravenna the more recent court titles found elsewhere, such as *protospatharius* or *spatharius*. Certainly 'Byzantine-sounding' titles had considerable cachet, but in the Ravenna area this implied, I believe, a more general nostalgia for the imperial past rather than a specific attachment to the Byzantine empire.[37] A broadly similar 'Byzantinizing snobbery' is of course found in Rome, as Toubert observed,[38] and extends to eastern clothes and luxury imports as well as names and titles.

Despite the nominal authority of the popes over the former Exarchate, in practice the archbishops maintained a powerful ecclesiastical lordship. This may in part have been based on the assumption of some public powers previously exercised by the exarch – one archbishop is described as ruling just like an exarch[39] – and certainly the episcopal palace complex expanded greatly, perhaps to perform the roles played by the now abandoned exarch's palace.[40] Undoubtedly central, however, were extensive landholdings, amounting to a massive land bank, used to bolster the archbishops' networks of patronage. Small plots were leased out to peasant farmers, usually for twenty-nine years, while larger estates were granted to powerful laymen on an emphyteutic basis, usually for minimal rents. Central to each kind of grant were conditions binding the recipient to loyalty to the archbishop.[41] The close ties between the archbishops and the local landed elites are reflected in the fact that the highly independent archbishop John VIII (850–878) had the support of his powerful brother,[42] Duke Gregory, and leading local families such as the Duchi and the Sergii clearly based their power on grants from the Church as well as the possession of traditional Romano-Byzantine titles. The ninth century also saw a further expansion of the archbishops' power and wealth by extensive land clearances in coastal and marsh areas, the

---

[36] De Lorenzi, *Storia del Notariato ravennate.*
[37] These issues are discussed in Brown, 'The interplay', and Brown, 'The background'. For more recent literature, see note 29.
[38] Toubert, *Les structures du Latium medieval,* I, p. 655, n.1.
[39] Sergius (744–769) *iudicavit iste … totum Pentapolim veluti exarchus* (Agnellus, *Liber Pontificalis ecclesiae Ravennatis,* c. 159).
[40] Miller, 'The development'.
[41] On the development of these grants, Brown, 'The church of Ravenna'.
[42] West-Harling, 'Proclaiming power in the city'.

setting up of monasteries (such as Pomposa, founded some time before 874) and the establishment of a network of baptismal churches throughout the countryside known as *pievi*.[43] The archbishops were clearly major beneficiaries of the economic expansion, which is well attested in the Exarchate in the seventh century.[44]

In view of the undoubted wealth and strategic importance of the Exarchate, therefore, it is perhaps time to reappraise its role in Carolingian Italy and in particular to question the notion that Ravenna and its hinterland constituted a 'semi-detached' backwater, largely 'off the radar' as far as the Frankish rulers were concerned. Little shall be said here about Ravenna's position under the early Carolingians, partly because papers by Jinty Nelson and this author offer useful pointers regarding the policies of Charlemagne and Louis the Pious, respectively.[45] Clearly, the papacy had considerable political claims and landed interests there and became involved in repeated conflicts about its authority, rights and patrimonies. However, in general rulers such as Charlemagne seem to have succumbed to the bribery and flattery of the archbishops through sporadic visits and the grant of privileges allowed the latter to defy papal authority and remain the dominant force. Charlemagne's will provides an interesting reflection of both the emperor's respect for Ravenna and his frustration at the disputes between rival ecclesiastics: he bequeathed to the see a silver table 'adorned with the likeness of the city of Rome'.[46] Clearly Pepin of Italy had close associations with the city; he was viewed as '*christianissimus*' in later tradition, and the *Pactum* that resolved his conflict with the Byzantines over Venice was issued at Ravenna in 810.[47] We know little of the city during the reign of his brother Louis the Pious, except that Archbishop Martin appears to have bribed a legate of Louis to avoid having to submit himself to papal authority.[48] Overall relations with both

[43] Samaritani, *Analecta Pomposiana*; Samaritani, *Presenza monastica;* Samaritani, Di Francesco, *Pomposa*; Rizzardi, 'Chiesa e Impero', and, on a more general level, various authors, *La bonifica benedettina*. On *pievi* Vasina, 'Pievi urbane'; Tabanelli, *Visita alle pievi*; Torricelli, *Centri plebani.*

[44] In addition to the various studies of Cirelli cited above, see his forthcoming paper 'Bishops and merchants: the economy of Ravenna at the beginning of the Middle Ages', an advanced copy of which I had the good fortune to read. See also Cosentino, 'Richezza', cited at n. 18.

[45] Nelson, 'Charlemagne and Ravenna'; Brown, 'Louis the Pious'.

[46] Brown, 'Louis the Pious', pp. 300–2. For another interpretation, Nelson, 'Charlemagne and Ravenna'.

[47] Rossi, *Historiarum Ravennatum Libri Decem*, v, pp. 234–5; *Pactum Lotharii*, c. 2.

[48] Brown, 'Louis the Pious', p. 302. Martin appears to have had close links with the Franks, since local tradition claimed that as a deacon he had guided Charlemagne's forces across the Alps in 773.

Louis and the papacy seem to have improved after the tensions of Pope Leo III's pontificate and Pope Paschal I granted a relatively generous privilege to the see of Ravenna in 824.[49] Relations were not always harmonious, however; the relics of one of the city's most eminent saints, Severus, were smuggled off to Mainz as a notorious *furtum sacrum* of the Frankish cleric Felix in 836.[50]

It is unfortunate for our reconstruction of the history of Ravenna in the early ninth century that several of the relevant episcopal lives are missing or fragmentary in Agnellus' gloriously opinionated text. After Louis' eldest son Lothar I assumed the government of Italy in 822, it is likely that Frankish interest in the important see of Ravenna increased. At first, evidence remains scanty, but we are fortunate, however, in having the life of Agnellus' particular *bête noir*, Archbishop George (834–846). George appears to have cooperated closely with Lothar when he exploited the wealth and power of Italian churches to advance his ambitions. Agnellus accompanied George when he attended as godfather the baptism in Pavia of Lothar's daughter. Then in 841, archbishop George travelled across the Alps together with the treasures and privileges of his see to support Lothar in his battle against his brothers Louis and Charles at the battle of Fontenoy in France. Agnellus bitterly attacks his subservience to Lothar and the cavalier policy that led to the loss of many of Ravenna's treasures and privileges.[51]

Lothar's eldest son and successor as emperor, Louis II, had much closer links with Ravenna than any previous Carolingian. He is known to have visited Ravenna on several occasions and held assemblies there.[52] He also encouraged the settlement of his Frankish and Lombard follow-ers from Tuscany and western Emilia in the Exarchate and marriage alliances between them and powerful local families as we shall see.

However, in his reign the earlier bitter and tangled disputes with Rome were revived by Archbishop John VIII (850–878). John sought to revive the claims to ecclesiastical autonomy (*autocephalia*), which his predeces-sor Maurus had briefly obtained from the Byzantine emperor in the late seventh century. The archbishop appears to have benefitted from the support of the local aristocracy in this struggle – for example, John VIII was strongly backed by his own brother Gregory who held the high lay rank of *magister militum*. In the face of Louis' support for John, Pope

---

[49] Brown, 'Louis the Pious', pp. 302–4. For a different interpretation, Nelson, 'Charlemagne and Ravenna'. See also Deliyannis, 'Charlemagne's silver tables'.

[50] Geary, *Furta Sacra*, p. 48.

[51] Brown, 'Louis the Pious', 305: Agnellus, *Liber Pontificalis ecclesiae Ravennatis*, cc. 171–4, and *Annals of St Bertin*, a. 841.

[52] E.g. *Annals of St Bertin*, a. 864 and a. 871.

Nicholas I stood his ground, accused John of heresy and of infringing the property rights of both the papacy and locals and deposed him early in 861. Despite further appeals to Louis, John was ultimately forced to submit to the pope later the same year, partly because the pope received support from Ravenna's suffragans and partly because when it came to the crunch, Louis backed the papacy's claims; Louis had too many enemies and problems to maintain his support for John.[53] Nevertheless, John seems to have continued to curry favour with Louis by supporting the latter's brother Lothar II in his bitter divorce case; Lothar visited Ravenna on his way to Rome in 864.[54]

Altogether, John pursued a much more proactive policy of cooperation with the emperor than any of his predecessors. One reason for this was of course his desire to throw off papal subjugation, but another possible factor was protection against the Arab threat. Muslim naval raids were common in the Adriatic, especially under the last emir of Bari, Sawdan (857–871).[55] The threat of such raids played a part in the transfer of the relics of the city's patron saint, Apollinaris, from Classe to the present church of S. Apollinare Nuovo in the city,[56] and also the building of bell towers (*campanili*), serving partly as watch towers, the earliest of which date from this period.[57]

After Louis II's death without leaving a direct male heir in 875, Ravenna assumed an even more prominent role in the kingdom. It was visited by successive kings and emperors, such as Charles the Bald in 877 and Charles the Fat in 880 and 882.[58] Perhaps because of its conveniently central position in Italy and its quasi-neutral status between the kingdom of Italy proper and Rome, the city became the venue for frequent assemblies, including lay diets, ecclesiastical synods and large-scale judicial hearings (*placita*).[59] The city became an even more common residence for the local Italian rulers from 888. For example, Lambert of Spoleto was crowned emperor alongside his father, Guy,

[53] On this episode Simonini, *Autocefalia*, pp. 175–7; Belletzkie, 'Pope Nicholas I and John of Ravenna'; Gantner, 'Kaiser Ludwig II. von Italien und Byzanz,' p. 108; West-Harling, 'Proclaiming power', p. 221; for a general survey Savigni, 'I Papi e Ravenna'.

[54] *Annals of St Bertin*, a. 864. John was also open to overtures from Patriarch Photius of Constantinople, who likewise sought Louis' support against Nicholas I: see n. 12 *supra*.

[55] Musca, *L'emirato di Bari*; Kreutz, *Before the Normans*, pp. 38–40; Metcalfe, *Muslims of Medieval Italy*, p. 21; Di Branco, 'Strategie di penetrazione islamica'.

[56] Verhoeven, *Early Christian Monuments*, pp. 65–71 and the discussion in Brown, 'Political use of the cult of saints' (forthcoming).

[57] Gardella, *I campanili di Ravenna*; Battistini, Bissi and Rocchi, *I campanili di Ravenna*.

[58] Groth, 'How to become an emperor?', and MacLean, 'Legislation and politics'.

[59] *Konzilien der karolingischen Teilreiche*, ed. Hartmann and Schroeder; *Placiti*, ed. Manaresi; MacLean, 'Legislation and politics'; MacLean, '"After his death"'.

there in 892.[60] There were several probable reasons for this. One was obviously the appeal of the imperial traditions and impressive monuments of the city to insecure rulers. Second, there was the convenience of the city for an emperor who was concerned with operations against the Lombards of Benevento and the Arabs, as in the case of Louis II, or whose power base adjoined the Exarchate, as was the case of rulers from the house of Spoleto. It is also possible that archbishops were able to offer Frankish rulers the military services of some of their lay tenants and clients.

Further research is needed before we can do full justice to the complex nature and extent of rulers' relations with the see of Ravenna in this tangled period from 888 to 924. Equally problematic are Ravenna's relations with the papacy after John VIII's death in 878. His successor Romanus appears to have pursued a more nuanced policy open to some cooperation with Rome. The degree and nature of the papacy's control in the Exarchate, which it claimed, remains mysterious; we find references to various papal officials, and they clearly attracted opposition at times.

According to a letter of Pope John VIII dated between 873 and 876 Maurinus, an opponent of the pope and apparent supporter of Formosus, attacked papal vestiaries in Ravenna, and forced them to give the keys of the city to the archbishop.[61] A few years later, in 880, archbishop Romanus sought to discredit and weaken a political opponent Deusdedit, the papal *consilarius*, by accusing him of having contracted an incestuous marriage.[62]

Overall, however, relations with the papacy appear to have improved from the late ninth century, as is demonstrated by archbishop John IX, a local figure, probably from Tossignano near Bologna, who was consecrated archbishop in 905. John was later crowned pope, somewhat confusingly as John X, in 914. He appears to have been active and successful, being best known for the role in the Christian league that finally expelled the Muslim pirates from their Garigliano base in 915. His surviving letters have still not been fully studied,[63] but his career reflects some important developments. First, Ravenna's relations with Rome became closer and positive, for several possible reasons. Some elements in Ravenna may have regarded the popes as more useful allies than the weak secular rulers of Italy after 888: some Ravennati clearly became

---

[60] Carpegna Falconieri, 'Guido'. Berengar I, emperor from 915 to 924, whose powerbase was Friuli the north-east, is only known to have issued one charter at Ravenna (in 916): Schoolman, *Rediscovering Sainthood*, p. 84.

[61] John VIII, *Fragmenta Registri*, no. 62, ed. Caspar, p. 312.

[62] Betti, 'Incestuous marriages'.

[63] John X, *Epistolae*, ed. Löwenfeld, 'Acht Briefe aus der Zeit König Berengars'.

involved with Roman factions. Second, the margraviate of Spoleto was increasingly powerful and played an important role in both Ravenna and Rome: John appears to have obtained the throne through his ties with Alberic of Spoleto. John, like most Ravenna prelates, also benefitted from powerful secular support, in his case his brother Peter, a powerful layman and *magister militum*.[64]

This points again to the main basis of the archbishops' power, their close ties with the local landed elite. At first these persons, to judge from names and titles, formed a cohesive group descended from the earlier exarchal aristocracy,[65] but from the 830s changes are evident. We find increased references to Germanic names, presumably nobles from neighbouring areas granted lands by the archbishops.[66]

In addition, during the ninth century, unions between members of the exarchal aristocracy and members of the Frankish aristocracy based in the *Regnum Italiae* were frequent. Possibly with archiepiscopal encouragement family groups chose to establish political, patrimonial and marital relations with the representatives of the Frankish aristocracy. Probably, the archbishops' aim was to establish a politically helpful network of alliances with the leading exponents of the Frankish aristocracy of the *Regnum* through families who were also mainly large leaseholders of the church of Ravenna. Archbishop John VIII, thanks to the marital union of his nephew, the dux Martinus, with Engelrada, daughter of Louis II's *comes palatii* Hucpold, had already been able to establish a bond of great political importance. Similarly the marriage between the dux Petronax, of the exarchal aristocracy, and Vulgunda, blood relative of Bishop Wibodus of Parma, surely fostered the relationship between archbishop Romanus and the bishop of Parma.[67] The valuable allies thus gained – such as the *comes palatii* Hucpold, loyal to Louis II, or the powerful Wibodus – could thus have supported the church of Ravenna in the face of Carolingian authority, ensuring Ravenna a key role on the Italian political chessboard.

---

[64] Wickham, 'The Romans according to their malign custom'; Wickham, *Roma medievale*, translated as *Medieval Rome*; Savigni, 'Sacerdozio e Regno'; Savigni, 'Giovanni IX da Tossignano'; Gnocchi, 'Giovanni X'. Liutprand of Cremona attributes his elevation as pope to a liaison with the infamous Marozia.

[65] Manarini, *I due volti*, pp. 149–58.

[66] Cosentino, 'Antroponomia', p. 179, describes the 830s as a 'turning point' and mentions the case of Bruningus, *vasso domni imperatoris* (sic), granted land near Adria in 838

[67] On Hucpold, Martin and Engelrada: Manarini, *I due volti*, pp. 37–49; Cosentino, 'Antroponomia', p. 180; Lazzari, *Comitato senza città*, pp. 51, 76, 83. On the marriage between Petr and Vulgunda, Lazzari, 'I "de Ermengarda"', pp. 598–608; Lazzari, *Comitato senza città*, pp. 109–16. On aristocratic relations between the regnum and the Exarchate see Lazzari, 'Tra Ravenna e Regno'.

In addition to this, the exogamic unions of the aristocracy close to the archbishop would have encouraged further opportunities to expand the landed patrimony of the church of Ravenna, through the recovery of influence over property unlawfully granted to *fideles* of the Carolingian rulers, or through donations of landed estates in other areas – and also strengthened its claims to metropolitan authority over areas such as western Emilia.

Clearly the story of Ravenna in the 'long ninth century' is complex, but progress is being made as scholars reconstruct a picture from the documents, letters, council *acta* and so forth of this period. Although it is unhelpful to regard the Exarchate as a 'Byzantine' enclave in any precise or narrow sense, it did retain distinctive traditions and institutions from the earlier period of exarchal rule. Because of its imperial associations and the survival of its grandiose monuments, Frankish kings from Charlemagne onwards had a stronger interest in it than is often realized. Its symbolic role was greatly valued along with its wealth and strategic importance. Ravenna itself, although hardly 'the Constantinople of the West', could be ideologically useful as an imperial capital, whose local masters, the archbishops, were consistently more compliant than the pontiffs of the other imperial city of the West, Rome.

In fact, the archbishops were extremely powerful figures, playing a major role in the affairs of the kingdom, not just through ingratiating themselves with Frankish rulers and hosting assemblies and synods, but through making alliances with a wide spectrum of the Frankish aristocracy, from local Tuscan landowners to claimants to the throne.

But in terms of the archbishops' local authority and the social cohesion of the Exarchate, there was a downside to this. Powerful families such as the Guidi who amassed landholdings in the Romagna and across the Apennines in Tuscany proved a disruptive threat for centuries.[68] Also the local elite lost its earlier unity and solidarity, and the kings' policy of involvement in the Exarchate served as a model for even greater intervention by the Ottonians. In the short term, this might strengthen the archbishops' power, but over the longer term it created tensions and alienation.

The Exarchate may never have been a 'Byzantine cuckoo in the Frankish nest', but ironically the opposite began to apply. Frankish incomers became prominent in the ninth century and eventually proved disruptive in what had traditionally been a stable and cohesive 'nest'. For all these changes, Ravenna and its hinterland retained an important but distinctive role in Carolingian Italy – a role that it partly owed to its symbolic position as an imperial capital, but not a purely Byzantine one.

[68] Canaccini, *La lunga storia.*

13   Urbanism as Politics in Ninth-Century Italy

Caroline Goodson

> See how well it [the city of Verona] was founded by evil men who knew
> not the law of our God and worshipped ancient images of wood and
> stone![1]

> Old Rome, your morals decay as do your walls. ... Now if the virtue of
> Peter and Paul do not favour you, you will long be wretched, little
> Rome.[2]

The author of the famous *Versus de Verona*, composed between 795 and
807, remarked upon the position of the city on the river, the walls and
temples of stone, its ancient bridges and roads, as well as beauty and the
history of its conversion and early Christian bishops and saints. For this
anonymous author, Verona's ancient architecture was a praise-worthy
asset as much as the relics of saints in its modern churches were. For the
translator of the pseudo-Dionysius, working in the Carolingian court,
there was an explicit correlation between the urban fabric of Rome and
the moral rectitude of those living there. Only the princes of apostles,
who had died in Rome and whose bodies lay there now, could redeem
the city.

Verona was not unique among medieval cities in Italy to have evolved
from its ancient civic form into a medieval centre and to be celebrated as
having a continuous tradition from ancient *civitas* to medieval city.[3] Nor
was Rome the only early medieval city to be criticized for lax morality,
exhorted to place its faith in the saints. In the tensions between ancient
Roman traditions and their socio-political forms, on the one hand, and

---

[1] *Versus de Verona*, ed. Pighi: *Ecce quam bene est fundata a malis hominibus / qui nesciebant
legem dei nostri atque uetera simulacra uenerabantur lignea lapidea!*; Godman, *Poetry of the
Carolingian Renaissance*, pp. 80–7.

[2] John Eriugena's translation of Ps. Dionysius the Areopagite's letter to the apostle John:
John Eriugena, *Joanni theologo apostolo et evangelistae determinate in Pathmos insulam*, PL
122, col. 1194: *Moribus et muris Roma uetusta cadis. ... Jam ni te meritum Petri Paulique
foueret, tempore iam longo Roma misella fores*; trans. Neil, *Seventh-Century Popes and
Martyrs*, pp. 89–90.

[3] Hyde, 'Medieval descriptions of cities'; Granier, 'À rebours des laudes civitatum'.

the fast-paced changing world and new power structures emerging in the ninth century, on the other, meant that urbanism and investment in cities were effective tools for Carolingian rulers of Italy and their contemporaries.

The legacy of Roman cities was enormous for the communities of the Italian peninsula in the eighth and ninth centuries. Roman cities were the principal places of governance, administration, much commerce, as well as the performance of civilized cultural values and status within imperial hierarchies. A dense network of cities, linked by roads and rivers, had developed during the Republic and became richer and more vibrant in the period of the principate.[4] There is no doubt that by the fifth century, the vibrancy of Italian cities had diminished and that some places that had thrived in antiquity were nearly nonexistent in the early Middle Ages. The intensity, chronology and regional variation of urban change in the early medieval period has been the subject of a significant body of literature over the past thirty years, as urban archaeology has provided surprising (if uneven) insights, and debate has sharpened our historiographical and methodological tools.[5] For the most part, at present it can be agreed that in the Italian peninsula, many long-lived cities endured from antiquity into the Middle Ages. They were trading places, royal seats and the targets of elite investment and residences.[6] They had large stone- or brick-built public churches and halls and high-status residences and they supported artisanal production and commercial exchange. Indeed, urbanism was (for the most part) so successful in Italy that the impetus to found new cities emerged in the eighth and ninth centuries, with new walled neighbourhoods at Benevento and Rome and further new foundations in the ninth century.[7]

North of the Alps and elsewhere in the empire, where the urban networks of antiquity had been more dispersed and civic centres themselves had been smaller, the decline and reordering of ancient cities and the civic structures of governance were significantly more comprehen-

---

[4] On the cities of Roman Italy, Cracco Ruggini, 'La città nel mondo antico'; Crawford, 'Italy and Rome from Sulla to Augustus'.

[5] For general discussion, see Cantino Wataghin, 'Quadri urbani nell' Italia settentrionale'; Liebeschuetz, *Decline and Fall of the Roman City*; La Rocca, 'Public buildings'; Marazzi, 'Cadavera urbium'. For a summary of the debate (as of 1996), see Ward-Perkins, 'Continuitists, catastrophists'.

[6] Brogiolo and Gelichi, *La città nell'alto medioevo italiano*; Augenti, *Le città italiane tra la tarda antichità e l'alto Medioevo*, especially La Rocca, 'Residenze urbane ed élites urbane'.

[7] Marazzi, 'Le città nuove pontificie e l'insediamento laziale nel IX secolo'; Gelichi, 'La storia di una nuova città attraverso l'archeologia'; Pani Ermini, 'Città fortificate e fortificazioni delle città italiane fra V e VI secolo'.

sive.[8] In southern Gaul, some port cities and episcopal centres, such as Marseille and Arles, persevered, but north of the Loire and east of the Rhine, the few ancient urban centres became even fewer in the early Middle Ages.[9] Centre-places were rural in northern Europe between c. 500 and c. 1100: trading places for the exchange of goods (sometimes even using money), royal seats and monasteries.[10]

Much earlier analysis of early medieval urbanism has aimed to define cities by scale or functional attributes, though these varied considerably by region and period.[11] Efforts expended to determine whether a place was a city or not have tended to overshadow the analysis of what roles the different characteristics of urban places might have played in life and the experience of living in those cities. Population density, demographic diversity, elite patronage, commerce, craft production and administrative capacity – all characteristics of urban centres all over the medieval world – were not simply the by-products of urban investment; they also shaped the nature of social interaction and governance in those cities. Thus modern geographers and urban historians of more modern periods have long recognized the ways in which the experience of a city, its diversity and its pressures might intensify competition among inhabitants, drive innovation and harden divides between some groups, despite the desires and advantages of heterogeneity and opportunity that the city provides.[12] Following a Foucauldian understanding of power structures in urban forms, we can recognize that cities house particular discursive strategies that make possible or impossible some individual and collective expressions and representations.[13] Investment in cities, therefore, further supports or limits certain kinds of discourse. To recognize the early medieval

---

[8] See the balanced depiction of this process in Loseby, 'Lost cities', where he stresses the survival of Gallic *civitates* as centres of territories. Compare Verhulst's characterization of the 'nadir of urban life' in Merovingian Gaul, Verhulst, *The Rise of Cities in North-West Europe*, p. 24. See also Verhaeghe, Loveluck and Story, 'Urban developments in the age of Charlemagne'; Henning, 'Early European towns '.

[9] These broad-brush statements inevitably obscure nuances of evidence and interpretation that have emerged in recent scholarship. For overview, Wickham, *Framing the Early Middle Ages*, pp. 665–6, 71–2, 74–88; Loseby, 'Reflections on urban space', pp. 665–6, 671–2, 674–88.

[10] Airlie, 'The palace complex', pp. 257–9.

[11] See discussion of the historiography in Goodson, Lester and Symes, 'Introduction,' pp. 5–6; the essays in Sami and Speed (eds.), *Debating Urbanism*; Loseby, 'Reflections on urban space'.

[12] On 'time-space compression' as an urban social characteristic, see Frisby, *Simmel and Since*; Simmel, 'The metropolis and mental life'. For a recent example of the gap between urban diversity and social isolation, see Butler and Robson, 'Social capital, gentrification and neighbourhood'.

[13] Parker, *Urban Theory*, p. 150.

rulers' efforts to create and sustain cities as a way of living is to acknowledge a kind of rulership and therefore a heuristic.[14]

In their provocative history of the Mediterranean in the *longue durée*, P. Horden and N. Purcell called for abandoning urbanism as an analytical category because no city exists wholly without a rural hinterland or wider territory.[15] For entirely different reasons, in 1959, E. Dupré Theseider had declared the study of the early medieval city to be 'a hopeless undertaking,' given the vastly different kinds of evidence that need to be considered in order to achieve a vision of the whole.[16] Both of these points are indeed true. No city existed entirely without a rural territory, but the category of 'urban' – as opposed to 'rural' – mattered in the Middle Ages. Thus, early medieval charters of property transactions never leave doubt about whether a property was inside or outside the walls or limits of a city or town. And the disparate evidence, whether textual or material, from and about cities of the early Middle Ages is rarely straightforwardly complementary, and often varies considerably in quality and quantity across the regions of Italy in our period. Chris Wickham argued (against Horden and Purcell) that '"cityness" has had a strong ideological element in much of history. It constituted culture.'[17] Thus, it merits examination. Indeed, I argue in what follows that analysis of the practice of urbanism, the investment in fostering 'cityness', is indeed a useful knife with which to slice through our understanding of early medieval Italy, in order to perceive similarities and differences, and strategies of distinction and alliance. It is worth considering urbanism both in terms of ideology as well as practice, in order to examine the ways in which urban communities attract attention and resources, and persuade or coerce those in their territories, or beyond those, to support the city.[18]

Advances have been made recently in the field of early medieval urban identities. Very recent scholarship has stressed the value of considering urbanism and urban identity in a transdisciplinary way, through archaeological, historical and literary evidence, and comparatively across different regions of the early medieval world. A 2015 volume, edited by Cristina La Rocca and Piero Majocchi, concentrated on the period between 800 and 1100 and northern Italy to reveal considerable variation within the *regnum Italiae*; another recent volume on the three 'Byzantine'

---

[14] On ruler representation, see Airlie, 'The palace complex'; MacLean, 'Palaces, itineraries and political order'.
[15] Horden and Purcell, *Corrupting Sea*, p. 90.
[16] Dupré Theseider, 'Problemi della città nell' alto medioevo'.
[17] Wickham, *Framing the Early Middle Ages*, p. 595.
[18] Moore, 'A global Middle Ages?'.

cities of early medieval north and central Italy, Venice, Ravenna and Rome, used those cities and their identities as a route into examining the durability of Byzantine rule and influence in Italy when its direct authority ceased.[19] These recent contributions have made clear that people in different cities approached relationships with central authority and practices of power differently, but commonalities emerged around the cultural capital of cityness, the strategic roles played by bishops – both those long dead, venerated as saints, and contemporary ones – and the production of texts, both literary and administrative.

In what follows, I will examine the diverse processes by which urbanism shaped and reshaped the society and politics across ninth-century Italy.[20] By 'urbanism' I mean the ways of life of cities and urban centres, which in our period included dense residential accommodation, the construction and preservation of communal fortifications like city walls, the financing and ongoing maintenance of religious communities and shrines within cities and may have included the legal or juridical regulation of urban communities, the dispensation of justice from urban courts, the composition of praise poetry about urban/civic entities and numerous other practices. As noted above, no city existed without a rural territory, of course, and every single city of the peninsula did not receive the same kind of attention from every ruler throughout our period: individual contexts and circumstances mattered in the past. That said, we can make some observations and distinctions about the value of cities and strategic choices made by rulers and populaces in relation to urban identities. Fundamentally, I consider urbanism to have been a field of cultural production, in Pierre Bourdieu's terms; rulers and leaders took specific positions around the role of cities. The impact and significance of those 'positions' related to other positions in the field and historical positions of a given place.[21] The very nature of cities – intensively populated – meant that when rulers or aristocrats did or did not build a new residence, support a certain church or pronounce on a given conflict, inhabitants of cities were more likely to know by observation than their rural counterparts might have been. I will first identify some of the differences in the practice of urbanism across the Italian peninsula, noting regional variations within and across geopolitical boundaries, and then consider the effects and implications of such variation.

---

[19] La Rocca and Majocchi, *Urban Identities in Northern Italy*; West-Harling, 'Introduction', p. 14.

[20] For an overview of recent historiography, see McCormick, 'Introduction'; Loseby, 'Reflections on urban space'; and essays in Henning (ed.), *Post-Roman Towns*.

[21] Bourdieu, 'The field of cultural production', reprinted with other essays in Bourdieu, *The Field of Cultural Production*.

Regional Overviews

Northern Italy

Life in the Lombard and then Carolingian kingdoms of Italy spread between cities and dispersed rural settlements; as we will see, the north was less focussed in urban centres than southern Lombard and Byzantine areas.[22] The origins of this distinction may lie in the early medieval political trajectories of the northern Lombard territories in the seventh and eighth centuries, as Lombard invasions may have destabilized cities in areas of political friction and indirectly encouraged rural investment.[23] In northern Italy, Lombard rulers' residences had been located both in cities (such as the royal centre of Pavia) and in the countryside at large estates where clients, petitioners and visiting embassies could be hosted (such as Corte Olona).[24] Pavia, effectively the capital, had been a relatively minor Roman town; it had assumed a regional significance in the Gothic period, which expanded under the Lombards. King Liutprand (r. 712–744) restored the palace there and rebuilt or founded anew a number of ecclesiastical buildings; into some of these he translated relics.[25] At Corte Olona, 15 km east of Pavia, Liutprand also built a royal palace, now lost, with ancient spolia reportedly from Rome, and founded a monastery in honour of Saint Anastasius, for whom he had particular devotion.[26] In both urban and rural contexts, Liutprand used secular and ecclesiastical patronage to convey his adherence to Lombard traditions and religious orthodoxy, as well as to broadcast his personal devotion; Milan might serve as another earlier example of this diffuse royal authority spread between urban and rural sites.[27] The political topography of the Lombard kingdom had three main networks: the gastaldates, run by royally appointed officials; the duchies, which were sometimes politically very close to, and sometimes very distant from,

---

[22] For characterization of the differences between north and south, see Goodson, 'City-states' and Martin, 'La longobardia meridionale'.

[23] So suggested Delogu, 'Longobardi e Romani'; but compare La Rocca, '*Castrum vel potius civitas*'.

[24] Calderini, 'Il palazzo di Liutprando a Corteolona'; Gasparri, 'I centri di potere dell' Italia longobarda e bizantina'; MacLean, *Kingship and Politics*, pp. 93–6; Bougard, 'Palais royaux et imperiaux de l'Italie carolingienne et ottonienne'.

[25] Paul the Deacon, *Historia Langobardorum* VI, 58, ed. Waitz, pp. 185–6; Gasparri, 'Pavia longobarda'.

[26] Calderini, 'Il palazzo di Liutprando a Corteolona', p. 179; Badini, 'La concezione della regalità' and on the political ritual of building churches, see Gasparri, 'Kingship rituals', p. 110.

[27] Brogiolo, 'Capitali e residenze regie nell'Italia longobarda'.

royal court; and episcopal centres of cathedrals and baptisteries.[28] The *civitates* themselves held a legal and ideological significance, which was based both on the physical aspects of cities and the territorial element of the *civitas* and its hinterland.[29] After 774, Carolingian rulers of the kingdom of Italy preserved, more or less, this system of administration spread between urban and rural centres in their *regnum*.[30] The itineraries of Frankish rulers deliberately moved between urban centres, such as Pavia and Mantua, and rural *palatia*, such as Corte Olona, Orcho (Cortereggio) and Marengo.[31] At key moments in the ninth century, Carolingian emperors and kings of Italy consolidated their rules by extending rights and privileges and endowing properties around palaces to aristocrats and bishops.[32]

Dispute resolution principally took place through urban networks, even when the dispute focussed on rural matters.[33] Using the example of Piacenza, Fumagalli showed some time ago that urban counts had extensive networks of representatives who participated in local politics, including hearing and witnessing *placita* even in very small scale localities.[34] The laws and customs invoked in these hearings may have become less Lombard and more Frankish over the course of the ninth century, but the system of deliberate spreading of government across both city and countryside established in the eighth century remained in place in the ninth.[35]

Ninth-century rulers in the *Regnum Italiae* relied upon the church both in practical and theological senses to carry out some of their administration, using the model in place north of the Alps.[36] After the 820s, many important bishops were Frankish appointments, such as Ratold of Verona (d. 840/847) and Angilbert of Milan (d. 859), and they worked with (or at times against) the counts in the service of the kings.[37] Both in

---

[28] Delogu, 'Lombard and Carolingian Italy', pp. 47–8.

[29] Cagiano de Azevedo, 'Milano longobarda'; Gasparri, 'Il regno dei Longobardi in Italia', p. 49; Gasparri, 'Langobardi e città'; La Rocca, 'Plus ça change, plus c'est la même chose'; Wickham, 'Aristocratic power in eighth-century Lombard Italy', esp. p. 158.

[30] Fumagalli, 'Le modificazioni politico-istituzionali'; Jarnut, 'La funzione centrale della città nel regno longobardo'.

[31] Bougard, 'Les palais royaux'.

[32] On this process, see the essays in *Formazione e strutture dei ceti dominanti nel medioevo*.

[33] Bruyning, 'Lawcourt proceedings'.

[34] Fumagalli, 'Città e distretti minori nell'Italia carolingia'.

[35] Keller, *Der Gerichtsort*; Wickham, 'Land disputes'.

[36] McKitterick, *The Frankish Church*; Reynolds, 'The organisation, law and liturgy of the Western Church, 700–900'.

[37] Wickham, *Early Medieval Italy*, p. 81. For a broad overview, see Bertolini, 'I vescovi del Regnum Langobardorum al tempo dei Carolingi'; Hlawitschka, *Franken, Alemannen, Bayern*, pp. 32–43 and now Davis, *Charlemagne's Practice of Empire*, pp. 230–1.

areas directly controlled by the Carolingian empire and in areas under less direct influence, the needs of the faithful and the aims of the rulers were exercised through ecclesiastical networks: urban episcopal webs as well as rural monastic and parish ones. Cathedrals, their bishops and chapters flourished through donations and concessions from emperors, kings and aristocrats. Where Italian bishops were not Frankish appointments (and many were), there was scope for those in the highest ecclesiastical office to muster power networks in opposition to Frankish counts and kings. Baptismal churches (*pievi*) were established in the countryside as a territorial web of episcopal powers rooted in *civitates*.[38] Some had been founded in late antiquity while others were established in northern Italy in the seventh and eighth centuries; in the Carolingian period, the *pievi* and their clergy participated in the integration of private churches and monasteries into the hierarchical administration of the episcopal churches and Frankish administration of the *regnum*.[39] If the *pievi* were part of the administrative apparatus of urban episcopal networks, which sometimes aligned with Frankish-appointed bishops and their aims, monasteries were by contrast often rural and independent – indeed, some were exempted from episcopal jurisdiction. Many of the monasteries of northern Italy had been Lombard royal or aristocratic foundations, and these continued to thrive with aristocratic support in the Carolingian period. Such was the case with Bobbio (founded 614 with Lombard royal support), Pomposa (early community of Columbanus' supporters, expanded in the ninth century), Nonantola (royal foundation of 752) and Monte Amiata (held to be a royal foundation of the mid-eighth century). However, the rural monasteries of the *regnum* were hardly the cultural and political power brokers that were the imperial monasteries north of the Alps; in Italy, it was to cathedral schools in cities and urban monasteries – not rural ones – that important Franks came to bolster educational and cultural centres.[40] Episcopal promotion of Carolingian educational principles gave cities key roles in education and transmission of learning in the *regnum*, as distinct from Francia, where rural monasteries were major centres of learning.[41] Recognizing the relative weakness of rural monasteries makes clear the extent to which Frankish rule of Italy

---

[38] Castagnetti, *L'organizzazione del territorio*.

[39] Stoffella, 'Aristocracy and rural churches in the territory of Lucca'; Stoffella, 'Local priests in early medieval rural Tuscany'. On rural private churches and their efficacy in promoting wealthy peasants, whose power was always rural, see Feller, 'Les élites rurales du haut Moyen Âge en Italie (IXe–Xe siècle)'.

[40] Sennis, 'Monasteries and cities'. See also the observations on urban monasteries versus rural ones in Balzaretti, 'Monasteries, towns and the countryside'.

[41] See Chapter 15 in this volume and Lazzari, 'Città e territori', pp. 347–9.

relied upon urban ecclesiastical networks for the cultural consolidation of their rule.

On the borders of the *regnum*, such as in the northeast, some cities expanded upon their earlier foundations, while entirely new centres were settled. Cividale (ancient Forum Iulii), the most important city in Friuli, had in the Lombard period consolidated the main branches of Lombard power (gastaldate, ducal/comital, and episcopal) in the ancient city. Its earlier Byzantine-period defensives were refurbished in the Lombard period, and three palaces were built in the city for the officials of three administrative branches. Coastal and fluvial settlements developed in the northern Adriatic as a result of trade or as challenges to existing power structures (such as bishops); few of these were located at the sites of Roman cities.[42] Some may have had significant populations that cohered into a collective 'civic' identity, such as the collective resentment of the duke famously conveyed by the residents of Istrian towns in the Placitus of Risano (804), so the politics of collective action worked even when people did not live with urban density. From a constellation of settlements in the lagoon, Venice emerged as a distinctly urban centre in the ninth century. It developed in its physical form, its political administration and its written histories of itself a modern expression of urban civility and a past that was not Roman, not Lombard and certainly not Frankish.[43] The ducal palace, churches with saints' relics and fortifications all were constructed on the Rialto in the course of the ninth century; the settlement and its trade networks were anchored by the dukes' urbanistic investment and their minting of coins in the names of Venice's rulers. Its independence notwithstanding, Venice's rulers were the beneficiaries of a certain number of pacts and concessions for urban religious houses, and at times they received the political support of Carolingians; Venice reproduced some Frankish principles of politics if not submitting to Frankish rule directly.[44] Its model of urbanism drew upon tendencies shared with other parts of Carolingian Italy, but remained unique unto itself and its geo-politics.

Because of its position between Venice and Rome, the urbanism of Ravenna took an exceptional path. Control over Ravenna in the late eighth and ninth centuries was disputed.[45] The archbishops were firmly based in Ravenna in the palace there, and preserved strong control on

---

[42] *I placiti*, ed. Manaresi, i, no. 17, p. 55; Cessi, 'L'occupazione longobarda e franca dell'Istria nei secc. VIII e IX'; Menis, 'Cultura in Friuli durante l'età carolingia'.

[43] Gasparri, 'The formation of an early medieval community'; Gelichi, 'La storia di una nuova città attraverso l'archeologia'.

[44] Bougard, 'Les Francs à Venise', pp. 230–1; Gasparri, 'Venezia fra l'Italia bizantina e il regno italico'.

[45] Brown, *Gentlemen and Officers*.

land, jurisdiction and power in the territory around Ravenna and the small cities that had been the Exarchate. The aristocracy, namely the ducal families who appear occasionally in the sources in the mid-ninth century, lived outside of Ravenna, at Jesi, Senigallia and Rimini.[46] The city of Ravenna, an imperial capital and the centre of Byzantine influence on Italy, was celebrated by Charlemagne, who famously sought ancient statues and materials from Ravenna, and Lothar, who granted the removal of more marble, as well as by Ravennate archbishops.[47] It was a city of the church, but not as powerful as Rome. As papal–Frankish relations ran hot and cold over the ninth century, the archbishops of Ravenna sought to leverage some independence from Rome through Frankish support, especially under Lothar and Louis II, but remained rather impotent in the face of both.[48]

Central Italy

Central Italy comprised territories under quite different systems of rule in the ninth century: Lombard principalities of Spoleto and Benevento (discussed in the section below) and the papal state. Each of these was a rather small territory, compared to the northern *Regnum*, and in each polity one main city played the key role in governance while other minor urban centres took supporting roles.[49] The dukes of Spoleto ruled from the ancient city of Spoleto, which had held some strategic military importance in the Roman period and had been strategic in Lombard military forays against Byzantines.[50] Spoleto remained the centre of a duchy under the control of the Franks throughout the ninth century; dukes ruled from an urban palace, the precise location of which is now not clear, though it was within the walls.[51] The area of the Sabina, between the duchy of Spoleto, the papal state and the territories of Ravenna, took on particular import. The landscape was dominated by the abbey of Farfa, which had, in the Lombard period, become the

---

[46] Carile, 'La società ravennate dall'esarcato agli Ottoni'; Haussig, 'L'arcivescovo di Ravenna, il papa ed il re dei Franchi', pp. 193–5.

[47] Bougard, 'Les Francs à Venise', pp. 233–4.

[48] Brown, 'Byzantine Italy, c.680–c.876', p. 449; Brown, 'Louis the Pious'. See, for example, Agnellus, *Liber Pontificalis ecclesiae Ravennatis*, cc. 172–3 and John VIII, *Registrum* 62, ed. Caspar, p. 55.

[49] On the rarity of villages in the territories of Spoleto and the Abruzzo, see Feller, 'L'économie des territoires', pp. 220–2.

[50] Gasparri, 'Il ducato e il principato di Benevento'; Gasparri, 'Il ducato longobardo di Spoleto'; Paroli, *L'Italia centro-settentrionale*; Peduto, 'Insediamenti longobardi del ducato di Benevento (secc. VI-VIII)'.

[51] Pani Ermini, 'Il ducato di Spoleto', p. 744.

largest landowner in the area and which preserved its assets through the assistance of Frankish immunities, concessions and income. Other monasteries were founded in the area, usually in proximity to a *civitas*: S. Salvatore at Rieti, S. Benedetto at Assisi, S. Arcangelo and S. Savino at Fermo, several monasteries in the hills around Spoleto itself.[52] The imperial foundation of Casauria in 873, at the southern limits of the kingdom of Italy, created a new pole for Frankish power in central Italy.[53]

Through the lens of the Farfa documents, we can catch a glimpse of the interaction between urban and rural in the Carolingian period:[54] the private charters and the notices of court reported in the *Regestum Farfense* were redacted at a number of different places, including Spoleto, Rome, the royal palace, in open fields near churches and – with some frequency – Rieti, the nearest small city to Farfa.[55] It was in the pronouncement and redaction of such documents that they gained their juridical value. The spread of locations between the capital of Spoleto, the *civitas* of Rieti, as well as several other places suggests that the geographical structures of power and justice in Carolingian-period Spoleto paralleled those of the more densely urbanized north: both rural and urban networks permitted the practice of governance.

Rome

The magnetic pole in central Italy in this period was undoubtedly the metropolis of Rome. Rome, of course, was *the* Urbs, an urban centre unlike anything else in the whole of medieval Europe.[56] Ninth-century Rome, even if at 1/40 (even at 1/100, if that is what it was) of its population in the first century, was still more populous and more economically vibrant than anywhere else, it was possibly more culturally diverse.[57] Part of its enormous scale in the Middle Ages is owed to the legacy of antiquity: Rome had been exceptionally populous and politically central in antiquity, so it remained. However, the concerted efforts of Rome's bishops, especially in the late eighth century and early ninth

---

[52] Ibid.   [53] Feller, *Les Abruzzes médiévales*.

[54] Costambeys, *Power and Patronage*; Costambeys, 'Disputes and courts in Lombard and Carolingian central Italy' and more generally, Bougard, *La justice*.

[55] On dukes and local urban society of Rieti, see Collavini, 'Duchi e società locali nei ducati di Spoleto e di Benevento nel secolo VIII', pp. 132–9.

[56] On Roman exceptionalism, see Witschel, 'Rom und die Städte Italiens in Spätantike und Frühmittelalter'; Zanini, 'Le città dell'Italia bizantina'.

[57] Sansterre, *Les moines grecs*; on Franks in particular, Bougard, 'Les Francs à Venise'; Delogu, 'I Romani e l'Impero (VII–X secolo)'; Schieffer, 'Charlemagne and Rome'.

century, to marshal the resources of Rome in terms of ecumenical authority, land and spiritual capital, made the city very powerful. The social and political capital of Rome and its leader, the pope, enabled the city and the idea of it in wider cultural imagination to punch above its weight. Its rulers advanced what modern sociologists would recognize as a 'metropolitan identity', fostering an intellectualized urban consciousness.[58] When considering early medieval Rome, we must grapple with the question of whether its very nature sets it so far apart that it must be considered by its own terms, or whether it was the best-formed and most-accomplished result of the aims of many early medieval rulers. I consider it to be the latter, and certainly the strategies of urban investment employed by early medieval popes align with the initiatives of other Italian rulers of this period, and were extremely successful in embodying a distinctly urban practice of power.

While Rome in antiquity had an extensive suburban area outside the walls, in the early Middle Ages most new building took place inside the walls. The neighbourhood around St Peter's became an extension of the urban fabric of Rome, and eventually it was enclosed within walls, too; there was also a small compound around St Paul's in the ninth century.[59] There are glimpses in our sources of the eighth century that suggest that there were rural bases of power in opposition to the papacy, such as Toto of Nepi, in Tuscia in the 760s, but by the ninth century these appear to have been overcome by the momentum of the papal state, and challenges to the papacy were based in the city.[60] The popes exerted direct influence on the bishops of smaller dioceses throughout the See of St Peter through active expression of jurisdictional authority (which we see in the *Liber Pontificalis*) and through networks of patronage, attested in both the *Liber Pontificalis* and the epigraphic record.

The city of Rome had a territory, the *terrae S. Petri*. The hinterland of Rome in the early Middle Ages was controlled by the Roman church in very direct ways for the most part: the land was owned by and worked on behalf of the Roman church, the papal court held juridical authority in the area of the Republic of St Peter and administrative bureaucracy

---

[58] Simmel, 'The metropolis and mental life' argued that the intensity of urban interactions as well as the predominance of economic market factors on human relations in cities that fostered these conditions; for the early medieval city we might argue more for the first condition than the second.

[59] Gibson and Ward-Perkins, 'The surviving remains of the Leonine Wall'; Hubert, 'L'organizzazione territoriale e l'urbanizzazione'; Meneghini and Santangeli-Valenzani, *Roma nell'altomedioevo*; Spera, 'Dalla tomba alla "città" di Paolo'; On the *suburbium*, see Osborne, 'Roman Catacombs'; Spera, *Il paesaggio suburbano*.

[60] On Toto and his brother, Pope Constantine, see now McKitterick, 'The damnatio memoriae of Pope Constantine II (767–768)'.

organized and recorded these processes and their economies.[61] The income that fuelled the city, decorated its churches and provided amenities for the poor, the clergy and for travellers came mostly from papal properties in the countryside around Rome.[62] Some of these are attested in contemporary sources and archaeology.[63] Their purpose, beyond the anchoring papal control of the territory around Rome, was to provide food for the charitable institutions run by the church for the people of Rome, the poor and the pilgrims. The consolidation of the Roman Church's ownership of lands, whether by shifting lands from family to papal ownership, direct purchase or acquisition of former imperial estates, seems to have focussed in the eighth and ninth centuries on blocs of lands in Lazio, and these efforts relate to the military and economic needs of the papacy as it refined its leadership of the papal state.[64] In the territory around Rome, however, the land was owned by the clergy of the urban churches that controlled tenancy and took rents.[65] Chris Wickham has observed the 'near total absence of rural elites' in the Agro Romano;[66] further afield, archaeology attests to some elite residences, but their material culture was closely connected to the city's elites.[67] The strong separation between urban elite administration and rural peasantry around Rome is markedly different from what is recorded in the northern Carolingian kingdoms and in the neighbouring Lombard duchies, and we will consider the effects of this separation below.

The attraction of the city as a place of work, a constellation of pilgrims' shines and eventually as the capital of the Papal State was unmistakable. While some of Rome's influence lay in its size and scale, many positive attributes of the city were elided into a cultural–spiritual package of episcopal authority attached to ancient events and religious traditions. The role of Rome and the papacy in the validation of bishoprics throughout Italy (and beyond) grew over the course of the eighth and ninth centuries, and the insoluble connections between the papacy and the city were promoted by regional bishops who expressed their relationship to

[61] Noble, *The Republic of Saint Peter*, pp. 215–55.

[62] Delogu, 'Rome in the ninth century'; this marks a slightly different view from that expressed in Delogu, 'The "Rebirth" of Rome'.

[63] On the *Domuscultae*, see Marazzi, *I 'Patrimonia'*, pp. 235–61; on S. Cornelia (*Domusculta Capracorum*), see Christie, *Three South Etrurian Churches*; Christie, 'Popes, pilgrims and peasants'; Goodson, 'Villamagna in the Middle Ages', p. 41; Noble, 'Paradoxes and possibilities'.

[64] Marazzi, *I 'Patrimonia'*, p. 260.

[65] Ibid.; Wickham, 'La struttura della proprietà fondiaria nell'Agro Romano, 900–1150', pp. 218–21.

[66] Toubert, *Les structures du Latium*, p. 966; Wickham, 'La struttura della proprietà fondiaria nell'Agro Romano, 900–1150', p. 185.

[67] Molinari, 'Siti rurali e poteri signorili nel Lazio (secoli X–XIII)'; Goodson, 'Villamagna in the Middle Ages'.

the pope, and strove to find apostolic origins for their sees in parallel to Rome. It has been argued that such attention to episcopal adherence to Rome reflects efforts to make Italian church networks and structures more like Frankish ones;[68] whether or not this is true, Rome provided an indelible model of an urban church as a political agent, and this image was powerful and widely used in the hagiography of other Italian cities.[69]

As at Rome, within the territories of southern Italy, comprising the southern Lombard duchy/principate of Benevento, the duchy of Naples and its subsidiaries, the catapanate as well as areas controlled by Muslims (not considered here for reasons of space, but in the main, urbanism was as critical to the role of Islamicate Italy as it was in other parts of the South, if not more so), cities and urban centres were far and away the main places of political and social organization and expression as well the centres of cult. Control of rural territories was essential to rule, even in the south, but the majority of landowners as well as rulers and aristocrats lived in cities, whether in so-called Byzantine, Roman or Lombard areas.[70]

Benevento was not governed by the Carolingians after their conquest of the rest of Lombard Italy; a tribute was presented to the emperor, and occasional gestures towards the authority of, on the one hand, the Franks and, on the other hand, the Byzantine emperors, were made through dating clauses of documents and the language around some kinds of rule.[71] Its geographic position on the peninsula, separated from the duchy of Spoleto by the papal state and including major ports both to the east and west, afforded the Duchy, then Principality of Benevento considerable independence, and though various concessions were made to the Franks in order to facilitate governance, the rulers of Benevento sustained a hostile campaign against the Franks and the papacy up to the mid-ninth century, during which time Benevento was a major centre of political, legal,, and cultural significance. Arechis II (r. 758–787) had established at Benevento a Lombard capital, based in part on the model of Pavia, the northern capital.[72] The princes of Benevento, Salerno and Capua governed the territories from their capital cities.[73] Subsequent princes of Benevento, and also of Salerno when it became a capital in

---

[68] Tabacco, 'L'ambiguità delle istituzioni nell'Europa costruita dai Franchi'.

[69] See examples of Pavia and Ravenna in Everett, 'The hagiography of Lombard Italy'.

[70] Granier, 'Napolitains et Lombards', p. 411. For a juxtaposition of the political and economic structures of Langobardia minor against those of the north, Martin, 'La longobardia meridionale'; Palmieri, 'Duchi, principi e vescovi'.

[71] Martin, 'Éléments préféodaux', pp. 559–60

[72] Belting, 'Studien zum Beneventanischen Hof im 8. Jahrhundert'; Bertolini, 'Arechis II'; Rotili, 'Benevento fra tarda Antichità e alto Medioevo', pp. 324–6.

[73] For Benevento and Salerno, see Peduto, 'Insediamenti longobardi del ducato di Benevento (secc. VI–VIII)'. On the political topography of the Principate of Salerno, see Taviani-Carozzi, La principauté lombarde, pp. 483–514.

851 and Capua in 862, resided in palaces in their cities, and owned princely houses in each of the other capitals. These royal residences were not simply the principal rulers' residences but also the sites of royal justice and, sometimes, in their chapels or associated monasteries, locations of shrines with relevance to the communal identities of the peoples governed.[74] The princes ruled with the support of Beneventan aristocracy and their agents in smaller cities. Very small towns, such as Avellino or Nocera, were referred to in contemporary sources as *civitates*, and the counts and gastalds of other *civitates* like Acerenza and Avellino could be instrumental to rulers, as they were to Sico (r. 817–832).[75]

The princes amassed considerable territories, whether by gift from their faithful, confiscation from traitors or those who died without heirs or military expansion.[76] Some of these lands were then redistributed to their followers, often urban palace officials or (urban) court artisans, though sometimes territorial or estate agents. In the latter half of the ninth century, these exchanges may have been an effort to adopt a Frankish sort of vassalage in southern Italy; diplomas and narrative sources attest to a growing consensus around the term *fidelis*, and a movement towards the regional private powers that characterize tenth-century Italy.[77] Vertical links were also established through religious houses, in that aristocratic daughters and sons went to royal monasteries, such as S. Sophia at Benevento or S. Maximus at Salerno.[78] Such relationships were hardly uncommon in our period throughout Italy and Francia, but it is worth recognizing that the royal monasteries in southern Italy were so resolutely located in cities, near the urban palaces, and this may have encouraged a sort of virtuous cycle of urban social links, between royal monasteries and parents of children in them, around the court.

There were few major rural religious centres in southern Italy. The three major monasteries, S. Vincenzo al Volturno Montecassino and Monte Sant' Angelo, all began before the Lombards or very early in the Lombard period, and while they continued through the Middle Ages as important cult centres, they were anomalous among newly founded

[74] Falkenhausen, 'I Longobardi meridionali', pp. 303–4. On Salerno, see Delogu, *Mito di una città meridionale (Salerno, secoli VIII–XI)*.

[75] Falkenhausen, 'I Longobardi meridionali', pp. 262–4; Gasparri, 'Il ducato e il principato di Benevento'.

[76] Martin, 'Éléments préféodaux', pp. 568–70.

[77] Ibid., pp. 562–6; Feller, 'L'économie des territoires', pp. 226–9, 240–1.

[78] Feller, 'L'économie des territoires', p. 240.

monasteries and churches, which were based nearly always in or very near to cities.[79] Bishops played central roles in the legitimization of rulers, and conversely, some rulers celebrated the cults of the earliest bishops of a city, such as Barbatus of Benevento, as a way of building consensus and celebrating the modern political entity of the city.[80]

Early medieval Naples went from being a medium-sized city under the Byzantine control to an autonomous city-state and then a capital of a territory in its own right. In the mid-eighth century, Neapolitan families succeeded in taking control of the title of *dux*, and what has been an imperially appointed position given to an agent of the Byzantine empire.[81] The duke of Naples controlled the coast up to the Duchy of Benevento, and ruled by dynastic succession and tight relations with the bishops; indeed, bishops were often brothers or nephews of the duke, and Athanasius II (878–898) was both duke and bishop.[82] The city had a substantial population inside and just outside the walled part of the ancient city; the late antique walls of the city had been maintained and partially rebuilt in the Middle Ages. The ducal palace was located within the walls, near the shore, though modern buildings have cancelled all traces of it. Aristocrats in the circle of the duke also lived in the city; they owned properties in the countryside, especially the grain fields east of the Bay of Naples, but the city was clearly the pole of aristocratic representation through religious patronage and consumption of the textiles, metalwork and foodstuffs made in the city.[83]

Early in the ninth century, Gaeta and Amalfi were small centres, with active trade and important families connected very directly to Naples.[84] Through the course of the ninth century, they both had become rich and powerful city-states seeking independence from the duchy of Naples and ruled by urban aristocracies. Like all medieval rulers, the ducal families of Naples and Gaeta were dependent upon the social capital provided by distributing rural landholdings among their supporters, but their main expression of leadership was in their urban residences.

Fundamentally, in the south, assembly politics and political representations took place in cities, within royal precincts or even in shared urban facilities. Some central and all the southern Italian polities cultivated urban ruling cultures, exclusively located in cities that housed palaces,

---

[79] Bloch, *Monte Cassino in the Middle Ages*; Marazzi, 'The early medieval alternative'.
[80] BHL 973–5; Everett, *Patron Saints of Early Medieval Italy*, pp. 39–49.
[81] Cassandro, 'Il ducato bizantino'; Galasso, 'L'eredità municipale del ducato di Napoli'.
[82] Kreutz, *Before the Normans*, p. 22.
[83] On the economy of the city in the tenth century, see Skinner, 'Urban communities in Naples, 900–1050'.
[84] Delogu, 'Il ducato di Gaeta'; Skinner, *Family Power in Southern Italy*.

courts, and major religious institutions. In southern Italy, disputes were resolved more often in urban spaces than in rural meeting grounds. The continuity of the pre-Lombard past of several cities was stressed in the preservation and extension of the city walls of Salerno and Benevento, for example. New investments in southern Lombard cities also projected cosmopolitan and worldly qualities of their patrons. The architectural vocabularies employed in, for example, Benevento, spoke to earlier Lombard models from northern Italy but also distant and relatively ancient Byzantine imperial models from Constantinople.[85]

In sum, throughout Italy, ancient cities remained political centres of power in the ninth century. In the northern half of the peninsula, in the *regnum* under the Carolingians and through the fracturing of Carolingian power in the ninth century, cities were key nodes in networks of royal and imperial administration that stretched across territories through rural centres as well as urban ones. In central and southern Italy, political authority and the practices of governance and justice were much more firmly rooted in urban society. Further, cities across the peninsula became increasingly independent one from another and more concentrated over the course of the late eighth and ninth centuries. These two trends can be registered in noting the itineraries of Carolingian emperors. Charlemagne's travels in Italy were rather exceptional among his itineraries in that they concentrated mostly on major cities: Milan, Pavia, Verona, Ravenna, Rome, Spoleto; some minor cities: Mantua, Treviso and Capua and the abbey of Montecassino;[86] Louis the Pious never came to Italy. Lothar avoided major cities in Italy, while Louis II and his successors frequented them.[87] The itineraries of Louis II took him to Pavia thirteen times; Rome, Mantua and Benevento six times; Brescia and Ravenna five times; Venosa three times; and twice each in the rural estates of Auriola, Corte Olona and Marengo.[88] The politics of Louis II's reign were different from Lothar's, of course, and Louis was necessarily in southern Italy more often, therefore interacting more often with emphatically urban rulers and administrations. We can nonetheless see in the itineraries the critical importance of cities in the highest levels of political interaction between Carolingian emperors and Italy, and different strategies at play in the engagement with cities and change over time.

---

[85] On Benevento, see Goodson, 'Basilicas and centralized churches in the Early Middle Ages'.

[86] On Charlemagne's itinerary, see now McKitterick, *Charlemagne*, pp. 178–86.

[87] Bougard, 'La cour et le gouvernement de Louis II (840–875)'; Bougard, 'Du centre à la périphérie'.

[88] Tondini, 'Un modello per il regno dei Carolingi in Italia', pp. 196–7; Brühl, *Fodrum, Gistum, Servitium Regis*, p. 403.

Paolo Delogu has highlighted the role played by cities in the social reorganization of the kingdom of Italy after 774 and through the changes in the structures of power within the kingdom over the course of the ninth century; as some counts of the *Regnum* exploited freemen as labourers, exacted arbitrary tolls and seized properties, the countryside of northern Italy became increasingly dominated by Frankish and then Italian counts, many of whom lived in cities but exercised their authority and secured their wealth in the countryside.[89] By contrast, inhabitants of cities – even cities that were comital capitals – sometimes organized for their own collective common good, securing the maintenance of public buildings, generating local income through artisanal and mercantile activity, and seeking the employment of local boys and men in episcopal courts and churches.[90] François Bougard and Tiziana Lazzari have shown through focussed regional studies of preserved documents that in some areas of the *Regnum*, royal power and urban authority had a poor grip on certain parts of the countryside.[91] Thus, while recognizing that political structures of northern Italy maintained a connection to the countryside, we must also recognize variations within regions of urban-rural models. The aim in fostering urbanism, whether by kings, dukes, bishops or abbots, was to assert a robust collective identity, with political, social and economic power unto itself and in opposition to others.

Conclusions

The Italian peninsula, in contrast to the Frankish empire north of the Alps, remained from antiquity to the early Middle Ages a dense constellation of cities. The concentration of settlement – the shape of society – created specific contexts and conditions for the transformations of the early medieval world in the Carolingian period, including an intensification of competition between cities and within cities. The nature of urban investment varied across different regions, in relation to different practices of power and governance though an urban network, with more deliberate urbanism in the south than the north. This reality was not simply motivated by the aspirations of ancient models, though that was no doubt a factor. It reflected alternative ways by which people organize themselves and each other, which had implications for social cohesion as

---

[89] Delogu, 'Lombard and Carolingian Italy', pp. 308–10, which signals some shifts in Delogu's thinking about the structures of comital power from his work on the topic in the 1960s.

[90] Angelis, 'Cittadini prima della cittadinanza'.

[91] Bougard, 'Lo stato e le élites fra 888 e 962'; Lazzari, 'Città e territori', esp. pp. 339, 345.

well as conflicts. These different positions reflect the extent and richness of the 'field' of urbanism for cultural production.

François Bougard has usefully distinguished several different uses of the past – and different positionings of the present – among some cities of Italy and their relationship to Carolingians. Thus the Veronese established a strong and durable relationship with Pippin through literary production and patronage of the built environment, including the location of the Frankish king's tomb, while Benevento from the mid-eighth century presented itself as distinctly anti-Carolingian, a 'refuge of the Lombard identity ... largely constructed through antithesis'.[92] Similar distinctions in the political character of Italian places can be observed by scrutinizing Latin hagiographic production in ninth-century Italy. Giorgia Vocino has shown that the cities of the *Regnum Italiae* promoted new ideas about religious behaviour and political authority emerging from Francia.[93] Thus, within the *Regnum* between the 770s and the 840s, there were a great number of saints' cults emerging around early bishops of northern Italian cities.[94] While a saintly bishop and his relics may have been celebrated in a place for centuries, in this period many relics were relocated to urban shrines and new tools for their veneration were composed, such as the new *vitae, passiones* or *translationes* for saints Philastrus of Brescia,[95] Syrus of Pavia,[96] Hermagoras of Aquileia,[97] Ilarus of Grado,[98] Ambrose of Milan[99] and Zeno of Verona[100] – all founding or very early bishops.[101]

Early bishops were also popular in the rest of Italy, though there is less of a direct connection with Carolingian/Frankish values in the cults of Naples, Rome and other southern cities. The relics of saints Fortunatus, Maximus, Efebus and Agrippinus, all early bishops of Naples, were brought from different catacombs outside the walls to the cathedral by Bishop John IV between 842 and 849.[102] In the early ninth century, the cult of the seventh-century Beneventan bishop Barbatus (d. 682) was

---

[92] Bougard, 'Les Francs à Venise', p. 228.   [93] Vocino, 'Under the aegis'.

[94] On cults of bishops in particular, see Picard, *Le souvenir des évêques*. Giorgia Vocino points out that 'martyrs and confessors ... seem to have been the only ones deserving newly written hagiography in Carolingian Italy'. Vocino, 'Under the aegis', p. 49.

[95] BHL 6797; Vocino, 'Triginta autem Brixienses sunt episcopi quos meminimus'.

[96] BHL 7976–8; Everett, 'The earliest recension of the life of S. Sirus of Pavia (Vat. Lat. 5771)'; Vocino, 'Under the aegis'; also Vocino, 'Hagiography'.

[97] BHL 3838; Vocino, 'Under the aegis'.

[98] BHL 3881, Cerno, 'Passio Helari et Tatiani'; Vocino, 'Under the aegis'.

[99] BHL 377d; Tomea, 'Ambrogio e i suoi fratelli'.   [100] BHL 9001–08d; BHL 9009.

[101] See translation of Saint Romulus from Villa Matutiana (S. Remo) to Genova between 889 and 916: Formentini, *Genova*.

[102] John the Deacon, *Gesta Episcoporum Neapolitanorum*, pars II, ed. Waitz; Strazzullo, 'Le due antiche cattedrali di Napoli', p. 229.

activated: his *Vita* dates from about then and there is also a cycle of paintings in the crypt of the Duomo.[103] The narrative sources attesting to these translations make clear the value of saints in competition between urban polities and the expression of cohesion between ruler, populace and divine figures. For example, the ninth-century *Translatio Ianuarii* reports a miraculous vision of Saint Ianuarius, an early bishop of Benevento then of Naples.[104] Ianuarius had been martyred in Pozzuoli with the deacon Festus, the lector Desiderius and others (Sossius, Proculus, Acutius and Eutichius); in the fifth century, Ianuarius's body had been translated to the catacombs outside of Naples, by the Neapolitan bishop Iohannes I.[105] The ninth-century *Translatio* reports that the Beneventan populace discovered the relics outside Naples and, along with the Neapolitan bishop Urso, brought them to Benevento in 839, in procession with hymns and lamps and placed them in the cathedral, in a small marble-lined oratory called 'Jerusalem'.[106] The reports of the translation must relate to Prince Sico's siege of Naples in 831, an episode of Benevento's long war with the Neapolitans, as well as to the relations between Bishop Urso and Prince Sicard.[107] Relics of the local Saint Festus, a deacon who had been martyred with Saint Ianuarius, and the lector Desiderius, buried outside Benevento, were also brought to the cathedral of Benevento, and the three who had been martyred together but buried separately were reunited.[108] The vision of the saint, the involvement of the populace and the bishop conveyed the consensus of the people of Benevento to dominate Naples, to seize it and overtake it, and to physically reunite the relics of the saints in the story, restoring coherence to a group of saints that had wrongfully been scattered.[109] Antonio Vuolo cites the composition of these *Translationes*, along with 'Vita Barbati', mentioned above, as markers of the beginning of an episcopal seat setting out autonomy from the Lombard court, no longer an agent of the princes.[110] That may have been the intent, but the epitaph of the Lombard Prince Sico (817–832) claimed his responsibility for the translation of Saint Ianuarius, describing the burial of the prince's body

---

[103] BHL 973–5; Everett, *Patron Saints of Early Medieval Italy*, pp. 39–49; Bove, 'L'architecture de la cathédrale de Bénévént', pp. 26–8.

[104] BHL 4140.   [105] *Gesta Episcoporum Neapolitanorum*, pars I, ed. Waitz, p. 406.

[106] BHL 4116, 4118; *Chronicon Salernitanum*, 57, ed. Westerbergh.

[107] Vuolo, 'Agiografia beneventana', pp. 220–6.

[108] BHL 4126. Other relics were moved from Alife to the Duomo of Benevento in a ceremony organized by Bishop Urso and Prince Sicard: BHL 2854–5; BHL 8318; Oldoni, 'Agiografia longobarda tra secolo IX e X'.

[109] Head, 'Discontinuity and discovery in the cult of saints'.

[110] Vuolo, 'Agiografia beneventana', pp. 223–4.

near that of the saint.[111] This example, with convoluted and competing narratives about ostensibly the same remains of a long-dead bishop, illustrates the strong potential they held for the expression of collective identities and potency against competitors. This example is also a useful reminder of the fact that urban communal identities were not necessarily singular or coherent, but urban contexts provided significant opportunities for competition between internal groups.

The 'explosion of writing' ignited by Carolingian influence and Frankish immigrants to Italy has encouraged a certain kind of research. Those manuscripts permit a detailed manuscript analysis for some regions, adhering strictly to contemporary, not later, accounts, but such study is simply not possible in the south, not even in Rome. This is worth pointing out, because it has fostered a certain circularity in argument that focuses exclusively on the saint veneration of northern Italy or the urban histories of northern Italy, for similar reasons. I have tried to show, however, that urbanism as a political strategy was not unique to northern Italy and the *regnum*, but rather it was a tool used in different ways by rulers across Italy. Investigating strategies employed by these rulers and the differences across regions helps us to recognize commonalities in the languages and topographies of power across the early medieval world and to consider the shapes and experiences of power among the people of early medieval Italy.

---

[111] *Carmina Varia*, ed. Dümmler, pp. 649–50.

14 Rome and the Others

Saints, Relics and Hagiography in Carolingian North-Eastern Italy

Francesco Veronese

Introduction: The Carolingians, Saints and Relics

In her recent and groundbreaking study on the formation and management of Charlemagne's empire, Jennifer Davis seriously challenged an idea widespread among historians of Carolingian times: that Charlemagne sought to impose a standardization of the practices and tools of government throughout the empire. Charlemagne, Davis underlined, was more interested in centralizing power, communications and the administration of justice than in standardizing them.[1] The aim was that of extending Carolingian authority to all the different peoples and social groups of the empire and having them acknowledge it. Yet in some fields of (broadly) political action, standardization, in Davis' eyes, was actually one of the goals pursued by Charlemagne.[2] In question here, as has long been highlighted by scholars, are very general issues of religious uniformity, such as the Christian identity of the empire and its rulers and the homogeneity of liturgy and belief, at least at a very basic level: everyone under Charlemagne's rule had to be baptized and to know the Lord's Prayer and the *Credo*.[3] Indeed, only Christian subjects could acknowledge the authority of a Christian king.[4] As Mayke de Jong has argued, the Carolingian empire was supposed to identify itself with the *ecclesia*, the community of the Christian faithful, ruled by a king anointed by God.[5]

One of the aspects that came under the closer control of royal power and its officers was the cult of saints. Two important stages in the process of its regulation can be detected. In 794 Charlemagne convoked and presided over an important meeting of bishops in Frankfurt. The council

---

I would like to thank Chiara Provesi for useful comments and suggestions over preliminary drafts of this article.
[1] Davis, *Charlemagne's Practice*, esp. ch. 6, pp. 293–335.   [2] Ibid., pp. 300–1.
[3] For a good overview, see de Jong, 'Charlemagne's church'; Nelson, 'Religion in the age of Charlemagne'.
[4] Innes, 'Immune from heresy'.   [5] de Jong, 'Ecclesia and the early medieval polity'.

dealt with several topics, as the resulting *Capitulare Francofurtense* attests: adoptianism, images and their cult, Tassilo of Bavaria's plea for royal pardon, food prices and more general issues of monastic and ecclesiastical life.[6] Among them, a certain amount of attention was paid to the cult of saints. Chapter 15 stipulated that every monastery hosting saints' relics should provide itself with a special *oratorium*, where divine service in their honour could be performed day and night.[7] In chapter 42, moreover, a strong limitation on the acknowledgement of new saints was introduced: only those figures supported by the *auctoritas passionum* or *vitae meritus* should be worshipped or have new monuments erected in their honour along the streets.[8] In other words, only saints whose cults were attested by written hagiographical traditions (*passiones, vitae*) could be venerated, and the creation of new saints was no longer allowed to serve as a tool for mastering space and defining, or changing, its identity. The second major step was taken almost twenty years later. In 813, Charlemagne convoked five regional councils in order to reassess and push forward his programme for the moral reform of the empire.[9] The Council of Mainz forbade transfers of saintly bodies that were not explicitly approved by rulers and/or a synod of bishops.[10] Paul Fouracre saw in these measures the clearest and most conscious expressions of an overall plan for centralizing the cult and the social uses of saints and relics.[11] In Fouracre's view, they were meant to put an end to the practice of sanctifying recently deceased and aristocratic figures, mostly bishops, who constituted an important part of the community of saints worshipped in the Merovingian kingdom and had a central role in the self-representation of aristocratic groups.[12] More recent studies have shown that in Merovingian times at least some kinds of hagiographical texts were conceived of and produced in order to teach young aristocrats to

---

[6] For a comprehensive overview of the synod of Frankfurt, see Berndt (ed.), *Das Frankfurter Konzil von 794*; with special consideration for the issue of the cult of images, Noble, *Images, Iconoclasm, and the Carolingians*, pp. 169–80.

[7] *De monasterio, ubi corpora sanctorum sunt: ut habeat oratorium intra claustra, ubi peculiare officium et diuturnum fiat; Capitulare Francofurtense*, c. 15, ed. Werminghoff, p. 168.

[8] *Ut nulli novi sancti colantur aut invocentur, nec memoria eorum per vias erigantur, sed hii soli in ecclesia venerandi sint, qui ex auctoritate passionum aut vitae merito electi sint; ibid.*, ch. 42, p. 170.

[9] Davis, *Charlemagne's Practice*, pp. 243–59, has argued that the idea of holding regional councils at the same time in different places derived from Bavarian precedents. See also Diesenberger, 'How collections shape the texts', esp. p. 200.

[10] *Deinceps vero corpora sanctorum de loco ad locum nullus transferre praesumat sine consilio principis vel episcoporum sanctaeque synodi licentia; Concilium Moguntinense*, c. 51, ed. Werminghoff, p. 272.

[11] Fouracre, 'The origins of the Carolingian attempt to regulate the cult of saints'.

[12] Fouracre and Gerberding, *Late Merovingian France*.

respect and serve the king.[13] Saints and hagiography in the Merovingian period were therefore not only social and political tools for aristocratic groups; they were also designed to be an instrument of government. In Carolingian times they retained this role; yet saints, hagiography and their uses were reshaped according to the new dynasty's need for self-legitimation. Preference was accorded to saints and relics belonging to a distant past and coming from distant places, especially from outside the Frankish kingdom. Issues of the centralization and regulation of cultic practices went hand in hand with the need to close the door on the making of new saints, who could boost their kinship groups' prestige and social power and thus present them as possible alternatives to the Carolingians as kings of the Franks. Not that surprisingly, at the same time the Carolingians themselves discovered the advantages of having a saint in their own family. In his *Liber de episcopis Mettensibus* of the late eighth century, Paul the Deacon established for the first time – as far as we know – a direct kinship tie between the ruling dynasty and St Arnulf, bishop of Metz in the first half of the seventh century, who is described as an ancestor of the Carolingians.[14] Damien Kempf argued that this scheme was orchestrated by Angilram, bishop of Metz, who wished to strengthen the connections between his see and the Carolingians, rather than by the royal court, as previously suggested by Walter Goffart.[15] In any case, Arnulf's membership in the royal kinship group received approval, and in ninth-century Carolingian genealogies he somehow appears as the founder of the royal family.[16] Sanctity was therefore no longer there for the taking. It was put firmly under the Carolingian rulers' control and was theirs to exploit. Only some kinds of saints were now acceptable, and they could only be put to a limited range of uses.

Despite such strong limitations on the use of saints and relics, these still remained very flexible tools for developing social and political strategies of self-representation and for the creation of identities. New ways of exploiting their multilayered meanings, as objects capable of connecting the material world with the spiritual one, resulted from negotiation with the new rules imposed by the Carolingians. As has been highlighted by numerous scholars, a new emphasis was placed on Roman relics.[17] They

---

[13] Helvétius, 'Hagiographie et formation politique'.

[14] Paul the Deacon, *Liber de episcopis Mettensibus*, ed. Santarossa, p. 137.

[15] Goffart, 'Paul the Deacon's *Gesta episcoporum Mettensium*'; Kempf, 'Paul the Deacon's *Liber de episcopis Mettensibus*'. Damien Kempf also published an edition with English translation of the text: Paul the Deacon, *Liber de episcopis Mettensibus*, ed. Kempf.

[16] Wood, 'Genealogy defined by women'.

[17] Smith, 'Old saints, new cults'; Herbers, 'Reliques romaines au IXe siecle'.

played a crucial role in the context of the Carolingian perception of Rome as a reservoir of authoritative traditions, objects and texts that gave rulers the ideal grounds for their programmes of moral and ecclesiastical reform.[18] Roman relics were requested, traded and stolen, and were transferred to the core of the Frankish kingdom by some of the most important Carolingian courtiers, such as Fulrad, Hilduin and Einhard. Hagiographical texts were produced in order to celebrate the arrival of relics coming from Rome and the miracles they performed in their new resting places. Yet not only Roman saints and relics were put to use. Our sources show that other networks involving the circulation of relics and texts were also at work in the different regions of the Carolingian domain, responding to the particular needs and features of the contexts in which they were used and of the participating social actors. In this chapter, I will focus on a quite limited geographical area, north-eastern Italy. I will examine some cases of social and political use of saints, relics and hagiography by the Carolingian public officers working there. On the one hand, I will show how they used them in order to build relationships with local elites and to try to get them involved in the Carolingian mechanisms of power; in other words, it was part of the attempt to make north-eastern Italy a Carolingian place. On the other hand, my attention will turn to how Italy, through its resources and perceptions, influenced the identities of the actors involved in exploiting relics, fostering cults and producing texts. The cases I will deal with are set at different times during the period of Carolingian rule in Italy, falling between the end of the eighth and the second half of the ninth century. Thus, it will also be possible to underline continuity and change in the use and meaning attributed to relics and saints by Carolingian agents in north-eastern Italy.

Re-editing the Past in Verona

At first sight and from an institutional point of view at least, the north-eastern part of the kingdom of Italy appears to be strongly Carolingian.[19] Between the 780s and the first half of the ninth century, public officers – counts, margraves and bishops – operating in the region were very frequently foreigners, mostly coming from Alamannia, Bavaria and, of

---

[18] de Jong, 'Charlemagne's church'; Costambeys, Innes and MacLean, *The Carolingian World*, pp. 136–7; Hen, 'The romanization of the Frankish liturgy'.
[19] See also Chapter 6 in this volume.

course, Francia.[20] They were chosen by Carolingian authorities, starting with Charlemagne himself, from among social and familial groups already integrated into the Carolingian mechanisms of power and versed in its logic. They were assigned to prestigious episcopal and comital offices in places far away from their native lands, where their positions of power depended only on their loyalty to the Carolingian rulers and the support they received from them. Their task was that of fostering the integration of local elites into the new political horizon in which they found themselves, the (still-forming) Carolingian empire. Carolingian rulers also directly intervened to modify the administrative and jurisdictional organization of the region, when they considered it necessary. The trend of imposing foreign officers has been mooted as a factor contributing to Hrotgaud's 776 revolt, and actually stepped up in its aftermath;[21] one of its main results was that the office of counts, typical of the Frankish kingdom since Merovingian times, replaced that of dukes, of Lombard tradition.[22] Moreover, in 828 the margrave Baldrich, who had not been able to prevent some Bulgarian raids into Friuli, was deposed and his march divided into four smaller jurisdictions, as we learn from the *Annales regni Francorum*.[23] Pippin of Italy was extremely active in this area from a military point of view. He fought and defeated the Avars in 796, and was celebrated for his military prowess in the poem *De Pippini regis victoria Avarica*.[24] He also tried several times to extend Frankish authority over the Venetian lagoons in the first decade of the ninth century.[25] His attempts were never entirely successful (or only for very short periods), but Carolingian pressure on the northern Adriatic was at the core of the negotiations held at Aachen in 812 between Charlemagne and the Byzantine emperor's ambassadors, who on that occasion agreed for the first time to call the Frankish ruler *imperatorem et basileum*.[26]

But how did the representatives of Carolingian power translate, or try to translate, institutional 'Carolingianness' into a socially diffused and

---

[20] Hlawitschka, *Franken, Alemannen, Bayern*; Beumann and Schröder (eds.), *Die transalpinen Verbindungen der Bayern*; Maurer, Schwarzmaier and Zotz (eds.), *Schwaben und Italien*; Pohl, '"*Gens ipsa peribit*"', esp. pp. 74–5. With a special focus on north-eastern Italy, Castagnetti, *Minoranze etniche dominanti*.

[21] On Hrotgaud's revolt, see Krahwinkler, *Friaul im Frühmittelalter*, pp. 126–34; Davis, *Charlemagne's Practice*, pp. 136–9.

[22] For more on the passage from Lombard to Frankish rule, see Gasparri, 'Il Passaggio dai Longobardi ai Carolingi'; Tabacco, 'L'Avvento dei Carolingi nel Regno dei Longobardi'; Gasparri, *Italia Longobarda*, pp. 100–42.

[23] *ARF*, s.a. 828, ed. Kurze, p. 174.   [24] *De Pippini regis victoria avarica*, ed. Berto.

[25] Berto, 'La "Venetia"'; Borri, 'L'Adriatico tra Bizantini, Longobardi e Franchi', pp. 41–50.

[26] *ARF*, s.a. 812, ed. Kurze, p. 136.

shared identity, at least among local elites? A central role in this process was assigned to local saints' cults and their exploitation by means of the production and/or diffusion of hagiographical texts.

Between the end of the eighth and the first half of the ninth centuries, Verona was in many ways a central place in Carolingian Italy. The succession of foreign bishops and counts that administered the town and its territory in this period suggests that Carolingian authorities were particularly eager to secure control over them. Since Roman times, Verona had lain in a strategic position at the intersection between north-south and east-west routes.[27] Under the Ostrogothic king Theoderic, Verona had become a *sedes regia*.[28] King Pippin, Charlemagne's son, spent some time there, though never very long periods.[29] Even later, especially during the reign of Emperor Berengar, Verona maintained the role of a place of residence for kings, and became the capital of the kingdom. Furthermore, some of its Carolingian bishops belonged to the upper imperial aristocracy. The Alamannian Egino was closely connected to the royal monastery of Reichenau, where he was buried.[30] He established channels for communication and the exchange of manuscripts, objects and texts across the Alps; as a result, Alamannian-like scripts are attested in Carolingian Verona's book and charter production.[31] His – likewise Alamannian – successor, Ratold, became one of the most loyal counsellors of Louis the Pious after his experience as bishop of Verona.[32] In 834, he was involved in securing the release of Empress Judith from her captivity in Tortona, where she had been confined by Lothar.[33] Noting, Ratold's successor, belonged to an aristocratic kinship group from the Middle Rhine Valley.[34] He maintained close relationships with the royal female monastery of San Salvatore in Brescia and with some of the most renowned intellectuals of his time, such as Hraban Maur. After his period in Verona, he served as bishop of Brescia. It is hard to say whether the subsequent career development of Ratold and Noting resulted from a job well done in Verona or from the personal prestige and social connections they enjoyed prior to taking office. Yet this seems to make little difference. In the first case, the see of Verona would have worked as a powerful launching pad

---

[27] de Feo, 'La *via Postumia*'; Azzara, 'Le vie di comunicazione'.
[28] Brogiolo, 'Capitali e residenze regie nell'Italia longobarda'.
[29] La Rocca, *Pacifico di Verona*, p. 175.
[30] Zettler, 'Die karolingische Grafen'. On Egino's grave in Reichenau, Hoffmann, Erdmann, Czarnetzki and Rottländer, 'Das Grab des Bischofs Egino von Verona'.
[31] Santoni, 'Scrivere documenti'.   [32] Hlawitschka, 'Ratold'.
[33] On this episode Hammer, *From Ducatus to Regnum*, pp. 327–37.
[34] Andenna, 'Notingo'.

for the self-promotion and social advance of its bishops. In the second, the see would have been seen as worthy of being assigned to highly powerful figures. In either case, being bishop of Verona in Carolingian times was a matter of power.

Carolingian Verona, especially its cathedral *scriptorium* and library, was a lively centre for the production, preservation and diffusion of written texts.[35] A whole range of historiographical, poetical and hagiographical texts has recently been assigned to Verona, and dated to between the second half of the eighth and the first half of the ninth centuries. A comparison of palaeographical and codicological elements of the so-called *Epitome phillipsiana* with other books crafted in Carolingian Verona has encouraged the attribution of the same provenance to this collection of excerpts from the Bible, the Fathers and early medieval historical texts.[36] The collection pays considerable attention to the succession of regimes that governed Italy since Roman times.[37] It contains texts concerning the Gothic king Theoderic, such as the famous (and probably sixth-century) *Anonimo Valesiano*, as well as selected parts of Paul the Deacon's *Historia Langobardorum*. A direct line linking Italy's political past to the Old Testament is traced; the Italian populace is thus presented as participating in the history of salvation in a way that clearly recalls contemporary Carolingian representations of the Franks as people chosen by God.[38] This collection seems designed to underline the antiquity, prestigious history and individuality of a territory that the Carolingians had recently conquered. The new rulers of Italy – that is, those who had inherited such a prestigious past – were most probably the addressees of the collection. This is also suggested by the presence of texts in the collection that can be read as models of good kingship (Constantine) and bad, or at least ambiguous, government (Theoderic). Establishing correct conduct for rulers was of the utmost importance to Carolingian ideology. Since the time of Charlemagne, the king had developed a new role for himself, one which contemporary sources described using a word usually connected to priests and bishops: *ministerium*; he had to drive his people to salvation in the afterlife. In

---

[35] On the history of the cathedral library of Verona, see Turrini, 'La Biblioteca Capitolare di Verona'; Marchi, 'Breve discorso storico sulla Biblioteca Capitolare di Verona'.

[36] For the attribution of this codex to Verona, see Rose, *Verzeichnis der lateinischen Handschriften*, pp. 299–307; Cessi, 'Di due miscellanee storiche medievali'. A more cautious opinion has been expressed by Pani, 'La trasmissione dell'*Historia Langobardorum*', pp. 379–85.

[37] For a comprehensive reading of the *Epitome*, see the unpublished thesis of Tondini, 'Un modello per il regno'.

[38] Garrison, 'The Franks as the New Israel?'. For an overview on the idea of 'chosen people' in the early Middle Ages, see Heydemann, 'People(s) of God?'.

Louis the Pious' time this duty was further emphasized; the ruler was to become the moral head of the empire, so that he could convey proper models of behaviour to his people and engage in *correctio*.[39] But only a morally proper head could correct the other members of the social body and legitimately show them how they had to live in order to be welcomed into the kingdom of heaven. Carolingian moralists produced *specula princi-pum* aiming to teach Christian morality and duties to contemporary kings.[40] The portraits of rulers of the past in the *Epitome phillipsiana* may have had the same function. Most probably, the somewhat eschatological description of Italy's past as part of a providential history was equally addressed to local elites, who were thus called on to accept a contemporary government that had inherited this past and had charged itself with the final accomplishment of salvation. The bishops of Verona had elaborated an ambitious scheme for rethinking the past in order to propose new and shared identities to rulers and ruled. Both sides were called upon to make their contribution: Italy had its glorious past, while the Carolingians were its glorious present.

A concern for the recovery of the local past and a conscious use of its resources is also evident in Carolingian Verona. This is where saints and relics played a prominent role. Sometime between the end of the eighth and the beginning of the ninth centuries, a Life of St Zeno, bishop of Verona, was composed by an otherly unknown *Coronatus notarius*.[41] Zeno lived in the fourth century; he was almost contemporary to Ambrose of Milan.[42] His cult in Verona is attested since the first half of the fifth century by both monument and text.[43] Coronatus' Life is composed of a series of miraculous episodes, some of which were already reported by older sources, such as Gregory the Great's *Dialogi* and Paul the Deacon's *Historia Langobardorum*. Most probably in the same period, a further hagiographical text, the *Passio et translatio sanctorum Firmi et Rustici*, was written in Verona.[44] It gives an account of the martyrdom of

---

[39] Guillot, 'Une *Ordinatio* Méconnue'; and, above all, de Jong, *The Penitential State*.

[40] Meens, 'Politics, mirrors of princes and the Bible'; Dubreucq, 'La litterature des *Specula*'; Dubreucq, 'Le prince et le peuple dans les miroirs des princes Carolingiens'.

[41] The *Sermo de vita Zenonis* is edited in Marchi, Orlandi and Brenzoni, *Il Culto di San Zeno nel Veronese*, pp. 18–23. For its date of composition, see Anti, *Verona e il Culto di San Zeno*, pp. 46–54.

[42] In a letter to Siagrius, successor of Zeno as bishop of Verona, Ambrose of Milan called Zeno *sanctae memoriae*: Ambrose of Milan, *Epistulae*, book 8, n. 56, ed. Banterle, vol. 2, p. 110.

[43] A sermon by Bishop Petronius of Verona (for others, of Bologna), who lived in that period, talks about the popular devotion focussed on Zeno's grave, also referring to *aedis istius ampliata sublimitas*: a (bigger) church had thus been erected over it. *Sermo Petronii Episcopi Veronensis in Natale Sancti Zenonis*, ed. Hamman, coll. 141–2.

[44] The text is edited in Golinelli, 'Passione e traslazione dei Santi Fermo e Rustico', esp. pp. 13–9.

Firmus and Rusticus in Verona at the beginning of the fourth century under Emperor Maximianus (but some manuscripts report Maximinus), and the journeys of their bodies after death. They were finally deposited at a church in Verona, 'not far from the river Adige', at the very end of the Lombard government, under the kings Desiderius and Adelchis.[45] The Carolingian period in Verona thus appears to have been marked by a strong and conscious investment in local sanctity. Saints belonging to earlier Christian centuries were now celebrated by means of hagiographical texts that emphasized the long-lasting connections between their protagonists and Verona. These connections may have been created *ex novo* in some cases. We have no elements linking Firmus and Rusticus to Verona before the second half of the eighth century at the earliest, for instance. Architectural works dated to that period in the church where they were interred, now San Fermo Maggiore, have been brought into connection with the arrival of their relics.[46] A textile decorated with little portraits of Verona's bishops, a sort of figurative episcopal list now known as the *Velo di Classe*, has equally been interpreted as a celebration of the two saints and their deposition in Verona.[47]

The hagiographical celebration of local saints in Verona between the late eighth and the early ninth centuries seems to have proceeded in strict accordance with Carolingian policies on saints' veneration as expressed in Frankfurt. Written texts were the means for assessing the merits of Zeno's life and the authority of the passion of Firmus and Rusticus, thus meeting the ideal and legal requirements for the validity of their cults in a Carolingian context; they also served to attest to their connections to Verona since ancient times.

Who promoted this written celebration of local saints, and why? Several hints point to the Carolingian bishops of Verona. Some of the ideas, images and messages emerging from the texts seem to respond to needs of these bishops for self-legitimation. The Life of a saintly bishop of the past, Zeno, in this case, was a chief means for promoting the authority and sanctity of his successors in the present.[48] In the *Passio et translatio Firmi et Rustici*, a decisive role in the recovery of the martyrs' relics is assigned to the last Lombard bishop of Verona, Anno.[49] In the

---

[45] On this text, see Veronese, 'Foreign bishops using local saints'.

[46] Hudson, 'I resti precedenti'.

[47] Picard, *Le souvenir des évêques*, pp. 515–9; Frattaroli, 'Il velo di classe'.

[48] In the same period, Zeno was also celebrated in a rhythmical composition, the *Rythmus de sancto Zenone*, which shares many episodes with Coronatus' *Sermo*. Vocino, 'Santi e luoghi santi', pp. 224–6; Vocino, 'Under the aegis of the saints', pp. 46–7.

[49] It is unclear whether he also piloted the transition of 774, as we do not know the date of his death. Anno was subsequently venerated as a saint in Verona. Tonolli, 'Annone, vescovo di Verona'.

text, Anno is depicted as the pivot of the whole local community, which gathers around him as he goes back to Verona with the relics he has bought in Trieste;[50] the foreign bishops of Carolingian Verona needed to develop exactly such a role for themselves in the eyes of local elites. Since they held control over the *scriptorium* and the cathedral library, they had at their disposal the means to express themselves and promote their strategies through written texts. They were themselves highly trained and cultivated figures, closely connected to a culturally prominent monastic milieu on the other side of the Alps, especially in the region of Lake Constance (Reichenau, St Gall) and the Middle Rhine Valley.[51] Recent studies by Francesca Santoni, Alfons Zettler, Giorgia Vocino and Giovanna Tondini have shown that these bishops established long-lasting channels for communication and the exchange of texts, books, objects and people across the Alps.[52] In order to create positive relation-ships with the social and political elites of Verona, they focussed on a recovery of the local past, both in its monumental (that is, Roman and pagan) and its Christian elements. This is shown, for instance, by the *Versus de Verona*, a poem in praise of the town in the shape of a *laus civitatis*, almost certainly written at Verona's cathedral during the reign of King Pippin of Italy (781–810).[53] One interesting aspect of this text lies in its sharing of narrative elements, sometimes even the same vocabulary and sentences, with the hagiographies of Zeno and of Firmus and Rusticus.[54] A relationship of some sort between these texts surely exists, even if it is difficult to determine precisely who was inspired by whom, as they all belong to the same period. Yet this is interesting per se, as it shows that the same ideas were expressed in the same ways and with similar formulations in texts of different literary character. The bishops most probably sought to address as wide as possible an audience. In so doing they aimed to prove their interest and ability in appreciating and preserving the central elements, or those they perceived to be and pre-sented as such, of local identity.

---

[50] The episode belongs to the tradition of hagiographical *adventus* passages, on which see Heinzelmann, *Translationsberichte*, pp. 66–77.

[51] Egino and Ratold's names were inscribed in Reichenau's *liber vitae*, produced in 823/4. Autenrieth, Geuenich and Schmid (eds.), *Das Verbrüderungsbuch der Abtei Reichenau*, p. 118, A4 (Egino) and p. 8, A3 (Ratold). On Carolingian *libri vitae*, see Butz and Zettler, 'The making of the Carolingian *libri vitae*'; with a specific focus in Reichenau's *liber*, Le Jan, 'Reichenau and its *Amici Viventes*'.

[52] Santoni, 'Scrivere documenti'; Zettler, 'Studien'; Vocino, 'Santi e Luoghi Santi'; Tondini, 'Un modello per il regno'.

[53] The text is edited in Pighi, *Versus de Verona*, pp. 152–4. On Italian *laudes civitatum*, see Granier, 'La *Renovatio*'.

[54] Avesani, 'Il Re Pipino'.

Local saints and relics, and their textual celebration, were crucial in this exploitation of the past by the bishops of Carolingian Verona. This investment in the veneration of Verona's saints was tied in with the new identity they were developing for themselves as bishops. Saints, texts and relics were the bishops' calling cards when it came to maintaining and feeding their connections to their region of origin, Alamannia. This is abundantly clear from the manuscript tradition of Carolingian Verona's hagiographical texts. The most ancient witness of Coronatus' *Sermo* about Zeno is a manuscript produced at the beginning of the ninth century in Reichenau.[55] It was sent there, probably from Verona, in the shape of a little *dossier* of hagiographical texts concerning saints from north-eastern Italy, mostly martyrs from Aquileia.[56] The oldest extant copy of the *Passio et translatio sanctorum Firmi et Rustici* comes likewise from the Lake Constance region;[57] even though it is more recent (end of the ninth century), it is conceivable that it or its template travelled along the routes of communications opened by the Carolingian and Alamannian bishops of Verona. The martyrology compiled by Hraban Maur towards the middle of the ninth century recalls Firmus and Rusticus on the day of their martyrdom (9 August), with their entry including details he almost certainly took from the *Passio et translatio*.[58] Not only did the bishops of Verona send copies of texts about local saints to their places of origin and to other transalpine contacts, they also sent pieces of their relics. In the *Tituli Fuldenses*, it is Hraban Maur, once again, who includes Verona's saints, Zeno, Firmus and Rusticus, in a list of all the relics preserved in the altars of the new monastic basilica of Fulda.[59]

Both relics and texts were at the core of the bishops' strategies for appropriating the local past. They promoted and diffused hagiographical narratives in which the antiquity of local saints and of their relationship with Verona was underlined or probably, in some cases, concocted. Bishops therefore reworked local cults in order that they meet all the requisites demanded by Carolingian rulers for a saintly cult to be accepted. In other words, they made local saints into Carolingian saints

---

[55] Ms Karlsruhe, Badische Landesbibliothek, Aug. perg. XXXII. For its description Holder, *Die Handschriften*, pp. 118–131.

[56] Chiesa, 'I manoscritti', pp. 109–10.

[57] Ms Sankt Gallen, Stiftsbibliothek, 566. Only the *Passio* was copied, not the *Translatio*. Its description is found in von Scarpatetti, *Die Handschriften*, pp. 61–5. It can be consulted online at www.e-codices.unifr.ch, accessed 14/02/2017.

[58] Hrabanus Maurus, *Martyrologium*, ed. McCulloh, p. 78.

[59] Hrabanus Maurus, *Carmina*, ed. Dümmler, pp. 205–16, esp. p. 208, *titulus* XIV, v. 8. On these metrical compositions, see Kloft, 'Hrabanus Maurus'.

in order to make them usable in the new ideological and institutional context of Carolingian Italy. In so doing, they aimed to demonstrate to local elites that they were able to take charge of and to promote important elements of local identity. Their own interests and needs were equally at stake. Carolingian public officers working in Italy were expected to ensure the involvement of Lombard elites in the social and political framework of the kingdom. This would only have been possible if their authority and their role as mediators with central power had been acknowledged by their local interlocutors. The appropriation, reconfiguration and celebration of local identities were the key to their expected audience's attention. Saints' remains and memories were the materials by which this key was made. By means of sanctification, relics and different sorts of texts, the bishops of Verona were trying to show that accepting Carolingian rules, authorities, representatives and identities could have advantages for both the rulers and the ruled.

Relics as Trial Witnesses: Aquileia versus Grado

The effort of 'Carolingianization' was not always that peaceful. Saints, relics and texts might also work as ideological weapons in order to impose Carolingian identity, and political control, over people and regions unwilling to embrace them. In 827, a synod of bishops from the provinces of *Aemilia*, *Liguria* and *Venetia* gathered in Mantua under the supervision of two papal legates and two imperial *missi*.[60] The central issue debated at the synod was the ecclesiastical jurisdictions of the two bordering and competing patriarchates of Aquileia and Grado, separated since the beginning of the seventh century. The patriarch of Aquileia, Maxentius, claimed the superior authority of his church over Grado and all its suffragans, the churches of the Venetian Lagoon and Istria. He was closely connected to the court at Aachen, as had been his predecessor, Paulinus; he was also granted by Charlemagne a property in Cividale once held by the rebel Hrotgaud.[61] The acts of the synod transmit an image of the proceedings that clearly reflects that of contemporary judicial assemblies: the floor was alternatively given to the two sides, which were called on to present the documents they believed would support their positions.[62] Maxentius deployed an extensive *dossier* made up of

---

[60] The acts of this synod are published by *Concilium Mantuanum*, ed. Werminghoff. For an introduction to the synod, see Azzara, 'Il Concilio di Mantova'.

[61] *DD Caroli Magni*, n. 214, ed. Mühlbacher, pp. 285–7. On this episode, see Everett, 'Paulinus', p. 145.

[62] La Rocca and Veronese, 'The Culture of Unanimity in Carolingian Councils'.

books of prayers (*libelli precum*) for the restoration of his church, Aquileia's sacred texts (*sacrae litterae*), and a letter by his predecessor John to the Lombard king Agilulf, in which he complained about the violent subordination of some of his Istrian suffragans to the patriarch of Grado.[63] Another text, a *decretum* from the people of Pula in Istria in which they asked Siguald of Aquileia, patriarch in the third quarter of the eighth century, to consecrate the bishop they had elected, was read at the synod and judged 'true and most proven', but the acts do not state whether it was also presented by Maxentius.[64] Moreover, a delegation of ecclesiastical and social elites from Istria attended the synod, begging that they be set free from the most unfair control of the Greeks and given back to their metropolis, Aquileia.[65] This huge provision of sources, proofs and 'very reliable authorities' (*auctoritates veracissimas*) was successful, and allowed Maxentius to reach his goal. Aquileia was not only recognized as the metropolis of Istria but also reclassified as the only patriarchal authority in the whole region; Grado was reduced to the status of one suffragan church among many.[66]

The acts underline that the assembly's decisions were also a result of the absence of Venerius, patriarch of Grado. Though he had been repeatedly invited to attend the council by royal and papal legates, Venerius decided not to go. As his substitute at the council he sent the *oeconomus* of his church, Tiberius, who was provided with what Venerius regarded as the documentary evidence supporting the legitimacy of the church of Grado's status. Unfortunately, their reading during the council scarcely had the results Venerius expected. The documents shown by Tiberius were judged not to be trustworthy, as they were *nullius manu roborati*, signed by no one's authority.[67] In any case, even if they had been seen as judicially acceptable, the council underlined that their content supported more the claims of Maxentius than of Venerius.[68] In the conciliar acts, the space taken up by the evidence given by Tiberius is

---

[63] The letter, which was inserted into the acts (*Concilium Mantuanum*, ed. Werminghoff, p. 586), is edited in *Epistolae Langobardicae Collectae*, n. 1, ed. Gundlach, p. 693.

[64] *Sed et populi Polensis, quae civitas caput est Histriae, decretum ab universo clero et cuncto populo missum ad Sigualdum, patriarcham Aquileiensem, qui usque ad Francorum tempora vixit, verum et probatissimum invenimus, ut electum ab eis episcopum ordinaret*; *Concilium Mantuanum*, ed. Werminghoff, p. 586.

[65] Ibid., pp. 586–7.

[66] *Statuit igitur sancta synodus, ut Aquileia metropolis, quae contra patrum statuta divisa in duos metropolitanos fuerat, deinceps secundum quod et antiquitus erat prima et metropolis habeatur*; ibid., p. 587.

[67] Ibid., p. 588.

[68] *Et quamvis ita sint, si essent firmata, magis Aquileiensi ecclesiae quam suae* [= Gradensi] *pertinerent*: ibid.

considerably shorter than that afforded the texts shown by Maxentius; a textual strategy aiming to emphasize the poverty and inefficacy of Venerius' defence was clearly elaborated. At the end of the debate, the acts also report a sort of confession by Tiberius, who openly acknowledged ('no one could deny') that the church of Aquileia was much older than that of Grado – that is, he was obliged to acknowledge that all the sources on which Maxentius had built his claims of superiority over Grado told the truth. Yet Tiberius added that Patriarch Helias had held a synod of his bishops in Grado after his flight from Aquileia;[69] with this he was suggesting that Helias had meant to locate the see of his patriarchate in Grado.

The Synod of Mantua was a clear and, most probably, well-prepared success for Maxentius. Yet its decrees were not the final and decisive step in the dispute between Aquileia and Grado. In 828 Venerius sent a letter to Pope Gregory IV appealing against the synod's decisions.[70] He never received an answer – as far as we know. The pope was probably incapable of resolutely taking a position in the matter, considering that his standing in Rome after his election was itself not very strong. Nonetheless, as Claudia Bolgia has argued, there are hints that in the following years a rapprochement between one of the territories subject to Grado's ecclesiastical authority, the Venetian duchy, and Rome took place. It was expressed, for instance, in the programme of mosaics commissioned by Gregory IV for the Roman basilica of San Marco, where 'Gregory depicted himself as protected and sponsored by the evangelist'.[71] But what has St Mark to do with this? And why should such an image signify a relationship with the Venetian lagoons?

In the years immediately following Mantua, the Venetian duchy undertook a propagandistic counter-attack against the synod's decrees. The evangelist was the figure around which it was built. Between 827 and 829, the dukes of Rivoalto, which had recently become the political core of the duchy, acquired a relic of the utmost importance: the body of St Mark. This was a coup that the Venetians believed would allow them to counter Maxentius' claims and turn upside down the strategies upon which they were grounded. The use of material sanctity was most probably associated with the production of texts written in response to

[69] *Negare non possum, quia ego et paene omnes sciunt Aquileiam civitatem primam et metropolim esse [...]. Sed propter oppressionem paganorum Helias Aquileiensis patriarcha ad Gradus veniens in diocesi et plebe sua habitavit et suorum episcoporum ibi synodum egit;* ibid., p. 589.
[70] *Epistolae Variorum*, n. 12, ed. Dümmler, pp. 315–6.
[71] Bolgia, 'The mosaics of Gregory IV', pp. 21–3 (the quotation at p. 22).

Maxentius' arguments in Mantua.[72] The transfer of Mark's body to Venice would later be celebrated in the *Translatio sancti Marci*, recently dated by Emanuela Colombi to the second half of the tenth century.[73] Significantly, this text includes a historical prologue into which an important part of the source material quoted by the decrees of Mantua was interpolated in order to support the legitimacy of the existence of the patriarchate of Grado.[74] It is therefore possible that the prologue was produced in the immediate aftermath of the Synod of Mantua and of the transfer of Mark's relics; later it would be attached to the narrative of their arrival in Venice. In any case, the appropriation of the evangelist's body has been read unanimously as a means of guarding both Rivoalto's ecclesiastical and political independence.[75] The affirmation of Aquileia's ecclesiastical jurisdiction over Grado – that is, also over its suffragan bishoprics in the Venetian lagoons – would have been a first step in the passage of that region into the Carolingian sphere of political control. Attempts to bring this about by military and diplomatic means in the first decade of the ninth century had failed.[76] In Mantua, Maxentius tried to bring the lagoons into the Carolingian political framework by means of a redefinition of ecclesiastical jurisdictions. He assigned a key role in this enterprise to St Mark, and the saint was important in the eyes of Rivoalto because he already featured in Maxentius' discourses.[77] Maxentius built his demonstration of Aquileia's superior dignity over Grado around a whole range of references to the evangelist. A local tradition, the origins of which have been traced back by Pier Franco Beatrice to the context of the Schism of the Three Chapters (sixth–seventh century), assigned the foundation of the church of Aquileia to St Mark.[78] Its first textual manifestation – as far as we know – appears at the beginning of Paul the Deacon's aforementioned *Liber de episcopis Mettensibus*.[79] In the acts of Mantua, the tradition was formulated in a very articulate manner,

---

[72] Veronese, 'Saint Marc entre Venise et Reichenau', pp. 301–4.

[73] Colombi, 'Translatio sancti Marci Venetias [BHL 5283–5284]', with a new edition of the *Translatio* at pp. 112–29. She endorsed arguments expressed previously by Cracco, 'I testi agiografici', pp. 937–40.

[74] On the prologue to the *Translatio*, see Colombi, 'Alcune riflessioni sull'*Istoria Veneticorum*'.

[75] Among a wide range of works, see Geary, *Furta Sacra*, pp. 107–13; Ortalli, 'Il ducato e la Civitas Rivoalti', pp. 736–9; Osborne, 'Politics, diplomacy and the cult of relics', pp. 385–6; Morini, 'Il Levante della Santità', pp. 875–84.

[76] Berto, 'La "Venetia"'.   [77] On what follows, see Vocino, 'Les saints en lice'.

[78] Beatrice, 'Agiografia e Politica'; Beatrice, '*Hermagorica Novitas*'.

[79] [Beatus Petrus] *Marcum vero, qui praecipuus inter eius discipulos habebatur, Aquilegiam destinavit; cuius civibus Hermagoram suum comitem Marcus praefecisset, ad beatum Petrum reversus, ab ao Alexandriam missus est*; Paul the Deacon, *Liber de Episcopis*, ed. Santarossa, p. 129.

responding to Maxentius' political and polemical needs. In this text, the connection between St Mark and the church of Aquileia is repeatedly stressed as a strong (maybe the strongest) argument supporting the apostolic origins – that is, the antiquity – of Maxentius' see. At the same time, the legend of Mark's foundation of the church of Aquileia is also used to build a connection to the Church of Rome, as it is said that the saint was sent to Italy on a mission of evangelization by St Peter himself.[80]

The legend of St Mark assumed different shapes, purposes and meanings in the acts of Mantua. From the beginning, Maxentius makes it a sort of calling card of his Church: 'We, who, according to an established truth, find that [...] the church of Aquileia was first founded in the faith of Christ by St Mark the Evangelist, who was St Peter the Apostle's spiritual and most beloved son, arisen from the womb of the baptismal source, and by the very elegant Hermachoras.'[81] Mark is therefore immediately linked to Peter through a tie of godparenthood.[82] Spiritual kinship, a very important way of shaping familial groups in the Carolingian (and also in the Merovingian) world, was thus recalled as the grounds of the connection between Aquileia and Rome.[83] But Mark is also linked to Hermachoras, who was supposed to have been his first successor at the see of Aquileia. The triangle of Mark, Peter and Hermachoras is perfected at the end of the acts: Hermachoras is equally shown to have been very close to Peter, whom he met in Rome after having been elected bishop in Aquileia *ab omni clero et populo* – that is, in accordance with the canonical requirements concerning bishops' elections.[84] The reference to Hermachoras' election is important, because it can be seen to stand in contrast to that of Candidianus, the first patriarch of Grado, who is presented as *haereticus*; the latter's election is said to have taken place through an act of violence and been contrary to canon

---

[80] *Concilium Mantuanum*, ed. Werminghoff, p. 588.

[81] *Nos qui veritate perfecta invenimus a beato evangelista Marco, qui spiritualis et ex sacro fontis utero ac carissimus sancti Petri apostoli fuit filius, necnon ab elegantissimo Hermachora Aquileiensem aecclesiam [...] in Christi fide prius fundatam esse; ibid.*, p. 585.

[82] The idea of a spiritual kinship tie between Peter and Mark seems to be grounded in the first epistle by Peter (1 Pt 5, 13), where Mark is called *filius meus*. Already the life of Peter contained in the Roman *Liber Pontificalis*, written at the beginning of the sixth century, established that Mark was "his [= Peter's] son by baptism": Davis, *The Book of Pontiffs*, p. 1. On the genesis of the *Liber Pontificalis* see now Verardi, *La Memoria Legittimante*.

[83] On ties of spiritual kinship Lynch, *Godparents*; Jussen, *Spiritual Kinship*.

[84] *Beatissimus igitur Marcus evangelista, Aquileiae residens, vultum beati Petri apostoli videre desiderans, Romam urbem regrediens et secum elegantem virum, Hermachoram nomine, ab omni electum clero et populo deferens et ab ipso beato Petro apostolo Aquileiae urbis ordinatus et constitutus est pontifex; Concilium Mantuanum*, ed. Werminghoff, p. 589.

law and therefore unlawful.[85] This passage was clearly designed to discredit the whole succession of the patriarchs of Grado from the very beginning. Maxentius' use of St Mark as a polemical tool continues with an excerpt from Paul the Deacon's *Historia Langobardorum* concerning the flight of his predecessor Paul to Grado when the Lombards conquered Italy in 568–569.[86] The passage is reported verbatim in the acts, and was interpolated in order to further underline the special relationship tying St Mark to Aquileia. When he went to Grado – which is defined as *plebs*, a dependent church – Paul took with him the treasure of his church, which included the seats used by St Mark and St Hermachoras.[87] This is where the acts differ from Paul the Deacon's text, which is silent on these relics. The acts proceed to say that the patriarch escaped to Grado 'not to build his see or the primacy of his church and ecclesiastical province there, but [only] to avoid the ferociousness of the barbarians';[88] this is another interpolation to the original text written by Paul the Deacon, who did evoke the patriarch's fear of the *Langobardorum barbaries*, but was silent on the nature (temporary or final) of his see's displacement. Finally, a full version of the legend of St Mark in Aquileia, the oldest surviving one to be rich in detail, was placed towards the end of the acts.[89] It collects all the elements already recalled in the previous sections of the acts: the missionary task given by Peter to Mark in respect of the north-east of Italy; the foundation of the church of Aquileia by Mark; the consecration of Hermachoras, once again called *elegans*, by Peter in Rome. On that occasion, the text says, Hermachoras was made *proton Italiae pontificem* – first bishop of Italy – most probably meaning *Italia Annonaria*, late-Roman northern Italy. Sometime later the patriarchs built a *munitio*, a fortified place, in Grado, that became their summer residence. The reconstruction of St Mark's legend and of the relationship between Aquileia and Grado leads to the synod's final statement: 'And one must underline that all the cities of Istria and the others recalled by

---

[85] *Hic enim Candidianus nec per consensum comprovintialium episcoporum nec in civitate Aquileia, sed in dioecesim et plebem Aquileiensem Gradus, quae est perparva insula, contra canonum statuta et sanctorum patrum decreta ordinatus est*; ibid., p. 586.

[86] Paul the Deacon, *Historia Langobardorum*, book 2, c. 10, ed. Capo, p. 88.

[87] *Paulus patriarcha [...], Longobardorum barbariem et immanitatem metuens, ex civitate Aquileiensi et de propria sede ad Gradus insulam, plebem suam, confugiens omnemque thesaurum et sedes sanctorum Marci et Hermachorae secum ad eamdem insulam detulit*; *Concilium Mantuanum*, ed. Werminghoff, p. 585. Underscores are mine, to underline the parts that were added to Paul the Deacon's text.

[88] *Non ut sedem aut primatum aecclesiae suaeque provintiae construeret inibi, sed ut Barbarorum rabiem possit evadere*; ibid.

[89] Ibid., p. 588–9.

this synod were subjected to the city of Aquileia, the chief and the first one of the whole of [northern] Italy.'[90]

In Mantua the whole arsenal connected to St Mark was exploited in order to support Aquileia's arguments. Decisions were taken on the grounds of the documentary evidence shown by Maxentius. As Giorgia Vocino has argued, the material also encompassed the *Passio Hermachorae et Fortunati*, recently written in the *milieu* of the church of Aquileia – it has been dated to the end of the eighth or the beginning of the ninth century;[91] the acts most probably borrowed from this text a qualification they use twice for Hermachoras: *elegantis*.[92] The composition of a *Passio* of Hermachoras and his fellow martyr Fortunatus by the church of Aquileia seems to answer the same needs that led to the production of Verona's texts: that is, to provide local cults with the textual support required by the Council of Frankfurt and necessary to attest to the actual sanctity of the individuals. The interpolation of passages from Paul the Deacon's *Historia Langobardorum* is another case in which the resources of the past – once again the Lombard past – were put at the service of strategies and needs in the present, something clearly recalling the use of historiographical texts (among them the *Historia* itself) in the *Epitome phillipsiana*. The choice of the texts presented at Mantua was thus driven by fully Carolingian principles, being either imposed by capitulary and/or conciliar legislation or forming part of a framework designed to create and spread models and ideas of identity. Maxentius' respect for Carolingian criteria also directed the choice of the form and documentary supports for the texts he provided. *Libelli precum*, collections of prayers, psalms and liturgical formulas, were central tools in the elaboration and diffusion of a shared Christian identity (one of the '"big ticket items" of Frankish governance' emphasized by Jennifer Davis) in the Carolingian empire for both clerics and laypeople.[93] Alcuin produced *libelli* for Saint-Martin of Tours, and he also circulated them among his correspondents.[94] Dhuoda, in her *Handbook*, urged her son William to read them every day.[95] The *libelli* of Alcuin (and

---

[90] *Et notandum, quod omnes Histriensium civitates ac reliquae, quas haec notat synodus, Aquileiae civitati, quae caput et prima est totius Italiae, subiectae sunt*; ibid., p. 589.

[91] The text is edited by P. Chiesa in Colombi (ed.), *Le passioni dei martiri*, 1, pp. 171–88. For its dating, see Colombi, 'Caratteristiche', p. 102. Also see Chiesa's introduction to his edition.

[92] Vocino, 'Les saints en lice', pp. 283–5.

[93] Boynton, '*Libelli Precum*'; Phelan, *The Formation*, pp. 249–52.

[94] See, for instance, Alcuin's letter to Arn of Salzburg of 802, which was accompanied by a *libellus* containing psalms and their exegetical explanations: Alcuin, *Epistolae*, n. 259, ed. Dümmler, p. 417, quoted by Phelan, *The Formation*, p. 250.

[95] Dhuoda, *Handbook for Her Warrior Son*, ed. Thiébaux, p. 362.

Maxentius) also share content and features with another strongly
Carolingian literary means of diffusing Christian culture, namely the
little handbooks containing liturgical formulas, prayers and exegetical
texts produced to help local priests in the performance of their everyday
pastoral duties.[96] Maxentius presented his case to a carefully selected
jury, as the absence of Venerius' suffragan bishops and his choice not to
attend the synod indicate. Nonetheless, the patriarch of Aquileia still felt
the need to collect a *dossier* of texts that could support his arguments on
the basis of both their content and their fully Carolingian character, or at
least on the strength of the fully Carolingian names (*libelli precum*) they
were given. The legend of St Mark in Aquileia was seen as a powerful
tool, not only for the prestige and saintly origins it assigned to the church
of Aquileia but also, perhaps primarily, because it responded, or was
presented as responding, to Carolingian rules in its textual nature and in
its strategies for exploiting the past and its resources. Its textual structure
was therefore as important as the arguments it brought – maybe more
important.

Rebuilding One's Repute through Roman Relics: Eberhard of Friuli, Gisla and Pope Callixtus

The cases of Verona and Mantua (Aquileia/Grado) show that material
and textual holiness, that is, saints' relics and hagiographical texts, had
important roles in the strategies and processes developed in order to
build a Carolingian identity for north-eastern Italy, its social elites and
its political and ecclesiastical structures. They were used according to the
rules set by Carolingian authorities concerning the validity of saints and
relics and the possibilities and limits of their exploitation. The saints
recalled were the ones traditionally linked, or presented as such, to the
local contexts of Verona and the patriarchate of Aquileia/Cividale. The
contribution of Rome and its saints to the cases we have seen until now
has been limited to the references to the privileged connections between
St Mark, St Hermachoras and St Peter contained in the acts of Mantua.
They were meant to earn papal support for Maxentius' position by
formulating a sort of dependence of Aquileia on Rome, to which the
initiative of converting north-eastern Italy was ultimately traced back.
But Rome and its saints were crucial to Carolingian concerns with
sanctity and its control. Roman relics and the possibilities of social and
political self-promotion they offered attracted the upper levels of the

---

[96] van Rhijn, 'The local church'; van Rhijn, 'Manuscripts'.

Carolingian aristocracy. Around the middle of the eighth century, in the context of Pippin III's expedition to Italy against the Lombards of King Haistulf, Fulrad, later Charlemagne's chancellor, obtained the relics of the SS Alexander and Hippolytus in Rome and transferred them to the royal monastery of Saint-Denis, where he was abbot.[97] In 826 Hilduin, equally abbot of Saint-Denis, obtained from Pope Eugenius the body of St Sebastian, which he placed in another monastery he controlled, Saint-Médard in Soissons.[98] This was the place where in 833 Louis the Pious underwent a public penance imposed on him by his son Lothar and a part of the Frankish bishops.[99] Concerning these events, the *Relatio Compendiensis*, composed some months later in Compiègne, reports that the ceremony had taken place *in basilica sanctae Dei genitricis Mariae, ubi sanctorum corpora requiescunt, Medardi uidelicet [...] nec non Sebastiani praestantissimi martyris*: a saint from Rome was somehow indicated as the witness of the emperor's deposition.[100] In the following year, Einhard, one of the main intellectuals of the Carolingian world since Charlemagne's time and lay abbot of several monasteries, ordered the theft of the relics of Marcellinus and Peter from their graves in Rome; after many adventures and stages, he deposited them in his newly built church and monastery at Seligenstadt.[101] From that moment on, the two saints are described in his letters as always working for the peace and health of the empire.[102] Roman relics were therefore one of the means by which central figures of the empire pursued their own strategies, intervened in the political context of their times and, in general, expressed themselves. Another comparable case is that of Eberhard, margrave of Friuli. Eberhard belonged to one of the most important noble families in Neustria, and married Gisla, daughter of Emperor Louis the Pious.[103] In 828 he succeeded Baldrich, punished for his military failures, and retained the office of margrave until his death in the 860s. His career does not therefore appear very different from that, for instance, of the

---

[97] On that occasion, according to the ninth-century *Translatio sancti Viti*, a relative of his also acquired the relics of St Vitus in Rome, which he then deposited in another church near Paris. In 836 – as is reported again by the *Translatio* – these relics were transferred again, this time to the Saxon monastery of Corvey. On this text, see Schmale-Ott, *Translatio sancti Viti martyris*, with its edition at pp. 30–70; Röckelein, *Reliquientranslationen*, pp. 100–8.

[98] *ARF*, s.a. 826, ed. Kurze, pp. 171–2.

[99] de Jong, *The Penitential State*; Booker, *Past Convictions*.

[100] The text of the *Relatio* has been recently re-edited in Booker, 'The public penance', pp. 11–19.

[101] These events are reported in his *Translatio et Miracula Sanctorum Marcellini et Petri*, ed. Waitz; trans. Dutton, *Charlemagne's Courtier*.

[102] Sot, 'Service de l'empire'.

[103] On Eberhard's life, see Fees, 'Eberardo'; La Rocca and Provero, 'The dead', pp. 235–8.

Alamannian bishops of Verona: he came from outside the kingdom of
Italy, where he was sent to work as a Carolingian public officer. Yet one
major difference emerges. He had the time and the chance to put down
roots in north-eastern Italy, and in the Italian context generally, where he
developed wide social and political networks. He had ties with the courts
of Lothar I and Louis II, and participated in imperial military expeditions
to central and southern Italy. His name was inserted into the *liber vitae* of
San Salvatore in Brescia, into both its regular lists and the special list of
those who offered women of their family to the monastic community.[104]
This female monastery was founded by the last king of the Lombards,
Desiderius, and his wife, Ansa; after the Carolingian conquest it
remained a royal monastery, where the women of the new ruling family
in Italy retained the office of abbess and developed for themselves scope
for political action as well as engaging in memory-keeping.[105] San
Salvatore's *liber vitae* tied Eberhard to the clergy of Brescia, whose names
are collected in a list of their own, starting at fol. 20r; in second place
among them, after the archbishop of Milan Angilbert, the aforementioned Noting is listed.[106] Noting and, even more so, Eberhard are also
the protagonists of a hagiographical text, the *Translatio Calixti Cysonium*.
It refers the transfer of the body of Pope Calixtus from Rome to the
Austrasian monastery of Cysoing, founded by Eberhard and Gisla, and
the miracles performed through the relics both during their journey and
in their new resting place.[107] The text has been dated to the years
immediately following Eberhard's death, and assigned to an initiative of
his widow, Gisla.[108] It says that Noting had initially requested the relics
from Pope Sergius II. The pope agreed, and the body of Calixtus was first
moved to a monastery named *Cella-aurea*. Yet this was meant to be just
an intermediate stage, as the relics' final destination was supposed to be a
monastery that Noting was building *in predio suo*; but when the bishop
tried to remove Calixtus' body fom *Cella-aurea*, it became so heavy that it
could not be lifted up by any means. Eberhard was informed of Noting's
troubles, and he asked to take the bishop's place in the transfer of
Calixtus, and to bring the body to his monastery in Cysoing. He obtained
the consent of both Noting and, much more important, of Calixtus,
whose relics immediately became very light. The journey to Cysoing

---

[104] *Der Memorial- und Liturgiecodex*, ed. Geuenich and Ludwig, f. 8r. On San Salvatore's
liber vitae, see Ludwig, 'Il Codice Memoriale'; Ludwig, 'Das Gedenkbuch'.
[105] Lazzari, 'Una mamma carolingia'; La Rocca, 'Monachesimo femminile'; Sereno,
'Bertilla e Berta'.
[106] *Der Memorial- und Liturgiecodex*, ed. Geuenich and Ludwig, f. 20r.
[107] *Translatio Sancti Calixti Cisonium*, ed. Holder-Egger.
[108] Mériaux, 'La *Translatio Calixti Cisonium* (BHL 1525)'.

was accomplished safely; along the way the relics showed their supernatural powers, performing many miracles.

The *Translatio Calixti* presents several points of interest. Many of them have been underlined quite recently by Charles Mériaux, who has strongly and convincingly supported the idea that the text was commissioned by Gisla, whose aim was most probably that of maintaining and celebrating her dead husband's memory.[109] Mériaux has also proposed that the text was composed at the *scriptorium* of Saint-Amand, not that far from Cysoing. A hagiographical text about a successful transfer of Roman relics was conceived as a tool to celebrate Eberhard's memory and to root it locally: Eberhard and Gisla were both buried in Cysoing, where forms of popular devotion developed around the figure of the margrave. The narrated events and the representation of Eberhard's figure and deeds are bound up with his experiences and relationships in Italy. His position as an imperial officer in north-eastern Italy is what allowed him to get in contact with the main actors in the transfer of the relics and to claim a role in the enterprise. The account of the displacement of prestigious relics is built around Eberhard's status as somebody thoroughly integrated into the political landscape of Carolingian Italy; this standing is central to the text's plausibility and, consequently, the relics' authenticity in the eyes of contemporaries. Once again, this instance of the textual and memorial exploitation of sanctity shows the utmost respect for Carolingian rules and social practices concerning saints and their cults. Calixtus' displacement takes place only after explicit consent has been asked from and granted by all the authorities involved, from the pope to the bishop originally controlling the relics to the saint himself, whose wishes deeply affect the events. Eberhard provides his and his wife's monastery with a relic coming from the Roman reservoir of sanctity, the one that the upper echelons of the Frankish aristocracy had been most eager to exploit since the second half of the eighth century in order to further their own social position and promote the monastic institutions they controlled. Finally, the very choice of the textual form of the account, a *Translatio*, reflects Gisla's acknowledgement of the more limited room for manoeuvre left by Carolingian rules on saints in respect of the use of cults and relics by aristocratic groups. Indeed, the text is a sort of hagiographical celebration of Eberhard built in a way that could be acceptable from a Carolingian perspective. The picture painted of the margrave by the hagiographer introduces him to his readers as a person very much worthy of praise. Eberhard is called

---

[109] Ibid.

miles Christi and depicted, with a pun, as a *marginalis miles ac limes*, a strenuous defender of Christianity's borders against pagan attacks – a reference to his participation in military campaigns against the Muslims in central and southern Italy.[110] If the *Translatio Calixti* had been written some 150 years before – that is, in a still Merovingian context – it would have most probably been shaped as a *Vita Evrardi*. Carolingian impositions strongly limited the making of new saints, but showing someone to be capable of moving supernatural objects such as relics was a way of saying that he or she was able to establish connections with saints, and to be acknowledged as their interlocutor. In other words, it could be seen as a way to suggest that he or she too was a saint.

Further textual features of the *Translatio Calixti* allow us to reconstruct Gisla's aims and better understand the elements she meant to emphasize in the description of her husband and his actions. Recent studies have focussed on Eberhard as a lay intellectual.[111] He asked for and received a copy of *De laudibus sanctae crucis* from Hraban Maur, which was attached to a letter that the abbot of Fulda sent him.[112] The will that Eberhard and Gisla composed as a couple contains a list of the books in their library.[113] They encompass liturgical as well as exegetical texts, works of the Church Fathers, historiographical books and collections of laws, the latter being closely connected to Eberhard's tasks as a public officer. In the couple's will the legal collections were assigned to Eberhard's intended successor as margrave, his first male son, Unroch.[114] One of them had been requested by Eberhard from Lupus, later abbot of Ferrières, another extremely learned figure.[115] Eberhard was therefore in touch with some of the most influential and renowned intellectuals of his time. He was integrated into wide-ranging networks of cultural communication, involving the exchange of books, texts and ideas. Yet being part of these networks could also bear risks. In the 840s, Eberhard briefly hosted Gottschalk of Orbais at his court, an oblate monk who had

---

[110] *Ea igitur tempestate vir nobilissimis Francorum natalibus oriundus nomine Evrardus ducatum Foriiuliensis divina ordinatione [...] nobiliter amministrabat. Hic itaque miles Christi non piger atque frigidus circa fidem ac dilectionem Dei, multitudinem gentis Sclavorum aliarumque paganarum gentium, ubi et ipse quasi quidam marginalis miles ac limes ad discernendum filios Dei a filiis diaboli fortiter astabat [...]. Nam sepe adversum Ismahelitas atque Agarenos, qui se Sarracenos gloriantur, dimicans contraque Numidarum ac Maurorum sevissimos populos resistens fortiter, non modicum ex ipsis reportaverat triumphum*; Translatio Calixti, ed. Holder-Egger, p. 419.
[111] Kershaw, 'Eberhard of Friuli'.
[112] Hrabanus Maurus, *Epistolae*, n. 42, ed. Dümmler, pp. 481–7.
[113] Eberhard and Gisla's will is edited in de Coussemaker (ed.), *Cartulaire*, n. 1, pp. 1–5. It has been recently translated into French in Lebecq, 'Le testament d'Evrard et Gysèle de Cysoing'.
[114] La Rocca and Provero, 'The dead'.   [115] Kershaw, 'Eberhard of Friuli', pp. 85–6.

studied in Fulda under Hraban Maur.[116] Later, no longer wishing to be a monk, Gottschalk tried to appeal against his oblation.[117] His case would prove extremely troublesome. It cast doubt on the whole practice of child oblation, the way in which monastic communities reproduced themselves, extended their landholdings and created social relationships in Carolingian times.[118] He was also the protagonist of a huge doctrinal debate that shook the Carolingian world towards the middle of the ninth century concerning predestination and individual responsibility for actions and sins.[119] On both issues he met the strong opposition of his former teacher Hraban, and was officially condemned as a heretic.[120] In the letter he sent to Eberhard, Hraban called Gottschalk *sciolus*, a know-it-all. This mocking nickname reflects the turmoil and *scandalum* caused by Gottschalk's views, the abbot admitting that *multos in desperationem suimet haec secta perduxit*.[121] The letter was composed both to respond to Eberhard's request for *De laudibus* and to refute Gottschalk's positions. A large part of it is constructed in the form of an exegetical and doctrinal treatise on the soul's destiny and the role of actions in determining it, which he supports by quotations from the Bible and the Church Fathers. Because Hraban Maur had heard that Gottschalk was at Eberhard's court at that time, his former student can be seen as the implicit recipient of his letter. It was, nevertheless, officially addressed to Eberhard. Hraban wished to convince him of the groundlessness of Gottschalk's doctrine by means of a rich dossier of biblical and patristic quotations.[122] Hraban expected that Eberhard, reading his letter (or listening to it being read aloud), would be able to follow his arguments and acknowledge their validity. On the one hand, the abbot's letter to Eberhard strengthens the latter's image as a skilled intellectual who could understand complicated arguments – even on theological and exegetical issues – and recognize the supporting sources and quotations, not always explicitly mentioned. On the other, Hraban's purpose was no doubt to convince Eberhard that he was harbouring a treacherous guest, who posed a risk to

---

[116] On Gottschalk's stay in Friuli, see Kershaw, 'Eberhard of Friuli'; Pezé, '*Primum in Italiam, deinde in Galliam*'.

[117] Recently, Matthew Gillis has applied an ethnic perspective to the claims made by Gottschalk in 829, the year in which he rejected his oblation: Gillis, 'Noble and Saxon'.

[118] de Jong, *In Samuel's Image*.

[119] The most recent and detailed analysis of the controversy on predestination is Pezé, *Le virus*.

[120] On Hraban's defence of child oblation against Gottschalk, see Patzold, 'Hraban'.

[121] Hrabanus Maurus, *Epistolae*, n. 42, ed. Dümmler, p. 481.

[122] *Haec ergo, amice karissime, ideo tibi scripsi, ut cognosceres, quale scandalum de illis partibus opinio veniens in hoc populo generarit, et si quis iuxta te manens inpudenter docet quae recte fidei sunt contraria, prohibeas eum, ut cesset ab hac secta*; ibid., p. 487.

his host. His words were effective: immediately after Hraban's letter, we no longer find Gottschalk in Friuli, but rather in Croatia.

Nonetheless, the protection that Eberhard accorded Gottschalk, though only for a short time, may have cast a shadow on the margrave and his orthodoxy. In the context of the Carolingian empire, in which the legitimacy of authority and power ideally rested on its holders' correct relationship with God and the Christian faith, being in any way connected to religious dissent could be easily read as a form of disobedience to Carolingian power and the ideology supporting it. Carolingian sources of the first half of the ninth century show that accusations of heresy were less a mirror of actual heretical tendencies in the empire than a way to attack political opponents; they were thus part of Carolingian political discourse and competition.[123] The sources on Eberhard produced in the following years, such as the *Translatio Calixti* and the *Carmina* composed in his praise by Sedulius Scottus, agree in building an image of Eberhard as an inexhaustible defender and even propagator of the Christian faith, both with weapons (fighting against Muslims and pagans) and with exemplary behaviour from the point of view of Christian morality.[124] The *Translatio*, in particular, insists on Eberhard's perfect adherence to all the canons and duties of the loyal Carolingian public officer. He is *non piger ac frigidus* about faith and the love of God. He is a soldier of Christ working on the borders, both protecting the faithful and conquering new lands and peoples for Christianity. He knows the dangers of the *fastus potentiae* and is able to avoid them; he thus manages to be loyal both to the emperor and to God. But the hagiographer went one step further. Eberhard's ability to establish relationships with the sphere of the divine is described as surpassing even that of a bishop (Noting), who, as a figure involved in the management of liturgy, sacraments, sacred objects and pastoral care, was a sort of professional in the dialogue between the material and the spiritual domains. The choice of showing Noting as the person who made the first, unsuccessful attempt to transfer the relics was most probably not random. In a letter he sent to Noting towards 840, Hraban Maur recalled that when they met sometime before the bishop had expressed his anxiety regarding the presence of groups of heretics in northern Italy. The text does not give names, yet it refers to 'quidam', who 'de predestinatione Dei inique contendunt'. It is tempting to identify, at least in part, the heretics referred to by Noting with Gottschalk.[125] In other words, the then bishop of Brescia may have warned Hraban

---

[123] Costambeys, Innes and MacLean, *The Carolingian World*, pp. 81–6.

[124] Sedulius Scottus, *Carmina*, nn. 37–8, ed. Meyers, pp. 65–7.

[125] This is the reading proposed by Kershaw, 'Eberhard of Friuli', p. 92.

Maur of Eberhard's ambiguous behaviour, thus casting a bad light on him. Whatever the case, Hraban's letter shows at least that Noting was active in locating and rebuking heretics, denouncing them to the most influential religious figure of Lothar's kingdom, the then abbot of Fulda and later archbishop of Mainz. Depicting Eberhard as being able to accomplish a relics transfer that Noting had been unable to perform, the hagiographer behind the *Translatio Calixti* seems to say that the margrave's familiarity with sacred objects was greater than that of a bishop strongly involved in the fight against heretics. Eberhard was thereby set on a higher spiritual level than a bishop. The Christian perfection of his moral behaviour allowed him to easily handle objects belonging to both the material and the spiritual worlds, such as saints' relics. His privileged relationship with sanctity, deriving from his way of living and fighting for Christianity, gave him new and powerful possibilities for social and political action, self-promotion and the construction of memory.

This is also true of his image as an imperial officer, as Eberhard's exemplarity as a loyal servant to the Carolingians is strongly emphasized in the *Translatio*. Talking about the journey from *Cella-aurea* to Cysoing, the hagiographer describes the miraculous intervention of Calixtus' relics in a place called *Aquilae silva*, one of the many such episodes. The passage concerns two brothers who were long in dispute concerning their parents' inheritance. Things risked turning badly wrong, as they had threatened to kill each other. When the relics briefly stopped there, however, the brothers were taken in front of them and were suddenly caught by so great a fear that they forgot their dispute and promised to reach a peaceful deal.[126] Calixtus acted therefore as a dispute settler, one of the most important duties of Carolingian officers. Of course, the merit was also Eberhard's, who was escorting the relics. The couple formed by the saint and the quasi-saint successfully administered justice, bringing peace and harmony wherever they went. They thereby put into practice ideas and values repeatedly emphasized by Carolingian capitularies as the

---

[126] *Cumque sanctum corpus ad locum qui Aquilae-silva dicitur deportassent locumque ipsum ad pernoctandum habilem repperissent, deposuerunt illud cum metu ac reverentia. [...] Cum interea nuntiatum est a dicentibus, quod ibi essent germani fratres, qui ob patrimonia derelicta adversum se dissidentes, alterutrum sibi mortem infligere querebant. Qui statim in conspectu aecclesiae adducti sunt. Et dum adhuc iniqua pleni cogitatione invidiaeque et iracundiae, ut Cain fratricida, facibus accensi ante presentiam martiris in medio constitissent, mirum in modum ita subito divinitus eos timor perculit, ut in facies suas ruerent veniamque de suis erratibus similiter exorarent. Tunc omnibus gratias Deo referentibus, qui salvat omnes et neminem vult perire, a terra sublevati sunt atque paternis ammonitionibus castigati, et viam pacis ingressi, ab illo die et deinceps unanimiter habitare ceperunt; Translatio Calixti*, ed. Holder-Egger, pp. 420–1.

specific tasks of the local representatives of the imperial authority. Counts and other officers were called upon to share a part of the emperor's *ministerium* [...] *in pace et iustitia facienda*, and to be seen as *nostri veri adiutores et populi conservatores*, as Louis the Pious' *Admonitio ad omnes regni ordines* puts it.[127]

In their celebration of Eberhard's memory by means of a hagiographical text, Gisla and the author worked on different but closely connected levels. Through the narrative of the transfer of relics, they emphasized the margrave's personal behaviour, his skills and successes as a Christian warrior, his special relationship with sacred things and his somehow miraculous efficiency as a dispute-settling public officer. All these elements converge to present Eberhard as fully, perfectly and unequivocally Carolingian. Encouraging moral behaviour among Carolingian lay magnates was the main goal of the *specula* written by Alcuin, Paulinus of Aquileia, Jonas of Orléans and Dhuoda between the end of the eighth and the first half of the ninth centuries.[128] They were responding to the more general issues of the moral reform of society expressed by Carolingian rulers.[129] Some of the texts, such as Paulinus' *Liber exhortationis* to Eiric of Friuli (a predecessor of Eberhard's), also presented the *miles terrenus* as 'a model of obedience and discipline for the would-be spiritual warrior'.[130] As *adiutores* of the emperor, counts and margraves were involved in fulfilling his religiously charged *ministerium*, that is, leading the Christian people to salvation; they were therefore equally supposed to enjoy some sort of familiarity with the spiritual sphere. Finally, good Carolingian officers were especially those who correctly administered justice, assigning priority to the cases of *viduae, pupilli* and *pauperes*.[131] The picture of Eberhard in the *Translatio* was built on the basis of Carolingian representations and justifications of public authority.

This image was first and foremost conveyed through the very choice of the medium expressing it. Textual accounts of relic transfers are hagiographical products strictly connected to and immediately resulting from Carolingian rules on the veneration of saints.[132] Calixtus, a Roman saint from the distant past, perfectly matched the criteria set in Frankfurt. His sanctity and his cult's antiquity were authenticated by ancient and

---

[127] *Admonitio ad omnes regni ordines*, ed. Boretius, p. 304. On this capitulary, see Guillot, 'Une *Ordinatio* Méconnue'.
[128] Dubreucq, 'La littérature des *Specula*'; Savigni, 'Gli *Specula* carolingi'.
[129] Stone, *Morality and Masculinity*.   [130] Ibid., p. 84.
[131] Some examples: *Duplex Legationis Edictum*, c. 17, ed. Boretius, p. 63; *Capitula Legibus Addenda*, c. 3, ed. Boretius, p. 281; *Admonitio ad omnes regni ordines*, c. 8, ed. Boretius, p. 304.
[132] Heinzelmann, *Translationsberichte*, pp. 94–99.

authoritative written texts, first of all his *Passio*, dating to the fifth or sixth century.[133] It is not surprising, therefore, that in all three surviving manuscripts containing the *Translatio* – the earliest dating to the tenth century – the text always follows the *Passio* of Calixtus.[134] It also opens with a sentence establishing a textual connection between the distant past of Calixtus' martyrdom and the far more recent past of his transfer to Cysoing.[135] The *Translatio* and the transfer it refers to were both thought of as a continuation and the conclusion of Calixtus' story. The new celebration of Calixtus (and Eberhard with him) in the ninth century was thus firmly tied to previous written traditions attached to him. That was the only way for Calixtus to be seen as a useful and exploitable saint in a Carolingian context. He thus became an effective tool for promoting Eberhard's memory and cleansing it of any disturbing suspicions of sympathies for heretics.

Conclusions

The public officers working in Carolingian north-eastern Italy used the cult of saints and relics in very different ways. The bishops of Verona invested in them in order to build up their own legitimacy and that of the central – Carolingian – authority they represented in the eyes of local elites. Securing the latter's support and their involvement in Carolingian politics and social processes was the principal aim of the enterprise. The patriarchs of Aquileia and Grado fought tenaciously (but in vain) to redefine the ecclesiastical hierarchy of the region; relics and hagiographical traditions were used as powerful weapons by both sides. Eberhard and, even more so, Gisla chose Roman relics not only to enrich their monastic foundation with a spiritual treasure and a new cult, but also to celebrate and rehabilitate the margrave's memory, strongly emphasizing his Christian exemplarity by means (among others) of hagiography. These cases let us perceive how flexible the cult of saints and their relics were in Carolingian times, and the many different social, political and memorial uses that were possible. The regulation or, in Jennifer Davis' words, centralization of the practices tied to the cult of saints and their relics imposed unprecedented limits upon their exploitation. But it also

---

[133] This is the dating proposed by Mériaux, 'La *Translatio Calixti*', p. 589. The *Acta martyrii* are published in *Acta Sanctorum Octobris*, vol. 6, pp. 439–41.

[134] Mériaux, 'La *Translatio Calixti*', p. 589; he also gives short descriptions of the three manuscripts at pp. 588–9.

[135] *Factum est igitur evolutis multis annorum curriculis, postquam gloriosa beati martyris Calixti et sociorum eius sub Macrino et Alexandro Romanorum principibus passio consummata est ...*; *Translatio Calixti*, ed. Holder-Egger, p. 418.

left some room to manoeuvre. Carolingian rules established the ways in which saints, relics and hagiography could be legitimately used. The rulers' purpose was not that of excluding or forbidding these practices, but rather of asserting their control over them – something typically Carolingian. If performed correctly – that is, if rules were respected – the celebration of saints and their relics acquired an unprecedented validity as a means to shape identities and pursue wider political purposes, precisely because it was legitimated and supported by Carolingian power.

In north-eastern Italy, the use of sanctity and its celebration in textual form were strong and varied. The flexible nature of saints and relics as tools of political and social action stood in correlation to the flexible nature, even the fantasy, of those using them, who turned to the saints in pursuit of different goals. Every solution they found was adapted to the local context. Old and new traditions, saintly figures and forms of communication were carefully chosen and mixed in the manner deemed most effective. In the cases of Aquileia and Verona, local sanctity was provided with new textual foundations that rested on an assertion of the relevant saints' antiquity and their long-standing connection to the locality. In other words, their memory was redefined according to the rules set at Frankfurt. In a Carolingian context, saintly cults had to be equipped with a long history rooted in a distant past and with written traditions bearing witness to that very past. When this was not actually the case, new hagiographical traditions concerning the antiquity of the saint had to be produced. In the case of Eberhard's celebration by Gisla and the author of the *Translatio Calixti*, the choice of Roman sanctity met different needs. It aimed to strengthen the family's memory in a place far away from north-eastern Italy (Cysoing) and to reassert the margrave's orthodoxy as spectacularly as possible. Nonetheless, it followed the same criteria. Calixtus was a late antique bishop of Rome, a saint who lived in the distant past and in a non-Frankish context. Furthermore, his sanctity was attested by authoritative texts, which provided the necessary prologue to the narrative of his transfer to Cysoing in the manuscript tradition of the *Translatio* – at least in the part of it that has survived. The text produced at Gisla's initiative was also coloured by the experiences of Eberhard as margrave of Friuli and, more broadly, as an officer of the Carolingian empire in north-eastern Italy, and by the relationships he developed. Roman sanctity seems to have exercised a strong fascination among the higher levels of the Carolingian aristocracy, most of all. Linking her husband to a Roman saint, Gisla wished to celebrate and shape his memory, presenting him as a lay magnate, who was as worthy and capable of establishing relationships with popes and their saints and relics as other Carolingian aristocrats before him.

Different contexts therefore required different choices; yet these were equally characterized by the care for respecting Carolingian rules. Not only were old saints revived and provided with new cults,[136] to recall the title of a famous article by Julia Smith, but sometimes new saints were also provided with ancient cults or, more accurately, with texts testifying to the antiquity of those cults. This was the case with Firmus and Rusticus in Verona and, in a way, with 'St Eberhard' in Cysoing. These processes of cultural, cultic and textual redefinition had a key role in the strategies of Carolingian officers to translate at a local level the designs and projects of the central Carolingian authorities to shape new identities for the former Lombard kingdom. In other words, they helped to make (north-eastern) Italy Carolingian.

Is it possible to determine how successful these strategies and efforts were? In other words: can we establish how Carolingian this region was in Carolingian times? What we have seen here, as far as the cult of saints is concerned, allows us to conclude that efforts to 'Carolingianize' north-eastern Italy were strong, in many ways sophisticated and often seen as a means of responding to different immediate needs. Yet some consideration must be given to the nature of the sources that underpin our analysis and the issue of how we should interpret them. The preliminary question to ponder is: how Carolingian are our sources on Carolingian Italy? As I have tried to show, the texts (not only hagiographies) that I focussed on here are all deeply Carolingian in their purposes, producers and forms of composition. Their audience was not entirely Carolingian, however, as it also encompassed the local elites of the kingdom. Yet the readers and listeners of these texts were the recipients of precisely these strategies aimed at redefining identities. They were therefore addressed by strongly Carolingian messages, in which every element that did not (yet) belong to a Carolingian identity was reshaped and presented in a Carolingian way and with a Carolingian vocabulary. There is a danger that the deeply Carolingian nature of these sources and the specific designs of their authors will result in a skewed image. If seen through this lens alone, the different roles assigned to the cult of saints and the various means by which it was exploited in Carolingian north-eastern Italy can only appear as very Carolingian. In other words, the cult of saints is a powerful key to fully appreciating the amount of effort expended by those who were charged with the diffusion of Carolingian

---

[136] Smith, 'Old saints, new cults'.

messages and identities in this region; but it is a much less effective key to fully appreciating how successful these efforts were. It is not easy to determine how truly Carolingian the north-eastern part of Carolingian Italy was on the basis of these sources, but, at the very least, they let us perceive that many people showed a strong interest in making the region Carolingian and invested important resources in the endeavour.

As Jennifer Davis (and Donald Bullough before her) underlined, Italy was in Charlemagne's eyes 'an arena for political experimentation' and 'a place to try out new tools of rulership'.[137] At the same time, Charlemagne would use to his advantage some of the political, administrative and judicial practices he learnt of in Italy, such as inquests.[138] The relationship between the Carolingian empire and Italy, one of its regions, was therefore one of mutual exchange, and one that brought significant consequences and profound changes for both parties, at least in Charlemagne's times. The case studies I have presented here show that relics, saints' cults and hagiographical texts had an important role in these processes; they can also give us useful hints on how these processes worked in practice. Saints, their cults and relics, and the texts written to celebrate them were powerful tools both in the integration of Italy into a Carolingian horizon and in the shaping of the identities of the Carolingian public officers operating there. The cases I have discussed are not limited to the period of Charlemagne's reign, thus showing that saints and relics were still seen as useful tools for integration and identity formation in the time of his successors – in other words, that the need for integration and the creation of shared identities was still felt in later generations. Indeed, the fact that saints and relics were again utilized shows that they continued to be seen as a tried and tested means of promoting the dialogue between Carolingian authorities and Italian social and political groups. Building a Carolingian – or as Carolingian as possible – identity for the former Lombard kingdom was a long and complicated process, and went hand in hand with the passage of Lombard elements and experiences to the Frankish world. Relics, a bridge between the material and the spiritual world, also served as a bridge connecting the two sides of the Alps.

---

[137] Bullough, '*Europae Pater*'; Davis, *Charlemagne's Practice*, p. 260.
[138] Davis, *Charlemagne's Practice*, pp. 259–78. For a general picture of justice in Carolingian Italy, see Bougard, *La justice*; Bougard, 'La justice'.

15 Between the Palace, the School and the Forum

Rhetoric and Court Culture in Late Lombard and Carolingian Italy

Giorgia Vocino

The cultural uniqueness of the Italian Middle Ages – or 'Italian exceptionalism', as the late Ronald Witt recently put it – is a long-standing historiographical paradigm.[1] The book and documentary cultures of medieval Italy appear to be distinct: the first privileged a literary, grammatical and exegetical approach to the written word, the second presupposed a knowledge of the law and judicial procedures as well as a familiarity with technical legal vocabulary and formulae. And yet, a discipline had once stood exactly at the crossroads between them: rhetoric, the art of persuasion. Placed at the convergence between literary theory and judicial training, the *ars bene dicendi* in the Ciceronian tradition was the most advanced, highly regarded and socially distinctive stage of education in the ancient and late antique world.[2] Although rhetoric was progressively marginalized during the early Middle Ages and areas that had once been covered by the *rhetor* integrated into grammatical teaching, eloquence remained both an essential skill in the toolbox of politically engaged individuals and an important criterion for social mobility.[3] Indeed, despite the disintegration of the ancient Roman educational system in the sixth century,[4] scholars formed in the late

---

[1] Witt, *The Two Latin Cultures*, esp. the introduction at pp. 1–13.

[2] At the *rhetor*'s school, students would work on the literary exegesis of classical authors – the so-called *enarratio auctorum* – and practise their rhetorical skills through the writing of declamations and the simulation of court debates. On education in the ancient world, see Clarke, *Higher Education in the Ancient World* and Bonner, *Education in Ancient Rome*. On the place of rhetoric in ancient education, see Kennedy, *Art of Rhetoric in the Roman World*.

[3] The predominant role of grammar in early medieval culture is studied in Irvine, *The Making*.

[4] The last paragons of the ancient *paideia* – that is, Cassiodorus, Boethius and Ennodius of Pavia – were remarkable orators and still benefitted from the scholastic system financed by the *res publica*. The succession crisis after the death of Theodoric (526), followed by Justinian's wars (535–553) and the Lombard conquest (568), had a dramatic impact on post-Roman Italy, and schools were among those institutions that could no longer count

Lombard kingdom stood out precisely for their skills in the arts of speech and were particularly renowned for their eloquence.[5] After the fall of Pavia at the hands of Charlemagne in 774, Italian masters (*magistri*) travelled, most likely carrying books, to the Frankish court, where some of the best intellectuals of the Latin west convened.[6] Through their mediation, particular texts, literary tastes and practices were injected into the networks shaped by the cultural elites gravitating around the royal court. This, in turn, created the conditions for the wider circulation of knowledge and for the revival of learning that came to be known as the 'Carolingian Renaissance'.[7]

In the following pages I shall be exploring the role played by the Lombard scholars who participated in the earliest cultural and intellectual endeavours of the Carolingians: the analysis of the rhetorical qualities of their literary output will be considered in connection to the store of knowledge and culture available in the Lombard kingdom where they were educated. This shall, on the one hand, shed new light on the nature of the Italian contribution to the literary production of the Carolingian court and, on the other, highlight the distinctiveness of the education and learning shared by those Italian scholars. The existence by the eighth century of a mature Lombard court culture that continued to thrive in the ninth-century kingdom will be thereby demonstrated. The 'Italian exceptionalism' postulated by Witt shall thus be tested against the surviving textual and manuscript evidence in order to better gauge the role of rhetorical education and training in the two Latin cultures that made Italy different from the rest of Carolingian Europe.

Italian *Magistri* at Charlemagne's Court

The very first generation of intellectuals that joined Charlemagne's court and contributed to his promotion of learning had three Italians at the forefront, all of them outstanding examples of eloquence. They were renowned scholars well before their attendance at the Frankish court and had been already engaged in teaching before the conquest of Pavia in 774.

---

on the public financial support. On culture and education in early sixth-century Italy, see Lozovsky, 'Intellectual culture'.

[5] Witt, *The Two Latin Cultures*, pp. 17–26.

[6] See, for instance, Villa, '"Itinera italica" nel secolo VIII'; Bullough, '*Aula renovata*'.

[7] On the 'Carolingian Renaissance' – a concept that is no longer considered to be a very helpful approach to understanding this period by many – see the recent article by Nelson, 'Revisiting the Carolingian Renaissance'.

The King's Tutor: Peter of Pisa

In a letter addressed to Charlemagne in 799, Alcuin remembered when
as a young cleric he had travelled to Rome in the 760s and stayed for a
few days in the royal city of Pavia (_Papia civitas regalis_).[8] There he
witnessed a public dispute (_disputatio_) between a Jew called Lullus (or
Iulius) and a Master Peter; the judicial speech (_controversia_) declaimed by
the latter had been recorded in writing in the same city, but Alcuin did
not have a copy. The Master Peter disputing with a Jew in Pavia was the
same grammarian who made his name teaching grammar in
Charlemagne's palace: Deacon Peter from Pisa.[9] Alcuin's memory of
Peter's _disputatio_ was interestingly triggered by the request received from
the Frankish ruler for the text of a debate between Bishop Felix of Urgell
and a Saracen. The bones of contention between the Jew, Lullus and
Master Peter as well as between Felix of Urgell and the learned Moslem
are not mentioned in Alcuin's letter, but their connection probably
resided in the trans-religious nature of the debates; it is therefore
tempting to assume that the _disputatio_ focussed on the correct interpretation of the Holy Scriptures. After all, Alcuin was writing to
Charlemagne to thank him for the correction of his doctrinal treatise
against the same adoptianist bishop, Felix of Urgell.[10] If the exact content of such disputations remains unknown, the letter unveils the existence of a scholarly practice in the royal city of Pavia that presupposed
both a rhetorical and a dialectical training. The debate was performed in
front of a public audience, and its transcript took the form of a _contro-
versia_ – that is, a judicial speech in the classical Ciceronian tradition. It
has been argued that Peter of Pisa's _quaestiunculae_ on the Book of Daniel
might be a reflection of the Pavia _disputatio_: the comparison between the
Latin (Jerome's) version of the Book of Daniel and its Hebrew counter-
part (which was two chapters shorter), as well as the interpretation of the
visions included in the text could indeed have provided a challenging
topic for a disputation between a Christian scholar and a Jew.[11] We have,
unfortunately, little information about the career of Peter of Pisa before

---

[8] Alcuin, _Epistolae_, 172, ed. Dümmler, p. 285.
[9] Ibid.: Alcuin, _Petrus fuit, qui in palatio vestro grammaticam docens claruit_. For the English
translation of this passage, see Gorman, 'Introduction', p. XVIII.
[10] Gorman, 'Introduction', pp. XVII–XIX.
[11] As argued in Bullough, 'Reminiscence and reality', esp. 193–201. Peter's didactic
commentary, which is organized in brief questions and answers, can in no way be
recording the actual _controversia_, however, although it might preserve a trace of the
object of debate, namely the correct understanding of an Old Testament book the
Christians shared with the Jews. The _quaestiunculae_ on Daniel are now edited in Krotz
and Gorman, _Grammatical Works_, pp. 203–21.

he became the tutor of Charlemagne, but he had most likely already worked as a teacher before joining the Frankish ruler's court: in the case of the grammatical works (Priscianus, Diomedes and Pompeius) explained by Peter in his *quaestiunculae*, for instance, the text versions used seem to have belonged to the respective Italian manuscript traditions, which in turn suggests that he worked on material acquired while still residing in Italy.[12] Thanks to Alcuin's testimony, however, we can take it that his activities in the *regnum Langobardorum* were not limited to the classroom: he was a scholar involved in public debates well before being recruited by Charlemagne, and he was also already acquainted with court life and literature.[13]

Peter's surviving poems confirm his familiarity with the literary genres, tastes and practices that were typical of a royal court: the ironic tone of his exchange with Paul the Deacon and the panegyric written in hexametres for Charlemagne highlight the applications outside the classroom of his grammatical learning as well as testify to his knowledge of versification techniques and declamatory poetry.[14] By the time he joined Charlemagne's court, Peter of Pisa was already an established and mature scholar – Einhard called him *senex*[15] – he could therefore rely on the knowledge, skills and techniques acquired in Italy to serve his new Frankish patron. Although Alcuin's fleeting mention and Peter's poems provide only indirect evidence, their testimony suggests that the Italian scholar had participated in the blossoming court life of the eighth-century Lombard capital, Pavia.[16] The same is confirmed by his fellow countrymen.

A Most Eloquent Theologian: Paulinus of Aquileia

Among the *amici* of Alcuin was another Italian master explicitly praised for his eloquence: the finest theologian of the late eighth century,

---

[12] Peter's exemplar of Priscian seems, for instance, to be related to a *codex* copied in ninth-century Tuscany (Bamberg, Staatsbibliothek, Msc. Class. 43). Also, a variant reading in the title of the *Quaestiunculae in Pompeium* is found in the sole surviving Carolingian witness in the family of Italian manuscripts transmitting Pompeius' commentary (family γ); see Gorman, *Introduction*, pp. XXIX–XXXIV and Holtz, 'Tradition et diffusion', and Holtz, 'Prolégomènes à une édition critique'.

[13] For an overview of Peter of Pisa's biography and literary output, see Sivo, 'Pietro da Pisa'.

[14] Schaller, 'Karl der Große'.

[15] Einhard, *Vita Karoli*, ch. 25, ed. Holder-Egger, p. 30: *in discenda grammatica Petrum Pisanum, diaconum senem audivit.*

[16] Considered one of the distinctive features of Carolingian culture, public debates have recently been the object of renewed scholarly interest. See, for instance, the articles gathered in the themed issue 'Carolingian cultures of dialogue, debate and disputation' edited by M. de Jong and I. van Renswoude, *Early Medieval Europe* 25/1 (2017).

Paulinus of Aquileia.[17] Paulinus had already earned Charlemagne's favour by 776: in a royal diploma granting him lands, Paulinus is presented with flattering words (*vir valde venerabilis*) and identified by his profession (*artis grammaticae magister*).[18] From that moment onwards, Paulinus spent long periods at Charlemagne's court, where he became one of the most active scholars and possibly the ruler's 'official panegyrist'.[19] In 787, he was appointed bishop of the metropolitan see of Aquileia in the north-eastern part of Italy and was thus put in charge of a liminal, and therefore strategically crucial, ecclesiastical province during the years of the military offensive against the Avars.[20] During his episcopate, Paulinus was repeatedly to the fore both in the fight against heresy and in missionary efforts among the new peoples brought under Charlemagne's rule. What made him the man for the job was not only his learning in doctrinal matters but also his knowledge of legal procedures and, probably the most important of his qualities, his skills as a communicator.

The rhetorical qualities of Paulinus are manifest in his verse compositions, in his doctrinal treatises, in his letters and in his pastoral writings. In a virtuoso *clausula excusatoria* appended to his *Regula fidei*, written in hexametres and probably composed around 791–792, Paulinus shows his learning and his grasp of the grammatical, metrical, rhythmic and rhetorical constructs necessary for the writing of correct and elegant verses.[21] Using a sophisticated Virgilian language, the poet mentions both the constituent parts of the *ars poetica* and their correspondent flaws, following thereby the order in which they were usually treated in grammatical treatises written for the classroom: syllables (short or long, common or natural), metrical feet, punctuated clauses, euphony, figures of speech (*schemata*) and tropes are explicitly evoked by Paulinus, who, in a rhetorical and mildly ironic profession of modesty, asks the reader to forgive the mediocrity of his versification.[22] Poetry with its rules,

---

[17] Seven letters addressed by Alcuin to Paulinus survive, while, unfortunately, none of the Italian scholar's responses has been preserved. Only three complete letters, two of which were addressed to Charlemagne, and four fragments written by Paulinus have come down to us; see Paulinus of Aquileia, *Epistolae*, ed. Dümmler.

[18] For the biography of Paulinus of Aquileia, see Chiesa, 'Paolino II'.

[19] Stella, 'Il ruolo di Paolino', esp. pp. 447–8.

[20] On Paulinus of Aquileia and his activities at Charlemagne's service, see Davis, *Charlemagne's Practice of Empire*, pp. 207–9.

[21] Paulinus also heavily relied on the *cursus* (prose rhythm) in his writings, which he may have learned in Friuli, where he was most likely educated, see Pollard, 'Paul, Paulinus and the rhythm of elite Latin'.

[22] Paulinus of Aquileia, *Regula fidei*, ed. Norberg, pp. 95–6: *cum aut per incuriam brevem pro lunga aut lungam pro brevi aut communem pro naturali aut naturalem pro communi syllaba at pedem pro pede aut scema pro scemate aut tropum pro tropo aut indiscretas membrorum cesuras*

allegorically personified by the Virgilian nymph Carmentis, is then compared to a harlot (*meretricula*) that should not be feared but rather faced down manfully (*viriliter*), in the same way one would deal with a duplicitous fox (*vulpicula*) whose pride needs to be tamed.[23] The formal beauty of poetry can therefore be deceptive – a common *topos* in Christian appreciations of rhetorically constructed writings – but its artistic quality could be put at the service of the communication of the truth, the form being subordinated to the substance. Paulinus did indeed apply rhetorical techniques to his preaching, and Alcuin's admiration for the Italian master's *lingua eloquentiae* went as far as to call him a *gallus in praedicatione*.[24]

The extent to which Paulinus relied not only on his grammatical knowledge but also on his rhetorical training is made manifest by the proceedings of the council he convened at Cividale in 796, which include a letter addressed to Charlemagne, Paulinus' opening address to the assembly and the fourteen canons promulgated on the occasion.[25] The Italian bishop employs a distinctively legalistic language in his report to the Frankish ruler, in which he declares that 'it is not allowed by the law (*non iuris fas est*), neither can whatever sanction written with the docile quill of a rational formula (*rationalis formule*) be considered valid, if it is not carefully tested through judicial vote (*iudiciali calculo*) and purged just like silver is seven times purified of the slags of its rust by fire'.[26] The reference to a *calculus iudicialis* can only be explained by assuming Paulinus' familiarity with legal vocabulary and, perhaps, a knowledge of Roman legislation.[27] The activities of the council are presented to the king in a distinctively juridical language: the assembled bishops are

incauta disidiae manu resectas aut inconsideratum colae defossum punctum aut comatum inaequales incisiones aut inconditos eufoniae melos aut si quid huiuscemodi reperiri potest in his inspexeris exaratum.

[23] Paulinus of Aquileia, *Regula fidei*, ed. Norberg, p. 96.

[24] Alcuin, *Epistola* 28, ed. Dümmler, p. 70; ibid., *Epistola* 86, ed. Dümmler, p. 130.

[25] *Concilium Foroiuliense*, ed. Werminghoff, pp. 177–95. The letter to Charlemagne is published separately; see Paulinus of Aquileia, *Epistolae*, ed. Dümmler , pp. 516–20. The entire dossier is transmitted in a tenth-century manuscript from St Peter of Beauvais, today Vatican City, BAV Vat. lat. 3827, ff. 39v–49r.

[26] Paulinus of Aquileia, *Epistolae*, ed. Dümmler, p. 517: *Non enim iuris fas est, nec potest quelibet docili digesta calamo rationalis formule sanctio perspicue rata putari, nisi fuerit iudiciali calculo exploratius examinata, argentique more a sui rubiginis scoria septimpliciter probati expurgata conbustione.* The image of the silver purified seven times by fire is derived from the Bible (Ps. 11:7) and was associated with God's pure words (*eloquia Domini*). The metaphor was used in several late antique and early medieval exegetical commentaries, but, interestingly, is also included in didactic treatises for the teaching of the *ars poetica*: see, for instance, Aldhelm, *De metris*, ed. Ehwald, p. 71.

[27] The *iudicialis calculus* is repeatedly mentioned in the *Epitome Iuliani*; see *Iuliani epitome novellarum Iustiniani*, ed. Hänel, *Const.* 1, 54, 78, 107, 108, 110; e.g. *Const.* 78, p. 103:

gathered in what is described as a judicial court in order to fulfil their duties to inquire 'about the state of practical issues, the cause of the orthodox faith (*de causa ortodoxae fidei*), the status and dignity of ecclesiastical leadership, the prejudicial loss of properties and all the urgent petitions brought forward by whispering requests (*necessariis susurrantium questionum petitionibus*), about which one can complain justly and rightfully, and the presentation (*exhibitio*) of which in querulous disputation (*querule disputationis*), complicated by intricacies, demanded to be thoroughly resolved with ecclesiastical discernment (*sacerdotali dirimatione*)'.[28] Through his choice of vocabulary, Paulinus underlines the judicial nature of the conciliar tasks and casts the king as the supreme arbiter and judge who, with the help of his trusted counsellors, is in charge of the whole *sancta ecclesia*.[29]

The rhetorical and dialectical skills deployed by the Italian bishop in his address to the assembled churchmen confirm and highlight Paulinus' mastery of the arts of speech. His skilful use of rhetorical techniques – rhetoric aimed at persuading – and dialectical argumentation – dialectic being the art of reasoning – allows him to modulate a discourse that targeted two distinct audiences: on the one hand, those who are not trained (the *simplices*) to understand the sophistic ornaments of words (*sophisticas verborum phaleras*) and dialectical reasoning (*isagogicas argumentorum inextricabiles conclusiones*) and, on the other, those who are familiar with sophisticated language and argumentation.[30] Paulinus' detailed explanation of the sacred mystery of the Trinity thus relies on

---

Haec autem constitutio non solum in futuris casibus teneat, sed etiam in praeteritis, nisi iudiciali calculo vel amicali compositione decisi sunt. The same expression was not unknown in Lombard territories and was used in the laws issued by Prince Arechis of Benevento in late eighth-century southern Italy; see *Principum Beneventi leges et pacta*, ed. G. H. Pertz, *MGH Leges* IV, p. 208.

[28] Paulinus of Aquileia, *Epistolae*, ed. Dümmler, p. 517: *de causa siquidem ortodoxae fidei, de statu quin etiam ac famosa ecclesiastici culminis dignitate, de rerum quarumcumque dispendiosa iactura, de quibuscumque necessariis susurrantium questionum petitionibus, de quibus iuste recteque conqueri potest, quarumque querule disputationis exhibitio, nodosa licium adligatione contorta, sacerdotali nichilominus desiderabat enodatim dirimatione resolvi.*

[29] Ibid., p. 517: *in vestrae potestatis arbitrio, in vestro nichilominus decrevimus reservare iudicio.*
   Ibid., p. 520: *Unde vestri est censura magisterii...quatinus sit sancta ecclesia vestris adiuta praesidiis libera et ab humano sanguine inpolluta.*

[30] *Concilium Foroiuliense*, ed. Werminghoff, p. 181: *de mysterio namque sanctae et inenarrabilis trinitatis planiore me repromisisse profiteor sermone dicturum, sophisticas per omnia verborum phaleras devitantes, sed et isagogicas argumentorum reliquentes inextricabiles conclusiones, simpliciter propter simplicium mentes liquidiusque [...] cultiore potius sensu quam stilo cupio recolere.*
   Ibid., p. 186: *Hucusque propter eos, qui nequeunt ad purum subtiliter intellegere, quid sit in sacro eloquio addere vel minuere. Nunc autem his ita digestis proposita nostrae repromissionis debita tandem aliquando pleno reddere calamo iam non differamus.*

his ability to apply rhetorical and dialectical techniques to the defence of the Catholic faith.[31] In doing so, he is implementing the instructions Gregory the Great had once given in his handbook for bishops (*Regula pastoralis*): the episcopal office was indissolubly bound by the duty of teaching and learning, and the mastery of speech was one of the necessary requirements to properly fulfil the pastoral duties attached to the job.[32] Gregory had dedicated an entire book of the *Regula* (*Liber* III) to the many ways in which bishops should adapt and adjust their discourse to suit different audiences, among which were the *simplices* and those 'who do not understand correctly the words of the sacred law' (*qui sacrae legis verba non recte intellegunt*). Doctrinal knowledge, rhetorical and dialectical skills as well as a thorough understanding of legal traditions and judicial procedures made Paulinus of Aquileia a resourceful man who could easily navigate and handle different public forums: a council, a judicial assembly (*placitum*) and, last but not least, the royal court.[33]

The attendance of the Frankish court and the ties established with scholars coming from different cultural backgrounds undoubtedly helped Paulinus enrich his literary repertoire.[34] His poetic models and sources reveal an impressive array of Christian and classical authors: while most of them belonged to the canon of poets that became standard in the Carolingian classroom (Virgil, Juvencus and Sedulius, above all others), rarer poets such as Nemesianus and Silius Italicus are less easily located within early medieval literary and scholastic traditions.[35] If the revival of epic and bucolic poetry can rightly be associated with the Carolingian court, the provenance of these 'rediscovered classical traditions' is less clear. It is therefore particularly intriguing that the earliest courtiers echoing Nemesianus' eclogues are the Italian masters at

---

[31] Ibid., p. 186: *De causa nempe fidei polliciti sumus contra eos disputare, qui variis erroribus inplicati non recte sentiunt de mysterio trinitatis.*

[32] Gregory the Great, *Regula pastoralis*, ed. Judic, Rommel and Morels, I, 1, p. 128: *Nulla ars doceri praesumitur, nisi intenta prius meditatione discatur.*

[33] On Paulinus' familiarity with the Lombard laws and judicial system, as shown by his exhortatory letter addressed to a Lombard layman named Aistulf, see Pohl, 'Le leggi longobarde nell'Italia carolingia'. The bishop of Aquileia also acted as royal *missus* on at least one occasion and, with Arn of Salzburg and Fardolfus of Saint-Denis, arbitrated upon a *placitum* addressing the complaints of the monastery of S. Bartolomeo near Pistoia against Pippin of Italy's *baiulus* Rotchild; see Stoffella, 'Le relazioni tra Baviera e Toscana', esp. on the *placitum* 74–5.

[34] Paulinus' acquaintance with Aldhelm of Malmesbury's works and with Paul the Deacon's *carmina* are, for instance, hard to explain outside the cultural exchanges taking place at court; see Colombi, 'Modelli poetici', on the parallels with Aldhelm's poetry esp. pp. 72–4.

[35] On the medieval transmission of these authors, see Reynolds, *Texts and Transmission*, pp. 246–7 and 389–91.

Charlemagne's court: allusions to the third-century poet have been noticed in Paulinus' verses,[36] in Paul the Deacon's mention of the pipe-playing shepherd (Nemesianus, Eccl. 1:3–4), in the poem Paul addressed to Peter of Pisa and in the latter's poetic reply.[37] Indirect evidence of the early medieval transmission of Silius Italicus' *Punica* also points to northern Italy as a region where it was still possible to read the Roman poet: the annotation 'Silus Italicus XV libri de bellis punicis' was, for instance, added to the upper margin of Bern, Burgerbibliothek 363, f. 147v by an Irish master who travelled to Italy, resided in the Milanese area in the 860s and here copied into his personal *vademecum* an intriguing selection of classical and late antique didactic treatises and poems.[38]

The renewed interest in epic and bucolic poetry observed in Carolingian literature probably owed more to Italian traditions than has been accounted for. As a matter of fact, the verse produced by Lombard scholars at the Frankish court shows both a knowledge of the Roman poets and a classical taste that must reflect their education.[39] The verse epistle addressed by Paulinus to the priest Zacharias is a firework of classical bucolic allusions, while his earliest production for Charlemagne – the Easter hymn *Regi regum* and the epic *De conversione Saxonum*, composed in the late 770s – highlights his mastery of celebratory poetry as well as the convergence between political and religious literature in praise of the Frankish ruler and his military accomplishments. The impression made on Charlemagne by the panegyrical quality of Paulinus' poetry has been stressed convincingly by Dieter Schaller: it was probably thanks to the Italian masters at court – Peter of Pisa also wrote a poem in praise of the Frankish king – that, in the late 770s and early 780s, Charlemagne became fully aware of the potential of poetry as

---

[36] Colombi, 'Modelli poetici', pp. 83–4.

[37] Neff, *Die Gedichte des Paulus Diaconus*, n. XVII, p. 84 (Peter of Pisa to Paul the Deacon) and n. XIX, p. 92 (Paul the Deacon to Peter of Pisa).

[38] On this manuscript, see now Vocino, 'A *peregrinus*'s vademecum'. The *Punica* were also listed in a tenth-century library catalogue from the Lake Constance area; see Bischoff, *Manuscripts*, p. 148. It should be stressed that cultural exchange between the Alamannian region and northern Italy saw a considerable increase in the late eighth century, when Alamannian men were appointed to key political positions in the former *regnum Langobardorum*. On the connections between Verona and Alamannia revealed by both books and documents, see, for instance, Santoni, 'Scrivere documenti'.

[39] The assumption that Virgil was rediscovered thanks to the cultural influence of the Anglo-Saxons at Charlemagne's court should not make us forget that the poet was read and continued to be copied in northern Italy: see, for instance, the late eighth-century fragment in Munich (Bayerische Staatsbibliothek Clm 29216/7), which is copied in Italian pre-Caroline minuscule.

a means of political propaganda and prestige.[40] The surge of poetical writing at Charlemagne's court as well as its preservation in ninth-century manuscripts are an eloquent indicator of the value placed on celebratory and occasional poetry; this applied not only to the court, where poems were most likely declaimed, but also to the bishoprics and monasteries where members of the ruler's entourage were educated in Carolingian and post-Carolingian times.[41]

A Poet for All Occasions: Paul the Deacon

In the verse epistles exchanged between Peter of Pisa and Paul the Deacon, the tight connection between rhetoric and poetry is made particularly visible: Paul is compared to Tertullus, for his mastery of the liberal arts, to Horace, for his metrical compositions, and to the elegiac poet Tibullus, for his eloquence.[42] The same is true of Paul's reply to Peter of Pisa: in a highly rhetorical and playful manner he dismisses the compliments 'thrown with irony in my face'.[43] Irony (yronia) was a powerful trope, and was thus listed and explained in classical, late antique and early medieval handbooks focussing on rhetorical figures of speech and thought.[44] Therefore, Paul the Deacon's aggressive reply, 'May I perish, should I wish to imitate any of them / who have gone into the impenetrable wilds; / I would rather compare them to mongrels',[45] which has been interpreted as a rejection of classical culture, should, on

---

[40] See again Schaller, 'Karl der Große'. For a critique of Schaller's attribution: Everett, 'Paulinus, the Carolingians and Famosissima Aquileia', esp. pp. 121–8. On the first phase of Carolingian encomiastic literature and the role of the 'visiting poets' at court, see also Stella, 'La dinamica del consenso', esp. pp. 361–4.

[41] On the re-emergence of political poetry at the late eighth- and ninth-century Carolingian court in general, see Godman, Poets and Emperors.

[42] Versus Petri grammatici, ed. Dümmler, p. 48: Tertullus in artibus, / Flaccus crederis in metris, Tibullus eloquio. Tertullus has often been identified with a biblical orator mentioned in the Acts of the Apostles (Acts 24:1), but it is the Christian author Tertullianus who is most likely intended here; see Mastandrea, 'Classicismo e Cristianesimo', esp. pp. 297–9.

[43] Versus Pauli, ed. Dümmler, p. 49: Totum hoc in meum caput dictum per hyroniam.

[44] Irony was, for instance, considered one of allegory's seven species in Donatus' De tropis and in Isidore's correspondent explanation in the Etymologies (Book I, ch. 37, 23), which relied on the definition included in a Christianized version of the late Roman grammarian's Ars Maior; see Irvine, The Making, pp. 225–34. Donatus, Ars Maior, III, 6, trans. Copeland and Sluiter, p. 98: Irony is the trope that shows what it attempts to say through the contrary. It should be added that Paul the Deacon was familiar with Donatus' Ars grammatica and that he wrote a commentary on the Ars Minor, which is today preserved in Vatican City, BAV Pal. lat. 1746.

[45] Latin text with English translation in Godman, Poetry, p. 86: Peream, si quenquam horum imitari cupio, / avia qui sunt sequuti pergentes per invium; / potius sed istos ego conparabo canibus!

the contrary, be understood as a discourse constructed with *yronia* and thus actually highlighting Paul's appreciation of classical authors and highly sophisticated versification.[46]

The poems written by Paul the Deacon are extremely varied in the chosen forms of versification (both metrical and rhythmic) and genre (inscriptions, epitaphs, praises, didactic and occasional poetry, enigmas and hymns).[47] The Italian scholar was comfortable writing verse in rare metrical feet (e.g. the serpentine elegiac couplets in praise of Lake Como or the sapphic stanzas of the hymn in honour of John the Baptist), which can only be a reflection of an excellent education in the ancient metres. The pronounced classicism of his verse production confirms the extent of his knowledge of the Roman and late antique poets (not only Virgil, Ovid and Martial but also Claudian and Venantius Fortunatus).[48] Furthermore, we most likely have Paul the Deacon's fondness for sophisticated versification and, more generally, the Italian epideictic tradition to thank for the survival of the rhetorical writings of Ennodius of Pavia (d. 521): the *opuscula, epistolae, dictiones* and *carmina* of the sixth-century bishop were gathered together in a collection compiled in eighth-century Pavia and from there brought to Charlemagne's court, in all likelihood by Paul the Deacon himself in 782.[49] One of the last paragons of ancient rhetorical culture in Ostrogothic Italy, Ennodius had been a *rhetor*, a poet, a panegyrist and a diplomat before his election to the episcopal see of Pavia. He considered rhetoric to be an art of practical use and utmost relevance in the exercise of power.[50] This view, as well as the equivalence between rhetoric and poetry cultivated by Ennodius, were positions that were certainly shared by Paul the Deacon and by others who had worked in connection with the Lombard court at Pavia before him.

---

[46] Peter Godman rightly stressed the ironic nature of the poetic exchange between Peter of Pisa and Paul the Deacon; see Godman, *Poetry*, pp. 9–10. On the innovative features of Paul's poetry, see Stella, 'La poesia di Paolo Diacono', esp. pp. 561–2.

[47] It should be stressed that the attribution of an important number of verse compositions is still controversial; see the synthetic overview in Valtorta, *Clavis Scriptorum Latinorum*, pp. 197–210.

[48] A systematic analytical study of Paul the Deacon's poems has yet to be carried out, but the influence of classical models on his poetry has been repeatedly stressed; see Giovini, '"Sophia" come "Daphnis", "Io" e "Alcimus"'; Giovini, '"Quel ramo del lago di Como" visto da Paolo Diacono'; Pucci, 'Paul the Deacon's Poem to Lake Como'; Giovini, 'Gli *inculta poemata* di Paolo Diacono'.

[49] The use of adonic verses in the poetic epistles exchanged between Charlemagne's courtiers is, for instance, a reflection of the circulation and study of Ennodius' works in the main centres of learning of the Carolingian empire; see Gioanni, 'Nouvelles hypothèses'.

[50] In his prosimetrum known as *Paraenesis didascalica*, Ennodius put the following words in the mouth of a personified Rhetoric talking to his students: *qui nostris servit studiis, mox imperat orbi, / nil dubium metuens ars mihi regna dedit*, ed. Vogel, p. 314.

A Distinctive Lombard Epideictic Culture

Once the boundaries between the territories dominated by the Lombards and those under Byzantine control had solidified in the second quarter of the seventh century, Pavia emerged as the capital of the kingdom and a residential administrative apparatus began to develop progressively in association with the royal palace.[51] Once again, the patronage of the kings became visible in the city: building programmes, memory politics and the promotion of learning increased considerably in the second half of the seventh century. During Cunipert's reign (680–700), a group of learned men and intellectuals worked for the royal palace and the ruler seems to have been keen to encourage their activities.[52] From that moment onwards, the existence of a school, a court and a chancery linked to the palace ensured that the most talented clerics and scions of the kingdom's elites were attracted to Pavia; among them were Paul the Deacon, Peter of Pisa and, possibly, Paulinus of Aquileia.[53]

A flourishing court life and culture encouraged the composition of an epideictic literature used for several purposes, some of the most prominent of which were political propaganda, entertainment, self-promotion, social prestige and scholarly competition. In Frankish territories, the tradition of politically invested poetry reached its peak in the sixth-century Merovingian kingdom, a time when the Italian poet Venantius Fortunatus crossed the Alps to offer his services to the Austrasian king, Sigebert, but celebratory poetry seems to have disappeared in the seventh and eighth centuries. If poems were still declaimed at the Merovingian court – which is not unlikely – they appear, nonetheless, not to have been considered worthy of being copied down, transmitted and studied in the classroom. The same cannot be said for Italy, where, even in those centuries that have left very little literary evidence, the epideictic genre continued to be *en vogue*: the *Rhythmus de synodo Ticinensi* commissioned by King Cunipert celebrated both the end of the Three Chapters controversy in 698 and the achievements of the Lombard ruler and his kin,

---

[51] Majocchi, 'Sviluppo e affermazione'.

[52] In the *Historia Langobardorum*, VI, 7, ed. Bethmann, p. 167, Paul the Deacon recalls how the king rewarded the grammarian Felix (uncle of Paul's preceptor at the palace) with the gift of a stick decorated with gold and silver. On the cultural blossoming of Pavia in the late seventh and eighth centuries, see also Cau and Casagrande Mazzoli, 'Cultura e scrittura a Pavia (secoli V–X)', esp. pp. 186–90.

[53] Paul the Deacon explicitly tells us that he attended the royal court (*Historia Langobardorum* II, 28, ed. Bethmann, pp. 87–9), and the epitaph composed by his pupil Ildericus situates his advanced education at Pavia under the aegis of King Ratchis (744–749); see *Epitaphium Pauli Diaconi*, ed. Dümmler, p. 85. For a biography of the Italian intellectual, see Capo, 'Paolo Diacono'.

while the *Versum de Mediolano*, written between 739 and 744, is the earliest surviving medieval example of a *laus urbis*, a rhetorical showpiece destined to achieve great popularity in medieval Italy.[54] Late antique panegyrical traditions did not die out in Lombard Italy and the surviving inscriptions from late seventh- and eighth-century Pavia offer precious evidence for the survival of sophisticated literary traditions and encomiastic writing. Epitaphs were dedicated not only to kings and members of their families but also to bishops and to other personages connected with the royal palace.[55] The court of Pavia was, therefore, still a place where the services of highly educated individuals continued to be available, requested and appreciated by the Lombard elites.[56] The Italian inscriptions reunited in the *Sylloge Laureshamense III* testify to the survival of both metrical and rhythmic verse composition and confirm the role of Pavia as a leading centre of culture and literary production in the late Lombard period.[57] The vocabulary as well as the rhetorical figures and tropes used in the eighth-century inscriptions imply the existence of schools where the study of the ancient and late antique poets continued to be prominent. After all, poetry had been a natural outlet for rhetorical training since the fall of the Roman Republic, a trend that became standard practice in the late imperial period, when the study of the classical poets – above all Virgil, Horace and Ovid – inherently implied learning how rhetoric could be applied to verse literature. This tradition continued to thrive in late antiquity, when poets and courtiers wrote in honour of the Roman emperors.[58] Not only could many examples of rhetorical figures of speech and thought be found in their verses, but also, more generally, their works came to be considered models for epideictic discourse.[59] Moreover, in Priscian's rhetorical exercises (*praeexercitamina*) – a pedagogic text that circulated in Lombard Italy[60] – poetry is

---

[54] On the *Rhythmus de synodo Ticinensi*, see Kamptner, '"Scripsi per prosa"'. On the *Versum de Mediolano* and the revival of the ancient rhetorical genre of the *Laudes urbium*, see Granier, 'La *renovatio* du modèle rhétorique antique'.

[55] On Lombard inscriptions, see the dedicated chapter in Everett, *Literacy*, pp. 235–76; Consolino, 'La poesia epigrafica'.

[56] For an overview of the surviving inscriptions connected to the Lombard royal family, see De Rubeis, 'Le iscrizioni dei longobardi'.

[57] The *Sylloge* is preserved in a ninth-century manuscript from Lorsch, now preserved in the Vatican library (Vatican City, BAV, Pal. lat. 833, ff. 41r-53v). The *codex* can be consulted online: https://digi.vatlib.it/view/bav_pal_lat_833. On the *Sylloge*, see again Consolino, 'La poesia epigrafica'; Everett, *Literacy*, pp. 243–8.

[58] The propagandistic quality of panegyrics written for late antique emperors is explored in Whitby, *The Propaganda of Power*.

[59] Prill, 'Rhetoric and poetics'.

[60] They were included in a didactic miscellany produced at Montecassino, most likely under Paul the Deacon's supervision (Paris, BnF lat. 7530, ff. 259v-265r).

defined as 'panegyric', and in the late antique tradition the poet came to be considered as the *rhetor summus*.[61] It does not come as a surprise, therefore, that Lombard poets studied and emulated precisely those authors renowned for the rhetorical quality of their verses, such as Claudian, Optatianus Porfirius, Ennodius of Pavia and Venantius Fortunatus.[62]

The Lombard scholars at the court of Charlemagne therefore shared an educational and cultural background that was rooted in the studies, experiences and practices of their years of residence at Pavia; they expressed a distinctive and coherent culture that can also be identified in the writings of less famous and prolific exiles, such as Peter's companion, Fiducia, and the Lombard abbot of St Denis, Fardolfus.[63] They both participated in the poetic exchanges between Charlemagne's courtiers, and their only surviving productions consist, unsurprisingly at this point, of metrical occasional poetry and inscriptions. Their grammatical and rhetorical skills transpire from their verse: the use of alliteration in the poem Fardolfus addressed to a friend and the insisted anaphoras in Fiducia's *Versus ad Angelramnum* reveal the familiarity of both authors with versification techniques and figures of speech.[64] It does not come as a surprise that one of the earliest manuscripts containing poems stemming from Charlemagne's court was produced at Saint-Denis at the time of Fardolfus' abbacy (Paris, BnF lat. 528).[65] This eclectic miscellany also contains didactic texts, many of which focus on grammatical and rhetorical aspects: copied alongside various introductory works relating to the understanding of the Sacred Scripture (Eucherius, Cassiodorus, Jerome, Isidore, Bede) were treatises focussing on figures of speech, tropes and versification (Bede's *De schematibus, De tropis* and *De arte metrica*) as well as grammatical compilations, glossaries and an anthology

---

[61] Prill, 'Rhetoric and poetics', p. 133.   [62] Consolino, 'Poesia epigrafica'.

[63] For a synthetic presentation of the evidence on Fiducia, see Villa, 'Berlin, Staatsbibliothek, Diez. B. 66'. Chiesa, 'Fardolfo'. Fiducia wrote a poem to Angilram of Metz, while Fardolfus has left four *carmina* (three inscriptions and a poem addressed to Charlemagne). In the compositions of both poets, classical allusions and, more particularly, borrowings from Virgil abound.

[64] *Fardulfi abbatis carmina*, III, ed. Dümmler, p. 353: *addit et aeternam per praemia plurima palmam.*

Versus Fiduciae, ed. Dümmler, p. 76: *Non sceptrum regis fero, nec mantilia lini; / Non manibus laticem mitto nec libamina sancta, / nec regum cerno proles nec pocula Bacchi / [...] Tu pius, alme pater, clarescis in ordine vatum, / tu florem meriti sequeris ad ardua regna; / Me vestrum foveas dictis factisque misellum.*

[65] The manuscript can be consulted online at http://gallica.bnf.fr/ark:/12148/btv1b9078378q.

of poems of diverse origin, genre and form.[66] The selection of texts and poems included in the manuscript suggests that the miscellany was put together by someone who shared the same tastes and interests of the Italian scholars attending Charlemagne's court. It therefore seems plausible to assume that the texts were indeed collected by Fardolfus (or at his request) and brought to Saint-Denis, where they were then studied in the monastic classroom.

The Italian masters who participated in the intellectual networks revolving around Charlemagne were already aware that the arts of speech could be put at the service of the king in various domains (teaching, propaganda, celebration, entertainment, debate). Their knowledge of the classical and late antique authors gave them the tools to impress and please, which they did with effect. In doing so, they poured a fair amount of their distinctive Lombard culture into the Carolingian melting-pot. Other questions are now left to be answered: What happened to the educational and cultural system so successfully represented by these intellectuals once the Carolingians settled in and ruled Lombard Italy? How did the cultural traditions of Lombard Italy evolve across the ninth century? Did the Carolingian kingdom of Italy lose its cultural distinctiveness?

'For Things to Remain the Same, Everything Must Change':[67] Court Culture in Carolingian Italy

Seven years after the fall of Pavia, a new king was crowned to rule over the *regnum Langobardorum* and, except for certain intervals (774–781, 818–822, 826–834), a Carolingian ruler resided in the Italian peninsula for the whole century following Charlemagne's conquest of 773–774.[68] Royal presence favoured the maintenance – or rapid reconstitution, if there was ever a rupture – of an associated chancery, a court and also,

---

[66] The anthology of poetic material was copied onto ff. 122r–134r and contains the following: the epitaphs of Emperor Constantius Chlorus and the sixth-century Byzantine general Droctulf (which is also transmitted in Paul the Deacon's *Historia Langobardorum*, III, 19); the verse epistles exchanged between Peter of Pisa and Paul the Deacon; the latter's poetic appeals to Charlemagne; the epitaph for his niece Sophia; Paul's letter to Abbot Theodemar of Montecassino; the anonymous abecedarian rhythms *De bonis sacerdotibus* and *De malis sacerdotibus* – which have been attributed to either Paul the Deacon or Paulinus of Aquileia; the hymn in honour of St Benedict attributed to Paul; a few poems written by Alcuin; Peter of Pisa's panegyric for Charlemagne.

[67] Tomasi di Lampedusa, *The Leopard*, p. 19.

[68] For a synthetic overview, see Wickham, *Early Medieval Italy*, pp. 47–63. For the account of Pippin's appointment as king in Italy, see *Annales Regni Francorum*, a. 781, ed. Kurze, p. 57

probably, a school.[69] Unfortunately, the destruction of the palace of Pavia in 1024 caused the irremediable loss of the archives and library sheltered there, which in turn led to the capital city of the Italian kingdom being almost absent from manuscript studies dedicated to the early medieval centres of learning and writing in early medieval Italy.[70] Two other cities that maintained a close association with royal power have preserved abundant manuscript and documentary evidence, however: Verona, intermittently a *sedes regia* since the time of the Ostrogothic king Theodoric (d. 526), and Milan, where the most powerful archbishop of the kingdom had his seat.[71]

The mention of King Pippin residing in Verona somewhere between 796 and 810 is included in the rhythmic praise of the city known as *Versus de Verona*, a poem composed following the rules of the epideictic genre of the *laudes urbium*.[72] The famous manuscript from Lobbes into which the *Versus* were copied, once belonging to Rather of Verona (d. 974), has been lost, but a poetic miscellany produced in the Italian city during the ninth century (Verona, Biblioteca Capitolare XC) preserves the model used for their composition: the *Versum de Mediolano*. The latter celebrated the city of Milan at the time of the *presul magnus* Theodorus during the last years of the pious king Liutprand (*pius rex*), and, in a similar fashion, the *Versus de Verona* commemorated the residence of the last Lombard bishop, the *presul inclitus* Anno, and Pippin *magnus rex piissimus* in the city.[73] The self-promotion of Carolingian Verona, a city intent on asserting its position as *sedes regia*, has also been observed in other literary endeavours, namely the compilation of the historical *compendium* known as *Epitome Philippsiana* and the production of three hagiographic texts celebrating the local patron saints (the bishop Zeno

---

[69] On the men responsible for the kingdom during Pippin's minority, see Bullough, '"Baiuli" in the Carolingian "regnum Langobardorum"'. If Pavia does not seem to have benefitted from Charlemagne's generosity in the late eighth and early ninth centuries, the notaries of the city continued to draft the records of the *placita* where the royal *missi* intervened; see Bougard, *La justice*, esp. pp. 130–3.

[70] On the early medieval 'punished city' of Pavia, see Settia, 'Pavia carolingia'. Pavia is conspicuously absent from the overview of Carolingian writing centres analyzed in Bischoff, *Manuscripts and Libraries*, esp. on Italy, pp. 44–53.

[71] On the Italian early medieval *sedes regiae*, see Brogiolo, 'Capitali e residenze regie nell'Italia longobarda'; Bougard, 'Les palais royaux et impériaux'.

[72] It would take too much space here to list all the relevant studies dedicated to this text: for further bibliographical references see Avesani, 'Il Re Pipino'. The text is edited under the title *Laudes Veronensis civitatis*, ed. Dümmler, pp. 118–22. For an English translation, see Godman, *Poetry*, pp. 180–6.

[73] *Versus de Verona*, p. 122: *Haec, ut valuit, paravit Anno praesul inclitus, / proba cuius flamma claret de bonis operibus / ab Austriae finibus terrae usque Neustriae terminos. [...] Magnus habitat in te rex Pipinus piissimus, / non oblitus pietatem aut rectum iudicium / qui bonis agens semper cunctis facit prospera.*

and the martyrs Fermus and Rusticus).[74] Furthermore, there is another celebratory poem that might be associated with Verona: the rhythmic *Carmen de Pippini regis victoria avarica*, which was composed by an anonymous author who probably participated in the military campaigns led by Pippin of Italy against the Avars in 796. The poem is transmitted in only one manuscript, a roughly contemporaneous miscellany also known as *Codex Diezianus* (Berlin, Staatsbibliothek, Diez. B. Sant. 66), which was copied by two scribes, one trained in a Frankish province – possibly Austrasia – and the other using a distinctively Italian pre-Caroline minuscule.[75] An analysis of its content sheds light on a school programme designed to form the elites of the Carolingian kingdom of Italy.

A Handbook for Future Office-Holders: Berlin, Staatsbibliothek Diez. B. Sant. 66

It was the northern Italian scribe working on the *Codex Diezianus* who copied down the panegyric in honour of Pippin as well as other poems written by Angilbert of St Riquier, Paul the Deacon, Peter of Pisa and Fiducia.[76] The insertion of this occasional poetry into a handbook focussing on grammar, prosody and rhetoric suggests that the poems had already become examples of versification to be read by students who were being educated in a centre connected to the Carolingian court in Italy.[77] Among the texts copied by the Italian scribe was also a list of classical authors and their works (ff. 218–219), which has been interpreted as either the catalogue of a section of Charlemagne's library or as a list of books available at Verona.[78] Given the coherence and the

---

[74] On the *Epitome Philippsiana*, see Tondini, 'Un modello per il regno dei Carolingi in Italia'. On the hagiography written in Carolingian Verona, see Vocino, 'Santi e luoghi santi', esp. pp. 215–42.

[75] The manuscript was produced at a centre with close connections to a Carolingian court. It was traditionally associated with Charlemagne's palace, but recent studies have convincingly argued for an Italian origin, with Verona as a likely candidate; see Villa, 'Die Horazüberlieferung'.

[76] Angilbert had been chosen as tutor of the young King Pippin and was the main chaplain at his Italian court, which implies his residence in the kingdom; see Villa, 'Die Horazüberlieferung', pp. 40–6.

[77] The manuscript contains an interesting selection of didactic material covering the basics of grammar (on the eight parts of speech), prosody (on syllables and metrical feet) and rhetoric (on figures of speech). Among them also a grammatical treatise (*Ars Dieziana*) compiled on the basis of Peter of Pisa's teaching material; see Gorman and Krotz, *Grammatical Works*, pp. XLIII–XLVII.

[78] Bischoff, *Manuscripts*, pp. 68–73; Villa, 'Die Horazüberlieferung', pp. 29–39; Gorman, 'The oldest lists of Latin books'.

pedagogic vocation of the *Codex Diezianus* as well as its compilation in early Carolingian Italy, it is more plausible to assume that the booklist was actually a well-thought-out list of further reading for students who had already acquired a solid education in grammatical basics, versification and rhetorical techniques, which were precisely the subjects covered by the texts gathered in the manuscript.[79] The first section of the booklist focusses on poetry, including the works of Lucan (*Pharsalia*), Statius (*Thebaid*), Terentius (six comedies), Juvenal (Satires), Tibullus (elegies), Horace (*Ars poetica*), Claudian (epic poems and invectives) and Martial (epigrams). The eclectic selection offers not only examples of different metres but also of different genres (epic, comic, elegiac, satiric, celebratory), styles and topics, thus providing an overview of the many fields covered by poetry. The second section of the booklist gathers prose writings and shows a pronounced focus on deliberative and judicial rhetoric: the handbook of Julius Victor (*Ars Rhetorica*), Cicero's orations (invectives, defence and prosecution speeches), *sententiae* excerpted from Sallust's historical works (*Bellum Catilinae* and *Bellum Iugurthinum*),[80] a *Liber Alchimi* (most likely fictional *controversiae*) and the *Exempla elocutionis* of Messius Arusianus (also known as *quadriga Messii*). Having followed the educational programme designed by the *Codex Diezianus*, students could approach the more complex works included in the booklist offering pertinent and excellent examples of the three genres of Ciceronian rhetoric. Such a curriculum fits the education of individuals destined to participate in court life and public affairs, a stage at which no distinction between ecclesiastical and lay status was made. At the highest level, the individuals belonging to the elites – churchmen and lay officials alike – needed to be familiar with the codes and customs of the royal court; writing elegant verses could provide them with a powerful means to win notice, to gain social prestige and to reach the ears of the most prominent political actors.[81] Moreover, those who managed to earn royal favour were generally entrusted with missions, tasks or offices that required them to act as arbiters, judges and advocates on behalf of their king or the community they served. The art of persuasion was therefore a crucial skill in their toolbox. While the *Codex Diezianus* addresses

---

[79] Also of the same opinion: McKitterick, *Charlemagne*, pp. 365–8. For the text of the booklist, see Bischoff, *Manuscripts*, pp. 71–2.

[80] The recorded *Sententia Catonis in senatu* most likely refers to the speech pronounced against Caesar by the Roman orator Cato Uticensis with regard to the Catiline conspiracy; see Sallust, *Bellum Catilinae*, ch. 52, ed. Ramsey, pp. 47–9.

[81] This is exactly what Paul the Deacon did when he addressed a poem to Charlemagne begging him to release his brother, Arechis; see *Versus Pauli ad regem precando*, ed. Neff, *Die Gedichte*, pp. 53–5.

precisely these requirements and the booklist's selected readings point to its composition at a centre connected to the court, it might be misguided to look for the exact city or an existing library that would be wholly reflected by the contents of the miscellany.[82] The court of Pippin of Italy was, after all, attended by scholars who travelled throughout the kingdom and beyond, not just to accompany the king but also to attend to the various affairs they had charge of. The *Codex Diezianus* would have been assembled by a well-connected scholar who had access to an intellectual network in which the court was the main, but not the only, hub, and which thus facilitated the wide circulation of learning and knowledge. Within this cultural horizon it was possible to gather together texts of diverse origin, such as poems compiled at Charlemagne's court, a reworking of Peter of Pisa's grammatical *compendium,* the panegyric celebrating Pippin of Italy's victory over the Avars and the Latin transliteration of the Greek *Magnificat,* which was transcribed from a Veronese manuscript. At least some of the rare authors and texts mentioned in the booklist were also available in the Italian kingdom: Claudian's *carmina minora* and the *Disticha Catonis* were, for instance, copied in late-eighth-century Verona (Verona, Biblioteca Capitolare CLXIII), while the local cathedral library also most likely owned a manuscript containing verses of the Roman poet Tibullus.[83] The lost *Liber Alchimi* was furthermore listed in the tenth-century library catalogue of the monastery at Bobbio,[84] where a copy of Arusianus Messius' *Exempla elocutionum* was also available.[85]

Deliberative and Judicial Rhetoric in Carolingian Italy

The booklist in the *Codex Diezianus* also includes an interesting selection of Roman political and forensic speeches that reveal an enduring concern for deliberative and judicial rhetoric. The survival of texts focussing precisely on these two rhetorical genres is a distinctive feature of Italian culture and literary traditions. The most technical handbook dedicated to judicial oratory, namely Consultus Fortunatianus' *Ars Rhetorica,* was included in the miscellany reflecting Paul the Deacon's teaching at

---

[82] Villa, 'La produzione libraria', on the *Codex Diezianus* esp. pp. 395–6.

[83] Villa, 'Die Horazüberlieferung', pp. 34–7.

[84] The *Liber Alchimi* is mentioned in the same entry as Cato; see Genest, 'Inventaire de la bibliothèque de Bobbio', p. 251 [420–1].

[85] Ferrari, 'Le scoperte a Bobbio nel 1493', esp. 145–6: a manuscript containing Arusianus Messius was listed in the catalogue of Bobbio compiled in 1461, and the description of the script as *littera longobarda obscura* suggests the *codex* was written in a pre-Caroline minuscule.

Montecassino (Paris, BnF lat. 7530), which most likely constituted a collection of texts the Lombard master had brought with him from northern Italy.[86] The same work was also copied into another ninth-century manuscript, compiled in Milan during the 860s (Bern, Burgerbibliothek 363, ff. 143r–153v). Both *codices* reflect teaching programmes that addressed the rhetorical nature of political and judicial debates: the Montecassino *summa* contains the only copy of a short didactic text focussing on definitions pertaining to the *quaestiones civiles* (ff. 258r–259v), while the Bern miscellany includes a compilation of excerpts tellingly gathered under the title *Ars Rhetorica de statibus* – the *status* being the central point at issue in a given case – and associated with an otherwise unknown Clodianus.[87] Also available in Carolingian Milan was a manuscript (Paris, BnF lat. 7900A) containing a collection of fictional *controversiae* known as the Pseudo-Quintilian *Declamationes maiores* and *minores* (forensic speeches used in rhetorical training). Unfortunately, they were scraped off around the year 900 to make room for a new, typically 'Carolingian', didactic programme focussing on the *enarratio poetarum* (Terence, Lucan, Horace and Martianus Capella), thus preventing us from studying what was most probably a unique rhetorical collection.[88] The manuscript size and the layout of the *scriptio inferior* in two columns are similar to the famous ninth-century Ambrosian copy of Quintilian's *Institutio oratoria* (Milan, Biblioteca Ambrosiana. E 153 sup.) and to the fragment of Cicero's *Brutus* today preserved at Cremona (Archivio Storico Comunale AC 295).[89] These three ninth-century *codices* – the palimpsest Pseudo-Quintilian, the Ambrosian Quintilian and the Cremona fragment – appear to belong to the same cultural milieu and, possibly, also writing, region, and show a keen interest not only in a thorough teaching of deliberative and judicial rhetoric but also in its possible applications to the writing of political and forensic speeches.

The association of the Ambrosian Quintilian with Pavia is particularly intriguing: the manuscript (or its apograph) was used in the tenth century to correct a mutilated copy of the *Institutio Oratoria*, which had been produced in northern Francia (now Bamberg, Staatsbibliothek, Msc.

---

[86] For a detailed analysis of the manuscript, see Holtz, 'Le Parisinus Latinus 7530'.

[87] Clodianus' *De statibus* is copied on ff. 165v–166v. On the Bern miscellany see now Vocino, 'A *peregrinus*'s vademecum'.

[88] On the palimpsest manuscript: Stramaglia, 'Le *Declamationes maiores* pseudo-quintilianee', esp. pp. 568–73 and 585–88.

[89] For a description and discussion of the possible origin of the Milanese manuscript, see Ferrari, 'Fra i "latini scriptores"', esp. pp. 267–72. On the fragment from Cremona, see Malcovati, 'La tradizione del *Brutus*'.

Class. 45) and later ended up in the library of the Ottonian king Henry II (d. 1024). In the fifteenth century the Milanese *codex* belonged to a monastery of Augustinian hermits, and since 1330 a community of this order had been living in the monastic compound adjacent to the basilica of S. Pietro in Ciel d'Oro at Pavia, where the body of St Augustine lay buried.[90] Founded by King Liutprand between 720 and 725, the monastery maintained close ties with the dynasty ruling over the Italian *regnum* across the eighth and the ninth centuries. While the existence of a local school and *scriptorium* is not documented at this early date, a library was certainly available on site. It would not therefore be too far-fetched to assume that books once belonging to the palace, or to an individual connected therewith, found their way, maybe through dona-tion, to the monastery.[91] The presence of short-hand annotations in the margins of the Ambrosian Quintilian also sits well with a centre where royal notaries and judges would have been trained; indeed, the use of this distinctive mode of writing has been observed in charters drafted and signed by personnel formed at Pavia.[92] The existence in the capital of a centre of learning that operated in close association with the palace is also confirmed by the well-known capitulary of Olona issued in 825. In this document, Lothar I entrusts the Irishman Dungal with the education of students coming from eleven cities in north-western Italy, thus clearly establishing Dungal's school as the most prominent one in the kingdom.[93]

That advanced studies in the arts of speech should be promoted at centres of education and learning that had direct links to the rulers and to the court is not particularly surprising, nor the relevance attached to rhetorical training for the future office-holders of the kingdom. The already-mentioned Bern miscellany compiled in the Milanese region offers some indirect evidence of the teaching and practical application of rhetoric. The manuscript is well known for its marginal annotations, in which the names of many contemporaneous individuals and eminent scholars are recorded – Sedulius Scottus and John Scottus Eriugena are, for example, mentioned more than a hundred times each. Among them also appears Hagano, bishop of Bergamo (837–867), whose name is added several times in relation to morphological, prosodic and syntac-tic explanations, but can also be found preceding a passage of Fortunatianus' *Ars Rhetorica*, where the late antique author is treating

---

[90] Ferrari, 'Fra i "latini scriptores"', pp. 277–8.
[91] Andenna, 'Un monastero nella vita di una città', esp. pp. 67–8.
[92] Petrucci and Romeo, 'Scrivere "in iudicio"'.
[93] Gavinelli, 'Dungal e l'organizzazione scolastica'. Stofferahn, '*Renovatio* abroad'.

the possible ambiguities of the law. Beside a fictional example is placed the annotation 'Agano intentio'.[94] *Intentio* in this context is a technical term belonging to judicial rhetoric and refers to an accusation made by the prosecutor which is rejected by the defence.[95] The didactic context of the Bern miscellany suggests that Hagano taught rhetoric and that the example given by Fortunatianus was used for the purposes of an exercise, maybe as the basis of a fictional *controversia*, for students practising their skills at debating.[96] Hagano's proximity to the Carolingian rulers (Lothar I and Louis II), his intellectual stature and his involvement in the heated debate about Lothar II's divorce certainly made him a teacher highly aware of the importance of judicial oratory, and Fortunatianus' *Ars rhetorica* focussed on that very genre. A further indication of the practical understanding and application of rhetoric is provided by an interpolation to the same treatise, which was probably copied into the Bern miscellany from its Italian antigraph. The issue at hand is the comparison of two conflicting laws and the choice of the one that ought to be approved, with the case provided by Fortunatianus being compared by an anonymous annotator to the existence of conflicting sentences in different canons.[97] The interpolation betrays the equivalence between the judicial setting described in the treatise – the Roman tribunal – and the activities taking place at a council. Rhetorical training could thus not only facilitate the task of addressing an ecclesiastical assembly (as Paulinus of Aquileia did in 796) but also be applied to the debates preceding the promulgation of the approved canons.

The availability in the cities of the *regnum Italiae* of books and texts dedicated to the teaching of the three genres of rhetoric confirms that those ancient and late antique traditions continued to be kept alive in Italian classrooms across the early Middle Ages. The distinctive Italian interest in didactic texts aiming at the formation of eloquent orators allowed the preservation of pedagogic material that would have otherwise been lost. The transmission of the treatises *De rhetorica* and *De dialectica* written by St Augustine during his stay in Milan in the late fourth

---

[94] Bern, Burgerbibliothek 363, f. 147r: *Ut "meretrices si ancillas habuerint, publicae sint": meritrices habent ancillas. Quaestio est qui debeant publicari id est decipi, utrum meritrices an ancillae earum an utraeque.*

[95] Quintilian, *Institutio Oratoria*, ed. Winterbottom, III, 6, 17: *sit enim accusatoris intentio: 'hominem occidisti'. Si negat reus, faciet statum qui negat.*

[96] On Hagano of Bergamo, see De Angelis, 'Aganone vescovo'; Lo Monaco, 'Aganone di Bergamo'.

[97] Bern, Burgerbibliothek 363, f. 146v: *Cum ita leges feruntur ut per comparationem quaerendum sit quae potius probanda sive sententia sive canon ut in canonibus diversis diversas sententias approbamus.*

century, for instance, originates in early medieval Italy.[98] From there
these didactic texts were distributed to other regions of the Latin west
and surviving manuscripts were produced in Carolingian times at centres
of learning such as Lorsch, Corbie and Fleury.[99] Both works also continued to be copied in the *regnum* during the ninth and tenth centuries,
which testifies to the sustained interest in teaching the three genres of
Ciceronian rhetoric there.[100]

Conclusions

The exploration of the rhetorical education of the Lombard scholars
attending Charlemagne's court combined with the study of the teaching
programmes and practices reflected by manuscript evidence highlights the
existence of a distinctive Italian tradition predating the Carolingian period.
An education preparing the intellectual elites for their political engagement
was already being promoted in the late Lombard period, at least in the
most important schools of the kingdom, such as Pavia, Verona, Milan and,
possibly, Cividale. For the first half century after Charlemagne's takeover
in 774, Italy contributed to the Carolingian 'revival of learning' more than
it was influenced by it. Very little is known about court life in Lombard
times, and yet it is possible that the palatine culture of Pavia did indeed
represent a model for Charlemagne's own court and may even have influenced his recruitment of Italian scholars in the 770s and 780s. The reversal
in trend, which saw the influence of Frankish culture and learning becom-
ing stronger in the Italian kingdom, seems to have been a relatively late
process, possibly starting only with Lothar I's residence in the kingdom in
the 820s. From this moment onwards, foreign masters were given the task
to 'reform' key centres of learning in the *regnum*. Dungal at Pavia and

---

[98] Augustine, *Retractationes*, ed. Knöll, I, 5, p. 27: *Per idem tempus, quo Mediolani fui
baptismum percepturus, etiam disciplinarum libros conatus sum scribere [...] sed earum
solum de grammatica librum absolvere potui, quam postea de armario nostro perdidi, et de
musica sex volumina [...] de aliis vero quinque disciplinis illic similiter incoatis, de dialectica,
de rhetorica, de geometrica, de arithmetica, de philosophia, sola principia remanserunt, quae
tamen etiam ipsa perdidimus, sed haberi ab aliquibus existimo.*

[99] Augustine's *De dialectica* enjoyed a more extensive manuscript transmission, whereas
his *De rhetorica* is only extant in three Carolingian *codices* (the already mentioned Bern,
Burgerbibliothek 363; Vatican City, BAV Pal. lat. 1588 from Lorsch; Paris, BnF
lat. 7730 from Fleury).

[100] The texts were copied into Bern, Burgerbibliothek 363, ff. 153v–165v from an Italian
exemplar that contained a coherent group of rhetorical texts (Fortunatianus' *Ars
Rhetorica*, Augustine's *De dialectica* and *De rhetorica*). The combination of
Fortunatianus with Augustine's *De rhetorica* can also be found in Cod. Bodmer 146, a
tenth-century *codex* produced in northern Italy, now at Cologny, Fondation Martin
Bodmer. On the transmission of the so-called *rhetores minores* in medieval Italy, see
Billanovich, 'Il Petrarca'.

Hildemar of Corbie at Milan, Brescia and Civate are well-known examples, but the appointment of learned bishops such as Joseph of Ivrea and Angilbert of Milan also had an impact on local didactic programmes, as can be appreciated from the surviving manuscripts connected to their episcopates.[101] It is in the central decades of the ninth century that the Carolingian classics – such as the *Liber Glossarum*, Martianus Capella and the commentaries on Terence – made their appearance in Italian libraries. The philological and exegetical approach that distinguished much of Carolingian didactic production thus met the poetic, rhetorical and legal traditions that constituted an important part of the culture and learning promoted at the Italian *sedes regiae*. Of course, one culture did not replace the other: they were not mutually exclusive, and could, on the contrary, merge nicely.[102] And yet, some of the peculiarities of the literary production of Carolingian Italy seem to be the result of divergent interests and traditions that were perpetuated across the early Middle Ages. Exegesis, for instance, which was such an essential part of Frankish court-related literature, was not a field in which Italian scholars excelled or even engaged.[103] On the other hand, rhetorically elaborated and politically engaged literature continued to be produced in the form of celebratory poetry – which was, after all, a means of writing history according to the ancient tradition. The rhythmic poems celebrating the victory of Pippin over the Avars, the captivity of Louis II at Benevento[104] and the coronation of Berengar I in 915 along with other panegyrical compositions stress the continuity in the Italian kingdom of the same court literary vein across the eighth to the tenth centuries.[105] Furthermore, these texts

---

[101] See Ferrari, '"In Papia conveniant ad Dungalum"'; Villa, '"Denique Terenti dultia legimus acta..."'; Ferrari, 'Manoscritti e cultura', esp. pp. 247–56; Gavinelli, 'Il vescovo Giuseppe di Ivrea'.

[102] The *Gesta Berengarii*, transmitted in a sole tenth-century manuscript together with the author's glosses (Venice, Biblioteca Marciana, lat. XII 45), are an excellent example of the happy marriage between Carolingian and Italian literary traditions; see Duplessis, 'Les sources des gloses'.

[103] See Chapter 5 in this volume.

[104] The abecedarian *Rhythmus de captivitate Lhuduici imperatoris* is a distinctively ironic poem, in which an imprisoned Emperor Louis II faces the accusations of a group of Beneventan conspirators in front of a public assembly. The judicial flavour of the *Rhythmus* comes repeatedly to the fore, not least through some telling word choices, such as the lemma *iudicare iudicium* that refers to Christ acting as the judge. For the edition of the text, see *MGH Poetae Latini Aevi Carolini III*, pp. 404–5.

[105] A fragment of a previously unknown panegyric for Louis II has been found in a twelfth-century manuscript from Thorney Abbey. The anonymous Italian author of the poem emulated the panegyric written by the grammarian Priscian for Emperor Anastasius I (d. 518), the transmission of which was limited to early medieval Italy; see Orth, 'Fragment einer historischen Dichtung'. Two poems celebrating Lothar I that were circulating in Milan were copied into Bern, Burgerbibliothek 363, f. 196v; see Staubach, 'Sedulius Scottus', esp. 572–5.

confirm the persistence of school traditions rooted in the study of epideictic oratory, the origins of which can be traced back to late antiquity.

The rhetorical qualities of the Italian intellectuals at the vanguard of the 'Carolingian Renaissance' and the analysis of manuscripts reflecting teaching programmes confirm such preferences and highlight the survival of an advanced education in the *ars bene dicendi* that also covered the most distinctive and technical Roman genre of judicial oratory. Ciceronian rhetoric was inherently a politically oriented discipline, and one in which orality played a crucial role. As trained poets, legal experts and disputers, the most learned members of the Italian elites often had occasion to put their rhetorical skills into practice. Their performances did not necessarily need to be written down or to be recorded in bulky manuscripts, however: a panegyric or poem declaimed on a special occasion or a speech or debate taking place in a public forum fulfilled their political function in the very moment communication took place. Only when such performances became models and were considered excellent and authoritative examples were they deemed worthy of being transcribed into the schoolbooks that ensured their survival. The scholars living in Carolingian Italy appear to have written less than their transalpine colleagues,[106] but this does not necessarily mean that they produced less in their day.[107] Their excellent education could find other ways to express itself, ways that need not be reflected in book or documentary evidence; at least a part of the literary output of the Italian intellectuals was not made, or considered worthy, to be preserved in the long term. There lies perhaps the undetectable cultural 'exceptionalism' of early medieval Italy: it was a country in which only a small fraction of the most learned literary production was entrusted to books.

---

[106] See again the overview provided by Bougard in Chapter 5 in this volume.

[107] Italian bishops and intellectuals do not seem to have been interested in collecting their letters in the same way as their colleagues north of the Alps (e.g. Alcuin, Einhard, Lupus of Ferrières, Frotharius of Toul, Hincmar of Rheims). It is, for instance, worth remembering that whereas Alcuin's letters to Paulinus of Aquileia survive, the replies of the Italian bishop have not been preserved.

Bibliography

Manuscripts (Vocino, Veronese)

Bamberg, Staatsbibliothek, Msc. Class. 43
Berlin, Staatsbibliothek, Diez. B. Sant. 66
Bern, Burgerbibliothek 363
Cologny, Cod. Bodmer 146
Karlsruhe, Badische Landesbibliothek, Aug. perg. XXXII
Munich, Bayerische Staatsbibliothek Clm 29216/7
Paris, BnF lat. 7530, ff. 259v–265r
Paris, BnF lat. 528
Paris, BnF lat. 7900A
Paris, BnF lat. 7730
Sankt Gallen, Stiftsbibliothek, 566
Vatican City, BAV Vat. lat. 3827
Vatican City, BAV Pal. lat. 1746
Vatican City, BAV, Pal. lat. 833
Vatican City, BAV Pal. lat. 1588
Venice, Biblioteca Marciana, lat. XII 45

Abbreviations

AB = Annales Bertiniani, ed. F. Grat, J. Vielliard and S. Clémencet (Paris, 1964)
AF = Annales Fuldenses. ed. F. Kurze, *MGH SRG* 7 (Hanover, 1891)
ARF = Annales Regni Francorum, ed. F. Kurze, *MGH SRG* 6 (Hanover, 1895)
BHL = Bibliotheca Hagiographica Latina
CCCM = Corpus christianorum continuatio medievalis (Turnhout, 1966)
CDA = Codice Diplomatico Aretino. Le carte della Canonica di Arezzo (649–998), ed. M. Calleri and F. Mambrini (Spoleto, 2014)
CDL = Codice Diplomatico Longobardo, ed. L. Schiaparelli, 2 vols., Fonti per la storia d'Italia dell'Istituto Storico Italiano (Rome, 1929–1933)
ChLA = Chartae Latinae Antiquiores. Facsimile-Edition of the Latin Charters prior to the Ninth Century, ed. A. Bruckner and R. Marichal (Dietikon-Zurich, 1954–1998), vols. 1–49

275

*ChLA*² = *Chartae Latinae Antiquiores. Facsimile-Edition of the Latin Charters. 2nd Series, Ninth Century*, ed. G. Cavallo and G. Nicolaj (Dietikon-Zurich, 1997 ff.), vols. 50 ff.

D = charter, diploma

DD = charters, diplomata

  B = Berengar

  K = Charles I–III

  L = Louis I–III

  Lo = Lothar I–II

LP = *Liber Pontificalis*, ed. L. Duchesne, *Le 'Liber Pontificalis': texte, introduction et commentaire*, 2 vols. (Paris, 1886–92; 2nd ed. With vol. III ed. C. Vogel, Paris 1955–7); trans. R. Davis, *Liber Pontificalis*, vol. 1: *The Book of Pontiffs: The Ancient Biographies of the First Ninety Roman Bishops to AD 715* (Liverpool, 1989), vol. 2: *The Lives of the Eighth-Century Popes. The Ancient Biographies of Nine Popes from AD 715 to AD 817* (Liverpool, 1992), vol. 3: *The Lives of the Ninth-Century Popes. The Ancient Biographies of Ten Popes from A.D. 817–891* (Liverpool, 1995).

MGH = *Monumenta Germania Historica*

  AA = *Auctores antiquissimi*

  Capit. = *Capitularia regum Francorum*, ed. A. Boretius and V. Krause, 2 vols. (Hanover, 1883–1890)

  Conc. = *Concilia. Legum Sectio* III

  DD = *Diplomata*

  Fontes iuris = *Fontes iuris Germanici Antiqui in usum scholarum separatism editi*

  Poet. = *Poetae latini aevi carolini*

  Epp. = *Epistulae* III±VIII (= *Epistolae Merovingici et Karolini aevi*, Hanover, 1892–1939)

  SRG = *Scriptores rerum Germanicarum in usum scholarum separatism editi*

  SRM = *Scriptores rerum Merovingicarum*

  SRL = *Scriptores rerum Langobardicarum et Italicarum, saec.* VI±IX, ed. G. Waitz (Hanover, 1885–1920)

  SS = *Scriptores* in Folio

PL = J.-P. Migne (ed.), *Patrologiae Cursus Completus, Series Latina*, 221 vols. (Paris 1841–64)

RI = *Regesta imperii* I: *Die Regesten des Kaiserreichs unter den Karolingern 751–918 (926)*, III: *Die Regesten des Regnum Italiae und der Burgundischen Regna*, I: *Die Karolinger im Regnum Italiae 840–887 (888)*, ed. H Zielinski (Cologne, Vienna, 1991)

Primary Sources

Acta martyrii, in *Acta Sanctorum Octobris*, vol. VI (Tongerloo, 1794), pp. 439–41

Admonitio ad omnes regni ordines (823–825), ed. A. Boretius, *MGH Capit. 1* (Hanover, 1883), n. 150, pp. 303–7

Agnellus, *Liber Pontificalis ecclesiae Ravennatis*, ed. D. M. Deliyannis, *Agnelli Ravennatis Liber Pontificalis ecclesiae Ravennatis* (Turnhout, 2006); trans. D. Deliyannis, *The Book of Pontiffs of the Church of Ravenna* (Washington, DC, 2004)

Agobard, *Epistolae*, ed. E. Dümmler, *MGH Epp.* v (Berlin, 1889), pp. 150–239

Alcuin, *Epistolae*, ed. E. Dümmler, *MGH Epp.* iv, (Berlin, 1895), pp. 1–493

Aldhelm, *De metris*, ed. E. Ehwald, *MGH AA* 15 (Berlin, 1919)

Ambrose of Milan, *Epistulae*, ed. G. Banterle, *Sancti Ambrosii Episcopi Mediolanensis Opera* 20 (Milan and Rome, 1988)

Anastasius Bibliothecarius, *Sermo Theodori Studitae de sancto Bartholomeo apostolo*, ed. U. Westerbergh, *Anastasius bibliothecarius: sermo Theodori Studitae de sancto Bartholomeo apostolo* (Stockholm, 1963)

Andreas of Bergamo, *Historia*, ed. G. Waitz, *MGH SRL* (Hanover, 1878), pp. 220–230

Annales Alamannici, ed. G.H. Pertz, *MGH SS* 1 (Hanover, 1826), pp. 19–60

Annales Bertiniani, ed. G. Waitz, *MGH SRG* 5 (Hannover 1883); ed. F. Grat, J. Vielliard and S. Clémencet, *Annales de Saint-Bertin* (Paris, 1964); trans. J. L. Nelson, *The Annals of St Bertin* (Ninth-Century Histories 1, Manchester 1991).

Annales qui dicuntur Einhardi, ed. G. H. Pertz, *MGH SS* 1 (Hanover, 1826), pp. 124–218

Annales Fuldenses, ed. F. Kurse, *MGH SRG* 7 (Hannover, 1891)

Annales Laureshamenses, Alamannici, Guelferbytani et Nazariani, ed. G. H. Pertz, *MGH SS* 1 (Hanover, 1826), pp. 19–60

Annales Laurissenses minores, ed. G. H. Pertz, *MGH SS* 1 (Hanover, 1826), pp. 112–123

Annales Mettenses priores, ed. B. von Simson, *MGH SRG* 10 (Hanover and Leipzig, 1905)

Annales Petaviani, ed. G. H. Pertz, *MGH SS* 1 (Hanover, 1826), pp. 7–18

Annales regni Francorum, ed. F. Kurze, *MGH SRG* 6 (Hanover, 1895)

Annales sancti Amandi, ed. G. H. Pertz, *MGH SS* 1 (Hanover, 1826), pp. 6–14

Astronomer, *Vita Hludowici imperatoris*, ed. E. Tremp, *Thegan. Die Taten Kaiser Ludwigs. Astronomus, Das Leben Kaiser Ludwigs*, *MGH SRG* 64 (Hanover, 1995)

Augustine, *Retractationes*, ed. P. Knöll, CSEL 36 (Vienna, 1902)

Benedetto di Sant'Andrea = *Il Chronicon di Benedetto e il Libellus de imperatoria potestate in Urbe Roma*, ed. G. Zucchetti, Fonti per la storia d'Italia dell'Istituto Storico Italiano (Rome, 1920)

I capitolari italici. Storia e diritto della dominazione carolingia in Italia, ed. C. Azzara and P. Moro (Rome, 1998)

Capitula Episcoporum III, ed. R. Pokorny, *MGH Capitula Episcoporum* iii (Hanover, 1995)

Capitula Episcoporum IV, ed. R. Pokorny, *MGH Capitula Episcoporum* iv (Hanover, 2005)

Capitula Legibus Addenda (818–819), ed. A. Boretius, *MGH Capit. 1* (Hanover, 1883), n. 139, pp. 280–5

Capitulare Francofurtense, ed. A. Werminghoff, *MGH, Conc.* ii/1 (Hanover and Leipzig, 1906), pp. 165–71

Carmina varia, ed. E. Dümmler, *MGH Poet.* 2, (Berlin, 1884)

Carte cremonesi, ed. E. Falconi, *Le Carte Cremonesi dei secoli VIII–XII* I (Cremona, 1979)

Le carte antiche di San Pietro in Castello di Verona (809/10–1196), ed. A. Ciaralli, Regesta Chartarum 55 (Roma, 2007)

Le carte degli archivi parmensi dei secoli X–XI, ed. G. Drei, vol. ⁱ (Parma, 1924)

Il chartarium Dertonense ed altri documenti del Comune di Tortona: 934–1346 (Pinerolo 1909)

Catalogus regum Langobardorum et Italicorum Brixiensis et Nonantulanus, ed. G. Waitz, *MGH SRL* (Hanover, 1878), pp. 501–4

CDA = *Codice Diplomatico Aretino. Le carte della Canonica di Arezzo (649–998)*, ed. M. Calleri and F. Mambrini (Spoleto, 2014)

Chronica sancti Benedicti Casinensis, ed. G. Waitz, *MGH SRL* (Hanover, 1878), pp. 467–89; ed. and trans. L. Berto, Edizione nazionale dei testi mediolatini 15 (Florence, 2006)

Chronicon Moissiacense, ed. G. H. Pertz, *MGH SS* 1 (Hanover, 1826), pp. 280–313

Chronicon Salernitanum, ed. U. Westerbergh, *Chronicon Salernitanum: A Critical Edition with Studies on Literary and Historical Sources and on Language*, Studia Latina Stockholmiensia 3 (Stockholm, 1956); trans. R. Matarazzo (Naples 2002)

Codex Bavarus: Breviarium ecclesiae Ravennatis (Codice Bavaro), ed. G. Rabotti (Rome, 1985).

Codex Carolinus, ed. W. Gundlach, *MGH Epp.* III (Berlin, 1891), pp. 469–657

Codex diplomaticus Langobardiae, ed. G. Porro-Lambertenghi, Monumenta Historiae Patriae 13 (Turin, 1873)

Codice diplomatico parmense, ed. U. Bernassi, vol I, (Parma, 1910)

Codice diplomatico Veronese. Dalla caduta dell'impero romano alla fine del periodo carolingio, ed. V. Fainelli Venezia, R. Deputazione di Storia Patria per le Venezie, N.S., 1 (Venice, 1940)

Concilia aevi Karolini 843–859/Die Konzilien der karolingischen Teilreiche 843–859, ed. W. Hartmann, *MGH Conc. III* (Hanover, 1984)

Concilium Foroiuliense, ed. A. Werminghoff, *MGH Conc.* II, 1, *Concilia aevi Karolini* (Hanover and Leipzig, 1906), pp. 177–95

Concilium Mantuanum, ed. A. Werminghoff, *MGH Conc.* II/2 (Hanover and Leipzig, 1908), pp. 583–9

Concilium Moguntinense, ed. A. Werminghoff, *MGH, Conc.* II/1 (Hanover and Leipzig, 1906), pp. 259–73

Constructio monasterii Farfensis, ristampa anastatica with foreword by U. Longo, Fonti e studi farfensi 1 (Rome, 2017)

Cronaca di Novalesa, ed. and trans. G. C. Alessio (Turin, 1982)

DD Arn = *Diplomata Arnolfi*, ed. P.F. Kehr, *MGH DD Arn* (Berlin, 1940)

DD B I = *I diplomi di Berengario I*, ed. L. Schiaparelli, (Rome, 1903).

DD G – L = *I diplomi di Guido e Lamberto*, ed. L. Schiaparelli, (Rome, 1906).

DD L III – DD R II = *I diplomi italiani di Ludovico III e di Rodolfo II*, ed. L. Schiaparelli (Rome, 1910).

DD K III = *Diplomata Karoli III*, ed. P. Kehr, *MGH DD Karl* (Berlin, 1937)

Diplomata Lotharii I et Lotharii II, ed. Th. Schieffer, *MGH DD Lo I / DD Lo II* (Berlin, Zurich, 1966)

Diplomata Ludovici Germanici, Karlomanni, Ludovici Iunioris, ed. P. Kehr, *MGH DD LD / DD Kn / DD Lj* (Berlin, 1934)

Diplomata Ludovici Pii, ed. T. Kölzer, *MGH DD Kar. II/1* (Wiesbaden, 2016)

Diplomata Ludovici II, ed. K. Wanner, *MGH DD L II* (Munich, 1994)

Diplomata Ottonis I, ed. T. Sickel, *MGH DD K I / DD H I / DD O I*, (Hanover, 1879–1884)

Diplomata Pippini, Carlomanni, Caroli Magni, ed. E. Mühlbacher, *MGH DD Kar. 1* (Hanover, 1906)

Diplomi inediti attinenti al Patriarcato di Aquileia dal 799 al 1082, ed. V. Joppi and E. Mühlbacher, Miscellanea della Regia Deputazione Veneta di Storia Patria, 3 (1885)

De Liutprando rege, ed. G. Waitz, *MGH SRL* (Hanover, 1878), p. 11

De Pippini regis victoria avarica, ed. E. Dümmler, *MGH Poet.* 1 (Berlin, 1881), 116–17; ed. L. A. Berto, *Testi Storici e Poetici dell'Italia Carolingia*, Medioevo Europeo 4 (Padova, 2002), pp. 67–71

Dhuoda, *Handbook for Her Warrior Son: Liber Manualis*, ed. M. Thiébaux, Cambridge Medieval Classics 8 (Cambridge, 1998)

Divisio principatus Beneventani, ed. J.-M. Martin, *Guerre, accords et frontières en Italie méridionale pendant le haut Moyen Âge: Pacta de Liburia, Divisio principatus Beneventani et autres actes* (Rome, 2005)

Donatus, *Ars Maior*, trans. R. Copeland and I. Sluiter, *Medieval Grammar and Rhetoric. Language Arts and Literary Theory, AD 300–1475* (Oxford, 2009)

Duplex Legationis Edictum (789), ed. A. Boretius, *MGH Capit. 1* (Hanover, 1883), n. 23, pp. 62–4

Einhard, *Epistolae*, ed. K. Hampe, *MGH Epp.* v (Berlin, 1899), pp. 105–45

Einhard, *Vita Karoli*, ed. O. Holder-Egger, *MGH SRG* 25 (Hanover, 1911)

Ennodius, *Paraenesis didascalica (Ennodius Ambrosio et Beato)*, ed. F. Vogel, *MGH AA 7* (Berlin, 1885), 310–5

Epistolae Langobardicae Collectae, ed. W. Gundlach, *MGH Epp.* iii (Berlin, 1892), pp. 691–715

Epistolae Variorum inde a Morte Caroli Magni usque ad Divisionem Imperii Collectae, ed. E. Dümmler, *MGH Epp.* v (Berlin, 1889), pp. 299–360

Epitaphium Pauli Diaconi, ed. E. Dümmler, *MGH Poet.* 1 (Berlin, 1881), pp. 85–6

Erchempert, *Historia Langobardorum Beneventanorum*, ed. G. H. Pertz and G. Waitz, *MGH SRL* (Hanover, 1878), pp. 231–64; ed. L. A. Berto, *Ystoriola Longobardorum Beneventum degentium* = *Piccola Storia dei Longobardi di Benevento* (Naples 2013)

Fardulfi abbatis carmina, ed. E. Dümmler, *MGH Poet.* 1 (Berlin, 1881), pp. 353–4

Flodoardi Annales, ed. Philippe Lauer, *Les Annales de Flodoard* (Paris, 1905)

Florus, *[Querela de divisione imperii]*, ed. E. Dümmler, *MGH Poet.* II (Berlin, 1884), pp. 559–64

Gesta Berengarii Imperatoris. Scontro per il regno nell'Italia del X secolo, ed. F. Stella (ed.), with an introduction by G. Albertoni (Pisa, 2009)

Gregorio di Catino, *Il Regesto di Farfa*, ed. I. Giorgi and U. Balzani, Biblioteca della Società Romana di Storia Patria 2, vol. III (Roma, 1883)

Gregory the Great, *Regula pastoralis*, ed. B. Judic, F. Rommel and C. Morels (Paris, 1992)

Gregory of Tours, *Decem libri historiarum*, ed. B. Krusch and W. Levison, *MGH SRM* I, 1 (Hanover, 1951)

Hadrian II, *Epistolae*, ed. E. Perels, *MGH Epp.* VI, *Karolini Aevi* IV (Berlin, 1925), pp. 691–765

Hincmar of Reims, *De ordine palatii*, ed. T. Gross and R. Schieffer, *MGH Fontes iuris* 3 (Hanover, 1980)

Historia Langobardorum codicis Gothani, ed. G. Waitz, *MGH SRL* (Hanover, 1878), pp. 7–11; ed. C. Azzari and S. Gasparri, *Le leggi dei Longobardi* (Milan, 1992), pp. 281–91; ed. and trans. L. A. Berto, *Testi storici e poetici dell'Italia carolingia* (Padova, 2002), pp. 1–19

Hrabanus Maurus, *Carmina*, ed. E. Dümmler, *MGH Poet.* II (Berlin, 1884), pp. 154–258

Hrabanus Maurus, *Epistolae*, ed. E. Dümmler, *MGH Epp.* V, Epistolae *Karolini Aevi* III, pp. 379–533

Hrabanus Maurus, *Martyrologium*, ed. J. McCulloh, *CCCM* 44 (Turnhout, 1979), pp. 1–161

Iuliani epitome novellarum Iustiniani, ed. G. Hänel (Leipzig, 1873)

John VIII, *Registrum*, ed. E. Caspar, *MGH Epp.* VIII, *Karolini Aevi* V (Berlin, 1928), pp. 1–272

John VIII, *Fragmenta Registri*, ed. E. Caspar, *MGH Epp.* VIII, *Karolini Aevi* V (Berlin, 1928), pp. 273–312

John X, *Epistolae*, ed. S. Löwenfeld, 'Acht Briefe aus der Zeit König Berengars', *Neues Archiv der Gesellschaft für ältere deutsche Geschichtskunde*, IX (1884), pp. 513–39.

John the Deacon (of Venice), *Istoria Veneticorum*, ed. A. Berto, *Fonti per la storia dell'Italia Medievale*, 2 (Rome, 1999)

John the Deacon (of Naples), *Gesta Episcoporum Neapolitanorum*, pars I, ed. G. Waitz, *MGH SRL* (Hanover, 1878), pp. 402–24

John the Deacon (of Naples), *Gesta Episcoporum Neapolitanorum*, pars II, ed. G. Waitz, *MGH SRL* (Hanover, 1878), pp. 424–35

John Eriugena, *Joanni theologo apostolo et evangelistae determinate in Pathmos insulam*, *PL* 122, cols. 1193–4

Konzilien der karolingischen Teilreiche 875–911, ed. W. Hartmann and I. Schroeder, *MGH Conc.* V (Hanover, 2012)

La cronaca della dinastia capuana, ed. N. Cilento, *Italia meridionale longobarda*, 2nd ed. (Naples, 1971), pp. 279–346

Laudes Veronensis civitatis, ed. E. Dümmler, *MGH Poet.* 1 (Berlin, 1881), pp. 118–22

Leo III, *Ep. 1, to Charlemagne*, ed. Karl Hampe, *MGH EE* 5 (Berlin, 1899), pp. 87f.

Leges Langobardorum, ed. Franz Beyerle, *Die Gesetze der Langobarden*, Germanenrechte Neue Folge 9 (Witzenhausen, 1962)

Libellus de imperatoria potestate in Urbe Roma, ed. G. Zucchetti, *Il Chronicon di Benedetto e il Libellus de imperatoria potestate in Urbe Roma*, Fonti per la storia d'Italia dell'Istituto Storico Italiano (Rome, 1920)

Liber historiae Francorum, ed. B. Krusch, *MGH SRM* 2 (Hanover, 1888)

Liutprand of Cremona, *Antapodosis*, ed. P. Chiesa, *Liutprandi Cremonensis Opera Omnia*, *CCCM* 156 (Turnhout, 1998)

Liutprand of Cremona, *Relatio de legatione Constantinopolitana*, ed. Joseph Becker, *MGH SRG* 41 (Hanover and Leipzig, 1915), pp. 175–212

Louis II, *Letter to Emperor Basil I*, ed. Walter Henze, *MGH EE* 7 (Berlin, 1928), pp. 385–394.

Marius of Avenches, *Chronica*, ed. Th. Mommsen, *MGH AA* 11, *Chronica minora* II (Berlin, 1894), pp. 225–39

Der Memorial- und Liturgiecodex von San Salvatore / Santa Giulia in Brescia, ed. D. Geuenich and U. Ludwig, *MGH Libri memoriales*, n.s., 4 (Hanover, 2000)

Memorie e documenti per servire alla storia del ducato di Lucca, V/2 (Lucca, 1837)

Monumenta Novaliciensia vetustioria, ed. C. Cipolla, Fonti per la storia d'Italia 31–2, 2 vols. (Roma, 1898–1901)

Nithard, *Historiae*, ed. P. Lauer, *Nithard. Histoire des fils de Louis le Pieux* (Paris, 1926)

Notitia Italica, ed. A. Boretius, *MGH Capitularia regum Francorum* I (Hanover, 1883)

Pactum Lotharii, ed. A. Boretius and V. Krause, *MGH, Capitularia regum Francorum* II, ed. A. Boretius and V. Krause, II (Hanover, 1897), 233, pp. 130–5

Paschasius Radbertus, *Epitaphium Arsenii*, ed. E. Dümmler, Abhandlungen der kaiserlichen Akademie der Wissenschaften zu Berlin, phil.-hist. Klasse (Berlin, 1900)

Passio Hermachorae et Fortunati, ed. P. Chiesa, in Colombi (ed.), *Le Passioni*, pp. 171–88

Paul the Deacon, *Historia Langobardorum*, ed. L. Bethmann and G. Waitz, *MGH SRL* (Hanover, 1878), pp. 12–187; ed. L. Capo (Milan, 1995)

Paul the Deacon, *Liber de episcopis Mettensibus*, ed. C. Santarossa, Edizione nazionale dei testi mediolatini d'Italia 38 (Florence, 2015); ed. D. Kempf, Dallas Medieval Texts and Translations 19 (Leuven, 2013)

Paulinus of Aquileia, *Epistolae*, ed. E. Dümmler, *MGH Epp.* II, *Epistolae variorum Carolo Magno regnante scriptae* (Berlin, 1895), pp. 516–27

Paulinus of Aquileia, *Regula fidei metrico promulgata stili mucrone*, ed. D. Norberg, *L'oeuvre poétique de Paulin d'Aquilée* (Stockholm, 1979)

Placiti = Placiti del Regnum Italiae I, ed. C. Manaresi, *I Placiti del 'Regnum Italiae'*, Fonti per la storia d'Italia, 92, 3 vols. (Rome, 1955–60)

Quellen zur karolingischen Reichsgeschichte, ed. R. Rau, Ausgewählte Quellen zur deutschen Geschichte des Mittelalters, 3 vols. (Berlin, 1955–60)

Principum Beneventi leges et pacta, ed. G. H. Pertz, *MGH Leges* IV (Hanover, 1868)

Pseudo-Liutprand, *Sergius II*, *PL*, vol. 129

Quintilian, *Institutio Oratoria*, ed. M. Winterbottom (Oxford, 1970)

RI: Regesta Imperii I: Die Regesten des Kaiserreichs unter den Karolingern 751–918 (926), III: Die Regesten des Regnum Italiae und der Burgundischen Regna, I: Die Karolinger im Regnum Italiae 840–887 (888), ed. H Zielinski (Cologne, Vienna, 1991)

Rhythmus de captivitate Lhuduici imperatoris, ed. L. Traube, *MGH Poet.* 3 (Berlin, 1896), pp. 404–5

Rossi, G., *Historiarum Ravennatum Libri Decem* (Venice, 1572)

Ss. Ilario e Benedetto e S. Gregorio, ed. L. Lanfranchi and B. Strina, *Fonti per la storia di Venezia*, II (Venice, 1965)

Sallust, *Bellum Catilinae*, ed. J. T. Ramsey, 2nd ed. (Oxford, 2007)

Sedulius Scottus, *Carmina*, ed. I. Meyers, *CCCM* 107 (Turnhout, 1991)

Sedulius Scottus, *De rectoribus christianis (On Christian Rulers)*, ed. and trans. R. W. Dyson (Woodbridge, 2010)

Sermo Petronii Episcopi Veronensis in Natale Sancti Zenonis, ed. A. Hamman, *PL Supplementum*, 3/1 (Paris, 1963), col. 141–142

Stansbury, M. and D. Kelly (eds.), *Earlier Latin Manuscripts*, https://elmss.nuilgalway.ie.

Thegan, *Gesta Hludowici imperatoris*, ed. E. Tremp, *Thegan. Die Taten Kaiser Ludwigs. Astronomus, Das Leben Kaiser Ludwigs, MGH SRG, 64* (Hanover, 1995)

Translatio et Miracula Sanctorum Marcellini et Petri, ed. G. Waitz, *MGH SS*, 15/1 (Leipzig, 1925), pp. 239–264; trans. P. E. Dutton, *Charlemagne's Courtier. The Complete Einhard* (Toronto, 1998), pp. 69–91

Translatio Sancti Calixti Cisonium, ed. O. Holder-Egger, *MGH SS* 15/1 (Hanover, 1887), pp. 418–22

Versus de Verona, ed. G. B. Pighi, *Versus de Verona: versum de Mediolano civitate* (Bologna, 1960)

Versus Fiduciae ad Angelramnum Presulem, ed. E. Dümmler, *MGH Poet.* I (Berlin, 1881), pp. 76–7

Versus Pauli, ed. E. Dümmler, *MGH Poet.* I (Berlin, 1881), p. 49

Versus Petri grammatici, ed. E. Dümmler, *MGH Poet.* I (Berlin, 1881), p. 48

Vita Walfredi, ed. H. Mierau, in K. Schmid (ed.), *Vita Walfredi und Kloster Monteverdi Toskanisches Mönchtum Zwischen Langobardischer und Fränkischer. Festschrift Gerd Tellenbach* (Tübingen, 1998), pp. 38–63

Widukind of Corvey, *Deeds of the Saxons*, ed. P. Hirsch and H.-E. Lohmann, *MGH SRG* 60 (Hanover, 1935)

Secondary Sources

Adriatic Connections: The Adriatic as a Threshold to Byzantium, c.600–1453 (Cambridge, forthcoming).

Airlie, S., 'The palace complex', in A. Rodríguez López and J. Hudson (eds.), *Diverging Paths?: The Shapes of Power and Institutions in Medieval Christendom and Islam* (Turnhout, 2014), pp. 255–90

Airlie, S., W. Pohl and H. Reimitz (eds.), *Staat im frühen Mittelalter*, Forschungen zur Geschichte des Mittelalters 11 (Vienna, 2006)

Albertoni, G., *L'Italia carolingia* (Rome, 1997)

'Il potere del vescovo. Parma in età Ottoniana' in R. Greci (ed.), *Parma Medievale*, vol. III.1, *Poteri e Istituzioni* (Parma, 2010), pp. 69–113

Vassalli, feudi, feudalesimo (Rome, 2015)

Albertoni, G. and F. Borri (eds.), *Spes Italiae: il regno di Pipino, i Carolingi e l'Italia (781-810)* (in preparation, Turnhout, 2021).

Albiero, L., 'Secundum Romanam consuetudinem: la riforma liturgica in epoca carolingia', in Pagani and Santi (eds.), Il secolo di Carlo Magno, pp. 151–76

Althoff, G., Inszenierte Herrschaft. Geschichtsschreibung und politisches Handeln im Mittelalter (Darmstadt, 2003)

Spielregeln der Politik im Mittelalter. Kommunikation in Frieden und Fehde, 2nd ed. (Darmstadt, 2014)

Ančić, M., J. Shepard and T. Vedriš (eds.), Imperial Spheres and the Adriatic. Byzantium, the Carolingians and the Treaty of Aachen (812) (Abingdon, 2018)

Andenna, C., 'Un monastero nella vita di una città. San Pietro in Ciel d'Oro fra riforme istituzionali, difficili equilibri politici e uso della memoria', in M. T. Mazzilli Savini (ed.), San Pietro in Ciel d'Oro a Pavia. Mausoleo santuario di Agostino e Boezio (Pavia, 2013), pp. 66–87

Andenna, G., 'Notingo', in Dizionario Biografico degli Italiani 78 (Rome, 2013), pp. 778–81

Angelis, G. de, 'Aganone vescovo e la scrittura carolina a Bergamo alla metà del IX secolo: dinamiche ed eredità di un'innovazione culturale', Scrineum – Rivista 4 (2006–2007), 5–34

'Cittadini prima della cittadinanza. Alcune osservazioni sulle carte altomedievali di area lombarda', in La Rocca and Majocchi (eds.), Urban Identities in Northern Italy, pp. 169–89

Anti, E. Verona e il Culto di San Zeno tra IV e XII secolo (Verona, 2009)

Arnaldi, G., 'Berengario', in Dizionario biografico degli Italiani 9 (Rome, 1967), pp. 1–26.

'Bertilla' in Dizionario Biografico degli Italiani 9 (Rome, 1967), p. 529.

'La tradizione degli atti dell'assemblea pavese del febbraio 876', in B. Paradisi (ed.), La Critica del Testo. Atti del II Congresso Internazionale della Società Italiana di Storia del Diritto. Venezia 1967, I (Florence, 1971), pp. 51–68

Natale 875: politica, ecclesiologia, cultura del papato altomedievale (Rome, 1990)

'Anastasio Bibliotecario, antipapa', in M. Bray (ed.), Enciclopedia dei papi, 3 vols. (Rome, 2000)

Italy and Its Invaders (Cambridge, MA, 2009)

Arnold, D., Johannes VIII. Päpstliche Herrschaft in den karolingischen Teilreichen am Ende des 9. Jahrhunderts (Frankfurt, 2005)

Augenti, A., Le città italiane tra la tarda antichità e l'alto Medioevo : atti del Convegno (Ravenna, 26–28 febbraio 2004) (Florence, 2006)

Autenrieth, J., D. Geuenich and K. Schmid (eds.), Das Verbrüderungsbuch der Abtei Reichenau, MGH Libri memoriales, n.s., 1 (Hanover, 1979)

Avesani, R., 'Il Re Pipino, il Vescovo Annone e il Versus de Verona', in Brenzoni and Golinelli (eds.), I Santi Fermo e Rustico, pp. 57–65.

Azzara, C., 'I capitolari dei Carolingi', in C. Azzara and P. Moro (eds.), I capitolari italici, pp. 31–45

'Le vie di comunicazione delle Venezie fra Tardo Antico e Alto Medioevo', in D. Gallo and F. Rossetto (eds.), Per Terre e per Acque. Vie di Comunicazione nel Veneto dal Medioevo alla Prima Età Moderna. Atti del Convegno, Castello di Monselice, 16 dicembre 2001, Carrubio 2 (Padua, 2003), pp. 79–92

'Il Concilio di Mantova del 6 Giugno 827', in G. Andenna and G. P. Brogiolo (eds.), Le Origini della Diocesi di Mantova e le Sedi Episcopali dell'Italia

Settentrionale (IV–XI secolo). Atti del Convegno di Mantova, Seminario Vescovile, 16–18 Settembre 2004 (Trieste, 2006), pp. 61–72

Azzara, C. and P. Moro (eds.), *I capitolari italici. Storia e diritto della dominazione carolingia in Italia* (Rome, 1998)

Bachrach, B. S., *Early Carolingian Warfare* (Philadelphia, 2001)

Badini, A., 'La concezione della regalità in Liutprando e le iscrizioni della chiesa di S. Anastasio a Corteolona' in *Atti del VI Congresso internazionale di studi sull'Alto Medioevo. Milano, 21–25 ottobre 1978* (Spoleto, 1980), pp. 958, I 283–302

Balzaretti, R., 'Monasteries, towns and the countryside: reciprocal relationships in the Archdiocese of Milan, 614–814', in G. P. Brogiolo, N. Gauthier and N. Christie (eds.), *Towns and Their Territories between Late Antiquity and the Early Middle Ages* (Turnhout, 2000), pp. 235–57

'Narratives of success and narratives of failure: representations of the career of King Hugh of Italy (c. 885–948)', *Early Medieval Europe* 24.2 (2016), 185–208

Barbero, A., 'Liberti, raccomandati, vassalli. Le clientele nell'età di Carlo Magno', *Storica*, 14 (1999), 7–60

Barbero, G., '*Credo sit Papias integer*: la ricezione del *Liber glossarum* in Italia presso gli Umanisti', *Les dossiers d'Histoire Épistémologie Langage* 10 (2016), 321–56, https://hal.archives-ouvertes.fr/hal-01473157

Bassetti, M., A. Ciaralli, M. Montanari and G. M. Varanini (eds.), *Studi sul medioevo per Andrea Castagnetti* (Bologna, 2011)

Battistini, G., L. Bissi and L. Rocchi, *I campanili di Ravenna: storia e restauri* (Ravenna, 2008)

Bautier, R.-H., 'Le règne d'Eudes (888–898) à la lumière des diplômes expédiés par sa chancellerie', *Comptes rendus des séances de l'Académie des Inscriptions et Belles-Lettres* 105 (1961), 140–57

Beatrice, P. F., 'Agiografia e Politica. Considerazioni sulla Leggenda Marciana Aquileiese', in M. Simonetti and P. Siniscalco (eds.), *Studi sul Cristianesimo Antico e Moderno in Onore di Maria Grazia Mara* (Rome, 1995), pp. 763–78

'*Hermagorica Novitas*. La Testimonianza di Colombano sullo Scisma dei Tre Capitoli', in *Aquileia e il Suo Patriarcato. Atti del Convegno Internazionale di Studio (Udine 21–23 Ottobre 1999)* (Udine, 2000), pp. 75–93

Becker, G., *Catalogi bibliothecarum antiqui* (Bonn, 1885)

Belletzkie, R., 'Pope Nicholas I and John of Ravenna: the struggle for ecclesiastical rights in the ninth century', *Church History* 49 (1980), 262–72

Belli Barsali, I., 'La topografia di Lucca nei secoli VIII–XI', in *Lucca e la Tuscia nell'alto medioevo*, pp. 461–554

Belting, H., 'Studien zum Beneventanischen Hof im 8. Jahrhundert', *Dumbarton Oaks Papers*, 16 (1962), 141–93

Benericetti, R., *Le carte ravennati dei secoli ottavo e nono* (Bologna, 2006)

Bernabo Brea, L., *Le Isole Eolie dal tardo antico ai normani* (Ravenna, 1988)

Berndt, R., (ed.), *Das Frankfurter Konzil von 794. Kristallisationspunkt Karolischer Kultur* (Mainz, 1997), 2 vols.

Bertelli, C. and G. Brogiolo (eds.), *Il futuro dei Longobardi: L'Italia e la costruzione dell'Europa di Carlo Magno: Saggi* (Milan, 2000)

Berto, L. A., 'La "Venetia" tra Franchi e Bizantini. Considerazioni sulle Fonti', *Studi Veneziani* 38 (1999), 189–202

Testi storici e poetici dell'Italia carolingia, Medioevo europeo, 3 (Padua, 2002)

'Remembering old and new rulers: Lombards and Carolingians in Carolingian Italy memory', *The Medieval History Journal* 13.1 (2010), 23–53

Bertolini, O., *Roma di fronte a Bisanzio e ai Longobardi*, Storia di Roma 9 (Bologna, 1941)

'I vescovi del Regnum Langobardorum al tempo dei Carolingi', in *Vescovi e diocesi in Italia nel Medioevo: (sec. IX–XIII): atti del II Convegno di Storia della Chiesa in Italia: (Roma, 5–9 sett. 1961)* (Padua, 1964), pp. 1–26; in O. Bertolini, *Scritti scelti di storia medioevale*, I (Livorno, 1968), pp. 71–92

'Benedetto IV' in *Dizionario Biografico degli Italiani*, vol. VIII (1968), pp. 347–52

Bertolini, P., 'Arechis II', in *Dizionario biografico italiano* (Rome, 1962), pp. 71–8

Betti, M., 'Incestuous marriages in late Carolingian Ravenna: the *causa Deusdedit* (878–81)', *Early Medieval Europe* 23 (2015), 457–77

Beumann, H. and W. Schröder (eds.), *Die transalpinen Verbindungen der Bayern, Alemannen und Franken bis zum 10. Jahrhundert*, Nationes 6 (Sigmaringen, 1987)

Billanovich, G., 'Il Petrarca e i retori latini minori', *Italia medioevale e umanistica* 5 (1962), 103–64

Bischoff, B., 'Das Güterverzeichnis des Klosters SS. Faustino e Giovita in *Brescia* aus dem Jahre 964', *Italia medioevale e umanistica* 4 (1972), 53–61.

'Italienische Handschriften des neunten bis elften Jahrhunderts in frühmittelalterlichen Bibliotheken ausserhalb Italiens', in Questa and Raffaelli (eds.), *Il libro e il testo*, pp. 170–94

Katalog der festländischen Handschriften des neunten Jahrhunderts (mit Ausnahme der wisigotischen), 3 vols. (Wiesbaden, 1998–2014)

Manuscripts and Libraries in the Age of Charlemagne (Cambridge, 1994)

Bischoff, B. and V. Brown, 'Addenda to *Codices latini antiquiores*', *Mediaeval Studies* 47 (1985), 317–66

Bischoff, B., V. Brown and J. J. John, 'Addenda to *Codices latini antiquiores* (II)', *Mediaeval Studies* 54 (1992), 286–307

Bloch, H., *Monte Cassino in the Middle Ages*, 3 vols. (Rome, 1986)

Bolgia, C., 'The mosaics of Gregory IV at S. Marco, Rome: papal response to Venice, Byzantium and the Carolingians', *Speculum* 81 (2006), 1–34

Bonaccorsi, I., 'Gregorio IV', in M. Bray (ed.), *Enciclopedia dei papi*, 3 vols. (Rome, 2000)

Bondiolo, L., 'A Carolingian frontier? Louis II, Basil I and the Muslims of Bari (840–871)' (forthcoming)

La bonifica benedettina (Rome, 1970)

Bonner, S., *Education in Ancient Rome* (Berkeley, 1977)

Booker, C., 'The public penance of Louis the Pious: a new edition of the *Episcoporum de Poenitentia, quam Hludowicus Imperator Professus Est, Relatio Compendiensis (833)*', *Viator* 39 (2008), 1–19

Past Convictions. The Penance of Louis the Pious and the Decline of the Carolingians (Philadelphia, 2009)

Borri, F., 'Gli Istriani e i loro parenti: Φράγγοι, Romani e Slavi nella periferia di Bisanzio', *Jahrbuch der Österreichischen Byzantinistik*, 60 (2010), 1–26

'L'Adriatico tra Bizantini, Longobardi e Franchi. Dalla conquista di Ravenna alla pace di Aquisgrana (751–812)', *Bullettino dell'Istituto Storico Italiano e Archivio Muratoriano* 112 (2010), 1–56

'Troubled times: narrating conquest and defiance between Charlemagne and Bernhard (774–818)', in C. Heath and R. Houghton (eds.), *Conflict and Violence in Medieval Italy 568–1154* (forthcoming)

Boshof, E. *Ludwig der Fromme* (Darmstadt, 1996)

Bouchard, C. B., 'The Bosonids or rising to power in the late Carolingian Age', *French Historical Studies* 15 (1988), 407–431

Bougard, F., 'Engelberga', in *Dizionario Biografico degli Italiani* 42 (Rome, 1993), pp. 668–76

'Elbungo', in *Dizionario Biografico deglit Italiani* 42 (Rome, 1993), pp. 379–80

La justice dans le Royaume d'Italie: de la fin du VIIIᵉ siécle au début du XIᵉ, Bibliothèque des Ècoles françaises d'Athènes et de Rome 291 (Rome, 1995)

'Les palais royaux et impériaux de l'Italie carolingienne et ottonienne', in A. Renoux (ed.), *Palais royaux et princiers au Moyen Âge : actes du colloque international tenu au Mans les 6–7 et 8 octobre 1994* (Le Mans, 1996), pp. 181–96

'La justice dans le Royaume d'Italie aux IXᵉ–Xᵉ siècle', in *La Giustizia nell'Alto Medioevo (secoli XI–XI)*, Settimane del CISAM 44 (Spoleto, 1997), pp. 133–76

'La cour et le gouvernement de Louis II, 840–875', in R. Le Jan (ed.), *La royauté et les élites dans l'Europe carolingienne (du début du IXe aux environs de 920)* (Lille, 1998), pp. 249–67

'Ludovico II re d'Italia, imperatore', in *Dizionario Biografico degli Italiani* 66 (Rome 2006), pp. 387–94

'Les Supponides: échec à la reine', in F. Bougard, L. Feller and R. Le Jan (eds.), *Les élites au Haut Moyen Âge: Crises et renouvellements*, Haut Moyen Âge 1 (Turnhout, 2006), pp. 381–401

'Adalhard de Corbie entre Nonantola et Brescia (813): commutatio, gestion des biens monastiques et marché de la terre', in E. Cuozzo, V. Déroche, A. Peters-Custot and V. Prigent (eds.), *Puer Apuliae. Mélanges offerts à Jean-Marie Martin* (Paris, 2008), pp. 51–68

'Tempore barbarici? La production documentaire publique et privée', in Gasparri (ed.), *774*, pp. 331–51

'Laien als Amtsträger: über die Grafen des *regnum Italiae*', in W. Pohl and V. Wieser (eds.), *Der frühmittelalterliche Staat – europäische Perspektiven*, Forschungen zur Geschichte des Mittelalters 16 (Vienna, 2009), pp. 201–15

'Notaires d'élite, notaires de l'élite dans le royaume d'Italie', in F. Bougard, R. Le Jan and R. McKitterick (eds.), *La culture au haut Moyen Âge: une question d'élites?*, Haut Moyen Âge 7 (Turnhout, 2009), pp. 438–60

'Le royaume d'Italie (jusqu'aux Ottons), entre l'empire et les réalités locales', in M. Gaillard, M. Margue, A Dierkens and H. Pettiau (eds.), *De la mer du Nord à la Méditerranée. Francia Media, une région au coeur de l'Europe (c. 840 – c. 1050)*, (Luxembourg, 2011), pp. 487–510

'I vescovi di Arezzo nei secoli IX–XI: tra le responsabilità locali e i destini "nazionali"', in G. Cherubini, F. Franceschi, A. Barlucchi and G. Firpo (eds.), *Arezzo nel Medioevo* (Roma, 2012), pp. 63–72

'Le couronnement impérial de Bérenger Ier (915) d'après les *Gesta Berengarii Imperatoris*', in M. Coumert, M.C. Isaïa, K. Krönert and S. Shimahara, *Rerum Gestarum Scriptor. Histoire et historiographie au Moyen Âge. Mélanges Michel Sot* (Paris, 2012), pp. 329–43

'Lo stato e le élites fra 888 e 962: il regno d'Italia a confronto (brevi considerazioni)', in M. Valenti and C. Wickham (eds.), *Italy, 888–962: a turning point. Italia, 888–962: una svolta. Atti del IV Seminario Internazionale (Cassero di Poggio Imperiale a Poggibonsi 2009)* (Turnhout, 2013), pp. 77–84

'Du centre à la périphérie: le "ventre mou" du royaume d'Italie de la mort de Louis II à l'avènement d'Otton Ier', in La Rocca and Majocchi (eds.), *Urban Identities in Northern Italy*, pp. 15–31

'Les Francs à Venise, à Ravenne et à Rome: un facteur d'identité urbaine?', in V. West-Harling (ed.), *Three Empires, Three Cities: Identity, Material Culture and Legitimacy in Venice, Ravenna and Rome, 750–1000* (Turnhout, 2015), pp. 227–54

'Diplômes et notices de plaid: dialogue et convergence', in A. Ghignoli, W. Huschner and M. Ulrike Jaros (ed.), *Europäische Herrscher und die Toskana im Spiegel der urkundlichen Überlieferung – I sovrani europei e la Toscana nel riflesso della tradizione documentaria (800–1100)* (Leipzig, 2016), pp. 15–22

'Italia infirma est patria et generat noxias "An non?" Le royaume d'Italie et Louis le Pieux', in P. Depreux and S. Esders (eds.), *La productivité d'une crise. Le règne de Louis le Pieux (814–840) et la transformation de l'Empire carolingien*, to be published.

Bougard, F., H.-W. Goetz and R. Le Jan (eds.), *Théories et pratiques des élites au haut Moyen Âge*, Collection Haut Moyen Âge 13 (Turnhout 2011)

Bourdieu, P., 'The field of cultural production or: the economic world reversed', *Poetics* 12.4 (1983), 311–56

The Field of Cultural Production (Cambridge, 1993)

Bourgain, P., 'Gregorius Turonensis ep.', in L. Castaldi and P. Chiesa (eds.), *La trasmissione dei testi latini del Medioevo. Medieval Texts and Their Transmission. TE. TRA. I*, Millennio medievale 50 (Florence, 2004), pp. 152–68

Bove, F., 'L'architecture de la cathédrale de Bénévént', in T. F. Kelly (ed.), *La cathédrale de Bénévént* (Ghent, 2000), pp. 15–44

Boyle, L., 'The site of the tomb of St Cyril in the Lower Basilica of San Clemente, Rome', in E. Farrugia, R. Taft and G. Piovesana (eds.), *Christianity among the Slavs: The Heritage of Saints Cyril and Methodius* (Rome, 1988), pp. 75–82

Boynton, S., '*Libelli Precum* in the central Middle Ages', in R. Hammerling (ed.), *A History of Prayer. The First to the Fifteenth Century* (Leiden and Boston, 2008), pp. 255–318

Bozóki, E., (éd.), *Hagiographie, idéologie et politique au Moyen Âge en Occident. Actes du colloque international du Centre d'Études Supérieures de Civilisation Médiévale de Poitiers, 11–14 Septembre 2008*, Hagiologia 8 (Turnhout, 2012)

Bozóky, E. and A.-M. L. Helvetius, *Les reliques: Objets, cultes, symboles* (Turnhout, 1999)

Braga, G. (ed.), *Il Frammento Sabbatini: un documento per la storia di San Vincenzo al Volturno* (Roma, 2003)

Branchi, M., *Lo* scriptorium *e la biblioteca di Nonantola*, Biblioteca 49 (Nonantola, 2011)

Brancoli Busdraghi, P., *La formazione storica del feudo lombardo come diritto reale*, (Milan, 1965 and Spoleto, 1999)

Brenzoni, C. G. and P. Golinelli (eds.), *I Santi Fermo e Rustico: Un Culto e una Chiesa in Verona. Per il 17° Centenario del loro Martirio* (Verona, 2004)

Brogiolo, G. P., 'Capitali e residenze regie nell'Italia longobarda', in G. Ripoll and J. M. Gurt (eds.), *Sedes regiae (ann. 400–800)* (Barcelona, 2000), pp. 135–62; also in S. Gasparri (ed.), *Alto medioevo mediterraneo* (Florence, 2005), pp. 233–50

Brogiolo, G. P. and S. Gelichi, *La città nell'alto medioevo italiano. Archeologia e storia* (Bari, 1998)

Brogiolo, G. P., N. Gauthier and N. Christie (eds.), *Towns and Their Territories between Late Antiquity and the Early Middle Ages* (Leiden, 2000).

Brovelli, F., 'La Expositio missae canonicae: edizione critica e studio liturgico-teologico', in *Ricerche storiche sulla chiesa ambrosiana* VIII, Archivio Ambrosiano 35 (Milan, 1979), pp. 5–151

Brown, T. S., 'The church of Ravenna and the imperial administration in the seventh century', *English Historical Review* 94 (1979), 1–28

Gentlemen and Officers. Imperial Administration and Aristocratic Power in Byzantine Italy 554–800 (London, 1984)

'*Romanitas* and *Campanilismo*, Agnellus of Ravenna's view of the past', in C. Holdsworth and T. P. Wiseman (eds.), *The Inheritance of Historiography 350–900* (Exeter, 1986) pp. 107–14

'The interplay between Roman and Byzantine traditions in the exarchate of Ravenna', *Bisanzio, Roma e l'Italia nell'alto medioevo 3–9 aprile 1986, Settimana di studio del Centro italiano di studi sull'alto medioevo* 34 (Spoleto, 1988), pp. 127–67

The background of Byzantine relations with Italy in the ninth century: legacies, attachments and antagonisms', in *Byzantium and the West, c.850–c.1200. Proceedings of the XVIIIth Spring Symposium of Byzantine Studies* (Amsterdam, 1988) (= *Byzantinische Forschungen* 13), pp. 27–45

'Louis the Pious and the papacy: a Ravenna perspective', in P. Godman and R. Collins (eds.), *Charlemagne's Heir. New Perspectives on the Reign of Louis the Pious (814–840)* (Oxford, 1990), pp. 297–307

'Ebrei ed orientali a Ravenna,' in A. Carile (ed.), *Storia di Ravenna*, II,1 (Venice, 1991), pp, 135–149

'Byzantine Italy', in McKitterick (ed.), *The New Cambridge Medieval History*, vol. II, pp. 320–48

'Byzantine Italy, c.680–c.876', in J. Shepard (ed.), *Cambridge History of the Byzantine Empire c. 500–1492* (Cambridge, 2008), pp. 433–65

'Culture and society in Ottonian Ravenna: imperial renewal and new beginnings', in Herrin and Nelson (eds.), *Ravenna*, pp. 335–54

'Ravenna – Constantinople of the west?', in the Festschrift for Paul Magdalino, *Constantinople: Queen of Cities* (Leiden, forthcoming)

'The political use of the cult of saints in Early Medieval Ravenna', in P. Kershaw and S. Gregorio (eds.), *Cities, Saints and Communities in Early Medieval Europe. Essays in Honour of Alan Thacker* (Turnhout, forthcoming)

'Ravenna and other early rivals of Venice: comparative urban and economic development in the upper Adriatic c. 751–1050' in *Adriatic Connections: The Adriatic as a Threshold to Byzantium (c.600–1453)* (Cambridge, forthcoming).

Brown, W. C., M. Costambeys, M. Innes and A. J. Kosto (eds.), *Documentary Culture and the Laity in the Early Middle Ages* (Cambridge, 2013)

Brugnoli, G., 'La biblioteca dell'abbazia di Farfa', *Benedictina* 5 (1951), 3–17

Brühl, C. 'Die Kaiserpfalz bei St. Peter und die Pfalz Otto III', in *Quellen und Forschungen aus italienischen Archiven und Bibliotheken* 34 (1954), 1–30

'Neues zur Kaiserpfalz bei St. Peter', *Quellen und Forschungen aus italienischen Archiven und Bibliotheken* 38 (1958), 266–68

Fodrum, Gistum, Servitium Regis. Studien zu den wirtschaftlichen Grundlagen des Königtums im Frankenreich und in den fränkischen Nachfolgestaaten Deutschland, Frankreich und Italien vom 6. bis zur Mitte des 14. Jahrhunderts (Cologne, 1968)

'Libellus de imperatoria potestate in urbe Roma', in *Lexikon des Mittelalters*, vol. 5 (Stuttgart), col. 1939

Brunhölzl, F., *Histoire de la littérature latine du Moyen Âge*, 3 vols. (Turnhout, 1991–6; 1st German ed. Munich, 1975–92)

Bruyning, L. F., 'Lawcourt proceedings in the Lombard kingdom before and after the Frankish Conquest', *Journal of Medieval History* 11 (1985), 193–214

Buc, P., 'Italian hussies and German matrons: Liutprand of Cremona on dynastic legitimacy', *Frühmittelalterliche Studien* 29 (1995), 207–25.

The Dangers of Ritual. Between Early Medieval Texts and Social Scientific Theory (Princeton, 2002)

'Text and ritual', in G. Althoff, J. Fried and P. J. Johannes (eds.), *Medieval Concepts of the Past. Ritual, Memory, Historiography* (Cambridge and Washington, DC, 2002)

Budriesi Trombetti, A. L., *Prime ricerche sul vocabolario feudale italiano* (Bologna, 1974)

Bührer-Thierry, G., *Évêques et pouvoir dans le royaume de Germanie. Les Églises de Bavière et de Souabe (876–973)* (Paris, 1997)

Bullough, D.A., 'Baiuli in the Carolingian regnum Langobardorum and the career of Abbot Waldo (†813)', *The English Historical Review* 77 (1962), 625–37

'*Europae Pater*: Charlemagne and his achievement in the light of recent scholarship', *English Historical Review* 85 (1970), 59–105

Bullough, D. A., 'Aula renovata: the court before the Aachen palace', in Bullough, *Carolingian Renewal: Sources and Heritage* (Manchester, 1991), pp. 123–60

'Reminiscence and reality. Text, translation and testimony of an Alcuin letter', *The Journal of Medieval Latin* 5 (1995), 174–201

Buringh, E., *Medieval Manuscript Production in the Latin West. Explorations with a Global Database*, Global Economics History Series 6 (Leiden and Boston, 2011)

Butler, T. and G. Robson, 'Social capital, gentrification and neighbourhood change in London: a comparison of three South London neighbourhoods', *Urban Studies*, 38 (2001), 2145–62

Butz, E. M. and A. Zettler, 'The making of the Carolingian *libri vitae*: exploring or constructing the past?', in E. Brenner, M. Cohen and M. Franklin-Brown (eds.), *Memory and Commemoration in Medieval Culture* (Farnham, 2013), pp. 79–92

Cagiano de Azevedo, M., 'Milano longobarda', *I Longobardi e la Lombardia: aspetti di civiltà longobarda* (Spoleto, 1980), pp. 131–50

Calderini, C., 'Il palazzo di Liutprando a Corteolona', *Contributi dell'Istituto di Archeologia (Milano)*, 5 (1975), 174–208

Cammarosano, P., *Nobili e re. L'Italia politica dell'alto Medioevo* (Rome and Bari, 1998)

Cammarosano, P. and S. Gasparri (eds.), *Langobardia* (Udine, 1990)

Canaccini, F., *La lunga storia di una stirpe comitale. I conti Guidi tra Romagna e Toscana* (Florence, 2009)

Cantino Wataghin, G., 'Quadri urbani nell' Italia settentrionale: tarda antichità e alto medioevo', in C. Lepelley (ed.), *La fin de la cité antique et le début de la cité médiévale* (Bari and Rome, 1996), pp. 239–71

Capo, L., 'Paolo Diacono', *Dizionario Biografico degli Italiani* 81 (2014), consulted online www.treccani.it/enciclopedia/paolo-diacono_%28Dizionario-Biografico%29/

Carile, A. (ed.), *Storia di Ravenna*, II: dall'età bizantina all'età ottoniana, 2 vols. (Venice, 1991–1992).

　'La società ravennate dall'esarcato agli Ottoni', in A. Carile (ed.), *Storia di Ravenna*, II/2: dall'età bizantina all'età ottoniana. Ecclesiologia, cultura e arte (Venice, 1992), pp. 379–404

Carile, M., 'Culto e commercio delle reliquie', in A. Augenti and C. Bertelli (eds.), *Ravenna tra Oriente e Occidente: storia e archeologia* (Ravenna, 2006), pp. 73–84

Carpegna Falconieri, T., 'Guido di Spoleto', in *Dizionario biografico degli Italiani* 61 (Rome, 2003), pp. 352–61

Carusi, E., 'Intorno al *Commemoratorium* dell'abate Teobaldo (1019–1022)', *Bullettino dell'Istituto storico italiano per il Medio Evo e Archivio muratoriano* 47 (1932), 173–90

Casadio, G., 'Romania e Romagna', *La Ludia: Bollettino dell'Associazione Istituto Friedrich Schürr per la Valorizzazione del Patrimonio Dialettale Romagnolo* 8 (2003), 2–3

Cassandro, G., 'Il ducato bizantino', in E. Pontieri (ed.), *Storia di Napoli II,1* (Naples, 1969)

Castagnetti, A., *L'organizzazione del territorio rurale nel Medioevo: circoscrizioni ecclesiastiche e civili nella Langobardia e nella Romania*, 2nd ed. (Bologna, 1982)

　Minoranze etniche dominanti e rapporti vassallatico-beneficiari. Alamanni e Franchi a Verona e nel Veneto in età carolingia e postcarolingia (Verona, 1990)

　Una famiglia di immigrati nell'alta Lombardia al servizio del regno (846–898) (Verona, 2004)

'Transalpini e vassalli in area milanese', in A. Castagnetti, A. Ciaralli and G. M. Varanini (eds.), *Medioevo. Studi e documenti* (Verona, 2005), vol. i, pp. 7–109

'Il conte Anselmo I: l'invenzione di un conte carolingio', *Studi storici Luigi Simeoni* 56 (2006), 9–60

'I vassalli imperiali a Lucca in età carolingia', in S. M. Pagano and P. Piatti (eds.), *Il patrimonio documentario della Chiesa di Lucca: Prospettive di ricerca. Atti del convegno internazionale di studi (Lucca, Archivio Arcivescovile, 14–15 novembre 2008)*, Toscana sacra 2 (Florence, 2010), pp. 211–84

'Giustizia partecipata. Lociservatores, scabini e astanti nei placiti lucchesi (785–822)', in *Studi Medievali*, ser. iii, 61/1 (2015), 1–40

Cau, E. and M. A. Casagrande Mazzoli, 'Cultura e scrittura a Pavia (secoli V–X)', in R. Bossaglia (ed.), *Storia di Pavia 2: L'Alto Medioevo* (Pavia, 1987), pp. 177–217

Cavallo, G., 'La trasmissione dei testi nell'area beneventano-cassinese', in G. Cavallo, *Dalla parte del libro. Storie di trasmissione dei classici*, Ludus philologiae 10 (Urbino, 2002), pp. 235–84

Cavarra, B., et al., 'Gli Archivi come fonti della storia di Ravenna: regesto dei documenti', in Carile (ed.), *Storia di Ravenna*, ii/1, pp. 401–547

Cerno, M., 'Passio Helari et Tatiani', in E. Colombi (ed.), *Le passioni dei martiri aquileiesi e istriani* (Rome, 2008), pp. 277–326

Cessi, R., 'Di due miscellanee storiche medievali', *Archivio Muratoriano* 13 (1913), 71–96

'L'occupazione longobarda e franca dell'Istria nei secc. VIII e IX', *Atti. Istituto Veneto di Scienze, Lettere ed Arti, Classe di Scienze Morali e Lettere*, 100 (1941), 289–313

Cherubini, G., F. Franceschi, A. Barlucchi and G. Firpo (eds.), *Arezzo nel Medioevo* (Roma, 2012)

Chiesa, P., 'Fardolfo', *Dizionario Biografico degli Italiani* 44 (1994) consulted online www.treccani.it/enciclopedia/fardolfo

'Le vie della cultura attraverso le Alpi fra VII e XI secolo', in Scalon and Pani (eds.), *Le Alpi porta d'Europa*, pp. 1–21

'I manoscritti delle Passiones Aquileiesi e Istriane', in Colombi (ed.), *Le Passioni*, pp. 105–25

'Paolino II, patriarca di Aquileia', *Dizionario biografico degli italiani* 81 (2014), consulted online www.treccani.it/enciclopedia/paolino-ii-patriarca-di-aquileia_%28Dizionario-Biografico%29/

Chiesa, P. (ed.), *Paolo Diacono: uno scrittore fra tradizione longobarda e rinnovamento carolingio: atti del convegno internazionale di studi, Cividale del Friuli, Udine, 6–9 maggio 1999* (Udine, 2000)

(ed.), *Paolino d'Aquileia e il Contributo Italiano all'Europa Carolingia. Atti del Convegno Internazionale di Studi, Cividale del Friuli-Premariacco, 10–13 ottobre 2002*, Libri e Biblioteche 12 (Udine, 2003)

Choy, R. S., *Intercessory Prayer and the Monastic Ideal in the Time of the Carolingian Reforms* (Oxford, 2016)

Christie, N., *Three South Etrurian Churches: Santa Corenlia, Santa Rufina and San Liberato* (London, 1991)

'Popes, pilgrims and peasants. The role of the domusculta Capracorum (Santa Cornelia, Rome)', in E. Dassmann and J. Engemann (eds.), *Akten des XII. Internationalen Kongresses für christliche Archäologie* (Rome, 1995), pp. 650–7

Cicco, G. G., 'La scuola cattedrale di Benevento e il vescovo Urso (secolo IX)', *Rivista di Storia della Chiesa in Italia*, 61 (2006), 341–73

Cilento, N., 'L'agiografia e le traduzione dal greco', in N. Cilento, *Civiltà napoletana del Medioevo nei secoli VI–XIII* (Naples, 1969), pp. 31–54

Cimino, R., 'Italian queens in the ninth and tenth centuries', PhD thesis, St Andrews and Bologna, 2013.

Remembering Bertha of Tuscany: Kingship, Land and Women's Legacy in the Tenth-Century Italy (forthcoming)

Cirelli, E., *Ravenna, Archeologia di una città* (Borgo San Lorenzo, 2008)

'Material culture in Ravenna and its hinterland between the 8th and the 10th century', in V. West-Harling (ed.), *Three Empires, Three Cities. Identity, Material Culture and Legitimacy in Venice, Ravenna and Rome, 750–1000* (Turnhout 2015), pp. 101–32

'Bishops and merchants: the economy of Ravenna at the beginning of the Middle Ages' (forthcoming)

Clarke, M. L., *Higher Education in the Ancient World* (London, 1972)

Collavini, S. M., 'Duchi e società locali nei ducati di Spoleto e di Benevento nel secolo VIII', in S. Gasparri (ed.), *I longobardi dei ducati di Spoleto e Benevento: atti del XVI Congresso internazionale di studi sull'alto Medioevo: Spoleto, 20–23 ottobre 2002, Benevento 24–27 ottobre 2002* (Spoleto, 2003), pp. 125–66

'Des Lombards aux Carolingiens: l'évolution des élites locales', in W. Fałkowski and Y. Sassier (eds.), *Le monde carolingien. Bilan, perspectives, champs de recherches. Actes du colloque international de Poitiers, Centre d'Études supérieures de Civilisation médiévale, 18–20 novembre 2004*, Culture et société médiévales 18 (Turnhout, 2009), pp. 263–300

Colombi, E., 'Modelli poetici nei componimenti di Paolino d'Aquileia', in Chiesa (ed.), *Paolino d'Aquileia*, pp. 71–92

'Alcune riflessioni sull'*Istoria Veneticorum* del Diacono Giovanni e il prologo della *Translatio Marci Evangelistae* (BHL 5283–5284)', *Studi Veneziani*, n.s., 64 (2011), 15–54

'Caratteristiche delle Passiones Aquileiesi e Istriane: un Primo Bilancio', in Colombi (ed.), *Le Passioni*, pp. 49–104

Colombi, E., (ed.), *Le passioni dei martiri aquileiesi e istriani*, vol. 1 (Rome, 2008)

'Translatio sancti Marci Venetias [BHL 5283–5284]', *Hagiographica* 17 (2010), 73–129

Consolino, F. E., 'La poesia epigrafica a Pavia longobarda nell'VIII secolo', in R. Bossaglia (ed.), *Storia di Pavia 2: L'Alto Medioevo* (Pavia, 1987), pp. 159–75

Cosentino, S., 'La percezione della storia bizantina nella medievistica italiana tra ottocento e secondo dopoguerra', *Studi Medievali*, ser.III, 39 (1998), 889–909

'Ricchezza ed investimento della chiesa di Ravenna tra la tarda antichità e l'alto medioevo', in S. Gelichi and R. Hodges (eds.), *From One Sea to Another. Trading Places in the European and Mediterranean Early Middle Ages*, (Turnhout) 2012, pp. 417–439

'Antroponomia, politica e società nell'Esarcato in età bizantina e post-bizantina', in J.-M. Martin et al. (eds.), *L' héritage byzantin* (Rome, 2012), II, pp. 173–85

Costambeys, M., *Power and Patronage in Early Medieval Italy: Local Society, Italian Politics and the Abbey of Farfa, c. 700–900* (Cambridge, 2007)

'Disputes and courts in Lombard and Carolingian central Italy', *Early Medieval Europe*, 15 (2007), 265–89

'Alcuin, Rome, and Charlemagne's imperial coronation', in F. Tinti (ed.), *England and Rome in the early Middle Ages: Pilgrimage, art and politics*, Studies in the Early Middle Ages, 40 (Turnhout, 2014), pp. 255–89.

'Disputes and documents in Early Medieval Italy', in K. Cooper and C. Leyser (eds.), *Making Early Medieval Societies. Conflict and Belonging in the Latin West, 300–1200* (Cambridge, 2016), pp. 104–24

Costambeys, M., M. Innes and S. MacLean, *The Carolingian World* (Cambridge, 2011)

Coussemaker, I. de (ed.), *Cartulaire de l'Abbaye de Cysoing* (Lille, 1885)

Cracco Ruggini, L., 'La città nel mondo antico: realtà e idea', in G. Wirth (ed.), *Romanitas-Christianitas: Untersuchungen zur Geschichte und Literatur der römischen Kaiserzeit Johannes Straub zum 70 Geburstag am 18. Oktober 1982 gewidmet* (Berlin, 1982), pp. 61–81

Cracco, G., 'I testi agiografici: religione e politica nella Venezia del mille', in L. Cracco Ruggini, M. Pavan, G. Cracco and Gh. Ortalli (eds.), *Storia di Venezia*, vol. 1, *Origini – Età Ducale* (Rome, 1992), pp. 923–61

Crawford, M. H., 'Italy and Rome from Sulla to Augustus', in A. Bowman, E. Champlin and A. Lintott (eds.), *The Cambridge Ancient History. Volume X. The Augustan Empire, 43 B.C – A.D. 69* (Cambridge, 1996), pp. 414–33

Davis, J. R., *Charlemagne's Practice of Empire* (Cambridge, 2015)

Day, W. R., M. Matzke and A. Saccocci, *Medieval European Coinage: With a Catalogue of the Coins in the Fitzwilliam Museum, Cambridge. 12, Italy. 1, Northern Italy* (Cambridge, 2016)

De Angelis, G., *Poteri cittadini e intellettuali di potere: scrittura, documentazione, politica a Bergamo nei secoli IX–XII* (Milan, 2009)

De Conno, A., 'L'insediamento longobardo a Lucca', in G. Rossetti (ed.), *Pisa e la Toscana occidentale nel Medioevo. A Cinzio Violante nei suoi 70 anni*, 2 vols. (Pisa, 1991), I, pp. 59–127

De Lorenzi, P., *Storia del Notariato ravennate*, 2 vols. (Ravenna, 1962)

De Rubeis, F., 'La capitale damasiana a Tours: esperimenti ed effimere primavere', *Scripta* 3 (2010), 57–72

De Rubeis, F., 'Sillogi epigrafiche: le vie della pietra in età carolingia', in Chiesa (ed.), *Paolino d'Aquileia*, pp. 93–114

Deliyannis, D. M., 'Charlemagne's silver tables: the ideology of an imperial capital', *Early Medieval Europe* 12 (2003), 159–77

Ravenna in Late Antiquity (Cambridge, 2010)

Delogu, P., 'Strutture politiche e ideologia nel regno di Ludovico II', *Bullettino dell'Istituto Storico Italiano per il Medio Evo* 80 (1968), 137–89

'Vescovi, conti e sovrani nella crisi del regno Italico', *Annali della Scuola speciale per archivisti e bibliotecari dell'Università di Roma* 8 (1968), 3–72

'L'istituzione comitale nell'Italia carolingia', *Bullettino dell'Istituto storico italiano per il Medio Evo e Archivio Muratoriano* 79 (1968), 53–114

Mito di una città meridionale (Salerno, secoli VIII–XI), (Naples, 1977)

'Il regno longobardo', in Galasso (ed.), *Storia d'Italia 1*, pp. 3–216

'Il ducato di Gaeta dal IX all' XI secolo: istituzioni e società', in G. Galasso and R. Romeo (eds.), *Storia del Mezzogiorno d'Italia* (Naples, 1986)

'The rebirth of Rome in the 8th and 9th centuries', in R. Hodges and B. Hobley (eds.), *The Rebirth of Towns in the West AD 700–1050* (London, 1988), pp. 32–42

'Lombard and Carolingian Italy', in McKitterick (ed.), *The New Cambridge Medieval History*, vol. II, pp. 290–319

'Longobardi e Romani: altre congetture', in S. Gasparri and S. Camarrosano (eds.), *Langobardia* (Udine, 2004), pp. 93–172

'Rome in the ninth century: the economic system', in J. Henning (ed.), *Post-Roman Towns, Trade and Settlement in Europe and Byzantium*, vol. I, *The Heirs of the Roman West* (Berlin and New York, 2007), pp. 105–22

'I Romani e l'Impero (VII–X secolo)', in V. West-Harling (ed.), *Three empires, Three Cities : Identity, Material Culture and Legitimacy in Venice, Ravenna and Rome, 750–1000* (Turnhout, 2015), pp. 191–225

'Ritorno ai Longobardi', in G. Archetti (ed.), *Desiderio. Il progetto politico dell'ultimo re longobardo. Atti del I Convegno Internazionale di Studi, Brescia, 21–24 marzo 2013* (Spoleto, 2015), pp. 19–50

Delumeau, J.-P., *Arezzo, espace et societés, 715–1230*, 2 vols. (Rome, 1996)

Dendorfer, J. and R. Deutinger (eds.), *Das Lehnswesen im Hochmittelalter. Forschungskonstrukte – Quellenbefunde – Deutungsrelevanz* (Ostfildern, 2010)

Depreux, P. 'Das Königtum Bernhards von Italien und sein Verhältnis zum Kaisertum', *Quellen und Forschungen aus italienischen Archiven und Bibliotheken*, 72 (1992), 1–24

'Tassilon III et le roi des Francs: examen d'une vassalité controversée', *Revue Historique* 293/1 (1995), 23–73

Prosopographie de l'entourage de Louis le Pieux (781–840) (Sigmaringen, 1997).

Deshusses, J., *Le sacramentaire grégorien. Ses principales formes d'après les manuscrits: édition comparative*, Spicilegium Friburgense 16, 24, 28, 3 vols. (Fribourg, 1971–82)

Desmulliez, J., 'Le dossier du groupe episcopal de Naples; etat actuel des recherches', *Antiquite tardive 6*, 6 (1998), 345–54

Deutinger, R., 'Seit wann gab es die Mehrfachvasallität?', *Zeitschrift für Rechtsgeschichte. Germ. Abt.* 119 (2002), 78–105

'Beobachtungen zum Lehnswesen im frühmittelalterlichen Bayern', *Zeitschrift für bayerische Landesgeschichte* 70 (2007), 57–83

Di Branco, M., 'Strategie di penetrazione islamica in Italia meridionale. Il caso dell'emirato di Bari,' in K. Herbers and K. Wolf (eds.), *Southern Italy as Contact Area and Border Region During the Early Middle Ages* (Cologne, 2018), pp. 149–64

Diehl, C., *Études sur l'administration Byzantine dans l'exarchat de Ravenne (568–751): Michel Apostolis. Publiées d'après les manuscrits des opuscules inédits du même auteur. Une introduction et des notes*, Bibliothèque des Écoles Françaises d'Athènes et de Rome 53 (Paris, 1888)

Diesenberger, M., 'How collections shape the texts: rewriting and rearranging *Passions* in Carolingian Bavaria', in M. Heinzelmann (ed.), *Livrets, Collections et Textes. Études sur la Tradition Hagiographique Latine* (Ostfildern, 2006), pp. 195–224

Dolbeau, F., 'Le rôle des interprètes dans les traductions hagiographiques d'Italie du Sud', *Traduction et traducteurs* 361 (1988–90), 145–62

'Naissance des homéliaires et des passionnaires. Une tentative d'étude comparative', in S. Gioanni and B. Grévin (eds.), *L'Antiquité tardive dans les collections médiévales. Textes et représentations, VIe–XIVe siècle*, Collection de l'École française de Rome 405 (Roma, 2008), pp. 13–35

Dubreucq, A., 'La littérature des *Specula*: delimitation du genre, Contenu, destinataires et reception', in M. Lauwers (ed.), *Guerriers et Moines. Conversion et Sainteté Aristocratiques dans l'Occident Médiéval*, Collection d'Études Médiévales de Nice 4 (Turnhout, 2002), pp. 17–39

'Le prince et le peuple dans les miroirs des princes Carolingiens', in H. Oudart, J.-M. Picard and J. Quaghebeur (eds.), *Le prince, son peuple et le bien commun. De l'antiquité tardive à la fin du moyen âge* (Rennes, 2013), pp. 97–114

Duby, G., *Les trois ordres ou l'imaginaire du féodalisme* (Paris, 1978)

Duplessis, F., 'Nam cuncta nequit mea ferre Thalia. Traitement de la matière historique par un panégyriste du Xeme siècle', in *Le poème et l'historien*, CEHTL 6 (2013), pp. 44–78

'Réseaux intellectuels entre France et Italie (IXe–Xe s.): autour des Gesta Berengarii imperatoris et de leurs gloses', unpublished PhD thesis, École pratique des hautes études, 2015

'Les sources des gloses des *Gesta Berengarii* et la culture du poète anonyme', *Aevum* 89/2 (2015), 205–63

Dupraz, Louis, 'Le capitulaire de Lothaire I, empereur, De expeditione contra Sarracenos facienda, et la Suisse romande (847)', *Zeitschrift für schweizerische Geschichte* 16 (1936), 241–93

Dupré Theseider, E., 'Problemi della città nell' alto medioevo', in *La città nell'alto Medioevo* (Spoleto, 1959), pp. 15–46

Dutton, P. E., *Carolingian Civilization. A Reader*, 2nd ed. (Peterborough, ON, 2004)

Eiten, G., *Das Unterkönigtum im Reiche der Merovinger und Karolinger* (Heidelberg, 1907)

Eldevik, J., 'Bishops in the medieval empire: new perspectives on the church, state and episcopal office', *History Compass*, 9/10 (2011), 776–90

Esders, S., 'Die römischen Wurzeln der fiskalischen Inquisitio der Karolingerzeit', in C. Gauvard (ed.), *L'enquête au Moyen Âge*, Collection de l'École française de Rome 399 (Roma, 2008), pp. 13–28

'Deux *libri legum* au service des fonctionnaires du royaume d'Italie à l'époque carolingienne', in C. Denoël, A.-O. Poilpré and S. Shimahara (eds.), *Imago libri. Représentations carolingiennes du livre* (Turnhout, 2018).

Everett, N., 'The hagiography of Lombard Italy', *Hagiographica: rivista di agiografia e biografia*, 7 (2000), 49–126

'The earliest recension of the life of S. Sirus of Pavia (Vat. Lat. 5771)', *Studi medievali*, 43 (2002), 857–958

Literacy in Lombard Italy, c. 568–774 (Cambridge, 2003)

'Paulinus, the Carolingians and Famosissima Aquileia', in Chiesa (ed.), *Paolino d'Aquileia*, pp. 115–54

Patron Saints of Early Medieval Italy AD c.350–800: History and Hagiography in Ten Biographies (Toronto, 2016)

Fainelli, V., 'Per l'edizione di un codice diplomatico veronese. Studio preparatorio sui documenti anteriori al Mille', in *Nuovo Archivio Veneto* 97 (1915), 5–72

Falkenhausen, V. v., 'I Longobardi meridionali', in A. Guillou and F. Burgarella (eds.), *Il Mezzogiorno dai Bizantini a Federico II* (Turin, 1983), pp. 249–326, 39–64

Fasoli, G., *I re d'Italia (888–962)* (Florence, 1949)

'Il dominio territoriale degli arcivescovi di Ravenna fra l'VIII e l'XI secolo', in *I poteri temporali dei vescovi in Italia e in Germania nel medioevo*, Annali dell'Istituto Storico Italo-Germanico di Trento (Bologna 1979), pp. 87–140

Fees, I., 'Eberardo', in *Dizionario Biografico degli Italiani* 42 (Rome, 1993), pp. 252–55

Feller, L., *Les Abruzzes médiévales: Territoire, économie et société en Italie centrale du IXe au XIIe siècle* (Rome, 1998)

'L'économie des territoires de Spolète et de Bénévent du VIe au Xe siècle', in *I Longobardi di Spoleto e di Benevento (Atti del XVI Congresso Internazionale di studi sull'alto medioevo)*, (2003), pp. 205–42

'Les élites rurales du haut Moyen Âge en Italie (IXᵉ–Xᵉ siècle), *Mélanges de l'École Française de Rome – Moyen Âge* 123.2 (2012), 327–43

Feo, F. de, 'La *via Postumia*', *Geographia Antiqua* 6 (1997), 79–105

Ferrari, M., 'Le scoperte a Bobbio nel 1493: vicende di codici e fortuna di testi', *Italia Medioevale e Umanistica* 13 (1970), 139–80

'"In Papia conveniant ad Dungalum"', *Italia Medioevale e Umanistica* 15 (1972), 1–52.

'La trasmissione dei testi nell'Italia nord-occidentale. I. Centri di trasmissione: Monza, Pavia, Milano, Bobbio', in *La cultura antica nell'Occidente latino dal VII all'XI secolo*, Settimane di studio del CISAM 22 (Spoleto, 1975), pp. 303–56

'Libri liturgici e diffusione della scrittura carolina nell'Italia settentrionale', in *Culto cristiano e politica imperiale carolingia*, Convegni del Centro di studi sulla spiritualità medievale 18 (Todi, 1979), pp. 265–79

'Fra i "latini scriptores" di Pier Candido Decembrio e biblioteche umanistiche milanesi: codici di Vitruvio e Quintiliano', in R. Avesani et al. (eds.), *Vestigia. Studi in onore di Giuseppe Billanovich* (Rome, 1984), pp. 247–96

'Manoscritti e cultura', in *Atti del 10° Congresso Internazionale di Studi sull'Alto Medioevo* (Spoleto, 1986), pp. 241–75

'La biblioteca del monastero di S. Ambrogio: episodi per una storia', in *Il monastero di S. Ambrogio nel Medioevo. Convegno di studio nel XII centenario: 784–1984* (Milano, 1988), pp. 82–164

'Libri e testi prima del Mille', in G. Cracco (ed.), *Storia della Chiesa di Ivrea dalle origini al XV secolo* (Roma, 1998), pp. 511–33

Il feudalesimo nell'alto medioevo, 8–12 aprile 1999, Settimane 47 (Spoleto, 2000)

Fichtenau, H., *Das Urkundenwesen in Österreich vom 8. bis zum frühen 13. Jahrhundert* (Vienna, 1971)

Fischer, J., *Königtum, Adel und Kirche im Königreich Italien (774–875)*, Habelts Dissertationsdrucke. Reihe Mittelalterliche Geschichte 1 (Bonn, 1965)

Fischer Drew, K., 'The Italian monasteries of Nonantola, San Salvatore and Santa Maria Teodota in the eighth and ninth centuries', *Manuscripta* 9 (1965), 131–54

Folz, R. *The Coronation of Charlemagne 25 December 800*, trans. J. E. Anderson (London, 1974)

Formentini, U., 'Genova nel basso impero e nell'alto medioevo,' in *Storia di Genova dalle origini al nostro tempo*, part 2 (Genova, 1941–42), pp. 7–278.

Forrai, R., 'Anastasius Bibliotecarius and his textual dossiers: Greek collections and their Latin transmission in 9th century Rome', in *L'Antiquité tardive dans les collections médiévales. Textes et répresentations* (2008), pp. 319–37.

Fouracre, P., 'The origins of the Carolingian attempt to regulate the cult of saints', in J. D. Howard-Johnston and P. A. Hayward (eds.), *The Cult of Saints in Late Antiquity and the Middle Ages. Essays on the Contribution of Peter Brown* (Oxford, 1999), pp. 143–65

Fouracre, P. and R. A. Gerberding, *Late Merovingian France. History and Hagiography* (Manchester and New York, 1996)

Frattaroli, P., 'Il velo di classe', in Brenzoni and Golinelli (eds.), *I Santi Fermo e Rustico*, pp. 45–55

Fried, J., 'Debate', *German Historical Institute London. Bulletin* 19/1 (1997), 28–40 *Charlemagne*, trans. P. Lewis (Cambridge, MA, 2016)

Frisby, D., *Simmel and Since: Essays on Georg Simmel's Social Theory* (London, 1992)

Fuchs F. and P. Schmid, *Kaiser Arnolf. Das ostfränkische Reich am Ende des 9. Jahrhunderts* (München, 2002)

Fumagalli, V., 'Città e distretti minori nell'Italia carolingia: un esempio', *Rivista storica italiana italiana*, 81 (1969), pp. 107–17

'L'amministrazione periferica dello stato nell'Emilia occidentale in età carolingia', *Rivista storica italiana* 83 (1971), 911–20

Il Regno italia, ed. G. Galasso, *Storia d'Italia*, vol. II (Turin, 1978)

'Le modificazioni politico-istituzionali in Italia sotto la dominazione carolingia', *Nascita dell'Europa ed Europa Carolingia. Un'equazione da verificare*, Settimane di studio del CISAM 27 (Spoleto, 1981), pp. 293–317

Galasso, G., 'L'eredità municipale del ducato di Napoli', *Mélanges de l'École Française de Rome – Moyen Âge* (1995) 107.1, 77–97

(ed.), *Storia d'Italia 1: Longobardi e bizantini* (Torino, 1980)

Gandino, G., 'Aspirare al regno: Berta di Toscana', in C. La Rocca (ed.), *Agire da donna. Modelli e pratiche di rappresentazione (secoli VI–X)* (Turnhout, 2007), pp. 249–68

Ganshof, F.-L., *Qu'est-ce que la féodalité?*, 4th ed. (Paris, 1984); English translation: F.-L. Ganshof, *Feudalism* (London, 1952)

'L'armée sous les Carolingiens', in *Ordinamenti militari in Occidente nell'alto Medioevo, 30 marzo–7 aprile 1967*, Settimane 15, 2 vols. (Spoleto, 1968), vol. I, pp. 394–419

Gantner, C., 'The Lombard recension of the Roman *Liber Pontificalis*', *Rivista di Storia del Cristianesimo* 10/1 (2013), 65–114

Freunde Roms und Völker der Finsternis: Die päpstliche Konstruktion von Anderen im 8. und 9. Jahrhundert (Vienna, 2014)

'Romana urbs: levels of Roman and imperial identity in the city of Rome', *Early Medieval Europa* 22 (2014), 461–75

'Kaiser Ludwig II. von Italien und Byzanz', in F. Daim, C. Gastgeber, D. Heher and C. Rapp (eds.), *Menschen, Bilder, Sprache, Dinge. Wege der Kommunikation zwischen Byzanz und dem Westen*, vol. 2, *Menschen und Worte*, Byzanz zwischen Orient und Okzident 9, 2 (Mainz, 2018), pp. 103–12

'"Our common enemies shall be annihilated!" How Louis II's relations with the Byzantine Empire shaped his policy in southern Italy', in K. Wolf and K. Herbers (eds.), *Southern Italy as Contact Area and Border Region during the Early Middle Ages: Religious-Cultural Heterogeneity and Competing Powers in Local, Transregional and Universal Dimensions* (Cologne, 2018), pp. 295–314

'The silence of the popes: Why King Pippin of Italy was hardly ever mentioned in the papal writings of the time', in Albertoni and Borri (eds.), *Pippin of Italy*. forthcoming

'Louis II and Rome: on the relationship of the Carolingian emperor of Italy with "his" popes Nicholas I and Hadrian II', in Mark Humphries and Giorgia Vocino (eds.), *Through the Papal Lens: Shaping History and Memory in Late Antique and Early Medieval Rome, 300–900* (forthcoming, Translated Texts for Historians Series, Liverpool 2021).

'The Saracen attack on Rome in 846 and its impact on the Italian Carolingian Empire', in: Walter Pohl and Andreas Fischer (eds.), *Social Cohesion and its Limits* (in print, Austrian Academy of Sciences Press, Vienna 2021)

Gardella, O., *I campanili di Ravenna* (Ravenna, 1902)

Garipzanov, I., *The Symbolic Language of Authority in the Carolingian World (c. 751–877)* (Leiden, 2008)

Garrison, M., 'The Franks as the New Israel? Education for an identity from Pippin to Charlemagne', in Y. Hen and M. Innes (ed.), *The Uses of the Past in the Early Middle Ages* (Cambridge, 2000), pp. 141–61

Gasparri, S., 'Il ducato longobardo di Spoleto. Istituzioni, poteri, gruppi dominanti', *Il ducato di Spoleto. Atti del 9 Congresso internazionale di studi sull'alto medioevo, Spoleto, 27 settembre – 2 ottobre 1982* (Spoleto, 1983), pp. 77–122

'Strutture militari e legami di dipendenza in Italia in età longobarda e carolingia', *Rivista storica italiana* 98 (1986), 664–726

'Pavia longobarda', in E. Cau (ed.), *Storia di Pavia, II (L'alto medioevo)* (Pavia, 1987), pp. 19–68

'Langobardi e città', *Società e Storia*, 46 (1989), pp. 973–79

'Il ducato e il principato di Benevento', in G. Galasso and R. Romeo (eds.), *Storia del Mezzogiorno*, vol. II, *Il Medioevo* (Naples, 1989), pp. 83–146

'Venezia fra i secoli VIII e IX. Una riflessione sulle fonti', in G. Ortalli and G. Scarabello (eds.), *Studi Veneti offerti a Gaetano Cozzi* (Venedig, 1992), pp. 3–18

'La frontiera in Italia (sec. V–VIII). Osservazioni su un tema controverso', in G. P. Brogiolo (ed.), *Città, castelli, campagne nei territori di frontiera (secoli VI–VII)* (Mantua, 1995), pp. 9–19

'Venezia fra l'Italia bizantina e il regno italico: la civitas e l'assemblea', in S. Gasparri, G. Levi and P. Moro (eds.), *Venezia. Itinerari per la storia della città* (Bologna, 1997), pp. 61–82

'Les relations de fidélité dans le royaume d'Italie au IX siècle', in R. Le Jan (ed.), *La royauté et les élites dans l'Europe carolingienne: début IXe siècle aux environs de 920* (Villeneuve-d'Ascq, 1998), pp. 145–57

'I centri di potere dell' Italia longobarda e bizantina: il regno, l'esarcato, i ducati', in G. P. Brogiolo and C. Bertelli (eds.), *Il futuro dei Longobardi. L'Italia e la costruzione dell'Europa di Carlo Magno* (Milan, 2000), pp. 229–32

'Kingship rituals and ideology in Lombard Italy', in J. Nelson and F. Theuws (eds.), *Rituals of Power: From Late Antiquity to the Early Middle Ages* (Leiden, 2000), pp. 95–114

'Il Passaggio dai Longobardi ai Carolingi', in C. Bertelli and G. P. Brogiolo (eds.), *Il Futuro dei Longobardi. L'Italia e la Costruzione dell'Europa di Carlo Magno. Saggi* (Milan, 2000), pp. 25–43

'Istituzioni e poteri nel territorio friulano in età longobarda e carolingia', in *Paolo Diacono e il Friuli altomedievale (secc. VI – X)* 1, Atti del XIV Congresso internazionale di studi sull'alto Medioevo (Spoleto, 2001), pp. 105–128

'The aristocracy' in La Rocca (ed.), *Italy in the Early Middle Ages*, pp. 59–84

'"Nobiles et credentes omines liberi arimanni'. Linguaggio sociale e tradizioni longobarde nel regno italico', *Bullettino dell'Istituto Italiano per il Medio Evo e Archivio Muratoriano* 105 (2003), 25–51

'Il regno dei Longobardi in Italia. Struttura e funzionamento di uno stato altomedievale', in Gasparri (ed.), *Il regno dei Longobardi in Italia*, pp. 1–92

'The fall of the Lombard Kingdom: facts, memory and propaganda', in Gasparri (ed.), *774. Ipotesi su una transizione*, pp. 41–65

'Italien in der Karolingerzeit', in Pohl and Wieser (eds.), *Der frühmittelalterliche Staat*, pp. 63–71

Italia longobarda. Il regno, i Franchi, il papato, Quadrante Laterza 179 (Rome and Bari, 2012)

'The formation of an early medieval community: Venice between provincial and urban identity', in V. West-Harling (ed.), *Three Empires, Three Cities: Identity, Material Culture and Legitimacy in Venice, Ravenna and Rome, 750–1000* (Turnhout, 2015), pp. 35–50

'L'identità dell'Italia nordorientale e Venezia. Dalla tarda età longobarda al regno di Berengario', in La Rocca and Majocchi (eds.), *Urban Identities in Northern Italy*, pp. 57–78

'The first dukes and the origins of Venice', in S. Gelichi and S. Gasparri, *Venice and Its Neighbors from the 8th to 11th Century*, The Medieval Mediterranean 111 (Leiden, 2017)

(ed.), *Il regno dei Longobardi in Italia. Archeologia, società e istituzioni* (Spoleto, 2004)

(ed.), *774: ipotesi su una transizione; atti del seminario di Poggibonsi. 16–18 febbraio 2006*, Seminari internazionali del Centro interuniversitario per la storia e l'archeologia dell'alto medioevo 1 (Turnhout, 2008)

Gasparri, S. and C. La Rocca, *Tempi barbarici. L'Europa occidentale tra antichità e medioevo (300–900)* (Rome, 2012)

Gavinelli, S., 'Per un'enciclopedia carolingia (codice Bernese 363)', *Italia med-ioevale e umanistica* 26 (1983), 1–25

'Una raccolta canonica a Livorno restituita al sec. IX', *Rivista di storia della Chiesa in Italia*, 60 (2006), 375–89

'Modelli librari e formazione ideologica centralizzata', in *Carlo Magno e le Alpi: atti del XVIII Congresso internazionale di studi sull'alto medioevo, Susa, 19–20 ottobre 2006, Novalesa, 21 ottobre 2006* (Spoleto, 2007), pp. 105–40

'Testi agiografici e collezioni canoniche in età carolingia attraverso codici dell'Ambrosiana', in M. Ferrari and M. Navoni (eds.), *Nuove ricerche su codici in scrittura latina dell'Ambrosiana*, Bibliotheca erudite 31 (Milano, 2007), pp. 53–78

'Tradizioni testuali carolingie fra Brescia, Vercelli e San Gallo: il *De civitate Dei* di s. Agostino', in A. Manfredi (ed.), *L'antiche e le moderne carte: studi in memoria di Giuseppe Billanovich*, Medioevo e Umanesimo 112 (Roma, 2007), pp. 263–84

'Transiti di manoscritti attraverso le Alpi occidentali in epoca carolingia: gli episcopati di Ivrea e Vercelli', in Scalon and Pani (eds.), *Le Alpi porta d'Europa*, pp. 381–408

'Dungal e l'organizzazione scolastica del regnum italicum in età carolingia', in D. G. Mantovani (ed.), *Almum Studium Papiense. Storia dell'Università di Pavia*, I, Dalle origini all'età spagnola (Milan, 2012), pp. 115–28

'Il vescovo Giuseppe di Ivrea nel circuito culturale carolingio', in Chiesa (ed.), *Paolino d'Aquileia*, pp. 167–96

Geary, P., *Furta Sacra. Thefts of Relics in the Central Middle Ages* (Princeton, 1978)

'Humiliation of Saints', in S. Wilson (ed.), *Saints and Their Cults: Studies in Religious Sociology, Folklore and History* (Cambridge, 1983), pp. 123–40

Furta sacra: Thefts of Relics in the Central Middle Ages (rev. ed.) (Princeton, NJ, 1990)

Gelichi, S., 'La storia di una nuova città attraverso l'archeologia: Venezia nell'alto medioevo', in V. West-Harling (ed.), *Three Empires, Three Cities: Identity, Material Culture and Legitimacy in Venice, Ravenna and Rome, 750–1000* (Turnhout, 2015), pp. 51–98

Genest, J.-F., 'Inventaire de la bibliothèque de Bobbio', in O. Guyotjeannin and E. Poulle (eds.), *Autour de Gerbert d'Aurillac: le pape de l'an mil* (Paris, 1996), pp. 251–62

Ghignoli, A., 'Su due famosi documenti pisani del secolo VIII', *Bullettino dell'Istituto Storico Italiano per il Medio Evo* 106 (2004), 1–69

Gibson, S. and B. Ward-Perkins, 'The surviving remains of the Leonine Wall', *Papers of the British School at Rome*, 47 (1979), 30–57

Gillis, M. B., 'Noble and Saxon: the Meaning of Gottschalk of Orbais' Ethnicity at the Synod of Mainz, 829', in R. Corradini, M. Gillis, R. McKitterick and I. van Renswoude (eds.), *Ego Trouble. Authors and Their Identities in the Early Middle Ages*, Forschungen zur Geschichte des Mittelalters 15 (Vienna, 2010), pp. 197–210

Heresy and Dissent in the Carolingian Empire: The Case of Gottschalk of Orbais (Oxford, 2017)

Gioanni, S., 'Nouvelles hypothèses sur la collection des oeuvres d'Ennode', in F. Gasti (ed.), *Atti della Terza Giornata Ennodiana* (Pisa, 2006), pp. 59–76

Giovini, M., '"Sophia" come "Daphnis", "Io" e "Alcimus": risonanze classiche in alcuni epicedi "al femminile" di Paolo Diacono', *Maia* 49 (1997), 109–18

'"Quel ramo del lago di Como" visto da Paolo Diacono', *Maia* 49 (1997), 119–28

'Gli *inculta poemata* di Paolo Diacono: Prudenzio e Virgilio in una dichiarazione di poetica del dissidio', *Maia* 52 (2000), 85–98

Glansdorff, S., 'L'évêque de Metz et archichapelain Drogon (801/802–855), *Revue belge de philologie et d'histoire* 81/4 (2003), 945–1014.

Gnocchi, C., 'Giovanni X', *Dizionario Biografico degli Italiani* 55 (Rome, 2001), cols. 568–71

Godman, P., *Poetry of the Carolingian Renaissance* (London, 1985)

Poets and Emperors. Frankish Politics and Carolingian Poetry (Oxford, 1987)

Goffart, W., 'Paul the Deacon's *Gesta episcoporum Mettensium* and the role of Metz in the Carolingian realm', *Traditio* 42 (1986), 59–93

Goldberg, E. J., *Struggle for Empire: Kingship and Conflict under Louis the German, 817–876* (Ithaca, 2006)

Golinelli, P., 'Passione e traslazione dei Santi Fermo e Rustico', in Brenzoni and Golinelli (eds.), *I Santi Fermo e Rustico*, pp. 13–23

Goodson, C., 'Material memory: rebuilding the Basilica of S. Cecilia in Trastevere, Rome', *Early Medieval Europe* 15 (2007), 2–34

The Rome of Pope Paschal I: Papal Power, Urban Renovation, Church Rebuilding and Relic Translation, 817–824 (Cambridge, 2010)

'Villamagna in the Middle Ages', in E. Fentress, C. Goodson and M. Maiuro (eds.), *Villa Magna: An Imperial Estate and Its Legacies: Excavations 2006–10* (Rome, 2016), pp. 410–19

'City-states in early medieval southern Italy', in Andreas Fischer and Walter Pohl (eds.), *Social Cohesion and its Limits*, Forschungen zur Geschichtes des Mittelalters (Vienna, forthcoming)

'Basilicas and centrally planned buildings,' in R. Ettlin (ed.), *The Cambridge Guide to the Architecture of Christianity: The Middle Ages*, (Cambridge, 2021) forthcoming

Goodson, C., A. Lester and C. Symes, 'Introduction', in C. Goodson, A. Lester and C. Symes (eds.), *Cities, Texts and Social Networks, 400–1500: Experiences and Perceptions of Medieval Urban Space* (Farnham/Burlington, 2010), pp. 1–17

Gorman, P. and E. Krotz (eds.), *Grammatical Works Attributed to Peter of Pisa, Charlemagne's Tutor* (Hildesheim, 2014)

Gorman, M. M., 'Peter of Pisa and the *Quaestiunculae* copied for Charlemagne in Brussels II 2572', *Revue bénédictine* 110 (2000), 238–50

Gorman, M., 'The oldest lists of Latin books', *Scriptorium* 58 (2004), 48–63

'Codici manoscritti della Badia amiatina nel secolo XI', in M. Marrocchi and C. Prezzolini (eds.), *La Tuscia nell'alto e pieno medioevo. In memoria di Wilhelm Kurze*, Millennio medievale 68 (Firenze, 2007), pp. 15–102

'Introduction', in P. Gorman and E. Krutz (eds.), *Grammatical works attributed to Peter of Pisa, Charlemagne's tutor* (Hildesheim, 2014)

Granier, T., 'Napolitains et Lombards aux VIIIe–XIe siècles. De la guerre des peuples à la guerre des saints en Italie du Sud', *Mélanges de l'Ecole française de Rome. Moyen-Age, Temps modernes*, 108 (1996), pp. 403–50

'À rebours des laudes civitatum: les Versus Romae et le discours sur la ville dans l'Italie du haut Moyen Âge', in C. Carozzi and H. Taviani-Carozzi (eds.), *Le médiéviste devant ses sources. Questions et méthodes* (Aix-en-Provence, 2004), pp. 131–54

'La captivité de l'empereur Louis II à Bénévent (13 août – 17 septembre 871) dans les sources des IXe–Xe siècles: l'écriture de l'histoire, de la fausse nouvelle au récit exemplaire', in C. Carozzi and H. Taviani-Carozzi (eds.), *Faire l'événement au Moyen Âge* (Aix-en-Provence, 2007), pp. 13–39

'La renovatio du modele rhetorique antique dans les éloges urbains de l'Italie du haut Moyen Âge', in M. Malard and M. Sot (ed.), *Au Moyen Âge, entre Tradition et Innovation. Actes du 131e Congres des Sociétés Historiques et Scientifiques, Grenoble, 2006* (Paris, 2009), pp. 35–56

Gravel, M., *Distances, rencontres, communications. Réaliser l'empire sous Charlemagne et Louis le Pieux* (Turnhout, 2012)

Grierson, P. and L. Travaini, *Medieval European Coinage: With a Catalogue of the Coins in the Fitzwilliam Museum, Cambridge. 14, Italy (III) South Italy, Sicily, Sardinia* (Cambridge, 1998)

Grondeux, A., 'Introduction', *Les dossiers d'Histoire Épistémologie Langage* 10 (2016), 3–8, https://hal.archives-ouvertes.fr/hal-01419929

Groth, S., 'How to become an emperor? John VIII and the role of the papacy in the 9th century', in J. Clauss, T. Gebhardt and C. Scholl (eds.), *Transcultural Approaches to the Concept of Imperial Rule in the Middle Ages* (Frankfurt am Main, 2017), pp. 117–38

Grumel, V., *Les regestes des actes du patriarcat de Constantinople*, I/2 (Paris, 1936)

Guglielmetti, R., 'Un'esegesi incontenibile', in Pagani and Santi (eds.), *Il secolo di Carlo Magno*, pp. 177–200

Guglielmotti, P., 'Ageltrude: dal ducato di Spoleto al cuore del regno italico', *Reti Medievali Rivista*, 13/2 (2012), 163–87

Guillot, O., 'Une *Ordinatio* Méconnue. Le Capitulaire de 823–825', in P. Godman and R. Collins (eds.), *Charlemagne's Heir. New Perspectives on the Reign of Louis the Pious (814–840)* (Oxford, 1990), pp. 455–86

Guillou, A., *Régionalisme et indépendance dans l'Empire byzantin au VIIe siècle. L'exemple de l'Exarchat et de la Pentapole d'Italie* (Rome, 1969)

Gullotta, G., *Gli antichi cataloghi e i codici della abbazia di Nonantola*, Studi e Testi 182 (Vatican City, 1955)

Guyotjeannin, O., 'Les pouvoirs publics de l'évêque de Parme au miroir des diplômes royaux et impériaux (fin IXe – début XIe siècle), in D. Barthélemy and J.-M. Martin, *Liber largitorius. Études d'Histoire Médiévale offertes à Pierre Toubert par ses élèves* (Geneva, 2003), pp. 15–34

Hack, A. T., *Das Empfangszeremoniell bei mittelalterlichen Papst-Kaiser-Treffen* (Cologne, 1999)

Codex Carolinus: Päpstliche Epistolographie im 8. Jahrhundert I (Stuttgart, 2006)

Haller, J., *Das Papsttum. Idee und Wirklichkeit: Der Aufbau*, vol. 2/1 (Reinbeck 1965 [1937])

Hammer, C. I., *From* Ducatus *to* Regnum. *Ruling Bavaria under the Merovingians and the Early Carolingians*, Haut Moyen Âge 2 (Turnhout, 2007)
'Christmas Day 800: Charles the Younger, Alcuin and the Frankish royal succession', *English Historical Review* 524 (2012), 1–23

Hannig, J., '*Pauperiores vassi de infra palatio?* Zur Entstehung der karolingischen Königsbotenorganisation', *Mitteilungen des Instituts für österreichische Geschichtsforschung* 91 (1983), 309–74

Hartmann, L. M., *Untersuchungen zur Geschichte der byzantinischen Verwaltung in Italien (540–750)* (Leipzig 1889)
Zur Wirtschaftsgeschichte Italiens im frühen Mittelalter. Analekten (Gotha, 1904)
Geschichte Italiens im Mittelalter, vol. III (1911, repr. Hildesheim, 1969)

Hartmann, W., *Die Synoden der Karolingerzeit im Frankenreich und in Italien* (Paderborn, 1989)

Haussig, H.-W., 'L'arcivescovo di Ravenna, il papa ed il re dei Franchi', *Corso di Cultura sull'Arte Ravennate e Bizantina*, 19 (1972), 187–218

Head, T., 'Discontinuity and discovery in the cult of saints: Apulia from Late Antiquity to the High Middle Ages', *Hagiographica: rivista di agiografia e biografia* 6 (1999), 171–211

Heene, K., 'Merovingian and Carolingian hagiography. Continuity or change in public and aims?', *Analecta Bollandiana* 107 (1989), 415–28

Hees, H., *Studien zur Geschichte Kaiser Ludwigs II* (Regensburg, 1973)

Heidecker, K. J., *The Divorce of Lothar II: Christian marriage and Political Power in the Carolingian World*, Conjunctions of Religion and Power in the Medieval Past (Ithaca, 2010).

Heil, M. W., 'Clerics, courts, and legal culture in Early Medieval Italy, c. 650 – c. 900', unpublished PhD thesis, Columbia University, 2013

Heinzelmann, M., *Translationsberichte und andere Quellen des Reliquienkultes*, Typologie des Sources du Moyen Âge Occidental 33 (Turnhout, 1979)

Heldmann, K. *Das Kaisertum Karls des Großen* (Weimar, 1928)

Helvétius, A.-M., 'Hagiographie et formation politique des aristocrates dans le monde franc (VIIe–VIIIe siècles)', in Bozóki (éd.), *Hagiographie, idéologie et politique*, pp. 59–79

Hen, Y., 'The annals of Metz and the Merovingian past', in Hen and Innes (eds.), *The Uses of the Past*, pp. 175–90
'The romanization of the Frankish liturgy: ideal, reality and the rhetoric of reform', in C. Bolgia, R. McKitterick and J. Osborne (eds.), *Rome across Time and Space. Cultural Transmission and the Exchange of Ideas* (Cambridge, 2011), pp. 111–24.

Hen, Y. and M. Innes (eds.), *The Uses of the Past in the Early Middle Ages* (Cambridge, 2000)

Henning, J., 'Early European towns – the development of the economy in the Frankish realm between dynamism and deceleration AD 500–1100', in J. Henning (ed.), *Post-Roman Towns, Trade and Settlement in Europe and Byzantium*, vol. 1, *The Heirs of the Roman West* (Berlin, 2007), pp. 3–40

Henning, J. (ed.), *Post-Roman Towns, Trade and Settlement in Europe and Byzantium*, vol. 1, *The Heirs of the Roman West* (Berlin, 2007)

Herbers, K., 'Der Konflikt Papst Nikolaus I. mit Erzbischof Johannes VII. von Ravenna (861)', in P.-J. Heinig (ed.), *Diplomatische und chronologische*

Studien aus der Arbeit an den Regesta Imperii (Cologne and Vienna, 1991), pp. 51–66

'Reliques romaines au IXe siècle : renforcements des liaisons avec la papauté?', in Bozóki (ed.), *Hagiographie, idéologie et politique*, pp. 111–26

'Der Konflikt Papst Nikolaus I. mit Erzbischof Johannes VII. von Ravenna, 860–861 (1991)', in K. Herbers, *Pilger, Päpste, Heilige: Ausgewählte Aufsätze zur europäischen Geschcichte des Mittelalters* (Tübingin, 2011), pp. 281–94.

Papst Leo IV. und das Papsttum in der Mitte des 9. Jahrhunderts. Möglichkeiten und Grenzen päpstlicher Herrschaft in der späten Karolingerzeit (Stuttgart, 2017)

Herrin, J., *Ravenna: Capital of Empire, Crucible of Europe* (London, 2020)

Herrin, J. and J. Nelson (eds.), *Ravenna: Its Role in Early Medieval Change and Exchange* (London, 2016)

Heydemann, G., 'People(s) of God? Biblical exegesis and the language of community in late antique and early medieval Europe', in E. Hovden, Ch. Lutter and W. Pohl (eds.), *Meanings of Community across Medieval Eurasia. Comparative Approaches* (Leiden and Boston, 2016), pp. 27–60

Hlawitschka, E., *Franken, Alemannen, Bayern und Burgunder in Oberitalien (774–962): Zum Verständnis der Fränkischen Königsherrschaft in Italien*, Forschungen zur Oberrheinische Landesgeschichte 8 (Freiburg im Breisgau, 1960)

'Die Widonen im Dukat von Spoleto (1983)', in *Quellen un Forschungen aus italienischen Archiven un Bibliotheken*, 63 (1983), 20–92

'Ratold, Bischof von Verona und Begründer von Radolfzell', *Hegau* 54/55 (1997/1998), 5–32

Hoffmann, F., W. Erdmann, A. Czarnetzki and R. Rottländer, 'Das Grab des Bischofs Egino von Verona in St. Peter und Paul zu Reichenau-Niederzell', in H. Maurer (ed.), *Die Abtei Reichenau* (Sigmaringen, 1974), pp. 545–75

Hofmeister, A., 'Markgrafen und Markgrafschaften im Italischen Königreich in der Zeit von Karl dem Großen bis auf Otto den Großen (774–962)', *Mitteilungen des Instituts für österreichische Geschichtsforschung* 7 (1907), 215–435

Holder, A., *Die Handschriften der Badischen Landesbibliothek in Karlsruhe. Neudruck mit Bibliographischen Nachträgen*, vol. 5/1, *Die Reichenauer Handschriften* (Wiesbaden, 1970)

Holtz, L., 'Tradition et diffusion de l'œuvre grammaticale de Pompée, commentateur de Donat', *Revue de philologie* 45 (1971), 48–83

'Le Parisinus Latinus 7530, synthèse cassinienne des arts libéraux', *Studi Medievali* 16 (1975), 97–152.

Prolégomènes à une édition critique du commentaire de Pompée, grammairien africain', in I. Taifakos (ed.), *The Origins of European Scholarship. The Cyprus Millennium International Conference* (Stuttgart, 2005), pp. 109–19

Horden, P. and N. Purcell, *The Corrupting Sea: A Study of Mediterranean History* (Oxford, 2000)

Hubert, É., 'L'organizzazione territoriale e l'urbanizzazione', in A. Vauchez (ed.), *Roma medievale* (Rome and Bari, 2001), pp. 160–86

Hudson, P. J., 'I resti precedenti la costruzione della chiesa inferiore benedettina di San Fermo Maggiore', in Brenzoni and Golinelli (eds.), *I Santi Fermo e Rustico*, pp. 305–7

Huschner, W., *Transalpine Kommunikation im Mittelalter: Diplomatische, kulturelle und politische Wechselwirkungen zwischen Italien und dem nordalpinen Reich (9.– 11. Jahrhundert)*, 3 vols. (Hannover, 2003)
'L'idea della cancelleria imperiale nella ricerca diplomatica. Diplomi ottoniani per destinatari in Toscana', in M. Marrocchi and C. Prezzolini, *La Tuscia nell'Alto e Pieno Medioevo. Fonti e temi storiografici territoriali e generali in memoria di Wilhelm Kurze* (Florence, 2007), pp. 183–97
Hyde, J. K., 'Medieval descriptions of cities', *Bulletin of the John Rylands Library* 48 (1966), 308–40
Inguanez, M., *Catalogi codicum Casinensium antiqui (saec. VIII–XV)*, Miscellanea cassinese 21 (Montecassino, 1941)
Innes, M., 'Charlemagne's government', in J. Story (ed.), *Charlemagne. Empire and Society* (Manchester, 2005), pp. 71–89
'"Immune from heresy". Defining the Boundaries of Carolingian Christianity', in P. Fouracre and D. Ganz (eds.), *Frankland. The Franks and the World of the Early Middle Ages. Essays in Honour of Dame Jinty Nelson* (Manchester and New York, 2008), pp. 101–25
Irvine, M., *The Making of Textual Culture* (Cambridge, 1994)
Jarnut, J., 'La funzione centrale della città nel regno longobardo', *Società e Storia*, 46 (1989), 967–71
'Ludwig der Fromme, Lothar I. und das Regnum Italiae', in P. Godman and R. Collins (eds.), *Charlemagne's Heir: New Perspectives on the Reign of Louis the Pious (814–840)* (Oxford, 1990), 349–62; reprinted in M. Becher et al. (eds.), *Jörg Jarnut, Herrschaft und Ethnogenese im Frühmittelalter: gesammelte Aufsätze von Jörg Jarnut: Festgabe zum 60. Geburtstag* (Münster, 2002), pp. 341–54
Jasper, D., 'Die Papstgeschichte des Pseudo-Liudprand', *Deutsches Archiv für Erforschung des Mittelalters* 31 (1975), 17–107
Jezierski, W., L. Hermanson, H. J. Oming and T. Småberg (eds.), *Rituals, Performatives and Political Order in Northern Europe, c. 650–1350* (Turnhout, 2015)
Jong, M. B. de, *In Samuel's Image. Child Oblation in the Early Medieval West* (Leiden, New York and Cologne, 1996)
'Charlemagne's church', in J. Story (ed.), *Charlemagne. Empire and Society* (Manchester and New York, 2005), pp. 103–35
'Ecclesia and the early medieval polity', in S. Airlie, W. Pohl and H. Reimitz (eds.), *Staat im Frühen Mittelalter* (Vienna, 2006), pp. 113–26
Jong, M. de, *The Penitential State. Authority and Atonement in the Age of Louis the Pious, 814–840* (Cambridge, 2009)
Jong, M. de and van Renswoude, I. (eds.), 'Carolingian cultures of dialogue, debate and disputation', *Early Medieval Europe* 25.1 (2017).
Jullien, M.-H., 'Alcuin et l'Italie', *Annales de Bretagne et des Pays de l'Ouest* 111 (2004), 393–406
Jussen, B., *Spiritual Kinship as Social Practice. Godparenthood and Adoption in the Early Middle Ages* (Newark and London, 2000)
Die Franken. Geschichte – Gesellschaft – Kultur (Munich, 2014)
Kamptner, M., '"Scripsi per prosa" (Stefanus, Rhythmus de Synodo Ticinensi, MGH Poet. IV/2, pp. 728–731)', in F. Stella (ed.), *Poesia dell'alto Medioevo*

europeo: manoscritti, lingua e musica dei ritmi latini (Florence, 2000), pp. 187–195.

Kantor, M. (ed.), *Medieval Slavic Lives of Saints and Princes* (Ann Arbor, 1983)

Kasten, B., *Adalhard von Corbie. Die Biographie eines karolingischen Politikers und Klostervorstehers* (Düsseldorf, 1986)

Königssöhne und Königsherrschaft. Untersuchungen zur Teilhabe am Reich in der Merowinger- und Karolingerzeit, MGH Schriften, 44 (Hanover, 1997)

'Aspekte des Lehnswesens in Einhards Briefe', in H. Schefers (ed.), *Einhard. Studien zum Leben und Werk. Dem Gedenken an Helmut Beumann gewidmet* (Darmstadt, 1997), pp. 247–67

'Das Lehnswesen – Fakt oder Fiktion?', in Pohl and Wieser (eds.), *Der frühmittelalterliche Staat*, pp. 331–53

Keefe, S. A., *Water and the World. Baptism and the Education of the Clergy in the Carolingian Empire*, 2 vols. (Notre Dame, 2002)

Keller, H., 'Zur Struktur der Königsherrschaft im karolingischen und nachkarolingischen Italien. Der "consiliarius regis" in den italienischen Königsdiplomen des 9. und 10. Jahrhunderts', *Quellen und Forschungen aus italienischen Archiven und Bibliotheken* 47 (1967), 123–223.

'Der Gerichtsort in oberitalienischen und toskanischen Städten: Untersuchungen zur Stellung der Stadt im Herrschaftssystem des Regnum Italicum vom 9. bis 11. Jahrhundert' in *Quellen und Forschungen aus italienischen Archiven und Bibliotheken* 49 (1969), 1–72

'Review of Delogu, P., 'L'istituzione comitale nell'Italia carolingia', *Bullettino dell'Istituto storico italiano per il Medio Evo e Archivio Muratoriano*, 79 (1968), 53–114', *Quellen und Forschungen aus italienischen Archiven und Bibliotheken* 49 (1969), 554–6

'La marca di Tuscia fino all'anno Mille', in *Lucca e la Tuscia nell'alto medioevo*, pp. 117–40

'I Placiti nella storiografia degli ultimi cento anni', in *Fonti medioevali e problemática storiografica. Atti del Congresso Internazionale tenuto in occasione del 90° Anniversario della fondazione dell'Istituto Storico Italiano 1883–1973*, vol. I (Rome 1976), pp. 41–68.

Adelsherrschaft und städtische Gesellschaft in Oberitalien. 9. bis 12. Jahrhundert (Tübingen, 1979)

Kempf, C., 'Paul the Deacon's *Liber de episcopis Mettensibus* and the Role of Metz in the Carolingian Realm', *Journal of Medieval History* 30 (2004), 279–99

Kennedy, G., *The Art of Rhetoric in the Roman World* (Princeton, 1972)

Kerneis, S., 'Les premiers vassaux', in É. Bournazel and J.-P. Poly (eds.), *Les féodalités* (Paris, 1998), pp. 18–46

Kershaw, P., 'Eberhard of Friuli, a Carolingian lay intellectual', in P. Wormald and J. L. Nelson (eds.), *Lay Intellectuals in the Carolingian World* (Cambridge, 2007), pp. 77–105

Kienast, W., *Die fränkische Vasallität. Von den Hausmeiern bis zu Ludwig dem Kind und Karl dem Einfältigen*, ed. P. Herde (Frankfurt am Main, 1990)

Kleinschmidt, H., 'Die Titulaturen englischer Könige im 10. und 11. Jahrhundert', in H. Wolfram and A. Scharer (eds.), *Intitulatio III. Lateinische Herrschertitel und Herrschertitulaturen vom 7. bis 13. Jahrhundert*,

Mitteilungen des Instituts für österreichische Geschichtsforschung Ergänzungsband 29 (Vienna, Cologne and Graz, 1988), pp. 75–129

Kloft, M. Th., 'Hrabanus Maurus, die "Tituli" und die Altarweihen', in Ph. Depreux, S. Lebecq, M. J.-L. Perrin and O. Szerwiniak (eds.), *Raban Maur et Son Temps*, Haut Moyen Âge 9 (Turnhout, 2010), pp. 367–87

Kohl, T., S. Patzold and B. Zeller (eds.), *Kleine Welten: Ländliche Gesellschaften im Karolingerreich* (Sigmaringen, 2017)

Koziol, R., *Begging Pardon and Favor. Ritual and Political Order in Early Medieval France* (Ithaca, 1992)

'The dangers of polemic: is ritual still an interesting topic of historical study', *Early Medieval Europe* 11/4 (2002), 367–88

'Is Robert I in Hell?', *Early Medieval Europe* 14/3 (2006), 233–67

The Politics of Memory and Identity in Carolingian Royal Diplomas. The West Frankish Kingdom (840–987) (Turnhout, 2012).

Krahwinkler, H., *Friaul im Frühmittelalter: Geschichte einer Region vom Ende des fünften bis zum Ende des zehnten Jahrhunderts*, Veröffentlichungen des Instituts für Österreichische Geschichtsforschung, 30 (Vienna, Cologne and Weimar, 1992)

... in loco qui dicitur Riziano ...: Zbor v Rižani pri Kopru leta 804 = Die Versammlung in Rižana/Risano bei Koper/Capodistria im Jahre 804, Knjižnica Annales 40 (Koper, 2004)

Kramer, R. 'Great expectations: imperial ideologies and ecclesiastical reforms from Charlemagne to Louis the Pious (813–822)', unpublished PhD Thesis, Free University of Berlin, 2014

Kreutz, B. M., *Before the Normans. Southern Italy in the Ninth and Tenth Centuries* (Philadelphia, 1991)

Kuhn, T., *The Structure of Scientific Revolutions* (Chicago, 1962)

Kurdziel, É., *Chanoines et institutions canoniales dans les villes du royaume d'Italie du milieu du IXe au milieu du XIe siècle*, unpublished thesis, University of Nanterre (2015)

Kurze, W., 'La Toscana come parte del regno longobardo', in W. Kurze, *Scritti di storia toscana. Assetti territoriali, diocesi, monasteri dai Longobardi all'età comunale* (Pistoia, 2008), pp. 13–61

La Rocca, C., 'Plus ça change, plus c'est la même chose: transformazioni della città altomedievale in Italia settentrionale', *Società e Storia*, 45 (1989), 721–28

'*Castrum vel potius civitas*. Modelli di declino urbano in Italia settentrionale durante l'alto medioevo', in R. Francovich and G. Noyé (eds.), *La Storia dell'Alto Medioevo italiano (VI–X secolo) alla luce dell'archeologia. Atti del Convegno Internazionale (Siena 1992)* (Florence, 1994), pp. 545–54

Pacifico di Verona. Il Passato Carolingio nella Costruzione della Memoria Urbana, Nuovi Studi Storici 31 (Roma, 1995)

La Rocca, C. (ed.), *Italy in the Early Middle Ages* (Oxford, 2002)

'Public buildings and urban change in northern Italy in the early medieval period', in J. Rich (ed.), *The City in Late Antiquity* (London, 2002), pp. 161–80

'Residenze urbane ed élites urbane tra VIII e X secolo in Italia settentrionale', in A. Augenti (ed.), *Le città italiane tra la tarda antichità e l'alto Medioevo: atti del Convegno (Ravenna, 26–28 febbraio 2004)* (Florence, 2006), pp. 255–65

'Monachesimo femminile e poteri delle regine tra VIII e IX secolo in Italia settentrionale', in G. Spinelli (ed.), *Il monachesimo italiano dall'età Longobarda all'età Ottoniana (secoli VIII–X). Atti del VII convegno di studi storici sull'Italia Benedettina. Nonantola (Modena), 10–13 Settembre 2003)*, Italia Benedettina 27 (Cesena, 2006), pp. 119–43

La Rocca, C. and P. Majocchi, *Urban Identities in Northern Italy, 800–1100 ca.* (Turnhout, 2015)

La Rocca, C. and L. Provero, 'The dead and their gifts. the will of Eberhard, Count of Friuli, and his wife Gisla, daughter of Louis the Pious', in F. Theuws and J. L. Nelson (eds.), *Rituals of Power. From Late Antiquity to the Early Middle Ages* (Leiden, 2000), pp. 225–80

La Rocca, C. and F. Veronese, *The Culture of Unanimity in Carolingian Councils*, in S. Ferente, L. Kunčević and M. Pattenden (eds.), *Cultures of Voting in Pre-Modern Europe* (London and New York 2018), pp. 39–57

Lazard, S., 'De l'origine des hellenismes d'Agnello,' *Revue de Linguistique Romaine* 40 (1976), 255–98

Lazzari, T., 'I "de Ermengarda". Una famiglia nobiliare a Bologna (secc. IX–XII)', *Studi medievali*, ser. III, 32 (1991), pp. 597–657

Comitato senza città: Bologna e l'aristocrazia del territorio: secoli IX–XI (Turin, 1998)

'Una mamma carolingia e una moglie supponide: percorsi femminili di legitti-mazione e potere nel regno italico, in G. Isabella (ed.), *'C'era una volta un re…'. Aspetti e momenti della regalità* (Bologna, 2005), pp. 41–57

'Dotari e beni fiscali', *Reti Medievali Rivista* 13/2 (2012), 123–39

'Città e territori: l'articolazione delle circoscrizioni pubbliche nell'Italia padana (secoli IX–XI)', in La Rocca and Majocchi (eds.), *Urban Identities in Northern Italy*, pp. 339–56

'Tra Ravenna e Regno: collaborazione e conflitti fra aristocrazie diverse', in *Rivaliser, coopérer: vivre en compétition dans les sociétés du haut Moyen Âge* (forthcoming)

Le Jan, R., 'Satellites et bandes armées dans le monde franc (VIIe–Xe siècles)', in *Actes des congrès de la Société des historiens médiévistes de l'enseignement supérieur public. 18e congrès* (Montpellier, 1987), pp. 97–105

'Reichenau and its *Amici Viventes*: competition and cooperation?', in R. Meens, D. van Espelo, B. van den Hoven van Genderen, J. Raijmakers, I. van Renswoude and C. van Rhijn (eds.), *Religious Franks. Religion and Power in the Frankish kingdom: Studies in Honour of Mayke de Jong* (Manchester, 2016), pp. 262–78

Lebecq, S., 'Le testament d'Evrard et Gysèle de Cysoing. Présentation et traduc-tion', in S. Joye, Th. Lienard, L. Jégou and J. Schneider (eds.), *Splendor Reginae. Passions, genre et famille. Mélanges en l'honneur de Régine Le Jan*, Haut Moyen Âge 22 (Turnhout, 2015), pp. 59–68

Leicht, P. S., 'Dal Regnum Langobardorum al Regnum Italiae', *Rivista di Storia del Diritto Italiano* 3 (1930), 3–20, reprinted in P. S. Leicht, *Scritti vari di storia del diritto italiano*, I (Milan, 1943), pp. 221–35

'Il feudo in Italia nell'età carolingia', in *I problemi della civiltà carolingia, 26 marzo–1 aprile 1953*, Settimane 1 (Spoleto, 1954), pp. 71–107

Lendi, W., (ed.), *Untersuchungen zur frühalemannischen Annalistik. Die Murbacher Annalen mit Edition*, Scrinium Friburgense 1 (Freiburg in der Schweiz, 1971)

Levison, W., 'Die Papstgeschichte des Pseudo-Liudprand und der Codex Farnesianus des Liber Pontificalis', *Neues Archiv der Gesellschaft für altere deutsche Geschichtskunde* 36 (1911), 415–38

Licciardello, P., *Agiografia aretina altomedievale. Testi agiografici e contesti socio-culturali ad Arezzo tra VI e XI secolo* (Florence, 2005)

Licht, T., 'Additional note on the "Library catalogue of Charlemagne's court"', *The Journal of Medieval Latin*, 11 (2001), 210–2.

'Einharts *Libellus de psalmis*', *Revue bénédictine* 122 (2012), 217–31

Liebeschuetz, J. H. W. G., *Decline and Fall of the Roman City* (Oxford, 2001)

Lo Monaco, F., 'Aganone di Bergamo e la Lombardia lotaringia', *Archivio Storico Bergamasco* 1 (1981), 9–23

Loseby, S., 'Reflections on urban space: streets through time', *Reti Medievali Rivista*, 12 (2011), 3–24

'Lost cities. The end of the *Civitas*-system in Frankish Gaul', in S. Diefenbach and G. M. Müller (eds.), *Gallien in Spätantike und Frühmittelalter: Kulturgeschichte einer Region* (Berlin, 2013), pp. 223–52

Lowe, E. A., *Codices Latini antiquiores: A Palaeographical Guide to Latin Manuscripts Prior to the Ninth Century*, 12 vols. (Oxford, 1934–71)

Lozovsky, N., 'Intellectual culture and literary practices', in J. J. Arnold, M. Shane Bjornlie and K. Sessa (eds.), *A Companion to Ostrogothic Italy* (Leiden, 2016), pp. 316–49

Lucca e la Tuscia nell'alto medioevo. Atti del 5° Congresso internazionale di studi sull'alto medioevo (Lucca, 3–7 ottobre 1971) (Spoleto, 1973)

Ludwig, U., 'Bemerkungen zu den Mönchslisten von Monteverdi', in K. Schmid, (ed.), *Vita Walfredi und Kloster Monteverdi Toskanisches Mönchtum Zwischen Langobardischer und Fränkischer. Festschrift Gerd Tellenbach* (Tübingen, 1998), pp. 122–45

'Il Codice Memoriale e Liturgico di San Salvatore/Santa Giulia. Brescia e Reichenau', in G. Andenna (ed.), *Culto e Storia in Santa Giulia* (Brescia, 2001), pp. 103–19

'Das Gedenkbuch von San Salvatore in Brescia. Ein Memorialzeugnis aus dem Karolingischen Italien', in M. Borgolte, C.D. Fonseca and H. Houben (eds.), MKemoria: *Erinnern und Vergessen in der Kultur des Mittelalters/Memoria: Ricordare e dimenticare nella cultura del Medioevo*, Annali dell'Istituto Storico Italo-Germanico in Trento 15 (Bologna and Berlin, 2005), pp. 169–200

Luongo, G., 'Alla ricerca del sacro. Le traslazione di santi in epoca altomedieo-vale', in A. Ruggiero (ed.), *il ritorno di Paolino. 80° dalla traslazione a Nola. Atti, documenti, testimonianze letterarie* (Naples, 1990), pp. 17–39

Lynch, J. H., *Godparents and Kinship in Early Medieval Europe* (Princeton, 1986)

MacLean, S., *Kingship and Politics in the Late Ninth Century: Charles the Fat and the End of the Carolingian Empire* (Cambridge, 2003)

'"*After his death a great tribulation came to Italy...*". Dynastic politics and aristocratic factions after the death of Louis II, c. 870–c. 890', *Millennium-Jahrbuch*, 4 (2007), 239–60

'Legislation and politics in late Carolingian Italy: the Ravenna Constitutions', *Early Medieval Europe* 18/4 (2010), 394–416

'Palaces, itineraries and political order in the post-Carolingian kingdoms', in A. Rodríguez López and J. Hudson (eds.), *Diverging Paths?: The Shapes of Power and Institutions in Medieval Christendom and Islam* (Turnhout, 2014), pp. 291–320

Magiorami, L., *Frammenti di manoscritti conservati ad arezzo. Archivio di Stato (2.1-2.51)* (Spoleto, 2016)

Magnou-Nortier, E., 'Quoi de neuf sur l'origine de la vassalité', *Cheiron. Materiali e strumenti di aggiornamento storiografico* 37 (2002), 169–210

Majocchi, P., *Le spolture regie del regno italico (secoli VI–X), repertorio digitale* (Florence, 2007)

Majocchi, M., 'Sviluppo e affermazione di una capitale altomedievale: Pavia in età gota e longobarda', *Reti medievali Rivista* XI/2 (2010), 169–79

Malcovati, E., 'La tradizione del *Brutus* e il nuovo frammento cremonese', *Athenaeum* 36 (1956), 30–47

Malfatti, B., *Bernardo re d'Italia* (Florence, 1876)

Manacorda, F., *Ricerche sugli inizi della dominazione dei Carolingi in Italia* (Rome, 1968)

Manarini, E., *I due volti di potere. Una parentela atipica di potere nel regno d' Italia* (Milan, 2016)

Manaresi, C., 'Alle origini del potere dei Vescovi sul territorio esterno delle città', *Bullettino dell'Istituto storico italiano per il Medio Evo e Archivio Muratoriano* 58 (1944), 221–334

Mancassola, N., *L'azienda curtense tra Longobardia e Romani: rapporti di lavoro e patti colonici dall'età carolingia al Mille* (Bologna, 2008)

Marazzi, F., 'Le città nuove pontificie e l'insediamento laziale nel IX secolo', in R. Francovich and G. Noyé (eds.), *La storia dell'alto medioevo italiano (VI–X secolo) alla luce dell'archeologia* (Florence, 1994), pp. 251–77

I *'Patrimonia Sanctae Romanae Ecclesiae' nel Lazio (secoli IV–X). Struttura amministrativa e prassi gestionali* (Rome, 1998)

'The early medieval alternative: monasteries as centres of non city-based economic systems in Italy between eighth and ninth century AD', in C. Virlouvet and B. Marin (eds.), *Nourrir les cités de Meditérranée* (Aix-en-Provence, 2003), pp. 739–67

'Cadavera urbium, nuove capitali e Roma aeterna: L'identità urbana in Italia fra crisi, rinascita e propaganda (secoli III–V)', in J. U. Krause and C. Witschel (eds.), *Italia fra crisi, rinascita e propaganda (secoli III–V)* (Stuttgart, 2006), pp. 33–65

Marchi, G. P., 'Breve discorso storico sulla Biblioteca Capitolare di Verona', in S. Marchi (ed.), *I Manoscritti della Biblioteca Capitolare di Verona. Catalogo Descrittivo Redatto da Don Antonio Spagnolo* (Verona, 1996), pp. 9–26

Marchi, G. P., A. Orlandi and M. Brenzoni, *Il Culto di San Zeno nel Veronese* (Verona, 1972)

Marrocchi, M., *Monaci scritori. San Salvatore al monte Amiata tra Impero e Papato (secoli VIII–XIII)*, Reti Medievali E-Book 18 (Firenze, 2014)

Martin, J.-M., 'Éléments préféodaux dans les principautés de Bénévent et de Capoue (fin du VIIIe siècle – début du XIe siècle): modalités de privatisation du pouvoir', *Structures féodales et féodalisme dans l'Occident méditerranéen (Xe–XIIIe siècles). Bilan et perspectives de recherche* (Rome, 1980), pp. 553–86

'La longobardia meridionale', in Gasparri (ed.), *Il regno dei longobardi in Italia*, pp. 327–67

Martin, J.-M., et al. (eds.), *L'Héritage byzantin en Italie (VIIIe–XIIe siècle)*, I±IV, (Rome, 2011–2017)

Mastandrea, P., 'Classicismo e Cristianesimo nella poesia di Paolo Diacono', in P. Chiesa (ed.), *Paolo Diacono. Uno scrittore tra tradizione longobarda e rinnovamento carolingio* (Udine, 2000), pp. 293–311

Maurer, H., H. Schwarzmaier and Th. Zotz (eds.), *Schwaben und Italien im Hochmittelalter*, Vorträge und Forschungen 52 (Stuttgart, 2001)

Mazzuconi, D., 'La diffusione dell'*expositio missae "primum in ordine"* e l'*expositio orationis dominicae* cosidetta milanese', in *Ricerche storiche sulla chiesa ambrosiana* XI, Archivio Ambrosiano 45 (Milan, 1982), pp. 208–66

McCormick, M., 'Byzantium and the West, 700–900', in R. McKitterick (ed.), *New Cambridge Medieval History* II (Cambridge, 1995), pp. 349–80

'Introduction', in H. Pirenne (ed.), *Medieval Cities: Their Origins and the Revival of Trade* (Princeton, 2014), pp. ix–xxx

McKitterick, R., *The Frankish Church and the Carolingian Reforms, 789–895* (London, 1977)

'Political ideology in Carolingian historiography', in Hen and Innes (eds.), *The Uses of the Past*, pp. 162–74

History and Memory in the Carolingian World (Cambridge, 2004)

Charlemagne. The Formation of a European Identity (Oxford, 2008)

'The damnatio memoriae of Pope Constantine II (767–768)', in R. Balzaretti, J. Barrow and P. Skinner (eds.), *Italy and Early Medieval Europe: Papers for Chris Wickham* (Oxford, 2018), pp. 231–48

McKitterick, R. (ed.), *The Uses of Literacy in Early Medieval Europe* (Cambridge, 1990)

The New Cambridge Medieval History, vol. II, *ca. 700–ca. 900* (Cambridge, 1995)

Old Saint Peter's, Rome (Cambridge, 2013)

Meens, R., 'Politics, mirrors of princes and the Bible. Sins, kings and the well-being of the realm', *Early Medieval Europe* 7 (1998), 345–57

Meens, R, D. van Espelo, B. van den Hoven van Genderen, J. Raijmakers, I. van Renswoude and C. van Rhijn (eds.), *Religious Franks: Religion and Power in the Frankish Kingdoms: Studies in Honour of Mayke de Jong* (Manchester, 2016)

Meneghini, R. and R. Santangeli-Valenzani, *Roma nell'altomedioevo: Topografia e urbanistica della città dal V al X secolo* (Rome, 2004)

Menis, G. C., 'Cultura in Friuli durante l'età carolingia', *Aquileia e le Venezie nell'alto medioevo (Antichità altoadriatiche 32)* (Udine, 1988), pp. 15–42

Mériaux, Ch., 'La *Translatio Calixti Cisonium* (BHL 1525). Une Commande de Gisèle, Fille de Louis le Pieux, au Monastère de Saint-Amand?', in M. Goullet (ed.), *Parva pro Magnis Munera. Études de Littérature Tardo-antique et Médiévale Offertes à François Dolbeau par ses Élèves*, Instrumenta Patristica et Mediaevalia 51 (Turnhout, 2009), pp. 585–611

Mersiowsky, M., 'Towards a reappraisal of Carolingian charters', in K. Heidecker (ed.), *Charters and the Use of the Written Word in Medieval Society* (Turnhout, 2000), pp. 15–26

Die Urkunde in der Karolingerzeit. Originale, Urkundenpraxis und politische Kommunikation, MGH Schriften, 60/I–II, 2 vols (Wiesbaden, 2015)

Metcalfe, A., *The Muslims of Medieval Italy* (Edinburgh, 2009)

Metzger, M. D., 'The *legimus* subscription of Charles the Bald and the question of Byzantine influence', *Viator* (1972), 52–8

Miller, M., 'The development of the episcopal palace in Ravenna. 300–1300,' *Felix Ravenna*, 141–4 (1991–2), 145–73

Mitchell, J. 'Literacy displayed: the use of inscriptions at the monastery of San Vincenzo al Volturno in the early ninth century', in McKitterick (ed.), *The Uses of Literacy*, pp. 186–225

'L'arte nell'Italia longobarda e nell'Europa carolingia', in Berttelli and Brogiolo (eds.), *Il futuro dei Longobardi*, pp. 173–87

'Artistic patronage and cultural strategies in Lombard Italy', in Brogiolo, Gauthier and Christie (eds.), *Towns and Their Territories*, pp. 347–70

'Karl der Große, Rom und das Vermächtnis der Langobarden', in Stiegemann and Wemhoff (eds.), *Kunst und Kultur der Karolingerzeit*, pp. 95–108

Moeglin, J.-M., '"Performative turn", "communication politique" et rituels au Moyen Âge. À propos de deux ouvrages récents', *Le Moyen Âge* 113/2 (2007), 393–406

Molinari, A., 'Siti rurali e poteri signorili nel Lazio (secoli X–XIII)', *Archeologia Medievale* 37 (2010), 129–42

Moore, R. I., 'A global Middle Ages?', in J. Belich, J. Darwin, M. Frenz and C. Wickham (eds.), *The Prospect of Global History* (Oxford, 2016), pp. 80–92.

Mordek, H., *Biblioteca capitularia regum Francorum manuscripta. Überlieferung und Traditionszusammenhang der fränkischen Herrschererlasse*, MGH Hilfsmittel 15 (Munich, 1995)

'Die Anfänge der fränkischen Gesetzgebung für Italien', *Quellen und Forschungen aus italienischen Archiven und Bibliotheken* 85 (2005), 1–34

Morini, E., 'Il Levante della Santità. I Percorsi delle Reliquie dall'Oriente all'Italia', in *Le Relazioni Internazionali nell'Alto Medioevo*, Settimane di Studio del CISAM 58 (Spoleto, 2011), pp. 873–940

Mostert, M., (ed.), *New Approaches to Medieval Communication*, (Turnhout, 1999)

Munding, E., *Abt-Bischof Waldo, Begründer des goldenen Zeitalters der Reichenau*, Texte und Arbeiten, 1/10–11 (Beuron and Leipzig, 1924)

Musca, G., *L'emirato di Bari, 847–871* (Bari, 1964)

Neff, K., *Die Gedichte des Paulus Diaconus. Kritische und erklärende Ausgabe* (Munich, 1908)

Neil, B., *Seventh-Century Popes and Martyrs: The Political Hagiography of Anastasius Bibliothecarius* (Turnhout, 2006)

'The politics of hagiography in ninth-century Rome', in C. Bishop (ed.), *Text and Transmission in Medieval Europe* (Newcastle, 2007), pp. 58–75

Nelson, J. L., 'The last years of Louis the Pious', in P. Godman and R. Collins, *Charlemagne's Heir. New Perspectives on the Reign of Louis the Pious* (Oxford, 1990), pp. 146–59, reprinted in J. L. Nelson, *The Frankish World 750–900* (London, 1996), pp. 37–50

'The reign of Charles the Bald. A survey', in M. T. Gibson and J. L. Nelson (ed.), *Charles the Bald. Court and Kingdom* (London, 1990), pp. 1–22

The Annals of St-Bertin (Manchester, 1991)

Charles the Bald (London and New York, 1992)

'Women at the court of Charlemagne: a case of a monstrous regiment?', in J. C. Parsons (ed.), *Medieval Queenship* (Stroud, 1993), pp. 43–61, reprinted in J. L. Nelson, *The Frankish World 750–900* (London, 1996), pp. 223–42

'Kingship and empire', in R. McKitterick (ed.), *Carolingian Culture: Emulation and Innovation* (Cambridge, 1994), pp. 52–87

'Kingship and royal government', in McKitterick (ed.), *The New Cambridge Medieval History*, vol. II, pp. 383–430

'The siting of the council at Frankfort: some reflections on family and politics', in R. Berndt (ed.), *Das Frankfurter Konzil von 794* (Frankfurt, 1997), pp. 149–65, reprinted in Janet L. Nelson, *Rulers and Ruling Families in Early Medieval Europe. Alfred, Charles the Bald, and Others* (Aldershot, 1999), no. XIII

'A tale of two princes: politics, text and ideology in a Carolingian annal', *Studies in Medieval and Renaissance History* 10 (1988), 105–41, reprinted in J. L. Nelson, *Rulers and Ruling Families in Early Medieval Europe. Alfred, Charles the Bald, and Others* (Aldershot, 1999), no. XVI

'Charlemagne – pater optimus?', in P. Godman, J. Jarnut and P. Johanek (eds.), *Am Vorabend der Kaiser Krönung* (Stuttgart, 2002), pp. 269–81, reprinted in J. L. Nelson, *Courts, Elites and Gendered Power in the Early Middle Ages. Charlemagne and Others* (Aldershot, 2007), no. XV

'Opposition to Charlemagne', *The 2008 Annual Lecture, German Historical Institute* (London, 2009)

'Religion in the age of Charlemagne', in J. Arnold (ed.), *The Oxford Handbook of Medieval Christianity* (Oxford, 2014), pp. 490–514

'Revisiting the Carolingian Renaissance', in J. Kreiner and H. Reimitz (eds.), *Motions of Late Antiquity: Essays on Religion, Politics and Society in Honour of Peter Brown* (Turnhout, 2016), pp. 331–46

'Charlemagne and Ravenna', in Herrin and Nelson (eds.), *Ravenna*, pp. 239–52

King and Emperor: A New Life of Charlemagne (Berkeley, 2019)

Noble, T. F. X., 'The revolt of King Bernard of Italy in 817: its causes and consequences', *Studi medievali* 15 (1974), 315–26

The Republic of St. Peter: The Birth of the Papal State 680–825 (Philadelphia, 1984)

'Paradoxes and possibilities in the sources for Roman society in the Early Middle Ages', in J. M. H. Smith (ed.), *Early Medieval Rome and the Christian West: Essays in Honour of David A Bullough* (Leiden, 2000), pp. 55–83

'The interests of historians in the tenth century', in Rollason, Leyser and Williams (eds.), *England and the Continent in the Tenth Century*, pp. 495–513

'Pope Nicholas I and the Franks: politics and ecclesiology in the ninth century', in Meens et al. (eds.), *Religious Franks*, pp. 472–88

Images, Iconoclasm, and the Carolingians (Philadelphia, 2009)

Odegaard, C. E., *Vassi and Fideles in the Carolingian Empire* (Cambridge, MA, 1945)

Offergeld, T., *Reges pueri: das Königtum Minderjähriger im frühen Mittelalter*, MGH Schriften 50 (Hanover, 2001)

Ohnsorge, W., 'Das Kaiserbündnis von 842–844 gegen die Sarazenen. Inhalt und politische Bedeutung des "Kaiserbriefs aus St. Denis"', *Archiv für Diplomatik* 1 (1955), 131

Oldoni, M., 'Agiografia longobarda tra secolo IX e X: La leggenda di Trofimena', *Studi medievali*, ser. III, 12 (1971), 583–636

Orselli, A. M., *L'idea e il culto del santo patron cittadino nella letteratura latina cristiana* (Bologna, 1965)

Ortalli, Gh., 'Venezia dalle origini a Pietro II Orseolo', in Galasso (ed.), *Storia d'Italia 1*, pp. 339–438

'Il ducato e la *Civitas Rivoalti*: tra Carolingi, Bizantini e Sassoni', in L. Cracco Ruggini, M. Pavan, G. Cracco and Gh. Ortalli (eds.), *Storia di Venezia*, vol. 1, *Origini – Età Ducale* (Rome, 1992), pp. 725–90

Orth, P., 'Fragment einer historischen Dichtung über Kaiser Ludwig. II. († 875)', *Mittellateinisches Jahrbuch* 52/3 (2017), 362–75

Osborne, J., 'The painting of the Anastasis in the Lower Church of San Clemente, Rome: re-examination of the evidence for the location of the Tomb of St. Cyril', *Byzantion* 51 (1981), 269–72

'The Roman catacombs in the Middle Ages', *Papers of the British School at Rome* 53 (1985), 278–328

'Politics, diplomacy and the cult of relics in Venice and the northern Adriatic in the first half of the ninth century', *Early Medieval Europe* 8 (1999), 369–86

Padoa Schioppa, A., 'Giudici e giustizia nell'Italia carolingia', in A. Padoa Schioppa, G. di Renzo Villlata and G. P. Massetto (eds.), *Amicitiae pignus, Studi in ricordo di Adriano Cavanna* (Milan, 2003), vol. III, pp. 1623–67, also in G. di Renzo Villata (ed.), *Il diritto tra scoperta e creazione. Giudici e giuristi nella storia della giustizia civile. Atti del Convegno di Napoli 18–20 ottobre 2001* (Neaples, 2003), pp. 357–408, now in A. Padoa Schioppa, *Giustizia medievale italiana. Dal Regnum ai Comuni*, Biblioteca del 'Centro per il collegamento degli studi medievali e umanistici in Umbria' 28 (Spoleto, 2015), pp. 29–73

Pagani, I. and Santi, F. (eds.), *Il secolo di Carlo Magno. Istituzioni, letterature e cultura del tempo carolingio*, mediEVI 11 (Florence, 2016)

Pagano, S. M. and P. Piatti (eds.), *Il patrimonio documentario della Chiesa di Lucca: Prospettive di ricerca. Atti del convegno internazionale di studi (Lucca, Archivio Arcivescovile, 14–15 novembre 2008)*, Toscana sacra 2 (Florence, 2010)

Palma, M., 'Antigrafo/apografo. La formazione del testo latino degli atti del Concilio Constantinopolitano dell'869–870', in Questa and Raffaelli (eds.), *Il libro e il testo*, pp. 307–35

Palmieri, S., ' Duchi, principi e vescovi nella Longobardia meridionale', in G. Andenna (ed.), *Longobardia e longobardi nell'Italia meridionale: le istituzioni ecclesiastiche* (Milan, 1996), pp. 43–100

Pani, L., 'La trasmissione dell'Historia Langobardorum di Paolo Diacono tra Italia e Regnum Francorum nel IX secolo', in Chiesa (ed.), *Paolino d'Aquileia*, pp. 373–403

'Manuscript production in urban centres: graphic and textual typologies', in La Rocca and Majocchi (eds.), *Urban Identities in Northern Italy*, pp. 273–306

Pani Ermini, L., 'Città fortificate e fortificazioni delle città italiane fra V e VI secolo', *Rivista di studi liguri*, 59–60 (1993–4), 193–206

'Il ducato di Spoleto: persistenze e trasformazioni nell'assetto territoriale (Umbria e Marche)', in S. Gasparri (ed.), *I Longobardi dei ducati di Spoleto e Benevento* (Spoleto, 2004), pp. 701–62

Pantarotto, M., 'La (ri)costruzione di un manoscritto nello scriptorium di Bobbio al tempo dell'abate Agilulfo (887–896)', *Scriptorium* 61 (2007), 46–73

Parker, S., *Urban Theory and the Urban Exxperience: Encountering the City* (London, 2004)

Paroli, L., *L'Italia centro-settentrionale in età longobarda: atti del convegno, Ascoli Piceno, 6–7 ottobre 1995* (1997)

Pasquali, G., *Agricoltura e società rurale in Romagna nel medioevo* (Bologna, 1984)
'Una signoria rurale assente o silente? Il caso anomalo della Romagna', in A. Spicciani and C. Violante (eds.), *La signoria rurale nel medioevo italiano*, Atti del Seminario di Pisa 1985, i (Pisa, 1997), pp. 63–80

Patetta, F., 'Il Breviario alariciano in Italia' [1891], in F. Patetta, *Studi sulle fonti giuridiche medievali*, ed. G. Astuti (Turin, 1967), pp. 601–44

Patzold, S., 'L'épiscopat du haut Moyen Âge du point de vue de la médiévistique allemande', *Cahiers de civilisation médiévale* 192/4 (2005), 341–58
'Normen im Buch. Überlegungen zu Geltungsansprüchen so genannten "Kapitularien"', *Frühmittelalterliche Studien* 41 (2007), 331–50
Episcopus. Wissen über Bischöfe im Frankenreich des späten 8. bis frühen 10. Jahrhunderts (Ostfildern, 2008)
'Hraban, Gottschalk und der Traktat *De Oblatione Puerorum*', in Ph. Depreux, S. Lebecq, M. J.-L. Perrin and O. Szerwiniak (eds.), *Raban Maur et son temps*, Haut Moyen Âge 9 (Turnhout, 2010), pp. 105–18
Das Lehnswesen (Munich, 2012)

Patzold, S. and C. van Rhijn (eds.), *Men in the Middle. Local Priests in Early Medieval Europe*, Ergänzungsbände zum Reallexikon der Germanischen Altertumskunde 93 (Berlin 2016)

Peduto, P., 'Insediamenti longobardi del ducato di Benevento (secc. VI–VIII)', in Gasparri (ed.), *Il regno dei Longobardi in Italia*, pp. 367–442

Pellegrini, M., *Vescovo e città. Una relazione nel Medioevo italiano (secoli II–XIV)* (Milan, 2009)

Perels, E., *Papst Nikolaus I. und Anastasius Bibliothecarius: Ein Beitrag zur Geschichte des Papsttums im neunten Jahrhundert* (Berlin, 1920)

Petrucci, A., 'Il codice e i documenti: scrivere a Lucca fra VIII e IX secolo', in Petrucci and Romeo, *'Scriptores in urbibus'*, pp. 77–108

Petrucci, A., 'Il codice n. 490 della Biblioteca Capitolare di Lucca: un problema di storia della cultura medievale ancora da risolvere', *Actum Luce. Rivista di studi lucchesi* 2 (1973), 159–75

Petrucci, A. and C. Romeo, 'Scrivere "in iudicio". Modi, soggetti e funzioni di scrittura nei placiti del Regnum Italiae (secc. IX–XI)', *Scrittura e civiltà* 13 (1989), 5–48
'Scriptores in urbibus'. Alfabetismo e cultura scritta nell'Italia altomedievale (Bologna, 1992)

Pezé, W., *'Primum in Italiam, deinde in Galliam*. La correspondance autour du passage de Gottschalk d'Orbais en Italie (835–848)', in S. Gioanni and P.

Cammarosano (ed.), *La corrispondenza epistolare in Italia/Les correspondances en Italie, 2: forme, stili e funzioni della scrittura epistolare nelle cancellerie italiane (secoli V–XV)/formes, styles et fonctions de l'écriture épistolaire dans les chancelleries italiennes (V^e–XVe siècle)*, Collection de l'École Française de Rome 475 (Rome, 2013), pp. 145–62

Le virus de l'erreur. La controverse carolingienne sur la double prédestination. Essai d'histoire sociale, Haut Moyen Âge 26 (Turnhout, 2017)

Picard, J.-C., *Le souvenir des évêques: sépultures, listes épiscopales et culte des évêques en Italie du Nord des origines au Xe siècle* (Rome, 1988)

Pierpaoli, M., *Storia di Ravenna: dalle origini all'anno Mille* (Ravenna, 1986)

Pierucci, C., 'Inventari dell'antica biblioteca di Fonte Avellana (secc. XI–XVIII)', in *Fonte Avellana nella società dei secoli XIII e XIV* (Urbino, 1980), pp. 141–234

Phelan, O. M., *The Formation of Christian Europe. The Carolingians, Baptism, and the Imperium Christianum* (Oxford, 2014)

Pighi, G. B., *Versus de Verona. Versum de Mediolano Civitate*, Studi Pubblicati dall'Istituto di Filologia Classica 7 (Bologna, 1960)

Pohl, W., 'Memory, identity and power in Lombard Italy', in Hen and Innes (eds.), *The Uses of the Past*, pp. 9–28

'Invasions and ethnic identity', in La Rocca (ed.), *Italy in the Early Middle Ages*, pp. 20–33

'Le leggi longobarde nell'Italia carolingia: contesto e trasmissione', in Chiesa (ed.), *Paolino d'Aquileia*, pp. 421–37

'Das Papsttum und die Langobarden', in M. Becher and J. Jarnut (ed.), *Der Dynastiewechsel von 751: Vorgeschichte, Legitimationsstrategien und Erinnerung* (Münster, 2004), pp. 145–161

'Gens ipsa peribit: Kingdom and identity after the end of Lombard rule', in Gasparri (ed.), *774*, pp. 67–78

Pohl, W. and V. Wieser (eds.), *Der frühmittelalterliche Staat – europäische Perspektiven*, Forschungen zur Geschichte des Mittelalters 16 (Vienna, 2009)

Pohl, W., I. Wood and H. Reimitz (eds.), *The Transformation of Frontiers. From Late Antiquity to the Carolingians*, The Transformation of the Roman World (Leiden, Boston and Cologne, 2001)

Pollard, R. M., 'Paul, Paulinus and the rhythm of elite Latin: prose rhythm in Paul the Deacon and Paulinus of Aquileia and its implication', in F. Bougard, R. Le Jan and R. McKitterick (eds.), *La culture du haut Moyen Âge: une question d'élites?* (Turnhout, 2009), pp. 63–99

Poly, J.-P., 'La corde au cou: les Francs, la France et la loi Salique', in *Genèse de l'État moderne en Méditerranée. Approches historique et anthropologique des pratiques et des représentations. Actes des tables rondes internationales tenues à Paris, 24–26 septembre 1987 et 18–19 mars 1988* (Rome, 1993), pp. 287–320

'Terra salica. De la société franque à la société féodale: continuité et discontinuité', in J. Perez and S. Aguade Neto (eds.), *Les origines de la féodalité. Hommage à Claudio Sánchez Albornoz. Actes du colloque international tenu à la Maison des Pays ibériques les 22 et 23 octobre 1993* (Madrid, 2000), pp. 183–96

Poly, J.-P. and E. Bournazel, *La mutation féodale. Xe–XIIe siècles* (Paris, 1980)

Prill, P. E., 'Rhetoric and Poetics in the Early Middle Ages', *Rhetorica: A Journal of the History of Rhetoric* 5/2 (1987), 129–47

Provero, L., 'Chiese e Dinastie', in R. Greci, *Parma Medievale*, III.1: *Poteri e Istituzioni* (Parma, 2010), pp. 41–67

Pucci, J., 'Paul the Deacon's Poem to Lake Como', *Latomus* 58/4 (1999), 872–84

Questa, C. and R. Raffaelli (eds.), *Il libro e il testo. Atti del Convegno Internazionale, Urbino, 20–23 settembre 1982*, Pubblicazioni dell'Università di Urbino. Scienze umane, atti di congressi 1 (Urbino, 1984)

Radding, C. M. and Ciaralli, A., *The Corpus Iuris Civilis in the Middle Ages. Manuscripts and Transmission from the Sixth Century to the Juristic Renewal*, Brill's Studies in Intellectual History 147 (Leiden, 2007)

Reekmans, L., 'Le développement topographique de la région du Vatican à la fin de l'antiquité et au début du Moyen Âge (300–850)', in *Mélanges d'archéologie et d'histoire de l'art : offerts au professeur Jacques Lavalleye*, Recueil de travaux d'histoire et de philologie 4, Sér. 45 (Louvain, 1970), pp. 197–234

Reuter, T., 'A Europe of bishops. The age of Wulfstan of York and Burchard of Worms', in L. Körntger and M. Waßerhoven (ed.), *Patterns of Episcopal Power: Bishops in Tenth- and Eleventh-Century Western Europe. Strukturen bischöflicher Herrschaft im westlichen Europa des 10. und 11. Jahrhunderts* (Berlin, 2011), pp. 17–38

Reynolds, L. D., *Texts and Transmission. A Survey of Latin Classics* (Oxford, 1983)

Reynolds, R. E., 'The organisation, law and liturgy of the Western Church, 700–900', in R. McKitterick (ed.), *The New Cambridge Medieval History: Volume 2: c.700–c.900* (Cambridge, 1995), pp. 587–621

Reynolds, S., *Fiefs and Vassals. The Medieval Evidence Reinterpreted* (Oxford, 1994)

'Fiefs and vassals after twelve years', in S. Bagge, M. H. Gelting and T. Lindkvist (eds.), *Feudalism. New Landscapes of Debate* (Turnhout, 2011), pp. 15–21

'Afterthoughts on "Fiefs and Vassals"', *Journal of the Haskins Society* 9 (1997), 1–15

'Susan Reynolds responds to Johannes Fried', *German Historical Institute London. Bulletin* 19/2 (1997), 30–40

'Carolingian Elopements as a Sidelight on Counts and Vassals', in B. Nagy and M. Sebök (eds.), *The Man of Many Devices, Who Wandered Full Many Ways. Festschrift in Honor of János M. Bak* (Budapest, 1999), pp. 340–46

'Ancora su feudi e vassalli', *Scienza e politica* 22 (2000), 3–21

Feudi e vassalli. Una nuova interpretazione delle fonti medievali, trans. S. Menzinger (Rome, 2004)

The Middle Ages without Feudalism. Essays in Criticism and Comparison on the Medieval West, Variorum Collected Studies Series 1019 (Farnham, 2012)

Rhijn, C. van, 'The Local Church, Priests' Handbooks and Pastoral Care in the Carolingian Period', in *Chiese Locali e Chiese Regionali nell'Alto Medioevo*, Settimane del CISAM 61 (Spoleto, 2014), pp. 689–706

'Manuscripts for local priests and the Carolingian reforms', in Patzold and van Rhijn (eds.), *Men in the Middle*, pp. 177–98

Rinaldi, R., 'A ovest di Ravenna: itinerari di conti, di vescovi e di giovani donne', in O. Capitani (ed.), *Bologna nel Medioevo* (Bologna, 2007), pp. 151–85

Rio, A., 'High and low: ties of dependence in the Frankish kingdoms', *Transactions of the Royal Historical Society*, Sixth Series, 18 (2008), 43–68

Rizzardi, C., 'Chiesa e Impero nel Medioevo: le Abbazie di Ravenna e dell'area padano-adriatica fra tradizione e innovazione', *Hortus artium medievalium* 13 (2007), 117–36

Röckelein, H., *Reliquientranslationen nach Sachsen im 9. Jahrhundert. Über Kommunikation, Mobilität und Öffentlichkeit im Frühmittelalter* (Stuttgart, 2002)

Rollason, D., C. Leyser and H. Williams (eds.), *England and the Continent in the Tenth Century: Studies in Honour of Wilhelm Levison*, Studies in the Early Middle Ages XXXVII (Turnhout, 2010)

Rose, V., *Verzeichnis der lateinischen Handschriften der Königlichen Bibliothek zu Berlin*, vol. 1, *Die Meerman-Handschriften des Sir Thomas Phillips* (Hildesheim, 1893), pp. 299–307

Rosenwein, B., 'Family politics of Berengar I, King of Italy (888–924), *Speculum* 71 (1996), 247–89

'Friends and family, politics and privilege in the kingship of Berengar I,' in S. K. Cohn, Jr. and S. A. Epstein (eds.), *Portraits of Medieval and Renaissance Living: Essays in Memory of David Herlihy* (Ann Arbor, 1996), pp. 91–106

Rossetti, G. (ed.), *Pisa e la Toscana occidentale nel Medioevo. A Cinzio Violante nei suoi 70 anni*, 2 vols. (Pisa, 1991)

Rotili, M., 'Benevento fra tarda Antichità e alto Medioevo', in A. Augenti (ed.), *Le città italiane tra la tarda antichità e l'alto Medioevo : atti del Convegno* (Ravenna, 26–28 febbraio 2004) (Florence, 2006), pp. 317–36

Rubeis, F. de, 'Le iscrizioni dei re longobardi', in F. Stella (ed.), *Poesia dell'alto Medioevo europeo: manoscritti, lingua e musica dei ritmi latini* (Florence, 2000), pp. 223–37

Rudolf, W., 'A tenth-century booklist in the Biblioteca Capitolare of Vercelli', *Manuscripta. A Journal for Manuscript Research* 62/2 (2018), 249–77

Rusconi, A., 'L'ordalia della croce per il primato del *cantus romanus* sull'*ambrosianus* nel cod. 318 di Montecassino', *Musica e storia* 13 (2005), 5–23

Salten, O., *Vasallität und Benefizialwesen im 9. Jahrhundert. Studien zur Entwicklung personaler und dinglicher Beziehungen im frühen Mittelalter* (Hildesheim, 2013)

Samaritani, A., *Analecta Pomposiana. Atti del Primo Convegno Internazionale di Studi Storici Pomposiani* (Codigoro, 1965)

Presenza monastica ed ecclesiale di Pomposa nell'Italia centrosettentrionale. Secoli X–XIV (Ferrara, 1996)

Samaritani, A. and C. Di Francesco (eds.), *Pomposa: storia, arte, architettura* (Ferrara, 1999)

Sami, D. and G. Speed (eds.), *Debating Urbanism within and beyond the Walls A.D. 300–700: Proceedings of a Conference held at the University of Leicester, 15th November 2008* (Leicester, 2010)

Santoni, F., 'Scrivere documenti e scrivere libri a Verona', in L. Pani and C. Scalon (eds.), *Le Alpi porta d'Europa. Scritture, uomini, idee da Giustiniano a Barbarossa* (Spoleto, 2009), pp. 173–211

Sansterre, J.-M., *Les moines grecs et orientaux à Rome aux époques byzantine et carolingienne (milieu du VIe–fin du IXe siècle)* (Brussels, 1983)

'Monaci e monasteri greci a Ravenna', in Carile (ed.), *Storia di Ravenna*, II, 1, pp. 323–30

'Scrivere documenti e scrivere libri a Verona', in Scalon and Pani (eds.), *Le Alpi porta d'Europa*, pp. 173–212

Santos Salazar, I., 'Crisis. What Crisis? Political articulation and government in the March of Tuscany through placita and diplomas from Guy of Spoleto to Berengar II', in I. Martín Viso (ed.), *The collapse of the early medieval European kingdoms (8th–9th centuries)*, Reti Medievali Rivista 17/2 (2016), 251–79

Savigni, R., 'I Papi e Ravenna. Dalla caduta dell'Esarcato alla fine del secolo decimo', in Carile (ed.), *Storia di Ravenna*, II, 2, pp. 331–68

'Sacerdozio e regno in età post-Carolingia; L'episcopato di Giovanni X, arcivescovo di Ravenna (905–914) e papa (914–928)', *Rivista della Storia della Chiesa in Italia* 46 (1992), pp. 1–29

'Giovanni IX da Tossignano (papa Giovanni X) e i suoi rapporti con la corte ducale spoletana', in M. Tagliaferri (ed.), *Ravenna e Spoleto, I rapporti tra due metropoli* (Bologna, 2007), pp. 215–46

'Gli *Specula* carolingi', in C. Leonardi, F. Stella and P. Stoppacci (eds.), *Un ponte fra le culture. Studi medievistici di e per I Deug-Su* (Firenze, 2009), pp. 23–48

Scalon, C., *Produzione e fruizione del libro nel basso medioevo: il caso Friuli*, Medioevo e Umanesimo 88 (Padua, 1995)

Scalon, C. and L. Pani (eds.), *Le Alpi porta d'Europa. Scritture, uomini, idee da Giustiniano al Barbarossa. Atti del convegno internazionale di studio dell'Associazione italiana dei paleografi e diplomatisti, Cividale del Friuli, 5–7 ottobre 2006*, Studi e ricerche 4 (Spoleto, 2009)

Scarpatetti, M. von, *Die Handschriften der Stiftsbibliothek St. Gallen*, vol. 1/4, 2nd ed. (Wiesbaden, 2003)

Schaller, D., 'Karl der Große im Licht zeitgenössischer politischer Dichtung', in P. Butzer et al. (eds.), *Karl der Grosse und sein Nachwirken 1200 Jahre Kultur und Wissenschaft in Europa* (Turnhout, 1997), I, pp. 193–219

Schäpers, M., *Lothar I. (795–855) und das Frankenreich*, Rheinisches Archiv (Wien [u. a.], 2018), vol. 159.

Scherer, Cornelia, *Der Pontifikat Gregors IV. (827–844): Vorstellungen und Wahrnehmungen päpstlichen Handelns im 9. Jahrhundert* (Stuttgart 2013).

Schieffer, R., 'Väter und Söhne im Karolingerhause', in R. Schieffer (ed.), *Beiträge zur Geschichte des Regnum Francorum*, Beihefte der Francia 22 (Sigmaringen, 1990), pp. 149–64

'Charlemagne and Rome', in J. M. H. Smith (ed.), *Early Medieval Rome and the Christian West: Essays in honour of Donald A. Bullough* (Leiden, 2000), pp. 279–95

Schmale-Ott, I., *Translatio sancti Viti martyris. Übertragung des hl. Märtyrers Vitus* (Münster, 1979)

Schmidinger, H., 'Eberhard, Markgraf von Friaul' in *Lexikon des Mittelalters*, vol. III (Munich, Zurich, 1986), p. 1513

Schoolman, E., *Rediscovering Sainthood in Italy. Hagiography and the Late Antique Past in Medieval Ravenna* (New York, 2016)

Schumann, R., *Authority and the Commune, Parma 833–1133* (Parma, 1973)

Schwarzmeier, H.-M., *Lucca und das Reich bis zum Ende des 11. Jahrhunderts. Studien zur Sozialstruktur einer Herzogstadt in der Toskana* (Tübingen, 1972)

Screen, E., 'Lothar I in Italy, 834–40: charters and authority', in J. Jarrett and A. Scott McKinley (eds.), *Problems and Possibilities of Early Medieval Charters*, International Medieval Research 19 (Turnhout, 2013), vol. 19, pp. 231–52

Sennis, A., 'Monasteries and cities: cultural encounters', in La Rocca and Majocchi (eds.), *Urban Identities in Northern Italy*, pp. 191–215

Sereno, C., 'Bertilla e Berta: il Ruolo di Santa Giulia di Brescia e San Sisto di Piacenza nel Regno di Berengario I', *Reti Medievali Rivista* 13/2 (2012), 187–202

Sergi, G., 'I rapporti vassallatico-beneficiari', in *Milano e i Milanesi prima del Mille (VIII–X secolo), Milano 26–30 settembre 1983*, Atti del X Congresso internazionale di studi sull'alto medioevo (Spoleto, 1986), pp. 137–63

'Feudalesimo senza sistema', *Prometeo* 10/43 (September 1993), 52–61

'Vassalli a Milano', in G. Sergi, *I confini del potere. Marche e signorie fra due regni medievali* (Turin, 1995), pp. 272–95

'Poteri temporali del vescovo: il problema storiografico', in G. P. Francesconi (ed.), *Vescovo e città nell'Alto Medioevo: Quadri generali e realtà toscane* (Pistoia, 2001), pp. 1–16

Antidoti all'abuso della storia. Medioevo, medievisti, smentite (Naples, 2010)

Settia, A. A., 'Pavia carolingia and postcarolingia', in R. Bossaglia (ed.), *Storia di Pavia 2: L'Alto Medioevo* (Pavia, 1987), pp. 69–155

Sigoillot, A., 'Destins d'hommes libres à l'époque carolingienne d'après les chartes de Saint-Sauveur de Monte Amiata', *Journal des savants* (janvier-juin 2013), 155–74

Simmel, G., 'The metropolis and mental life', in R. Sennett (ed.), *Classic Essays on the Culture of Cities* (Englewood Cliffs, N.J., 1969 [orig. pub. 1950])

Simonini, A., *Autocefalia ed Esarcato in Italia* (Ravenna, 1969)

Sirantoine, H., *Imperator Hispaniae: les idéologies impériales dans le royaume de León (IX\ᵉ–XII\ᵉ siècles)*, Bibliothèque de la Casa de Velázquez 58 (Madrid, 2012)

Sivo, V., 'Pietro da Pisa', *Dizionario Biografico degli Italiani* 83 (2015), consulted online www.treccani.it/enciclopedia/pietro-da-pisa.

Skinner, P., 'Urban communities in Naples, 900–1050', *Papers of the British School at Rome*, 62 (1994), 279–99

Family Power in Southern Italy: The Duchy of Gaeta and Its Neighbours, 850–1139 (Cambridge, 2003)

Smith, J. M. H., 'Old saints, new cults: Roman relics in Carolingian Francia', in J. M. H. Smith (ed.), *Early Medieval Rome and the Christian West: Essays in Honour of David A Bullough* (Leiden, 2000), pp. 317–39

Europe after Rome. A New Cultural History (Oxford, 2005)

Sot, M., 'Service de l'empire et culte des saints dans la correspondance d'Éginhard', in B. Dumézil and L. Vissière (eds.), *Épistolaire Politique 1. Gouverner par les lettres* (Paris, 2014), pp. 91–105

Spera, L., *Il paesaggio suburbano di roma dall'antichità al Medioevo: il comprensorio tra le vie Latina e Ardeatina dale mura aureliane al III miglio*, Bibliotheca archaeologica (Roma) 27 (Roma, 1999).

'Dalla tomba alla "città" di Paolo: profilo topografico della Giovannipoli', in O. Bucarelli and P. Morales (eds.), *Paulo apostolo martyri. L'apostolo San Paolo nella storia, nell'arte e nell'archeologia, Atti della giornata di studi (Università Gregoriana, 19 gennaio 2009)* (Rome, 2011), pp. 119–61

Spieß, K.-H. (ed.), *Ausbildung und Verbreitung des Lehnswesens im Reich und in Italien im 12. und 13. Jahrhundert* (Ostfildern, 2013)

Staubach, N., 'Sedulius Scottus und die Gedichte des Codex Bernensis 363', *Frühmittelalterliche Studien* 20 (1986), 549–98

Stella, F., 'La poesia di Paolo Diacono: nuovi manoscritti e attribuzioni incerte', in Chiesa (ed.), *Paolo Diacono*, pp. 551–71

'Il ruolo di Paolino nell'evoluzione della poesia politica e religiosa dell'Europa carolingia alla luce delle recenti attribuzioni', in Chiesa (ed.), *Paolino d'Aquileia*, pp. 439–52

'La dinamica del consenso nelle lodi imperiali dei poeti carolingi e postcarolingi', in G. Urso (ed.), *'Dicere laudes'. Elogio, comunicazione, creazione del consenso. Atti del Convegno internazionale. Cividale del Friuli, 23–25 settembre 2010* (Pisa, 2011), pp. 359–81

Stiegemann, C. and M. Wemhoff (eds.), *799—Kunst und Kultur der Karolingerzeit: Karl der Große und Papst Leo III in Paderborn. Beiträge zum Katalog der Ausstellung Paderborn 1999* (Mainz, 1999)

Stoffella, M., 'Crisi e trasformazione delle élites nella Toscana nord-occidentale nel secolo VIII: esempi a confronto', *Reti Medievali Rivista* 8 (2007), 1–50

'Aristocracy and rural churches in the territory of Lucca between Lombards and Carolingians: a case study', in Gasparri (ed.), *774*, pp. 289–311

'Le relazioni tra Baviera e Toscana tra VIII e IX secolo: appunti e considerazioni preliminari', *Mélanges de l'École Française de Rome. Moyen Âge* 120/1 (2008), pp. 73–85

'Per una categorizzazione delle élites nella Toscana altomedievale nei secoli VIII–X', in Bougard, Goetz and Le Jan (eds.), *Théories et pratiques des élites*, pp. 325–50

'*Lociservatores* nell'Italia carolingia: l'evidenza Toscana', in M. Bassetti, A. Ciaralli, M. Montanari and G. M. Varanini (eds.), *Studi sul medioevo per Andrea Castagnetti* (Bologna, 2011) pp. 345–82

'Società longobarda a Lucca e chiesa romana tra fine VIII e inizio IX secolo', in *Rivista di Storia del Cristianesimo* 10/1 (2013), pp. 29–48

'Ecclesiastici in città e in campagna. La competizione per le istituzioni religiose minori nell'Italia centro-settentrionale (VIII–X secolo)', in P. Depreux, F. Bougard and R. Le Jan (eds.), *Compétition et sacré au haut Moyen Âge: entre médiation et exclusion*, Collection Haut Moyen Âge 21 (Turnhout, 2015), pp. 103–22

'Ufficiali pubblici minori nella Toscana di fine VIII–inizio IX secolo: alcuni esempi', in L. Jégou, T. Lienhard, S. Joye and J. Schneider (eds.), *Faire lien. Aristocratie, réseaux et échanges compétitifs. Mélanges en l'honneur de Régine Le Jan*, coll. Histoire ancienne et médiévale (Paris, 2015), pp. 227–35

'Peredeo', in *Dizionario Biografico degli Italiani* 82 (Rome, 2015), pp. 318–9

'Local priests in early medieval rural Tuscany', in Patzold and van Rhijn (eds.), *Men in the Middle*, pp. 98–124

'In a periphery of empire: Tuscany between Lombards and Carolingians', in R. Große and M. Sot (eds.), *Charlemagne. Les temps, les espaces, les hommes. Construction et déconstruction d'un règne* (Turnhout, 2018), pp. 319–36

'Condizionamenti politici e sociali nelle procedure di risoluzione dei conflitti nella Toscana occidentale tra età longobarda e carolingia', in Studi Medievali [Italics] 3a serie, 59/I (2018), 35–63

'Kleine Welten in der Toskana: eine ländliche Gesellschaft in Italien', in Kohl, Patzold and Zeller (eds.), *Kleine Welten*

'Pipino e la Divisio regnorum del 6 febbraio 806' in Albertoni and Borri (eds.), *Spes Italiae: il regno di Pipino*, forthcoming. 'In Threatening Times. A Comparison of the urban Communities of Verona and Lucca immediately after the Frankish Conquest', in A. Grabowsky, S. Patzold, G. Bührer-Thierry (eds), *Les communautés menacées au haut Moyen Âge* (Turnhout, 2020), forthcoming

Stofferahn, S. A., '*Renovatio* abroad: the politics of education in Carolingian Italy', in C. H. Chandler and S. A. Stofferahn (eds.), *Discovery and Distinction in the Early Middle Ages* (Kalamazoo, MI, 2013), pp. 149–63

Stone, R., *Morality and Masculinity in the Carolingian Empire* (Cambridge, 2012)

Stramaglia, A., 'Le *Declamationes maiores* pseudo-quintilianee: genesi di una raccolta declamatoria e fisionomia della sua trasmissione testuale', in E. Amato (ed.), *Approches de la Troisième Sophistique. Hommages à Jacques Schamp* (Brussels, 2006), pp. 555–88

Strazzullo, F., 'Le due antiche cattedrali di Napoli', *Campania Sacra* 4 (1973), 177–241

Supino Martini, P., 'Aspetti della cultura grafica a Roma fra Gregorio Magno e Gregorio VII', in *Roma nell'alto medioevo*, Settimane di studio del CISAM 48 (Spoleto, 2001), pp. 921–68

Tabacco, G., 'Arezzo, Siena, Chiusi nell'Alto Medioevo', in *Lucca e la Tuscia nell'Alto Medioevo*, pp. 163–89

'La storia politica e sociale. Dal tramonto dell'Impero alle prime formazioni di Stati regionali', in R. Romano and C. Vivanti (eds.), *Storia d'Italia*, II, *Dalla caduta dell'Impero Romano al secolo XVIII*, 1 (Turin, 1974), pp. 1–274

'L'ambiguità delle istituzioni nell'Europa costruita dai Franchi', *Rivista storica italiana* 87 (1975), 392–425

'Il feudalesimo', in *Storia delle idee politiche, economiche e sociali* II/2 (Turin, 1983), pp. 55–115

'Vassalli, nobili e cavalieri nell'Italia precomunale', *Rivista storica italiana* 99 (1987), 247–68

Struggle for power in medieval Italy. Structures of political rule (Cambridge, 1990)

'Il volto ecclesiastico del potere in età carolingia' [1986], in G. Tabacco, *Sperimentazioni del potere nell'alto medioevo* (Turin, 1993), pp. 164–208

'L'avvento dei Carolingi in Italia', in Gasparri and Cammarosano (eds.), *Langobardia*, pp. 375–403; now in Gasparri (ed.), *Il regno dei Longobardi in Italia*, pp. 443–79

Medievistica del Novecento. Recensioni e note di lettura. 2 vols. (Florence, 2007)

Tabanelli, M., *Visita alle pievi di Romagna* (Brescia, 1982)

Taviani-Carozzi, H., *La principauté lombarde de Salerne (IXe–XIe siècle) : pouvoir et société en Italie lombarde méridionale* (Rome, 1991)

Thacker, A., 'The making of a local saint', in Thacker and Sharpe (eds.), *Local Saints and Local Churches*, pp. 45–73

Thacker, A. and R. Sharpe (eds.), *Local Saints and Local Churches in the Early Medieval West* (Oxford, 2002)

Tirelli, V., 'Gli inventari della biblioteca della cattedrale di Cremona (sec. X–XIII) e un frammento di glossario latino del secolo X', *Italia medioevale e umanistica* 7 (1964), 1–76

Tischler, M., *Einharts* Vita Karoli: *Studien zur Entstehung, Überlieferung und Rezeption*, MGH Schriften 48, 2 vols. (Hanover, 2001)

Tomasi di Lampedusa, G., *The Leopard* (London, 2007)

Tomea, P., 'Ambrogio e i suoi fratelli. Note di agiografia milanese medievale', *Filologia mediolatina*, (1998), pp. 149–232

Tomei, P., 'Chiese, vassalli, concubine. Su un inedito placito lucchese dell'anno 900', in P. Cammarosano and P. Chastang (eds.), *Codicologie et langage de la norme dans les statuts de la Meditérranée Occidentale a la fin du Moyen Âge (XII–XV sec.)*, *Mélanges de l'École française de Rome – Moyen Âge*, 126/2 (2014), pp. 1–23

Tondini, G., 'Un modello per il regno dei Carolingi in Italia. L' *Epitome Phillipsiana* e l' identità urbana di Verona dopo il 774', unpublished PhD thesis, Università delgi Studi di Padova, 2011

Tonolli, S., 'Annone, vescovo di Verona', in *Bibliotheca Sanctorum*, vol. 1 (Rome, 1961), pp. 1314–7

Torricelli, M. P., *Centri plebani e strutture insediative nella Romagna medievale* (Bologna, 1989)

Toubert, P., *Les structures du Latium médiéval: le Latium méridional et la Sabine du IXe siècle à la fin du XIIe siècle* (Rome, 1973)

L'Europe dans sa première croissance. De Charlemagne à l'an mil (Paris, 2004)

Tramontin, S., 'Realtà e leggende nei racconti marciani veneti', *Studi Veneziani* 12 (1970), 35–58

Tristano, C., 'Un nuovo testimone dei *Commentaria in Genesim* di Rabano Mauro', *Studi medievali*, 51 (2010), pp. 839–891

Turrini, G., 'La Biblioteca Capitolare di Verona', *Italia Medioevale e Umanistica* 5 (1962), 401–23

Twyman, S., *Papal Ceremonial at Rome in the Twelfth Century* (Woodbridge, 2002)

Ubl, K., *Die Karolinger. Herrscher und Reich* (Munich, 2014)

Unfer Verre, G.E., 'Ancora sul manoscritto 490. Precisazioni e problemi aperti', in *Rivista di Storia del Cristianesimo* 10/1 (2013), pp. 49–63

Valtorta, B. (ed.), *Clavis Scriptorum Latinorum Medii Aevi. Auctores Italiae (700–1000)*, Edizione nazionale dei testi mediolatini, Serie 1, 10 (Florence, 2006).

Vasina, A. (ed.), *Storia di Ravenna*, III: Dal Mille alla fine della signoria polentana (Venice, 1993)

Vasina, A., 'Pievi urbane in Romagna prima e dopo il Mille', *Felix Ravenna*, 127–30 (1984–5), pp. 481–506

Verardi, A. A., *La Memoria Legittimante. Il Liber Pontificalis e la Chiesa di Roma nel VI secolo*, Nuovi Studi Storici 99 (Rome, 2016)

Verhaeghe, F., C. Loveluck and J. Story, 'Urban developments in the age of Charlemagne', in J. Story (ed.), *Charlemagne: Empire and Society* (Manchester, 2005), pp. 259–88

Verhoeven, M., *The Early Christian Monuments of Ravenna: Transformations and Memory* (Turnhout, 2011)

Verhulst, A. E., *The Rise of Cities in North-West Europe* (Cambridge, 1999)

Veronese, F., 'Foreign bishops using local saints. The *Passio et Translatio Sanctorum Firmi et Rustici* (BHL 3020–3021) and Carolingian Verona', in M.C. Ferrari (ed.), *Saints and the City. Beiträge zum Verständnis Urbaner Sakralität in Christlichen Gemeinschaften (5.–17– Jh.)* (Erlangen, 2015), pp. 85–114

'Saint Marc entre Venise et Reichenau: les reliques de l'évangeliste comme objet et enjeu de compétition', in Ph. Depreux. F. Bougard and R. Le Jan (dir.), *Compétition et sacré: entre médiation et exclusion*, Haut Moyen Âge 21 (Turnhout, 2015), pp. 295–312

Vespignani, G., *La Romania italiana dall'esarcato al patrimonium: il Codex parisinus (BNP, NAL 2573) testimone della formazione di società locali nel secoli IX e X* (Spoleto, 2001)

Vignodelli, G., *The King and the Cathedral Canons: Hugh of Arle's Policies towards Local Aristocracies in the Kingdom of Italy (926–945)* (forthcoming)

Villa, C., '"Denique Terenti dultia legimus acta...": una "lectura Terenti" a S. Faustino di Brescia nel secolo IX', *Italia Medioevale e Umanistica* 22 (1979), 1–44

'Die Horazüberlieferung und die "Bibliothek Karls des Großen". Zum Werkverzeichnis der Handschrift Berlin, Diez B. 66', *Deutsches Archiv für Erforschung des Mittelalters* 51 (1995), 29–52

'"Itinera italica" nel secolo VIII: i libri e i viaggi', in P. Chiesa (ed.), *Paolino d'Aquileia e il contributo italiano all'Europa carolingia* (Udine, 2003), pp. 453–70

'La produzione libraria, prima e dopo il 774', in S. Gasparri (ed.), *774*, pp. 387–401

'Berlin, Staatsbibliothek, Diez. B. 66. Una cronaca bibliografica e una scheda per Fiducia "clericus et locopositus"', *Filologia mediolatina* 23 (2016), 1–12

Violante, C., 'Le strutture organizzative della cura d'anime nelle campagne dell'Italia centrosettentrionale (secoli V–X)', in *Cristianizzazione e organizzazione ecclesiastica delle campagne nell'Alto Medioevo: espansione e resistenze. Atti della XXVIII Settimana di studio, Spoleto, 10–16 aprile 1980*, 2 vols. (Spoleto, 1982), II, pp. 963–1156

Vocino, G., 'Santi e luoghi santi al servizio della politica carolingia (774–877): *Vitae* e *Passiones* del regno italico nel contesto europeo', unpublished PhD thesis, University Ca' Foscari of Venice, 2010

'Hagiography as an Instrument for Political Claims in Carolingian Northern Italy: The Saint Syrus Dossier (BHL 7976 and 7978)', in P. Sarris, P. Booth and M. Dal Santo (eds.), *An Age of Saints? Power, Conflict and Dissent in Early Medieval Christianity* (Turnhout, 2011), pp. 169–86

'Triginta autem Brixienses sunt episcopi quos meminimus. Mémoire épiscopale et hagiographie à l'époque carolingienne: le dossier de saint Filastre évêque de Brescia', in M. Coumert, M.-C. Isaïa, K. Krönert and S. Shimahara (eds.), *Rerum gestarum scriptor. Histoire et historiographie au Moyen Âge* (Paris, 2012), pp. 313–28

'Under the aegis of the saints. Hagiography and power in early Carolingian northern Italy', *Early Medieval Europe* 22 (2014), 26–52

'Les saints en lice: hagiographie et reliques entre Cividale et Grado à l'époque Carolingienne', in Ph. Depreux. F. Bougard and R. Le Jan (dir.), *Compétition et sacré: entre médiation et exclusion*, Haut Moyen Âge 21 (Turnhout, 2015), pp. 273–93

'A *peregrinus*'s vademecum: MS Bern 363 and the "circle of Sedulius Scottus"', in M. Teeuwen and I. van Renswoude (eds.), *The Annotated Book in the Early Middle Ages: Practices of Reading and Writing* (Turnhout, 2017), pp. 87–123

Vuolo, A., 'Agiografia beneventana', in G. Andenna and G. Picasso (eds.), *Longobardia e longobardi nell'Italia meridionale : le istituzioni ecclesiastiche : Atti del 2. convegno internazionale di studi promosso dal Centro di cultura dell'Università cattolica del Sacro Cuore : Benevento, 29–31 maggio 1992* (Milan, 1996)

Vita et Translatio s. Athanasii neopolitani episcopi (BHL 735 e 737). *Sec. IX*, Fonti per la storia d'Italia Medievale, Antiquitates (Rome, 2001)

Ward-Perkins, B., 'Continuitists, catastrophists, and the towns of post-Roman northern Italy', *Papers of the British School at Rome* 65 (1997), 157–76

Werner, K. F., 'Missus – Marchio – Comes. Entre l'administration centrale et l'administration locale de l'Empire carolingien', in W. Paravicini and K. F. Werner (eds.), *Histoire comparée de l'administration (IVᵉ – XVIIIᵉ siècles)* (Zürich and Munich, 1980), pp. 191–239

West, C., *Reframing the Feudal Revolution. Political and Social Transformation between Marne and Moselle. c. 800–c. 1100* (Cambridge, 2014)

West-Harling, V., 'Introduction', in West-Harling (ed.), *Three Empires, Three Cities*, pp. 13–31

'Proclaiming power in the city; the archbishops of Ravenna and the doges of Venice', in La Rocca and Majocchi (eds.), *Urban Identities in Northern Italy*, pp. 221–34

Rome, Ravenna and Venice, 750–1000, (Oxford, 2020)

West-Harling, V., (ed.). *Three Empires, Three Cities. Identity, Material Culture and Legitimacy in Venice, Ravenna and Rome, 750–1000* (Turnhout 2015)

Whitby, M. (ed.), *The Propaganda of Power. The Role of Panegyric in Late Antiquity* (Leiden, 1998)

Wickham, C., *Early Medieval Italy: Central Power and Local Society, 400–1000* (London, 1981)

'Land disputes and their social framework in Lombard-Carolingian Italy, 700–900', in W. Davies and P. Fouracre (eds.), *The Settlement of Disputes in Early Medieval Europe* (Cambridge, 1986), pp. 105–24, now published also in C. Wickham, *Land and Power. Studies in Italian and European Social History, 400–1200* (London, 1994), pp. 229–56

'Aristocratic power in eighth-century Lombard Italy', in A. C. Murray (ed.), *After Rome's Fall: Narrators and Sources of Early Medieval History* (Toronto, 1998), pp. 153–70

'Le forme del feudalesimo', in *Il feudalesimo nell'alto medioevo, 8–12 aprile 1999*, Settimane 47 (Spoleto, 2000), pp. 15–46

'"The Romans according to their malign custom": Rome in Italy in the late ninth and tenth centuries', in J. M. H. Smith (ed.), *Early Medieval Rome and the Christian West. Essays in Honour of Donald A. Bullough* (Leiden, 2000), pp. 151–67

'Rural economy and society', in La Rocca, (ed.), *Italy in the Early Middle Ages*, pp. 118–43

Framing the Early Middle Ages: Europe and the Mediterranean, 400–800 (Oxford, 2005)

'Public court practice: the eighth and twelfth centuries compared', in S. Esders (ed.), *Rechtsverständnis und Konfliktbewältigung. Gerichtliche und außergerichtliche Strategien im Mittelalter* (Cologne, Weimar and Vienna, 2007), pp. 17–30

The Inheritance of Rome. A History of Europe from 400 to 1000 (London, 2009)

'La struttura della proprietà fondiaria nell'Agro Romano, 900–1150', *Archivio della Società Romana di Storia Patria* 132 (2009), 181–239

Roma medievale. Crisi e stabilità di una città 950–1150 (Rome, 2013), translated as *Medieval Rome: Stability and Crisis of a City, 900–1150* (Oxford, 2015)

'Consensus and assemblies in the Romano-Germanic kingdoms: a comparative approach', in V. Epp and C. F. Weber (eds.), *Recht und Konsens im frühen Mittelalter*, Vorträge und Forschungen 82 (Ostfildern, 2017), pp. 389–424

Wieczinski, J., 'The anti-papal conspiracy of the patriarch Photius in 867', *Byzantine Studies* 1/2 (1974), 180–9

Winkelmüller, M., 'Politische Unifikationsbestrebungen im Konflikt mit der Wahrung lokaler Tradition: *Gallia tota* im Gedicht *Olim romulea* (Montecassino 318)', in F. Hentschel (ed.), *Nationes-Begriffe im mittelalterlichen Musikschrifttum. Politische und regionale Gemeinschaften in musikbezogenen Quellen, 900–1400* (Berlin, 2016), pp. 41–50

Witschel, C., 'Rom und die Städte Italiens in Spätantike und Frühmittelalter', *Bonner Jahrbücher* 159 (2001), 113–62

Witt, R., *The Two Latin Cultures and the Foundation of Renaissance Humanism in Medieval Italy* (Cambridge, 2012)

Wolf, G. (ed.), *Zum Kaisertum Karls des Großen* (Darmstadt, 1972)

Wolfram, H., *Intitulatio. I. Lateinische Königs- und Fürstentitel bis zum Ende des 8. Jahrhunderts* (Graz, Vienna and Cologne, 1967)

'Karl Martell und das fränkische Lehnswesen', in J. Jarnut, U. Nonn and M. Richter (eds.), *Karl Martell in seiner Zeit* (Sigmaringen, 1994), pp. 61–78

'Political theory and narrative in charters', *Viator* 26 (1995), 39–51

Wood, I., 'Genealogy defined by women: the case of the Pippinids', in L. Brubaker and J. M. H. Smith (eds.), *Gender in the Early Medieval World. East and West, 300–900* (Cambridge, 2004), pp. 234–56

Zanini, E., 'Le città dell'Italia bizantina: qualche appunto per un'agenda della ricerca', *Reti Medievali Rivista* 11 (2010), pp. 1–22

Zarotti, G. and M. Turchi, *Le epigrafi della Cattedrale nella storia di Parma*, (Parma, 1988)

Zechiel-Eckes, K., 'Florus Polemik gegen Modoin. Unbekannte Texte zum Konflikt zwischen dem Bischof von Autun und dem Lyoner Klerus in den dreißiger Jahren des 9. Jahrhunderts', *Francia* 25 (1998), 19–38

Zettler, A., 'Die Ablösung der langobardischen Herrschaft in Verona durch die Karolinger – eine Spurensuche', in U. Ludwig und T. Schilp (eds.), *Nomen et fraternitas: Festschrift für Dieter Geuenich zum 65. Geburtstag,* Ergänzungsbände zum Reallexikon der Germanischen Altertumskunde 62 (Berlin and New York, 2008), pp. 595–623

'Die karolingischen Grafen von Verona I. Studien zu Bischof Egino († 802)', in S. Brather, D. Geuenich and Ch. Huth (eds.), *Historia Archaeologica. Festschrift für Heiko Steuer zum 70. Geburtstag,* Ergänzungsbände zum Reallexikon der Germanischen Altertumskunde 70 (Berlin and New York, 2009), pp. 363–85

Zielinski, H., 'Ludwig II. von Italien', in *Neue Deutsche Biographie 15* (Berlin, 1987), pp. 323–27

'Ein unbeachteter Italienzug Kaiser Lothars I. im Jahre 847', *Quellen und Forschungen aus Italienischen Archiven und Bibliotheken* 70 (1990), 1–22

'Art. Ludwig der Blinde, Kaiser († 928)' in *Lexikon des Mittelalters* (1991), vol. 5, S 2177–8.

'Reisegeschwindigkeit und Nachrichtenübermittlung als Problem der Regestenarbeit am Beispiel eines undatierten Kapitulars Lothars I. von 847 Frühjahr (846 Herbst?)', *Studien aus der Arbeit an den Regesta Imperii* (1992), 37–49

Böhmer, J. F., *Regesta Imperii I. Die Regesten des Kaiserreichs unter den Karolingern 751–918 (926: 962). Bd. 3. Die Regesten des Regnum Italiae und der burgundischen Regna. Tl. 2. Das Regnum Italiae in der Zeit der Thronkämpfe und Reichsteilungen 888 (850) – 926,* Regesta Imperii (Cologne [u.a.], 1998), vol. 3

Zimmermann, H., 'Imperatores Italiae', in H. Beumann (ed.), *Historische Forschungen für Walter Schlesinger* (Cologne and Vienna, 1974), pp. 379–99

Zimmermann, M., '*Sicut antiquus sanctium est...* Tutelle des Anciens ou protection de l'innovation? L'invocation du droit et la terminologie politique dans les représentations médiévales en Catalogne (IXᵉ–XIIᵉ siècle)', in J.-M. Sansterre (ed.), *L'autorité du passé dans les sociétés médiévales* (Rome, 2004), pp. 27–56.

Index

For EU product safety concerns, contact us at Calle de José Abascal, 56–1°,
28003 Madrid, Spain or eugpsr@cambridge.org.

www.ingramcontent.com/pod-product-compliance
Ingram Content Group UK Ltd.
Pitfield, Milton Keynes, MK11 3LW, UK
UKHW020400140625
459647UK00020B/2578